A. T. Robertson, John Albert Broadus

A harmony of the Gospels in the revised version:

With some new features

A. T. Robertson, John Albert Broadus

A harmony of the Gospels in the revised version:
With some new features

ISBN/EAN: 9783337713850

Printed in Europe, USA, Canada, Australia, Japan

Cover: Foto ©ninafisch / pixelio.de

More available books at **www.hansebooks.com**

A HARMONY

OF THE

GOSPELS,

IN THE REVISED VERSION.

WITH SOME NEW FEATURES.

By JOHN A. BROADUS, D.D., LL.D.

THE NOTES AT THE END OF THE VOLUME
BY A. T. ROBERTSON, D.D.

SECOND EDITION.

New York.
A. C. ARMSTRONG AND SON,
51 EAST 10TH STREET.
1894.

COPYRIGHT BY JOHN A. BROADUS,
1893.

COMPOSITION BY BAPTIST BOOK CONCERN, } LOUISVILLE, KY.
ELECTROTYPING BY ROBERT ROWELL,

PREFACE.

This work is the fruit of more than thirty years spent in teaching the English New Testament. I first used as a text-book the Harmony of Dr. Ed. Robinson, and for some twenty years past that of Dr. G. W. Clark. Both are valuable works, deserving their wide reputation. But I have become more and more convinced that most harmonists seriously err in laying stress on the division of our Lord's ministry into Passover years. It is quite impossible to determine with any great confidence whether the feast of John 5:1 was a passover, and the two known passovers of John 2:13 and 6:4 have really no important relation to the development of our Lord's ministry. Besides, the length of his ministry, and the dates of his birth and death, cannot be precisely fixed. But cease to labor for an exact chronology, quit regarding the feasts (except the last Passover) as important epochs in his work, and you presently perceive that his ministry divides itself easily into well-defined periods, in each of which you can trace a gradual progress, (a) in our Lord's self-manifestation, (b) in the hostility of his enemies, and (c) in his training of the Twelve Apostles. Thus we become able to follow the *inner movements* of the history, towards that long-delayed, but foreseen and inevitable collision, in which, beyond all other instances, the wrath of man was made to praise God.

The chief marks of this historical progress in the Life of our Lord I have tried to indicate by brief foot-notes, and other notes in italic letters placed here and there between the sections. Many of these brief notes also touch various points of harmonizing, of chronology, and other matters, so that the reader may quickly get the most important necessary information or help, and move forward. Questions requiring more elaborate discussion have been treated by my colleague, Dr. A. T. Robertson, in longer notes placed at the end of the volume, which in my judgment are remarkably complete and discriminating, and will greatly aid the careful student.

PREFACE.

It has seemed best to print the Harmony in the Revised Version, commonly known as the Canterbury, or Anglo-American Revision, which is nowadays given in many lesson helps and commentaries along with the Common or King James translation. In printing this revised text some use has been made of Waddy's Harmony.

Probably most persons look upon a Harmony of the Gospels as useful only to Bible class work or other regular forms of study. But I invite any one who takes pleasure in reading his Bible to try the experiment of reading this Harmony as a connected and complete Life of Christ, moving steadily on through the successive periods, and striving to come ever nearer to him as our Teacher, Exemplar, Redeemer, Lord. It is hoped also that Y. M. C. A. classes, in Colleges and elsewhere, may in many cases like to take up a series of lessons in that great Life, which is the focus of human history, and the centre of Scripture. When Sunday School lessons are taken from any one of the Gospels, it is an important advantage for all teachers, and the more intelligent pupils, to compare every such lesson with the other Gospels as presented in a Harmony; while for regular lessons on the Life of Christ a Harmony is indispensable to thorough treatment. In Theological Seminaries, not merely students who use only the English Bible, but those who study the Gospels in Greek, would be much profited by first making a survey of the Harmony in English. And no minister can afford to prepare a sermon on any text from a Gospel without looking up the parallel passages from other Gospels, and also considering where his text stands in the gradual unfolding of the Saviour's teaching and work.

J. A. B.

Southern Bapt. Theol. Seminary,
Louisville, Ky., June 15, 1893.

INDEX.

FOR THE INTERNATIONAL SUNDAY-SCHOOL LESSONS ON THE LIFE OF CHRIST, JULY 1, 1894, TO JUNE 30, 1895.

1894.			Page.
July 1.	The Birth of Jesus	Luke 2:1-16	7, 8
8.	Presentation in the Temple	Luke 2:25-38	8, 9
15.	Visit of the Wise Men	Matt. 2:1-12	9, 10
22.	Flight into Egypt	Matt. 2:13-23	10
29.	The Youth of Jesus	Luke 2:40-52	11
Aug. 5.	The Baptism of Jesus	Mark 1:1-11	12-16
12.	Temptation of Jesus	Matt. 4:1-11	16, 17
19.	First Disciples of Jesus	John 1:35-49	18, 19
26.	First Miracle of Jesus	John 2:1-11	19
Sept. 2.	Jesus Cleansing the Temple	John 2:13-25	20
9.	Jesus and Nicodemus	John 3:1-16	20, 21
16.	Jesus at Jacob's Well	John 4:9-26	23
Oct. 7.	Jesus at Nazareth	Luke 4:16-30	26, 27
14.	The Draught of Fishes	Luke 5:1-11	27, 28
21.	A Sabbath in Capernaum	Mark 1:21-34	28-30
28.	A Paralytic Healed	Mark 2:1-12	32, 33
Nov. 4.	Jesus Lord of the Sabbath	Mark 2:23-28 and 3:1-5	41-43
11.	The Twelve Chosen	Mark 3:6-19	43-45
18.	The Sermon on the Mount	Luke 6:20-31	46-48
25.	Opposition to Christ	Mark 3:22-35	58-60
Dec. 2.	Christ's Testimony to John	Luke 7:24-35	54, 55
9.	Christ Teaching by Parables	Luke 8:4-15	60-63
16.	The Twelve Sent Forth	Matt. 10:5-16	72, 73
1895.			
Jan. 6.	John the Baptist Beheaded	Mark 6:17-29	75
13.	Feeding the Five Thousand	Mark 6:30-44	76-78
20.	Christ the Bread of Life	John 6:26-35	81, 82
27.	The Great Confession	Matt. 16:13-24	89-91
Feb. 3.	The Transfiguration	Luke 9:28-36	92, 93
10.	Christ and the Little Child	Matt. 18:1-11	98-100
17.	The Good Samaritan	Luke 10:25-37	111, 112
24.	Christ and the Man Born Blind	John 9:1-11	108
Mar. 3.	The Raising of Lazarus	John 11:35-45	127
10.	The Rich Young Ruler	Mark 10:17-27	132, 133
17.	Zacchæus the Publican	Luke 19:1-10	138
24.	Missionary Lesson	Luke 10:1-9	110, 111
Apr. 7.	The Triumphal Entry	Mark 11:1-11	140-143
14.	The Wicked Husbandman	Mark 12:1-12	149-151
21.	Watchfulness	Matt. 24:42-51	166
28.	The Lord's Supper	Mark 14:12-26	172-179
May 5.	The Agony in Gethsemane	Mark 14:32-42	184-186
12.	Jesus Before the High Priest	Mark 14:53-64	190-194
19.	Jesus Before Pilate	Mark 15:1-15	195-203
26.	Jesus on the Cross	Mark 15:22-37	208-213
June 2.	The Resurrection of Jesus	Mark 16:1-8	218, 219
9.	The Walk to Emmaus	Luke 24:13-32	223, 224
16.	Peter and the Risen Lord	John 21:4-17	226, 227
23.	The Saviour's Parting Words	Luke 24:44-53	229-231

SYNOPSIS OF THE HARMONY.

PART I.

MATTERS CONNECTED WITH OUR LORD'S BIRTH AND CHILDHOOD.

Sect.   Page.

1. Introductory portions of the several Gospels.
   (a) Dedication of Luke's Gospel............................. 1
   (b) Introduction to John's Gospel........................... 1
   (c) The Genealogies in Matthew and Luke.................. 2
2. Annunciation of the Birth of John the Baptist................... 3
3. Annunciation to the Virgin Mary of the Birth of Jesus.......... 4
4. Visit of Mary to Elisabeth....................................... 5
5. Birth of John the Baptist, and his Desert Life.................. 6
6. Annunciation to Joseph of the Birth of Jesus................... 7
7. Birth of Jesus... 7
8. Angels proclaim to Shepherds that the Messiah is born at Bethlehem... 8
9. Circumcision of Jesus, and Presentation in the Temple.......... 8
10. Magi visit the new-born King of the Jews...................... 9
11. The Child Jesus carried to Egypt, and the Children of Bethlehem slain.. 10
12. The Child brought from Egypt to Nazareth..................... 10
13. Jesus lives at Nazareth, and visits Jerusalem when 12 years old.. 11

PART II.

BEGINNING OF THE FORERUNNER'S MINISTRY.

14. John the Baptist preaches the near approach of the Messianic reign, and baptizes in the Jordan those who repent and believe.. 12

PART III.

BEGINNINGS OF OUR LORD'S MINISTRY.

Sect.   Page.

15. Jesus baptized by John in the Jordan............................ 15
16. Jesus tempted in the Wilderness 16
17. John testifies to Jesus.. 18
18. Jesus makes his first disciples.................................... 18
19. Jesus works his first miracle, at Cana........................... 19
20. Jesus makes a first sojourn at Capernaum, accompanied by his kindred and his early disciples............................. 20
21. Jesus attends the first Passover during his Ministry.
    (a) He cleanses the Temple. (Comp. § 106.)................. 20
    (b) During the Passover, many believe on Jesus, including the ruler Nicodemus. Conversation with Nicodemus. 20
22. Early Ministry in Judea, and John's renewed testimony.......... 21
23. Jesus removes from Judea through Samaria to Galilee.
    (a) Reasons for leaving Judea................................ 22
    (b) Conversation at Jacob's well, and sojourn at Sychar..... 22
    (c) Arrival in Galilee.. 24

PART IV.

OUR LORD'S GREAT MINISTRY IN GALILEE.

24. General account of his teaching in Galilee...................... 25
25. He heals at Cana the son of a courtier of Capernaum............ 26
26. Rejected at Nazareth, he makes Capernaum his residence. (Comp. § 20.)... 26
27. He calls four fishermen to follow him............................ 27
28. He heals a demoniac in the synagogue at Capernaum............ 28
29. He heals Peter's mother-in-law, and many others................ 29
30. He journeys about Galilee, preaching and healing................ 30
31. A leper healed, and much popular excitement................... 31
32. Thronged in Capernaum, he heals a paralytic lowered through the roof... 32
33. The call of Matthew, who makes him a great entertainment..... 34
34. Jesus discourses on fasting..................................... 35
35. He raises Jairus' daughter, and heals a woman who only touched his garment... 36
36. He heals two blind men, and a dumb demoniac................. 39

SYNOPSIS OF THE HARMONY.

Sect.		Page.
37.	Attending a feast in Jerusalem (probably the Passover), Jesus heals a man on the Sabbath, and defends his action	39
38.	The disciples of Jesus pluck ears of grain on the Sabbath, and he defends them	41
39.	Jesus heals a withered hand on the Sabbath, and defends it. (Comp. § 88.)	42
40.	Great multitudes attend him beside the sea of Galilee	44
41.	After a night of prayer, Jesus selects Twelve Apostles	44
42.	The Sermon on the Mount. Privileges and Requirements of the Messianic Reign	45
43.	Jesus heals a centurion's servant at Capernaum	52
44.	He raises a widow's son at Nain	53
45.	A message comes from John the Baptist, and our Lord discourses as to John, and various other matters suggested	54
46.	The woman that was a sinner anoints the Saviour's feet. (Comp. § 117.)	56
47.	Further journeying about Galilee. (Comp. § 30.)	57
48.	Blasphemous accusation of league with Beelzebub. (Comp. § 84.)	57
49.	Scribes and Pharisees demand a sign	59
50.	Christ's mother and brethren	59
51.	The first great group of Parables	60
52.	In crossing the lake, Jesus stills the tempest	66
53.	Beyond the lake, he heals two Gadarene demoniacs	67
54.	Returning, he visits Nazareth, and is again rejected. (Comp. § 26.)	70
55.	Jesus yet again journeys about Galilee (comp. §30 and 47), and now sends the Twelve before him (comp. § 80), after instructing them	71
56.	Herod Antipas supposes Jesus to be John the Baptist risen, whom he had beheaded	74

PART V.

SEASON OF RETIREMENT INTO DISTRICTS AROUND GALILEE.

57.	The Twelve return, and Jesus retires with them beyond the lake to rest. Feeding of the Five Thousand	76
58.	The Twelve try to row back, and Jesus comes walking on the water	79
59.	He discourses in the crowded Synagogue at Capernaum, on eating spiritual food, and on the necessity of a divine teaching and drawing in order to true discipleship. (Comp. § 92.)	81

VIII SYNOPSIS OF THE HARMONY.

Sect. Page.
60. Emissaries from Jerusalem reproach him for disregarding Tradition 83
61. He retires to the region of Tyre and Sidon, and heals a Phoenician woman's daughter....................................... 85
62. He goes farther North, and then East and South into Decapolis—heals multitudes, and feeds the Four Thousand.............. 86
63. After crossing to Galilee, he again retires into the tetrarchy of Philip. A blind man healed............................... 88
64. In the neighborhood of Cæsarea-Philippi, the Twelve avow (through Peter) their belief that he is the Messiah.......... 89
65. Jesus distinctly foretells that he, the Messiah, will be rejected and killed, and will rise the third day.................... 91
66. The Transfiguration, and discourse in descending................ 92
67. The demoniac boy, whom the disciples could not heal........... 94
68. Returning privately through Galilee, he again foretells his death and resurrection. (Comp. § 65, 66, 101.)..................... 97
69. Jesus, the Messiah, pays the half-shekel for the Temple......... 97
70. The Twelve contend as to who shall be the greatest under the Messiah's reign. His subjects must be childlike. (Comp. § 99.) 98
71. Right treatment of a brother who has sinned against one, and duty of patiently forgiving.................................... 100
72. The Messiah's followers must give up everything for his service. 101
73. The unbelieving brothers of Jesus counsel him to exhibit himself in Judea, and he rejects the advice........................ 102
74. He goes privately to Jerusalem through Samaria............... 102

PART VI.

CLOSING MINISTRY, IN ALL PARTS OF THE HOLY LAND.

75. At the Feast of Tabernacles Jesus teaches in the Temple, and people wonder whether he is the Messiah. Attempt of the rulers to arrest him...................................... 104
[76. Story of an adulteress brought to Jesus for judgment.]......... 105
77. Jesus claims to be the Son of God, and to have existed before Abraham. Attempt of the people to stone him............ 106
78. Jesus heals a man born blind. The rulers forbid his being recognized as the Messiah.................................... 108
79. Jesus intimates that he is going to die for his flock, and come to life again.. 109
80. Mission of the Seventy, and their return. (Comp. § 55.)........ 110

Sect.		Page.
81.	Jesus answers a lawyer's question as to eternal life, giving the parable of the Good Samaritan...	111
82.	Jesus the guest of Martha and Mary...	112
83.	Jesus again gives a model of prayer (comp. §42,d), and encourages his disciples to pray...	112
84.	Blasphemous accusation of league with Beelzebub. (Comp. §48.)	113
85.	While breakfasting with a Pharisee, Jesus severely denounces the Pharisees and lawyers, and excites their enmity...	114
86.	He speaks to his disciples and a vast throng, about hypocrisy, worldly anxieties (comp. §42,e), watchfulness, and his own approaching Passion...	115
87.	All must repent or perish. Parable of the barren fig tree...	118
88.	Jesus heals on the Sabbath, and defends himself. (Comp. §37–39, 91.) Parables of the mustard seed and the leaven. (Comp. §51,d.)...	118
89.	At the Feast of Dedication, Jesus will not yet openly say that he is the Messiah. They try to stone him, and he retires to Perea...	119
90.	Teaching in Perea, on a journey toward Jerusalem. Warned against Herod Antipas...	120
91.	While breakfasting with a chief Pharisee, Jesus again heals on the Sabbath, and defends himself. (Comp. §88 and 37–39.) Three lessons suggested by the occasion...	121
92.	Great crowds follow him, and he warns them to count the cost of discipleship to him. (Comp. §59.)...	122
93.	Five great Parables—the lost sheep, the lost coin, the lost son—the unrighteous steward—the rich man and the beggar Lazarus. Some other lessons...	123
94.	Jesus raises Lazarus of Bethany from the dead...	126
95.	The Sanhedrin plot his death, and he retires again...	127
96.	Journeying through Samaria and Galilee towards Jerusalem, he teaches that the Messianic reign will come unexpectedly...	128
97.	Parables of the importunate widow, and of the Pharisee and the Publican...	129
98.	Going from Galilee through Perea, he teaches concerning divorce...	129
99.	He blesses some infant children, and teaches that subjects of the Messianic reign must be childlike. (Comp. §70.)...	131
100.	The rich young ruler, and the perils of riches. The rewards of forsaking all to follow the Messiah (comp. §72) will be great, but will be sovereign...	132

Sect.		Page.
101.	Jesus again foretells to the disciples his death and resurrection (comp. ₰ 65-67), and rebukes the selfish ambition of James and John	135
102.	Blind Bartimæus and his companion healed near Jericho	137
103.	Jesus visits Zacchæus, speaks the Parable of the pounds, and sets out for Jerusalem	138

PART VII.

LAST WEEK OF OUR LORD'S MINISTRY, AND HIS CRUCIFIXION.

104.	Jesus arrives at Bethany, near Jerusalem	140
105.	His triumphal entry into Jerusalem as the Messiah	140
106.	The barren fig tree cursed, and the second cleansing of the Temple. (Comp. ₰ 21,a.)	144
107.	Some Greeks wish to see Jesus, and he foretells that by being "lifted up" he will draw all men to him	145
108.	The barren fig tree found to have withered	146
109.	The rulers question the authority of Jesus. He refuses to explain, and sets forth their wickedness by three Parables—the two sons, the wicked husbandmen, the marriage feast of the king's son	147
110.	The Pharisees and the Herodians try to ensnare Jesus about paying tribute to Cæsar	152
111.	The Sadducees ask him a puzzling question about the resurrection	153
112.	A Pharisee who is a lawyer questions him, and then Jesus asks the Pharisees a question about the Messiah, which they cannot answer	155
113.	In his last public discourse, Jesus solemnly denounces the Scribes and Pharisees. (Comp. ₰ 85.)	156
114.	Jesus closely observes the contributions in the Temple, and commends the poor widow's gift	159
115.	Sitting on the Mount of Olives, Jesus speaks to his disciples about the destruction of Jerusalem, and his own second coming	160
116.	Conclusion of this discourse, as to the second coming—Parable of the Ten Virgins, and of the Talents—the Final Judgment	167

Sect.		Page.
117.	Jesus again predicts, and the rulers plot, his death. Mary anoints him beforehand for burial (comp. § 46), and Judas bargains to betray him.	169
118.	Preparation for the Paschal meal, and contention among the Twelve as to precedence under the Messianic reign	172
119.	During the Paschal meal, Jesus washes the feet of his disciples.	174
120.	Jesus foretells that Judas will betray him, and Peter will deny him	174
121.	Jesus institutes the Memorial of eating bread and drinking wine.	178
122.	Farewell discourse to his disciples	179
123.	Going forth to Gethsemane, Jesus suffers long in agony	183
124.	Jesus is betrayed, arrested, and forsaken	186
125.	Jesus first examined by Annas, the ex-High Priest	190
126.	Tried and Condemned by Caiaphas and the Sanhedrin	190
127.	Peter thrice denies his Lord	193
128.	After dawn, Jesus is formally condemned by the Sanhedrin, and led away to Pilate	195
129.	Remorse and suicide of Judas the betrayer	197
130.	Jesus before Pilate the first time	197
131.	Jesus before Herod Antipas the tetrarch of Galilee	200
132.	Brought back to Pilate, who slowly and reluctantly consents that he shall be crucified	201
133.	The Crucifixion	207

PART VIII.

OUR LORD'S RESURRECTION, APPEARANCES, AND ASCENSION.

134.	Angels announce to certain women that Jesus is risen, and Peter and John enter the empty tomb	218
135.	The risen Lord appears to the women, and separately to Mary Magdalene. These report to the Apostles	220
136.	Some of the guard report to the Jewish Rulers	222
137.	Jesus appears to Simon Peter, and to two disciples on the way to Emmaus	223
138.	He appears to the Apostles (except Thomas), to the two returned from Emmaus, and others, and gives a Commission	224
139.	He appears again to the Apostles, including Thomas	226
140.	He appears to seven disciples beside the sea of Galilee	226

XII SYNOPSIS OF THE HARMONY.

Sect. Page.
141. He meets the Apostles and above five hundred on an appointed mountain in Galilee, and gives a Commission............... 228
142. He appears to James; then to all the Apostles, and gives them a Commission... 229
143. The Ascension.. 230

INDEX TO NOTES (AT THE END) ON POINTS OF
SPECIAL DIFFICULTY.

On § 1,c. The Genealogies of Christ.............................. 232
On § 7. Probable time of the Saviour's Birth.................... 235
On § 37. The Feast of John 5:1, and the Duration of our Lord's Ministry.. 241
On § 41. The four lists of the Twelve Apostles.................. 244
On § 42. The Sermon on the Mount................................ 246
On § 75. The Combination of Luke and John...................... 249
On § 118. Did Christ eat the Passover?........................... 253
On § 132. The Hour of the Crucifixion............................ 258
On § 134. Time of the Resurrection of Christ..................... 260
On § 134. Length of our Lord's Stay in the Tomb................. 263

TABLE

FOR FINDING ANY PASSAGE IN THE HARMONY.

MATTHEW.

Chap.	Verse.	Section.	Page.	Chap.	Verse.	Section.	Page.
1	1–17	1(c)	2	9	1	54	70
1	18–25	6	7	9	2–8	32	32
2	1–12	10	9	9	9–13	33	34
2	13–18	11	10	9	14–17	34	35
2	19–23	12	10	9	18–26	35	36
3	1–12	14	12	9	27–34	36	39
3	13–17	15	15	9	35–38	55	71
4	1–11	16	16	10	1–42	55	71
4	12	23(a)	22	11	1	55	74
4	13–16	26	27	11	2–30	45	54
4	17	24	25	12	1–8	38	41
4	18–22	27	27	12	9–14	39	42
4	23–25	30	30	12	15–21	40	44
5	1,2	42	45	12	22–37	48	57
5	3–12	42(a)	46	12	38–45	49	59
5	13–16	42(b)	46	12	46–50	50	59
5	17–48	42(c)	46	13	1–3	51	60
6	1–18	42(d)	48	13	3–23	51(a)	61
6	19–34	42(e)	49	13	24–30	51(c)	64
7	1–6	42(f)	50	13	31–35	51(d)	64
7	7–12	42(g)	51	13	36–53	51(e)	65
7	13–23	42(h)	51	13	54–58	54	70
7	24–29	42(i)	52	14	1–12	56	74
8	1	43	52	14	13–21	57	76
8	2–4	31	31	14	22–36	58	79
8	5–13	43	52	15	1–20	60	83
8	14–17	29	29	15	21–28	61	85
8	18	52	66	15	29–38	62	86
8	19–22	72	101	15	39	63	88
8	23–27	52	66	16	1–12	63	88
8	28–34	53	67	16	13–20	64	89

XIV TABLE FOR FINDING ANY PASSAGE IN HARMONY.

MATTHEW—Continued.

Chap.	Verse.	Section.	Page.	Chap.	Verse.	Section.	Page.
16	21–28	65	91	25	1–46	116	167
17	1–13	66	92	26	1–16	117	169
17	14–20	67	94	26	17–20	118	172
17	22, 23	68	97	26	21–25	120	174
17	24–27	69	97	26	26–29	121	178
18	1–14	70	98	26	30	123	183
18	15–35	71	100	26	31–35	120	176
19	1–12	98	129	26	36–46	123	183
19	13–15	99	131	26	47–56	124	186
19	16–30	100	132	26	57	126	190
20	1–16	100	134	26	58	127	193
20	17–28	101	135	26	59–68	126	190
20	29–34	102	137	26	69–75	127	194
21	1–11	105	140	27	1, 2	128	195
21	12, 13	106	144	27	3–10	129	197
21	14–17	105	143	27	11–14	130	197
21	18, 19	106	144	27	15–30	132	201
21	19–22	108	146	27	31–34	133 (a)	207
21	23–46	109	147	27	35–44	133 (b)	209
22	1–14	109	151	27	45–56	133 (c)	212
22	15–22	110	152	27	57–66	133 (d)	215
22	23–33	111	153	28	1–8	134	218
22	34–46	112	155	28	9, 10	135	220
23	1–39	113	156	28	11–15	136	222
24	1–51	115	160	28	16–20	141	228

MARK.

Chap.	Verse.	Section.	Page.	Chap.	Verse.	Section.	Page.
1	1–8	14	12	2	18–22	34	35
1	9–11	15	15	2	23–28	38	41
1	12, 13	16	16	3	1–6	39	42
1	14	23(a)	22	3	7–12	40	44
1	14, 15	24	25	3	13–19	41	44
1	16–20	27	27	3	19–30	48	57
1	21–28	28	28	3	31–35	50	59
1	29–34	29	29	4	1, 2	51	60
1	35–39	30	30	4	3–25	51(a)	61
1	40–45	31	31	4	26–29	51(b)	64
2	1–12	32	32	4	30–34	51(d)	64
2	13–17	33	34	4	35–41	52	66

MARK—CONTINUED.

Chap.	Verse.	Section.	Page.	Chap.	Verse.	Section.	Page.
5	1–20	53	67	12	18–27	111	153
5	21	54	70	12	28–37	112	155
5	22–43	35	36	12	38–40	113	156
6	1–6	54	70	12	41–44	114	159
6	6–13	55	71	13	1–37	115	160
6	14–29	56	74	14	1–11	117	169
6	30–44	57	76	14	12–17	118	172
6	45–56	58	79	14	18–21	120	174
7	1–23	60	83	14	22–25	121	178
7	24–30	61	85	14	26	123	183
7	31–37	62	86	14	27–31	120	176
8	1–9	62	87	14	32–42	123	184
8	10–26	63	88	14	43–52	124	186
8	27–30	64	89	14	53	126	190
8	31–38	65	91	14	54	127	193
9	1	65	92	14	55–65	126	190
9	2–13	66	92	14	66–72	127	194
9	14–29	67	94	15	1	128	195
9	30–32	68	97	15	2–5	130	197
9	33–50	70	98	15	6–19	132	201
10	1–12	98	129	15	20–23	133(a)	207
10	13–16	99	131	15	24–32	133(b)	209
10	17–31	100	132	15	33–41	133(c)	212
10	32–45	101	135	15	42–47	133(d)	215
10	46–52	102	137	16	1–8	134	218
11	1–11	105	140	16	9–11	135	220
11	12–18	106	144	16	12, 13	137	223
11	19–25	108	146	16	14	138	224
11	27–33	109	147	16	15–18	141	228
12	1–12	109	149	16	19, 20	143	230
12	13–17	110	152				

LUKE.

Chap.	Verse.	Section.	Page.	Chap.	Verse.	Section.	Page.
1	1–4	1(a)	1	2	21–38	9	8
1	5–25	2	3	2	39	12	10
1	26–38	3	4	2	40–52	13	11
1	39–56	4	5	3	1–18	14	12
1	57–80	5	6	3	19, 20	23	22
2	1–7	7	7	3	21, 22	15	15
2	8–20	8	8	3	23–38	1(c)	2

XVI TABLE FOR FINDING ANY PASSAGE IN HARMONY.

LUKE.—CONTINUED.

Chap.	Verse.	Section.	Page.	Chap.	Verse.	Section.	Page.
4	1–13	16	16	11	1–13	83	112
4	14, 15	23	22	11	14–36	84	113
4	14, 15	24	25	11	37–54	85	114
4	16–31	26	26	12	1–59	86	115
4	31–37	28	28	13	1–9	87	118
4	38–41	29	29	13	10–21	88	118
4	42–44	30	30	13	22–35	90	120
5	1–11	27	27	14	1–24	91	121
5	12–16	31	31	14	25–35	92	122
5	17–26	32	32	15	1–32	93	123
5	33–39	34	35	16	1–31	93	124
6	1–5	38	41	17	1–10	93	125
6	6–11	39	42	17	11–37	96	128
6	12–16	41	44	18	1–14	97	129
6	17–19	42	45	18	15–17	99	131
6	20–26	42(a)	46	18	18–30	100	132
6	27–36	42(c)	46	18	31–34	101	135
6	31	42(g)	51	18	35–43	102	137
6	37–42	42(f)	50	19	1–28	103	138
6	47–49	42(i)	52	19	29–44	105	140
7	1–10	43	52	19	45–48	106	144
7	11–17	44	53	20	1–19	109	147
7	18–35	45	54	20	20–26	110	152
7	36–50	46	56	20	27–40	111	153
8	1–3	47	57	20	41–44	112	156
8	4	51	60	20	45–47	113	156
8	5–18	51(a)	61	21	1–4	114	159
8	19–21	50	59	21	5–36	115	160
8	22–25	52	66	21	37, 38	108	146
8	26–39	53	67	22	1–6	117	169
8	40	54	70	22	7–16	118	172
8	41–56	35	36	22	17–20	121	178
9	1–6	55	71	22	21–23	120	174
9	7–9	56	74	22	24–30	118	173
9	10–17	57	76	22	31–38	120	176
9	18–21	64	89	22	39–46	123	183
9	22–27	65	91	22	47–53	124	186
9	28–36	66	92	22	54	126	190
9	37–43	67	94	22	54–62	127	193
9	43–45	68	97	22	63–65	126	192
9	46–50	70	98	22	66–71	128	195
9	51–56	74	102	23	1	128	196
9	57–62	72	101	23	2–5	130	197
10	1–22	80	110	23	6–12	131	200
10	25–37	81	111	23	13–25	132	201
10	38–42	82	112	23	26–33	133(a)	207

LUKE.—CONTINUED.

Chap.	Verse.	Section.	Page.	Chap.	Verse.	Section.	Page.
23	33–43	133 (b)	209	24	13–35	137	223
23	44–49	133 (c)	212	24	36–43	138	224
23	50–56	133 (d)	215	24	44–49	142	229
24	1–8	134	218	24	50–53	143	230
24	9–11	135	220				

JOHN.

Chap.	Verse.	Section.	Page.	Chap.	Verse.	Section.	Page.
1	1–18	1(b)	1	12	1	104	140
1	19–34	17	18	12	2–8	117	169
1	35–51	18	18	12	9–11	104	140
2	1–11	19	19	12	12–19	105	141
2	12	20	20	12	20–50	107	145
2	13–22	21(a)	20	13	1–20	119	174
2	23–25	21(b)	20	13	21–38	120	174
3	1–21	21(b)	20	14	1–31	122(a)	179
3	22–36	22	21	15	1–27	122(b)	180
4	1–4	23(a)	22	16	1–33	122(b)	181
4	5–42	23(b)	22	17	1–26	122(c)	182
4	43–45	23(c)	24	18	1	123	183
4	46–54	25	26	18	2–12	124	186
5	1–47	37	39	18	12–14	125	190
6	1–14	57	76	18	15–18	127	193
6	15–21	58	79	18	19–23	125	190
6	22–71	59	81	18	24	126	190
7	1	60	83	18	25–27	127	194
7	2–9	73	102	18	28	128	196
7	10	74	102	18	28–38	130	197
7	11–52	75	104	18	39, 40	132	202
7	53	76	105	19	1–16	132	203
8	1–11	76	105	19	16, 17	133(a)	207
8	12–59	77	106	19	18–27	133(b)	209
9	1–41	78	108	19	28–30	133(c)	213
10	1–21	79	109	19	31–42	133(d)	215
10	22–42	89	119	20	1–10	134	218
11	1–46	94	126	20	11–18	135	220
11	47–54	95	127	20	19–25	138	224
11	55–57	104	140	20	26–31	139	226
				21	1–25	140	226

PART I.

MATTERS CONNECTED WITH OUR LORD'S BIRTH AND CHILDHOOD.

§ 1. INTRODUCTORY PORTIONS OF THE SEVERAL GOSPELS.

Matthew, writing for Jewish readers, begins with a genealogy (comp. Gen. 5:1; 6:9; 10:1, etc.). Luke, writing like a Greek historian, begins with a dedication to a friend (so also in Part II of his history, Acts 1:1). John begins in a thoroughly unique manner, not (as in many biographies) with the birth of the subject, but with his eternal pre-existence, and the fact that the entire universe owes its existence to him; adding that he finally became incarnate, and we knew him well (comp. 1 John 1:1). Mark begins his narrative without any formal Introduction.

(a) DEDICATION OF LUKE'S GOSPEL.
Luke 1:1–4.

1 FORASMUCH as many have taken in hand to draw up a narrative con-
2 cerning those matters which have been ¹fulfilled among us, even as they delivered them unto us, which from the beginning were eyewitnesses
3 and ministers of the word, it seemed good to me also, having traced the course of all things accurately from the first, to write unto thee in order,
4 most excellent Theophilus; that thou mightest know the certainty concerning the ²things ³wherein thou wast instructed.

1 Or. *fully established.* 2. Gr. *words.* 3. Or, *which thou wast taught by word of mouth.*

(b) INTRODUCTION TO JOHN'S GOSPEL.
John 1:1–18.

1 In the beginning was the Word, and the Word was with God, and
2 the Word was God. The same was in the beginning with God.
3 All things were made ¹by him; and without him ²was not anything
4 made that hath been made. In him was life; and the life was the light
5 of men. And the light shineth in the darkness; and the darkness ³ap-
6 prehended it not. There came a man, sent from God, whose name was
7 John. The same came for witness, that he might bear witness of the
8 light, that all might believe through him. He was not the light, but
9 came that he might bear witness of the light. ⁴There was the true
10 light, *even the light* which lighteth ⁵every man, coming into the world.

He was in the world, and the world was made ¹by him, and the world
11 knew him not. He came unto ⁶his own, and they that were his own

John 1:1-18.

12 received him not. But as many as received him, to them gave he the
13 right to become children of God, *even* to them that believe on his name:
which were ⁷born, not of ⁸blood, nor of the will of the flesh, nor of the
14 will of man, but of God. And the Word became flesh, and ⁹dwelt
among us (and we beheld his glory, glory as of ¹⁰the only begotten
15 from the Father), full of grace and truth. John beareth witness of
him, and crieth, saying, ¹¹This was he of whom I said, He that com-
16 eth after me is become before me: for he was ¹²before me. For of his
17 fulness we all received, and grace for grace. For the law was given
18 ¹by Moses; grace and truth came ¹by Jesus Christ. No man hath seen
God at any time; ¹³the only begotten Son, which is in the bosom of
the Father, he hath declared *him*.

1. Or, *through*. 2. Or, *was not anything made. That which hath been made was life in him; and the life, &c.* 3. Or, *overcame*. 4. Or, *The true light, which lighteth every man, was coming*. 5. Or, *every man as he cometh*. 6. Gr. *his own things*. 7. Or, *begotten*. 8. Gr. *bloods*. 9. Gr. *tabernacled*. 10. Or, *an only begotten from a father*. 11. Some ancient authorities read (*this was he that said*). 12. Gr. *first in regard of me*. 13. Many very ancient authorities read *God only begotten*.

(c) THE GENEALOGIES IN MATTHEW AND LUKE.

| Matt. 1:1-17. | Luke 3:23-38. |

1 ¹The book of the ²generation of Jesus Christ, the son of David, the son of Abraham.
2 Abraham begat Isaac; and Isaac begat Jacob; and Jacob begat Ju-
3 dah and his brethren; and Judah begat Perez and Zerah of Tamar; and Perez begat Hezron; and Hez-
4 ron begat ³Ram; and ³Ram begat Amminadab; and Amminadab begat Nahshon: and Nahshon
5 begat Salmon; and Salmon begat Boaz of Rahab; and Boaz begat
6 Obed of Ruth; and Obed begat Jesse; and Jesse begat David the king.
And David begat Solomon of her *that had been the wife* of Uriah;
7 and Solomon begat Rehoboam; and Rehoboam begat Abijah;
8 and Abijah begat ⁴Asa; and ⁴Asa begat Jehoshaphat; and Jehoshaphat begat Joram; and Joram
9 begat Uzziah; and Uzziah begat Jotham; and Jotham begat Ahaz;
10 and Ahaz begat Hezekiah; and Hezekiah begat Manasseh; and Manasseh begat ⁵Amon; and
11 ⁵Amon begat Josiah; and Josiah begat Jechoniah and his breth-

Being the son (as was supposed)
24 of Joseph, the *son* of Heli, the *son* of Matthat, the *son* of Levi,
25 the *son* of Jannai, the *son* of Joseph, the *son* of Mattathias, the *son* of Amos, the *son* of Nahum, the *son* of Esli, the *son* of Nag-
26 gai, the *son* of Maath, the son of Mattathias, the *son* of Semein, the *son* of Josech, the *son* of
27 Joda, the *son* of Joanan, the *son* of Rhesa, the *son* of Zerubbabel, the *son* of ⁷Shealtiel, the *son* of
28 Neri, the *son* of Melchi, the *son* of Addi, the *son* of Cosam, the
29 *son* of Elmadam, the *son* of Er, the *son* of Jesus, the *son* of Eliezer, the *son* of Jorim, the *son* of
30 Matthat, the *son* of Levi, the *son* of Symeon, the *son* of Judas, the *son* of Joseph, the *son* of Jonam,
31 the *son* of Eliakim, the *son* of Melea, the *son* of Menna, the *son* of Mattatha, the *son* of Nathan,
32 the *son* of David, the *son* of Jesse, the *son* of Obed, the *son* of Boaz, the *son* of ⁸Salmon, the *son* of
33 Nahshon, the *son* of Amminadab,
⁹the *son* of ¹⁰Arni, the *son* of Hez-
34 ron, the *son* of Perez, the *son* of

OUR LORD'S BIRTH AND CHILDHOOD.

Matt. 1:1-17.	Luke 3:23-38.
ren, at the time of the ⁶carrying away to Babylon.	Judah, the *son* of Jacob, the *son*
12 And after the ⁶carrying away to Babylon, Jechoniah begat ⁷Shealtiel; and ⁷Shealtiel begat	35 of Isaac, the *son* of Abraham, the *son* of Terah, the *son* of Nahor, the *son* of Serug, the *son* of Reu, the *son* of Peleg, the *son* of Eber,
13 Zerubbabel; and Zerubbabel begat Abiud; and Abiud begat Eli-	36 the *son* of Shelah, the *son* of Cainan, the *son* of Arphaxad, the
14 akim; and Eliakim begat Azor; and Azor begat Sadoc; and Sa-	*son* of Shem, the *son* of Noah,
15 doc begat Achim; and Achim begat Eliud; and Eliud begat Eleazar; and Eleazar begat Matthan; and Matthan begat Jacob;	37 the *son* of Lamech, the *son* of Methuselah, the *son* of Enoch, the *son* of Jared, the *son* of Ma-
16 and Jacob begat Joseph the husband of Mary, of whom was born Jesus, who is called Christ.	38 halaleel, the *son* of Cainan, the *son* of Enos, the *son* of Seth, the *son* of Adam, the *son* of God.

17 So all the generations from Abraham unto David are fourteen generations; and from David to the ⁶carrying away to Babylon fourteen generations; and from the ⁶carrying away to Babylon unto the Christ fourteen generations.*

1 Or, *The Genealogy of Jesus Christ.* 2 Or, *The birth;* as in ver. 18. 3 Gr. *Aram.* 4 Gr. *Asaph.* 5 Gr. *Amos.* 6 Or, *removal to Babylon.* 7 Gr. *Salathiel.* 8 Some ancient authorities write *Sala.* 9 Many ancient authorities insert *the son of Admin:* and one writes *Admin* for *Amminadab.* 10 Some ancient authorities write *Aram.*

The first events of the history are the several Annunciations and related matters, and the birth of John the Forerunner, and of Jesus the Messiah. §§ 2-8.

§ 2. ANNUNCIATION† OF THE BIRTH OF JOHN THE BAPTIST.

Jerusalem, in the Temple.   Probably B.C. 6.

Luke 1:5-25.

5 There was in the days of Herod, king of Judea, a certain priest named Zacharias, of the course of Abijah: and he had a wife of the
6 daughters of Aaron, and her name was Elisabeth. And they were both righteous before God, walking in all the commandments and or-
7 dinances of the Lord blameless. And they had no child, because that Elisabeth was barren, and they both were *now* ¹well stricken in years.
8 Now it came to pass, while he executed the priest's office before
9 God in the order of his course, according to the custom of the priest's
10 office, his lot was to enter into the ²temple of the Lord and burn incense. And the whole multitude of the people were praying without
11 at the hour of incense. And there appeared unto him an angel of the
12 Lord standing on the right side of the altar of incense. And Zacha-
13 rias was troubled when he saw *him*, and fear fell upon him. But the angel said unto him, Fear not, Zacharias: because thy supplication is

*Observe that Matthew's three divisions of the genealogy represent three great periods in the history of Israel. Luke's genealogy is strikingly different (see Note in the latter part of this volume, on § 1, c).
†Observe that there are three annunciations: §2, §3, §6, and §§4 and 5 are virtually connected with these. Trace this connection throughout §§2-7.

MATTERS CONNECTED WITH

Luke 1:5–25.

heard, and thy wife Elisabeth shall bear thee a son, and thou shalt 14 call his name John. And thou shalt have joy and gladness; and many 15 shall rejoice at his birth. For he shall be great in the sight of the Lord, and he shall drink no wine nor [3]strong drink; and he shall be 16 filled with the [4]Holy Ghost, even from his mother's womb. And many 17 of the children of Israel shall he turn unto the Lord their God. And he shall [5]go before his face in the spirit and power of Elijah, to turn the hearts of the fathers to the children, and the disobedient *to walk* in the wisdom of the just; to make ready for the Lord a people pre-18 pared *for him*. And Zacharias said unto the angel, Whereby shall I know this? for I am an old man, and my wife [6]well stricken in years. 19 And the angel answering said unto him, I am Gabriel, that stand in the presence of God; and I was sent to speak unto thee, and to bring 20 thee these good tidings. And behold, thou shalt be silent and not able to speak, until the day that these things shall come to pass, because thou believedst not my words, which shall be fulfilled in their 21 season. And the people were waiting for Zacharias, and they mar-22 velled [7]while he tarried in the [2]temple. And when he came out, he could not speak unto them: and they perceived that he had seen a vision in the [2]temple: and he continued making signs unto them, and 23 remained dumb. And it came to pass, when the days of his ministration were fulfilled, he departed unto his house.
24   And after these days Elisabeth his wife conceived; and she hid her-25 self five months, saying, Thus hath the Lord done unto me in the days wherein he looked upon *me*, to take away my reproach among men.

1. Gr. *advanced in their days*.   2. Or, *sanctuary*.   3. Gr. *sikera*.   4. Or, *Holy Spirit;* and so throughout all the Gospels.   5. Some ancient authorities read *come nigh before his face*.   6. Gr. *advanced in her days*.   7. Or, *at his tarrying*.

§ 3. ANNUNCIATION TO THE VIRGIN MARY OF THE BIRTH OF JESUS.

Nazareth.   Probably B.C. 5.

Luke 1:26–38.

26 Now in the sixth month the angel Gabriel was sent from God unto 27 a city of Galilee, named Nazareth, to a virgin betrothed to a man whose name was Joseph, of the house of David; and the virgin's name 28 was Mary. And he came in unto her, and said, Hail, thou that art 29 [1]highly favoured, the Lord *is* with thee.[2] But she was greatly troubled at the saying, and cast in her mind what manner of saluta-30 tion this might be. And the angel said unto her, Fear not, Mary: 31 for thou hast found [3]favor with God. And behold, thou shalt conceive in thy womb, and bring forth a son, and shalt call his name 32 Jesus. He shall be great, and shall be called the Son of the Most High: and the Lord God shall give unto him the throne of his father 33 David: and he shall reign over the house of Jacob [4]forever; and of his 34 kingdom there shall be no end. And Mary said unto the angel, How 35 shall this be, seeing I know not a man? And the angel answered and said unto her, The Holy Ghost shall come upon thee, and the power of the Most High shall overshadow thee: wherefore also [5]that which

Luke 1:26–38.

36 ⁶is to be born ⁷shall be called holy, the Son of God. And behold,
Elisabeth thy kinswoman, she also hath conceived a son in her old
37 age: and this is the sixth month with her that ⁸was called barren.
38 For no word from God shall be void of power. And Mary said, Behold, the ⁹handmaid of the Lord; be it unto me according to thy word. And the angel departed from her.

1. Or, endued with grace. 2. Many ancient authorities add blessed art thou among women. (See ver. 42.) 3. Or, grace. 4. Gr. unto the ages. 5. Or, the holy thing which is to be born shall be called the son of God. 6. Or, is begotten. 7. Some ancient authorities insert of thee. 8. Or, is. 9. Gr. bondmaid.

§ 4. VISIT OF MARY TO ELISABETH.

Hill Country of Judea.

Luke 1:39–56.

39 And Mary arose in these days and went into the hill country with
40 haste, into a city of Judah; and entered into the house of Zacharias and
41 saluted Elisabeth. And it came to pass, when Elisabeth heard the salutation of Mary, the babe leaped in her womb; and Elisabeth was filled
42 with the Holy Ghost; and she lifted up her voice with a loud cry, and said, Blessed *art* thou among women, and blessed *is* the fruit of thy
43 womb. And whence is this to me, that the mother of my Lord should
44 come unto me? For behold, when the voice of thy salutation came
45 into mine ears, the babe leaped in my womb for joy. And blessed *is* she that ¹believed; for there shall be a fulfilment of the things which
46 have been spoken to her from the Lord. And Mary said,
   My soul doth magnify the Lord,
47 And my spirit hath rejoiced in God my Saviour.
48 For he hath looked upon the low estate of his ²handmaiden:
   For behold, from henceforth all generations shall call me blessed.
49 For he that is mighty hath done to me great things;
   And holy is his name.
50 And his mercy is unto generations and generations
   On them that fear him.
51 He hath shewed strength with his arm;
   He hath scattered the proud ³in the imagination of their heart.
52 He hath put down princes from *their* thrones,
   And hath exalted them of low degree.
53 The hungry he hath filled with good things;
   And the rich he hath sent empty away.
54 He hath holpen Israel his servant,
   That he might remember mercy
55 (As he spake unto our fathers)
   Toward Abraham and his seed for ever.
56 And Mary abode with her about three months, and returned unto her house.

1. Or, believed that there shall be. 2. Gr. bondmaiden. 3. Or, by.

§ 5. BIRTH OF JOHN THE BAPTIST, AND HIS DESERT LIFE.
Hill Country of Judea.
Luke 1:57-80.

57 Now Elisabeth's time was fulfilled that she should be delivered;
58 and she brought forth a son. And her neighbors and her kinsfolk heard that the Lord had magnified his mercy toward her; and they
59 rejoiced with her. And it came to pass on the eighth day, that they came to circumcise the child; and they would have called him Zacha-
60 rias, after the name of his father. And his mother answered and
61 said, Not so; but he shall be called John. And they said unto her,
62 There is none of thy kindred that is called by this name. And they
63 made signs to his father, what he would have him called. And he
64 asked for a writing tablet, and wrote, saying, His name is John. And they marvelled all. And his mouth was opened immediately, and his
65 tongue *loosed*, and he spake, blessing God. And fear came on all that dwelt round about them: and all these sayings were noised abroad
66 throughout all the hill country of Judea. And all that heard them laid them up in their heart, saying, What then shall this child be? For the hand of the Lord was with him.
67 And his father Zacharias was filled with the Holy Ghost, and prophesied, saying,
68 Blessed *be* the Lord, the God of Israel;
For he hath visited and wrought redemption for his people,
69 And hath raised up a horn of salvation for us
In the house of his servant David
70 (As he spake by the mouth of his holy prophets which have been since the world began),
71 Salvation from our enemies, and from the hand of all that hate us;
72 To show mercy towards our fathers,
And to remember his holy covenant;
73 The oath which he sware unto Abraham our father,
74 To grant unto us that we being delivered out of the hand of our enemies
Should serve him without fear,
75 In holiness and righteousness before him all our days.
76 Yea and thou, child, shalt be called the prophet of the Most High:
For thou shalt go before the face of the Lord to make ready his ways;
77 To give knowledge of salvation unto his people
In the remission of their sins,
78 Because of the [1] tender mercy of our God,
[2] Whereby the dayspring from on high [3] shall visit us,
79 To shine upon them that sit in darkness and the shadow of death;
To guide our feet into the way of peace.
80 And the child grew, and waxed strong in spirit, and was in the deserts till the day of his shewing unto Israel.*

1. Or, *heart of mercy*. 2. Or, *Wherein*. 3. **Many** ancient authorities read *hath visited us*.

*Dwell on this summary statement as to John's retired life in the wild regions of Judea, whence he will come forth 30 years later, § 14.

OUR LORD'S BIRTH AND CHILDHOOD.

§ 6. ANNUNCIATION TO JOSEPH OF THE BIRTH OF JESUS.
Nazareth.
Matt. 1:18-25

18 Now the [1]birth [2]of Jesus Christ was on this wise: When his mother Mary had been betrothed to Joseph, before they came together she
19 was found with child of the [3]Holy Ghost. And Joseph her husband, being a righteous man, and not willing to make her a public example,
20 was minded to put her away privily. But when he thought on these things, behold, an angel of the Lord appeared unto him in a dream, saying, Joseph, thou son of David, fear not to take unto thee Mary
21 thy wife: for that which is [4]conceived in her is of the Holy Ghost. And she shall bring forth a son; and thou shalt call his name JESUS;
22 for it is he that shall save his people from their sins. Now all this is come to pass, that it might be fulfilled which was spoken by the Lord through the prophet, saying,
23 Behold, the virgin shall be with child, and shall bring forth a son, And they shall call his name [5]Immanuel;
24 which is, being interpreted, God with us. And Joseph arose from his sleep, and did as the angel of the Lord commanded him, and took unto
25 him his wife; and knew her not till she had brought forth a son.

1. Or. *generation:* as in ver. 1 in § 3.   2. Some ancient authorities read *of the Christ.*
3. Or, *Holy Spirit.*   4. Gr. *begotten.*   5. Gr. *Emmanuel.*

§ 7. BIRTH OF JESUS.
Bethlehem.   Probably B.C. 5.
Luke 2:1-7.

1 Now it came to pass in those days, there went out a decree from
2 Cæsar Augustus, that all the [1]world should be enrolled. This was the first enrolment made when Quirinius was governor of Syria.
3 And all went to enrol themselves, every one to his own city.* And
4 Joseph also went up from Galilee, out of the city of Nazareth, into Ju-
5 dea, to the city of David, which is called Bethlehem, because he was of the house and family of David; to enrol himself with Mary, who was
6 betrothed to him, being great with child. And it came to pass, while they were there, the days were fulfilled that she should be delivered.
7 And she brought forth her firstborn son; and she wrapped him in swaddling clothes, and laid him in a manger, because there was no room for them in the inn.

1. Gr. *inhabited earth.*

*Observe how the ruler of the civilized world is unconsciously bringing it about that the Messiah, the son of David, shall be born at Bethlehem, though his mother's home was Nazareth. All the previous history of Rome and of Israel gathers about this manger. As to Quirinius, and as to the probable time of the Saviour's birth, see Note at the end of the book, § 7.

§ 8. ANGELS PROCLAIM TO SHEPHERDS THAT THE MESSIAH IS BORN AT BETHLEHEM.

Near Bethlehem.
Luke 2:8–20.

8 And there were shepherds in the same country abiding in the field,
9 and keeping [1]watch by night over their flock. And an angel of the Lord stood by them, and the glory of the Lord shone round about
10 them, and they were sore afraid. And the angel said unto them, Be
11 not afraid; for behold, I bring you good tidings of great joy which shall be to all the people: for there is born to you this day in the city
12 of David, a Saviour which is [2]Christ the Lord. And this is the sign unto you; Ye shall find a babe wrapped in swaddling clothes, and lying
13 in a manger. And suddenly there was with the angel a multitude of the heavenly host praising God, and saying,
14 Glory to God in the highest,
And on earth [3]peace among [4]men in whom he is well pleased.
15 And it came to pass, when the angels went away from them into heaven, the shepherds said one to another, Let us now go even unto Bethlehem, and see this [5]thing that is come to pass, which the Lord
16 hath made known unto us. And they came with haste, and found
17 both Mary and Joseph, and the babe lying in the manger. And when they saw it, they made known concerning the saying which was spok-
18 en to them about this child. And all that heard it wondered at the
19 things which were spoken unto them by the shepherds. But Mary
20 kept all these [6]sayings, pondering them in her heart. And the shepherds returned, glorifying and praising God for all the things that they had heard and seen, even as it was spoken unto them.

1. Or, *night-watches.* 2. Or, *Anointed Lord.* 3. Many ancient authorities read *peace, good pleasure among men.* 4. Gr. *men of good pleasure.* 5. Or, *saying.* 6. Or, *things.*

Next, in §§ 9–13 we find certain events connected with Jesus' infancy and childhood.

§ 9. CIRCUMCISION OF JESUS, AND PRESENTATION IN THE TEMPLE.

Bethlehem and Jerusalem.
Luke 2:21–38.

21 And when eight days were fulfilled for circumcising him, his name was called JESUS, which was so called by the angel before he was conceived in the womb.
22 And when the days of their purification according to the law of
23 Moses were fulfilled, they brought him up to Jerusalem, to present him to the Lord (as it is written in the law of the Lord, Every male that openeth the womb, shall be called holy to the Lord), and to offer
24 a sacrifice according to that which is said in the law of the Lord, A
25 pair of turtledoves, or two young pigeons. And behold, there was a man in Jerusalem, whose name was Simeon; and this man was righteous and devout, looking for the consolation of Israel: and the Holy
26 Spirit was upon him. And it had been revealed unto him by the Holy Spirit, that he should not see death, before he had seen the Lord's

OUR LORD'S BIRTH AND CHILDHOOD.

Luke 2:21-38.

27 Christ. And he came in the Spirit into the temple: and when the parents brought in the child Jesus, that they might do concerning
28 him after the custom of the law, then he received him into his arms, and blessed God and said,*
29   Now lettest thou thy [1]servant depart, O [2]Lord,
    According to thy word, in peace;
30   For mine eyes have seen thy salvation,
31   Which thou hast prepared before the face of all the peoples;
32   A light for [3]revelation to the Gentiles,
    And the glory of thy people Israel.
33 And his father and his mother were marvelling at the things which
34 were spoken concerning him; and Simeon blessed them, and said unto Mary his mother, Behold, this *child* is set for the falling and rising
35 up of many in Israel; and for a sign which is spoken against; yea and a sword shall pierce through thine own soul; that thoughts out of many
36 hearts may be revealed. And there was one Anna, a prophetess, the daughter of Phanuel, of the tribe of Asher (she was [4]of a great age,
37 having lived with a husband seven years from her virginity, and she had been a widow even for four-score and four years), which departed not from the temple, worshipping with fastings and supplications night
38 and day. And coming up at that very hour she gave thanks unto God, and spake of him to all them that were looking for the redemption of Jerusalem.

1. Gr. *bondservant.* 2. Gr. *Master.* 3. Or, *the unveiling of the Gentiles.* 4. Gr. *advanced in many days.*

§ 10. MAGI VISIT THE NEW-BORN KING OF THE JEWS.

Jerusalem and Bethlehem.

Matt. 2:1-12.

1   Now when Jesus was born in Bethlehem of Judea in the days of
2 Herod the king, behold, [1]wise men from the east came to Jerusalem, saying, [2]Where is he that is born King of the Jews? for we saw his
3 star in the east, and are come to worship him. And when Herod the
4 king heard it, he was troubled, and all Jerusalem with him. And gathering together all the chief priests and scribes of the people, he
5 inquired of them where the Christ should be born. And they said unto him, In Bethlehem of Judea: for thus it is written [3]by the prophet,
6   And thou Bethlehem, land of Judah,
    Art in no wise least among the princes of Judah;
    For out of thee shall come forth a governor,
    Which shall be shepherd of my people Israel.
7 Then Herod privily called the [1]wise men, and learned of them
8 carefully [4]what time the star appeared. And he sent them to Bethlehem, and said, Go and search out carefully concerning the young child; and when ye have found *him*, bring me word, that I also may
9 come and worship him. And they, having heard the king, went their way; and lo, the star, which they saw in the east, went be-

* Notice the four Psalms here occurring, those of Elisabeth and Mary in § 4, of Zacharias in § 5, of Simeon in § 9.

Matt. 2:1-12.

fore them, till it came and stood over where the young child was.
10 And when they saw the star, they rejoiced with exceeding great joy.
11 And they came into the house and saw the young child with Mary his mother; and they fell down and worshipped him; and opening their treasures they offered unto him gifts, gold and frankincense
12 and myrrh. And being warned *of God* in a dream that they should not return to Herod, they departed into their own country another way.

1. Gr. *Magi.* Compare Esther 1:13; Dan. 2:12. 2. Or, *Where is the King of the Jews that is born?* 3. Or, *through.* 4. Or, *the time of the star that appeared.*

§ 11. THE CHILD JESUS CARRIED TO EGYPT, AND THE CHILDREN AT BETHLEHEM SLAIN.

Probably B.C. 4.

Matt. 2:13-18.

13 Now when they were departed, behold, an angel of the Lord appeareth to Joseph in a dream, saying, Arise and take the young child and his mother, and flee into Egypt, and be thou there until I tell
14 thee: for Herod will seek the young child to destroy him. And he arose and took the young child by night, and departed into Egypt;
15 and was there until the death of Herod: that it might be fulfilled which was spoken by the Lord through the prophet, saying, Out of
16 Egypt did I call my son. Then Herod, when he saw that he was mocked of the ¹wise men, was exceeding wroth, and sent forth, and slew all the male children that were in Bethlehem, and in all the borders thereof, from two years old and under, according to the time
17 which he had carefully learned of the ¹wise men. Then was fulfilled that which was spoken ²by Jeremiah the prophet, saying,
18 A voice was heard in Ramah,
Weeping and great mourning,
Rachel weeping for her children;
And she would not be comforted, because they are not.

1. Gr. *Magi.* 2. Or, *through.*

§ 12. THE CHILD BROUGHT FROM EGYPT TO NAZARETH.

Probably B.C. 4.

Matt. 2:19-23.

19 But when Herod was dead, behold, an angel of the Lord appeareth in a dream to Joseph in
20 Egypt, saying, Arise and take the young child and his mother, and go into the land of Israel:
21 for they are dead that sought the young child's life. And he arose and took the young child and his mother, and came into the land of Is-
22 rael. But when he heard that Archelaus was

Luke 2:39.

39 And when they had accomplished all things that were according to the law of the Lord, they returned into

OUR LORD'S BIRTH AND CHILDHOOD.

Matt. 2:19–23.

reigning over Judea in the room of his father Herod, he was afraid to go thither; and being
23 warned *of God* in a dream, he withdrew into the parts of Galilee, and came and dwelt in a city called Nazareth: that it might be fulfilled which was spoken ¹by the prophets, that he should be called a Nazarene.

Luke 2:39.

Galilee, to their own city Nazareth.*

1. Or, *through*.

§ 13. JESUS LIVES AT NAZARETH, AND VISITS JERUSALEM WHEN 12 YEARS OLD.

Probably A.D. 7 or 8.

Luke 2:40-52.

40 And the child grew, and waxed strong, ¹filled with wisdom; and the grace of God was upon him.
41 And his parents went every year to Jerusalem at the feast of the
42 passover. And when he was twelve years old, they went up after the
43 custom of the feast; and when they had fulfilled the days, as they were returning, the boy Jesus tarried behind in Jerusalem; and his
44 parents knew it not; but supposing him to be in the company, they went a day's journey; and they sought for him among their kinsfolk
45 and acquaintance: and when they found him not, they returned to
46 Jerusalem, seeking for him. And it came to pass, after three days they found him in the temple, sitting in the midst of the ²doctors,
47 both hearing them, and asking them questions: and all that heard
48 him were amazed at his understanding and his answers. And
49 when they saw him, they were astonished: and his mother said unto him, ³Son, why hast thou thus dealt with us? behold, thy father and
50 I sought thee sorrowing. And he said unto them, How is it that ye
51 sought me? wist ye not that I must be ⁴in my Father's house? And they understood not the saying which he spake unto them. And he went down with them, and came to Nazareth: and he was subject unto them: and his mother kept all *these* ⁵sayings in her heart.
52 And Jesus advanced in wisdom and ⁶stature, and in ⁷favor with God and men.

1. Gr *becoming full of wisdom*. 2. Or, *teachers*. 3. Gr. *Child*. 4. Or, *about my Father's business*. Gr. *in the things of my Father*. 5. Or, *things*. 6. Or, *age*. 7. Or, *grace*.

* After the return to Nazareth, in § 12, we know nothing of Jesus' life at that place beyond the general statements of Luke 2:40, 52, with the knowledge and dispositions indicated in the narrative of § 13, and the fact that he was a carpenter, until he comes forth to be baptized by John his forerunner, § 15. The social and political conditions of this period in Galilee are described by Edersheim, Geikie, and other writers on the Life of Jesus, and briefly stated in the author's commentary on Matthew, p. 30 f. Dwell on the general statement of Luke 2:52 (§ 13).

PART II.

BEGINNING OF THE FORERUNNER'S MINISTRY.

Several months. Probably A.D. 25 or 26.

In the wilderness of Judea, and beside the Jordan.

§ 14. JOHN THE BAPTIST PREACHES THE NEAR APPROACH OF THE MESSIANIC REIGN, AND BAPTIZES IN THE JORDAN THOSE WHO REPENT AND BELIEVE.

Matt. 3:1-12.	Mark 1:1-8.	Luke 3:1-18.
	1 The beginning of the gospel of Jesus Christ ⁶the Son of God.	1 Now in the fifteenth year of the reign of Tiberius Cæsar, Pontius Pilate being governor of Judea, and Herod being tetrarch of Galilee, and his brother Philip tetrarch of the region of Ituræa and Trachonitis, and Lysanias tetrarch of Abilene, 2 in the highpriesthood of Annas and Caiaphas, the word of God came unto John the son of Zacharias in the wilderness. 3 And he came into all the region round about Jordan, preaching the baptism of repentance unto remission of 4 sins; as it is written in the book of the words of Isaiah the prophet, The voice of one crying in the wilderness, Make ye ready the way of the Lord, Make his paths straight. 5 Every valley shall be filled, And every moun-
1 And in those days cometh John the Baptist, preaching in the wilderness of 2 Judea, saying, Repent ye; for the kingdom of heaven is at 3 hand. For this is he that was spoken of ¹by Isaiah the prophet, saying, The voice of one crying in the wilderness, Make ye ready the way of the Lord, Make his paths straight. 4 Now John himself had his raiment of camel's hair, and a leathern girdle about his loins; and	2 Even as it is written ⁵in Isaiah the prophet, Behold, I send my messenger before thy face, Who shall prepare thy way; 3 The voice of one crying in the wilderness, Make ye ready the way of the Lord, Make his paths straight; 4 John came, who baptized in the wilderness and preached the baptism of repentance unto remission of sins. And 5 there went out unto him all the country	

Matt. 3:1-12.	Mark 1:1-8.	Luke 3:1-18.
his food was locusts and wild honey. 5 Then went out unto him Jerusalem, and all Judea, and all the region round about 6 Jordan; and they were baptized of him in the river Jordan, confessing their 7 sins. But when he saw many of the Pharisees and Sadducees coming to his baptism, he said unto them, Ye offspring of vipers, who warned you to flee from the wrath 8 to come? Bring forth therefore fruit worthy of ²repent-9 ance: and think not to say within yourselves, We have Abraham to our father: for I say unto you, that God is able of these stones to raise up children un-10 to Abraham. And even now is the axe laid unto the root of the trees: every tree therefore that bringeth not forth good fruit is hewn down, and cast into the fire.	of Judea, and all they of Jerusalem; and they were baptized of him in the river Jordan, confessing their sins. 6 And John was clothed with camel's hair, and *had* a leathern girdle about his loins, and did eat locusts and wild honey.	tain and hill shall be brought low; And the crooked shall become straight, And the rough ways smooth; 6 And all flesh shall see the salvation of God. 7 He said therefore to the multitude that went out to be baptized of him, Ye offspring of vipers, who warned you to flee from the wrath to 8 come? Bring forth therefore fruits worthy of ²repentance; and begin not to say within yourselves, We have Abraham to our father: for I say unto you, that God is able of these stones to raise up children unto Abra-9 ham. And even now is the axe also laid unto the root of the trees: every tree therefore that bringeth not forth good fruit is hewn down, and cast into 10 the fire. And the multitudes asked him, saying, What then must we do? 11 And he answered and said unto them, He that hath two coats, let him impart to him that hath none; and he that hath food, let him 12 do likewise. And there came also ³publicans to be baptized,

Matt. 3:1-12.	Mark 1:1-8.	Luke 3:1-18.
		and they said unto him, [9]Master, what must we do? And he said unto them, Extort no more than that which is appointed you. And [10] soldiers also asked him, saying, And we, what must we do? And he said unto them, Do violence to no man, neither [11]exact *anything* wrongfully; and be content with your wages.
		13
		14
		15 And as the people were in expectation, and all men reasoned in their hearts concerning John, whether haply he were the Christ; John answered, saying unto them all, I indeed baptize you with water: but there cometh he that is mightier than I, the latchet of whose shoes I am not [4]worthy to unloose: he shall baptize you [3]with the [7]Holy Ghost and *with* fire:
		16
11 I indeed baptize you [3]with water unto repentance: but he that cometh after me is mightier than I, whose shoes I am not [4]worthy to bear: he shall baptize you [3]with the [7]Holy Ghost and *with* fire:	7 And he preached, saying, There cometh after me he that is mightier than I, the latchet of whose shoes I am not [4]worthy to stoop down and unloose. I baptized you [3]with water; but he shall baptize you [3]with the [7]Holy Ghost.	
12 whose fan is in his hand, and he will throughly cleanse his threshing-floor; and he will gather his wheat into the garner, but the chaff he will burn up with unquenchable fire.	8	17 whose fan is in his hand, throughly to cleanse his threshing-floor, and to gather the wheat into his garner: but the chaff he will burn up with unquenchable fire.
		18 With many other exhortations therefore preached he

FORERUNNER'S MINISTRY.

Luke 3:1-18.
¹²good tidings unto the people.*

1 Or, *through*. 2 Or, *your repentance*. 3 Or, *in-* 4 Gr. *sufficient*. 5 Some ancient authorities omit *the Son of God*. 6 Some ancient authorities read *in the prophets*. 7 Or, *Holy Spirit*. 8 That is, *collectors or renters of Roman taxes;* and so elsewhere. 9 Or, *Teacher*. 10 Gr. *soldiers in service*. 11 Or, *accuse any one*. 12 Or. *the gospel*.

PART III.

BEGINNINGS OF OUR LORD'S MINISTRY.†

In all parts of the Holy Land, lasting several months.

For the most part probably in A.D. 27.

This early ministry divides itself into the Baptism and Temptation (§ 15, 16), the first calling of disciples (§ 17, 18), the beginning of his work in Galilee (§ 19, 20), the opening ministry in Judea (§ 21, 22), the ministry in Samaria and return to Galilee (§ 23).

§ 15. JESUS BAPTIZED BY JOHN IN THE JORDAN.

Bethany beyond Jordan.

Matt. 3:13-17.	Mark 1:9-11.	Luke 3:21, 22.
13 Then cometh Jesus from Galilee to the Jordan unto John, to be baptized of him. 14 But John would have hindered him, saying, I have need to be baptized of thee, and comest thou to 15 me? But Jesus answering said unto him, Suffer ¹it now: for thus it becometh us to fulfil all righteousness. Then he	9 And it came to pass in those days, that Jesus came from Nazareth of Galilee, and was baptized of John ⁴in the Jordan.	

* One may easily put together all that we are told of John the Baptist, in Sections 2, 4, 5, 14, 15, 17, 18, 22, 23(a), 45, 56. Comp. § 109, and Acts 13:25; 19:1-7; and the general introductory statement in John 1:6-15.

† The precise duration of this early ministry cannot be determined. Our Lord's baptism must have been at least two months *before* the Passover (§ 16, 20), and may have been some weeks or months earlier. Then the highly successful ministry in Judea *after* the Passover must have lasted several months, John 3:22 (§ 22); 4:1-3 (§ 21). If the "yet four months" in John 4:35 (§ 21) be understood to be not a common saying as to the usual interval between seedtime and harvest, but a statement that it was *then* just four months before harvest, that would make the Judean ministry extend eight months after the Passover. But this interpretation is upon the whole improbable, and we can only say that the opening ministry lasted several months. The time occupied makes very little difference for our understanding the events and discourses.

BEGINNINGS OF

Matt. 3:13-17.	Mark 1:9-91.	Luke 3:21, 22.
16 suffereth him. And Jesus, when he was baptized, went up straightway from the water: and lo, the heavens were opened [2]unto him, and he saw the Spirit of God descending as a dove, and coming 17 upon him; and lo, a voice out of the heavens, saying, [3]This is my beloved Son, in whom I am well pleased.	10 And straightway coming up out of the water, he saw the heavens rent asunder, and the Spirit as a dove descending 11 upon him: and a voice came out of the heavens, Thou art my beloved Son, in thee I am well pleased.	21 Now it came to pass, when all the people were baptized, that Jesus also having been baptized, and praying, the heaven was 22 opened, and the Holy Ghost descended in a bodily form, as a dove, upon him, and a voice came out of heaven, Thou art my beloved Son; in thee I am well 23 pleased. And Jesus himself, when he began *to teach*, was about thirty years of age.

1 Or. *me*. 2 Some ancient authorities omit *unto him*. 3 Or, *This is my son; my beloved in whom I am well pleased*. 4 Gr. *into*.

§ 16. JESUS TEMPTED IN THE WILDERNESS.

Matt. 4:1-11.	Mark 1:12, 13.	Luke 4:1-13.
1 Then was Jesus led up of the Spirit into the wilderness to be tempted of the devil. 2 And when he had fasted forty days and forty nights, he afterward hungered. 3 And the tempter came and said unto him, If thou art the Son of God, command that these stones become 4 [1]bread. But he answered and said, It is written, Man shall not live by bread alone, but by every word that proceedeth out of the mouth 5 of God. Then the devil taketh him into the holy city; and he set him on the [2]pinnacle of the tem-6 ple, and saith unto him, If thou art the	12 And straightway the Spirit driveth him forth into the 13 wilderness. And he was in the wilderness forty days tempted of Satan; and he was with the wild beasts;	1 And Jesus, full of the Holy Spirit, returned from the Jordan, and was led [3]by the Spirit in the wilderness during 2 forty days, being tempted of the devil. And he did eat nothing in those days: and when they were completed, he hun-3 gered. And the devil said unto him, If thou art the Son of God, command this stone that it be-4 come [4]bread. And Jesus answered unto him, It is written, Man shall not live by 5 bread alone. And he led him up, and shewed him all the kingdoms of [5]the world in a moment 6 of time. And the devil said unto him,

Matt. 4:1-11.	Mark 1:12, 13.	Luke 4:1-13.

Son of God, cast thyself down: for it is written,
  He shall give his angels charge concerning thee:
  And on their hands they shall bear thee up,
  Lest haply thou dash thy foot against a stone.
7 Jesus said unto him, Again it is written, Thou shalt not tempt the Lord thy God.
8 Again the devil taketh him unto an exceeding high mountain, and sheweth him all the kingdoms of the world, and the glory of 9 them; and he said unto him, All these things will I give thee, if thou wilt fall down and worship 10 me. Then saith Jesus unto him, Get thee hence, Satan: for it is written, Thou shalt worship the Lord thy God, and him only shalt thou serve.
		To thee will I give all this authority, and the glory of them: for it hath been delivered unto me; and to whomsoever I will I give it.
		7 If thou therefore wilt worship before me, it shall all be thine.
		8 And Jesus answered and said unto him, It is written, Thou shalt worship the Lord thy God, and him only shalt thou 9 serve. And he led him to Jerusalem, and set him on the pinnacle of the temple, and said unto him, If thou art the Son of God, cast thyself down from hence:
		10 for it is written,
		  He shall give his angels charge concerning thee, to guard thee:
		11 And on their hands they shall bear thee up,
		  Lest haply thou dash thy foot against a stone.
		12 And Jesus answering said unto him, It is said, Thou shalt not tempt the Lord thy God.

11 Then the devil leaveth him; and behold angels came and ministered unto him.	and the angels ministered unto him	13 And when the devil had completed every temptation, he departed from him [6]for a season.

1. Gr. *loaves.*   2. Gr. *wing.*   3. Or, *in.*   4. Or, *a loaf.*   5. Gr. *the inhabited earth.*
6. Or, *until.*

§ 17. JOHN TESTIFIES TO JESUS.

At Bethany beyond the Jordan.

John 1:19-34.

19 And this is the witness of John, when the Jews sent unto him from
20 Jerusalem priests and Levites to ask him, Who art thou? And he
21 confessed, and denied not: and he confessed, I am not the Christ. And
they asked him, What then? Art thou Elijah? And he saith, I am not.
22 Art thou the prophet? And he answered, No. They said therefore
unto him, Who art thou? that we may give an answer to them that
23 sent us. What sayest thou of thyself? He said, I am the voice of one
24 crying in the wilderness, Make straight the way of the Lord, as said
25 Isaiah the prophet. [1]And they had been sent from the Pharisees.
And they asked him, and said unto him, Why then baptizest thou, if
thou art not the Christ, neither Elijah, neither the prophet? John
26 answered them, saying, I baptize [2]with water: in the midst of you
standeth one whom ye know not, *even* he that cometh after me, the
27 latchet of whose shoe I am not worthy to unloose. These things were
28 done in [3]Bethany beyond Jordan, where John was baptizing.
29 On the morrow he seeth Jesus coming unto him, and saith, Behold,
30 the Lamb of God, which [4]taketh away the sin of the world! This is
he of whom I said, After me cometh a man which is become before me:
31 for he was [5]before me. And I knew him not; but that he should be
32 made manifest to Israel, for this cause came I baptizing [2]with water.
And John bare witness, saying, I have beheld the Spirit descending
33 as a dove out of heaven; and it abode upon him. And I knew him not:
but he that sent me to baptize [2]with water, he said unto me, Upon
whomsoever thou shalt see the Spirit descending, and abiding upon
34 him, the same is he that baptizeth [2]with the Holy Spirit. And I have
seen, and have borne witness that this is the son of God.*

1. Or, *And* certain *had been sent from among the Pharisees*. 2. Or, *in*. 3. Many ancient authorities read *Bethabarah*, some *Betharabah*. 4. Or, *beareth the sin*. 5. Gr. *first in regard of me*.

§ 18. JESUS MAKES HIS FIRST† DISCIPLES.

At Bethany beyond the Jordan.

John 1:35-51.

35 Again on the morrow John was standing, and two of his disciples;
36 and he looked upon Jesus as he walked, and saith, Behold, the Lamb
37 of God! And the two disciples heard him speak, and they followed
38 Jesus. And Jesus turned, and beheld them following, and saith unto
them, What seek ye? And they said unto him, Rabbi (which is to say,
39 being interpreted, [1]Master), where abidest thou? He saith unto them,
Come, and ye shall see. They came therefore and saw where he abode;

*Put together John the Baptist's testimonies to Jesus, § 14, 15, 17, 18, 22, 45. Comp. John 1: 6-15. Add the testimony of Jesus to John, § 45. Notice here the *four successive days* in John 1:19, 29, 35, 43, and the third day from this last in John 2:1. Even the *hour* is retained among these vivid recollections in John 1:39.

† Notice here a series of First Things: first testimony of John (§ 17), first disciples (§ 18), first miracle (§ 19), first residence at Capernaum (§ 20), first passover during his ministry (§ 21, a), first extended discourse (§ 21, b).

John 1:25-51.

and they abode with him that day: it was about the tenth hour. One
40 of the two that heard John *speak*, and followed him, was Andrew,
41 Simon Peter's brother. He findeth first his own brother Simon, and
saith unto him, We have found the Messiah (which is, being inter-
42 preted, ²Christ). He brought him unto Jesus. Jesus looked upon
him, and said, thou art Simon the son of ³John: thou shalt be called
Cephas (which is by interpretation, ⁴Peter).
43 On the morrow he was minded to go forth into Galilee, and he findeth Philip: and Jesus saith unto him, Follow me. Now Philip was
44 from Bethsaida, of the city of Andrew and Peter. Philip findeth Na-
45 thanael, and saith unto him, We have found him, of whom Moses in
the law, and the prophets, did write, Jesus of Nazareth, the son of
46 Joseph. And Nathanael said unto him, Can any good thing come out
47 of Nazareth? Philip saith unto him, Come and see. Jesus saw Nathanael coming to him, and saith of him, Behold, an Israelite indeed,
48 in whom is no guile! Nathanael saith unto him, Whence knowest
thou me? Jesus answered and said unto him, Before Philip called
thee, when thou wast under the fig tree, I saw thee. Nathanael an-
49 swered him, Rabbi, thou art the son of God; thou art King of Israel.*
50 Jesus answered and said unto him, Because I said unto thee, I saw
thee underneath the fig tree, believest thou? thou shalt see greater
51 things than these. And he saith unto him, Verily, verily, I say unto
you, Ye shall see the heaven opened, and the angels of God ascending
and descending upon the Son of man.

1. Or, *Teacher*. 2. That is, *Anointed*. 3. Gr. *Joanes*: called in Matt. 16:17, *Jonah*.
4. That is, *Rock or Stone*.

§ 19. JESUS WORKS HIS FIRST MIRACLE.

At Cana in Galilee.
John 2:1-11.

2 And the third day there was a marriage in Cana of Galilee: and the
2 mother of Jesus was there: and Jesus also was bidden, and his disci-
3 ples, to the marriage. And when the wine failed, the mother of Jesus
4 saith unto him, They have no wine. And Jesus saith unto her, Wo-
5 man, what have I to do with thee? mine hour is not yet come. His
mother saith unto the servants, Whatsoever he saith unto you, do it.
6 Now there were six waterpots of stone set there after the Jews' man-
7 ner of purifying, containing two or three firkins apiece. Jesus saith
8 unto them, Fill the waterpots with water. And they filled them up
to the brim. And he saith unto them, Draw out now, and bear unto
9 the ¹ruler of the feast. And they bare it. And when the ruler of the
feast tasted the water ² now become wine, and knew not whence it was
(but the servants which had drawn the water knew), the ruler of the
10 feast calleth the bridegroom, and saith unto him, Every man setteth
on first the good wine; and when *men* have drunk freely, *then* that
11 which is worse: thou hast kept the good wine until now. This beginning of his signs did Jesus in Cana of Galilee, and manifested his
glory; and his disciples believed on him.

1. Or, *steward*. 2. Or, *that it had become*.

*Notice that these first disciples at once believed that Jesus was the Messiah (ver. 41, 45, 49). Compare on ¶ 21 (c) and ¶ 64.

BEGINNINGS OF

§ 20. JESUS MAKES A FIRST SOJOURN AT CAPERNAUM, ACCOMPANIED BY HIS KINDRED AND HIS EARLY DISCIPLES.

(Comp. § 26, where Capernaum will become his home.)

John 2:12.

After this he went down to Capernaum, he, and his mother, and *his* brethren, and his disciples: and there they abode not many days.

§ 21. JESUS ATTENDS THE FIRST PASSOVER DURING HIS MINISTRY.

Jerusalem.* Probably A.D. 27.

(a) He cleanses the Temple. (Comp. § 106.)

John 2:13-22.

13 And the passover of the Jews was at hand, and Jesus went up to
14 Jerusalem. And he found in the temple those who sold oxen and
15 sheep and doves, and the changers of money sitting: and he made a scourge of cords, and cast all out of the temple, both the sheep and
16 the oxen; and he poured out the changers' money, and overthrew their tables; and to them that sold the doves he said, Take these things
17 hence; make not my Father's house a house of merchandise. His dis-
18 ciples remembered that it was written, The zeal of thine house shall eat me up. The Jews therefore answered and said unto him, What
19 sign shewest thou unto us, seeing thou doest these things? Jesus answered and said unto them, Destroy this ¹temple, and in three days I
20 will raise it up. The Jews therefore said, Forty and six years was
21 this ¹temple in building, and wilt thou raise it up in three days? But
22 he spake of the ¹temple of his body. When therefore he was raised from the dead, his disciples remembered that he spake this; and they believed the scripture, and the word which Jesus had said.

1. Or, *sanctuary*.

(b) During the Passover, many believed on Jesus, including the ruler Nicodemus. Conversation with Nicodemus.

John 2:23 to 3:21.

23 Now when he was in Jerusalem at the passover, during the feast,
24 many believed on his name, beholding his signs which he did. But
25 Jesus did not trust himself unto them, for that he knew all men, and because he needed not that any one should bear witness concerning ¹man: for he himself knew what was in man.
3 Now there was a man of the Pharisees, named Nicodemus,† a ruler
2 of the Jews: the same came unto him by night, and said to him, Rabbi, we know that thou art a teacher come from God: for no man
3 can do these signs that thou doest, except God be with him. Jesus

*Observe the successive *scenes* of this early ministry—beside the Jordan, on the eastern side (§ 18), at Cana of Galilee (§ 19), at Capernaum (§ 20), at Jerusalem (§ 21), in Judea (§ 22), in Samaria (§ 23).

†Nicodemus appears as an exception to the statement of 2:24, as one whom Jesus did trust, and who amid all difficulties of temperament and station proved not unworthy of the trust (§ 75, and § 133 d).

John 2:23 to 3:21.

answered and said unto him, Verily, verily, I say unto thee, Except a
4 man be born ²anew, he cannot see the kingdom of God. Nicodemus
saith unto him, How can a man be born when he is old? can he enter
5 a second time into his mother's womb, and be born? Jesus answered,
Verily, verily, I say unto thee, Except a man be born of water and
6 the Spirit, he cannot enter into the kingdom of God. That which is
born of the flesh is flesh; and that which is born of the Spirit is spirit.
7 Marvel not that I said unto thee, Ye must be born ²anew. ³The wind
8 bloweth where it listeth, and thou hearest the voice thereof, but
knowest not whence it cometh, and whither it goeth: so is every one
9 that is born of the Spirit. Nicodemus answered and said unto him,
10 How can these things be? Jesus answered and said unto him, Art
thou the teacher of Israel, and understandest not these things?
11 Verily, verily, I say unto thee, We speak that we do know, and bear
12 witness of that we have seen; and ye receive not our witness. If I
told you earthly things, and ye believe not, how shall ye believe, if I
13 tell you heavenly things? And no man hath ascended into heaven,
but he that descended out of heaven, *even* the Son of man, ⁴which is in
14 heaven. And as Moses lifted up the serpent in the wilderness, even
so must the Son of man be lifted up: that whosoever ⁵believeth may
15 in him have eternal life.
16 For God so loved the world, that he gave his only begotten Son,
that whosoever believeth on him should not perish, but have eternal
17 life. For God sent not the Son into the world to judge the world; but
18 that the world should be saved through him. He that believeth on
him is not judged; he that believeth not has been judged already, because he hath not believed on the name of the only begotten Son of
19 God. And this is the judgement, that the light is come into the
world, and men loved the darkness rather than the light; for their
20 works were evil. For every one that ⁶doeth ill hateth the light, and
21 cometh not to the light, lest his works should be ⁷reproved. But he
that doeth the truth cometh to the light, that his works may be made
manifest, ⁸that they have been wrought in God.

1. Or, *a man, for....the man.* 2. Or, *from above.* 3. Or, *The Spirit breatheth.* 4. Many ancient authorities omit *which is in heaven.* 5. Or, *believeth in him may have.* 6. Or, *practiseth.* 7. Or, *convicted.* 8. Or, *because.*

§ 22. EARLY MINISTRY IN JUDEA, AND JOHN'S RENEWED TESTIMONY.

Judea and Ænon.

John 3:22-36.

22 After these things came Jesus and his disciples into the land of
23 Judea; and there he tarried with them, and baptized. And John also
was baptizing in Ænon near to Salim, because there ¹was much water
24 there; and they came, and were baptized. For John was not yet cast
25 into prison. There arose therefore a questioning on the part of John's
26 disciples with a Jew about purifying. And they came unto John, and
said to him, Rabbi, he that was with thee beyond Jordan, to whom
thou hast borne witness, behold, the same baptizeth, and all men
27 come to him. John answered and said, A man can receive nothing,
28 except it have been given him from heaven. Ye yourselves bear me

John 3:22-36.

witness, that I said, I am not the Christ, but, that I am sent before
29 him. He that hath the bride is the bridegroom: but the friend of
the bridegroom, which standeth and heareth him, rejoiceth greatly
because of the bridegroom's voice: this my joy therefore is fulfilled.
30 He must increase, but I must decrease.
31 He that cometh from above is above all: he that is of the earth is of
the earth, and of the earth he speaketh: ²he that cometh from heaven
32 is above all. What he hath seen and heard, of that he beareth wit-
33 ness; and no man receiveth his witness. He that hath received his
34 witness hath set his seal to *this*, that God is true. For he whom God
hath sent speaketh the words of God: for he giveth not the Spirit by
35 measure. The Father loveth the Son, and hath given all things
36 into his hand. He that believeth on the Son hath eternal life; but he
that ³obeyeth not the Son shall not see life, but the wrath of God
abideth on him.

1. Gr. *were many waters*. 2. Some ancient authorities read *he that cometh from heaven beareth witness of what he hath seen and heard*. 3. Or, *believeth not*.

§ 23. JESUS REMOVES FROM JUDEA THROUGH SAMARIA TO GALILEE.

(a) Reasons for leaving Judea.

John 4:1-4.

1 When therefore the Lord knew how that the Pharisees had heard
2 that Jesus was making and baptizing more disciples than John*
3 (although Jesus himself baptized not, but his disciples), he left
4 Judea, and departed again into Galilee. And he must needs pass
through Samaria.

Luke 3:19,20.

19 But Herod the tetrarch, being reproved by him for Herodias his
brother's wife, and for all the evil things which Herod had done,
20 added yet this above all, that he shut up John in prison.†

Matt. 4:12.	Mark 1:14.	Luke 4:14.
Now when he heard that John was delivered up he withdrew into Galilee.	Now after that John was delivered up Jesus came into Galilee.	And Jesus returned in the power of the Spirit into Galilee.

(b) Conversation at Jacob's Well, and sojourn at Sychar.

John 4:5-42.

5 So he cometh to a city of Samaria, called Sychar, near to the parcel
of ground that Jacob gave to his son Joseph; and Jacob's ¹well was

*Up to this point, our Lord's ministry has run parallel to that of John. His first disciples were gained in § 18, probably some others at the Passover, § 21, and certainly many in Judea, § 22, until at length he is surpassing John, § 23 (a).
†The place of John's imprisonment was Machaerus, east of the Dead Sea.

John 4:5–42.

6 there. Jesus therefore, being wearied with his journey, sat ²thus by
7 the well¹. It was about the sixth hour. There cometh a woman of
8 Samaria to draw water: Jesus saith unto her, Give me to drink. For
9 his disciples were gone away into the city to buy food. The Samaritan woman therefore saith unto him, How is it that thou, being a Jew, askest drink of me, which am a Samaritan woman? (³For Jews
10 have no dealings with Samaritans.) Jesus answered and said unto her, If thou knewest the gift of God, and who it is that saith to thee, Give me to drink; thou wouldest have asked of him, and he would
11 have given thee living water. The woman saith unto him, 'Sir, thou hast nothing to draw with, and the well is deep: from whence then
12 hast thou that living water? Art thou greater than our father Jacob, which gave us the well, and drank thereof himself, and his sons, and
13 his cattle? Jesus answered and said unto her, Every one that drink-
14 eth of this water shall thirst again: but whosoever drinketh of the water that I shall give him shall never thirst; but the water that I shall give him shall become in him a well of water springing up unto
15 eternal life. The woman saith unto him, 'Sir, give me this water,
16 that I thirst not, neither come all the way hither to draw. Jesus
17 saith unto her, Go, call thy husband, and come hither. The woman answered and said unto him, I have no husband. Jesus saith unto
18 her, Thou saidst well, I have no husband: for thou hast had five husbands; and he whom thou now hast is not thy husband: this hast thou
19 said truly. The woman saith unto him, 'Sir, I perceive that thou
20 art a prophet. Our fathers worshipped in this mountain; and ye say,
21 that in Jerusalem is the place where men ought to worship. Jesus saith unto her, Woman, believe me, the hour cometh, when neither
22 in this mountain, nor in Jerusalem, shall ye worship the Father. Ye worship that which ye know not; we worship that which we know: for
23 salvation is from the Jews. But the hour cometh, and now is, when the true worshippers shall worship the Father in spirit and truth:
24 ⁴for such doth the Father seek to be his worshippers. ⁵God is a
25 Spirit: and they that worship him must worship in spirit and truth. The woman saith unto him, I know that Messiah cometh (which is called Christ): when he is come, he will declare unto us all
26 things. Jesus saith unto her, I that speak unto thee am *he*.
27 And upon this came his disciples; and they marvelled that he was speaking with a woman; yet no man said, What seekest thou? or, Why
28 speakest thou with her? So the woman left her waterpot, and went
29 away into the city, and saith to the men, Come, see a man, which told
30 me all things that *ever* I did: can this be the Christ? They went out
31 of the city, and were coming to him. In the mean while the disciples
32 prayed him, saying, Rabbi, eat. But he said to them, I have meat to
33 eat that ye know not. The disciples therefore said one to another,
34 Hath any man brought him *aught* to eat? Jesus saith unto them, My
35 meat is to do the will of him that sent me, and to accomplish his work. Say not ye, There are yet four months, and *then* cometh the harvest? behold, I say unto you, Lift up your eyes, and look on the fields, that
36 they are ⁷white already unto harvest. He that reapeth receiveth wages, and gathereth fruit unto life eternal; that he that soweth and
37 he that reapeth may rejoice together. For herein is the saying true,
38 One soweth and another reapeth. I sent you to reap that whereon

John 4:5-42.

ye have not laboured: others have laboured, and ye are entered into their labour.

39 And from that city many of the Samaritans believed on him *because of the word of the woman, who testified, He told me all things that
40 *ever* I did. So when the Samaritans came unto him, they besought
41 him to abide with them: and he abode there two days. And many
42 more believed because of his word; and they said to the woman, Now we believe, not because of thy speaking: for we have heard for ourselves, and know that this is indeed the Saviour of the world.†

1. Gr. *spring:* and so in ver. 14; but not in ver. 11, 12.   2. Or, *as he was.*   3. Some ancient authorities omit *For Jews have no dealings with Samaritans.*   4. Or, *Lord.*
5. Or, *for such the Father also seeketh.*   6. Or, *God is spirit.*   7. Or, *white unto harvest. Already he that reapeth, &c.*

(c) Arrival in Galilee.

John 4:43-45.

43 And after the two days he went forth from thence into Galilee.
44 For Jesus himself testified, that a prophet hath no honour in his own
45 country. So when he came into Galilee, the Galileans received him, having seen all the things that he did in Jerusalem at the feast: for they also went unto the feast.

*Notice that John also had recently been preaching to Samaritans (§ 22), and compare hereafter Philip's work in the city of Samaria (Acts 8:5 ff.)

† In this early ministry Jesus allowed himself to be regarded as the Messiah by his first disciples, § 18, and personally declared that he was the Messiah to the woman at the well, § 23 b (John 4:26), which many other Samaritans also personally believed (John 4:39, 42). He never declared this to the Jewish rulers at Jerusalem till the very end, § 126, doubtless because such an avowal would lead them to kill him, and so must not be made till his work in teaching the people and training his disciples should be completed. Compare what he says in § 64.

PART IV.

OUR LORD'S GREAT MINISTRY IN GALILEE.

Probably more than a year,* in A.D. 27 and 28.

The matters presented by this great ministry may be grouped *as follows:*
(1) He revisits Cana and Nazareth (§25-26), then settles at Capernaum, and recalls four disciples (§27-29). (2) He makes a journey about Galilee, teaching and healing on a large scale (§30), afterwards performing various miracles at Capernaum, and calling Matthew (§31-36). (3) While attending a feast at Jerusalem he heals on the Sabbath, and afterwards does the same in Galilee, in both cases awakening a desire to kill him (§37-39). (4) Great crowds now attend his ministry in Galilee, and he chooses the twelve disciples, giving to them and the multitude the Sermon on the Mount (§40-42). (5) Various miracles, especially the one at Nain, spread his fame over all the land, and then comes a message of inquiry from John the Forerunner, which occasions special discourses (§43-46). (6) Now we find him again journeying about Galilee (§47), and presently meet with the blasphemous accusation of league with Satan, and the opposition of his mother and brothers (§48-50). (7) Then comes the first great group of Parables (§51), immediately after which he crosses the Lake, heals the Gadarene demoniacs, and returning to Galilee revisits Nazareth (§52-54). (8) Finally, he makes a third journey about Galilee, with the Twelve sent in advance (§55), and presently the miracles of Jesus and his disciples excite the jealous fears of Herod Antipas (§56).

§ 24. GENERAL ACCOUNT OF HIS TEACHING IN GALILEE.

Matt. 4:17.	Mark 1:14,15.	Luke 4:14,15.
From that time began Jesus to preach, and to say, Repent ye: for the kingdom of heaven is at hand.	14 [Now after that John was delivered up, Jesus came into Galilee,] preaching the gospel of God,	14 [And Jesus returned in the power of the Spirit into Galilee:] and a fame went out concerning him

*We cannot confidently determine the length of the ministry in Galilee. We are not sure whether it began in summer or late autumn (see footnote on § 15). If the feast of John 5:1 was a Passover (see note at the end of the book on § 37), the Galilean ministry lasted at least 16 months, for it ended when another Passover was near, John 6:4 (§ 57). Otherwise we should not certainly know that it lasted more than some 6 or 8 months. About the two subsequent periods of our Lord's ministry we shall find no room to question that each lasted 6 months; but here we have to admit much uncertainty as to the time. After all, a determination of the time employed would be a matter of very little importance to our study of this period.
Throughout this great ministry in Galilee, and the periods that will follow after, the reader ought to trace carefully the progress of the history along several lines: (1) the Saviour's progressive self-manifestation; (2) the gradual training of the Twelve who are to carry on his teaching and work after his death; (3) the deepening and spreading hostility of the Jewish influential classes and official rulers. By constantly observing these parallel lines of progress, it will be seen that the history and teachings of our Lord exhibit a vital growth, moving on to an end by him foreseen (Luke 12:50), when the hostility of the rulers will culminate as he before the Sanhedrin avows himself to be the Messiah, and the Twelve will be almost prepared to succeed him.*

Mark 1:14,15.	Luke 4:14,15.
15 and saying, The time is fulfilled, and the kingdom of God is at hand: repent ye, and believe in the gospel.	through all the region round about. 15 And he taught in their synagogues, being glorified of all.

In § 25-27 he revisits Cana and Nazareth (comp. § 19, 20), then settles at Capernaum, and recalls four disciples.

§ 25. HE HEALS AT CANA THE SON OF A COURTIER OF CAPERNAUM.

John 4:46-54.

46 He came therefore again unto Cana of Galilee, where he made the
47 water wine. And there was a certain [1]nobleman, whose son was sick at Capernaum. When he heard that Jesus was come out of Judea into Galilee, he went unto him, and besought *him* that he would come
48 down, and heal his son; for he was at the point of death. Jesus there-
49 fore said unto him, Except ye see signs and wonders, ye will in no
50 wise believe. The [1]nobleman saith unto him. [2]Sir, come down ere my child die. Jesus saith unto him, Go thy way; thy son liveth. The man believed the word that Jesus spake unto him, and he went his
51 way. And as he was now going down, his [3]servants met him, saying,
52 that his son lived. So he inquired of them the hour when he began to amend. They said therefore unto him, Yesterday at the seventh
53 hour the fever left him. So the father knew that *it was* at that hour in which Jesus said unto him, Thy son liveth: and himself believed,
54 and his whole house. This is again the second sign that Jesus did, having come out of Judea into Galilee.

1. Or, *king's officer.* 2. Or, *Lord.* 3. Gr. *bondservants.*

§ 26. REJECTED AT NAZARETH, HE MAKES CAPERNAUM HIS RESIDENCE.

(Comp. § 20.)

Luke 4:16-31.

16 And he came to Nazareth, where he had been brought up: and he entered, as his custom was, into the synagogue on the sabbath day,
17 and stood up to read. And there was delivered unto him [1]the book of the prophet Isaiah. And he opened the [2]book, and found the place where it was written,
18   The Spirit of the Lord is upon me,
        [3]Because he anointed me to preach [4]good tidings to the poor:
        He hath sent me to proclaim release to the captives,
        And recovering of sight to the blind,
        To set at liberty them that are bruised,
19   To proclaim the acceptable year of the Lord.
20 And he closed the [2]book, and gave it back to the attendant, and sat down: and the eyes of all in the synagogue were fastened on him.

Luke 4:16–31.

21 And he began to say unto them, To-day hath this scripture been ful-
22 filled in your ears. And all bare him witness, and wondered at the
words of grace which proceeded out of his mouth: and they said, Is
23 not this Joseph's son? And he said unto them, Doubtless ye will say
unto me this parable, Physician, heal thyself: whatsoever we have
heard done at Capernaum, do also here in thine own country. And
24 he said, Verily I say unto you, No prophet is acceptable in his own
25 country. But of a truth I say unto you, There were many widows in
Israel in the days of Elijah, when the heaven was shut up three years
and six months, when there came a great famine over all the land;
26 and unto none of them was Elijah sent, but only to ⁵Zarephath, in the
land of Sidon, unto a woman that was a widow. And there were many
27 lepers in Israel in the time of Elisha the prophet; and none of them
was cleansed, but only Naaman the Syrian. And they were all filled
28 with wrath in the synagogue, as they heard these things; and they
29 rose up, and cast him forth out of the city, and led him unto the brow
of the hill whereon their city was built, that they might throw him
30 down headlong. But he passing through the midst of them went his
31 way. And he came down to Capernaum, a city of Galilee.

Matt. 4:13–16.

13 And leaving Nazareth* he came and dwelt in Capernaum, which is
14 by the sea, in the borders of Zebulun and Naphtali; that it might be
fulfilled which was spoken ⁶by Isaiah the prophet, saying,
15   The land of Zebulun and the land of Naphtali,
    ⁷Toward the sea, beyond Jordan,
    Galilee of the ⁸Gentiles,
16   The people which sat in darkness
    Saw a great light,
    And to them which sat in the region and shadow of death,
    To them did light spring up.

1. Or, *a roll.*   2. Or, *roll.*   3. Or, *wherefore.*   4. Or, *the gospel.*   5. Gr. *Sarepta.*
6. Or, *through.*   7. Gr. *the way of the sea.*   8. *Nations,* and so elsewhere.

§ 27. HE CALLS FOUR FISHERMEN TO FOLLOW HIM.

By the Sea of Galilee, near Capernaum.

Matt. 4:18–22.	Mark 1:16–20.	Luke 5:1–11.
18 And walking by the sea of Galilee, he saw two brethren, Simon who is called Peter, and Andrew his brother, casting a net into the sea;	16 And passing along by the sea of Galilee, he saw Simon and Andrew the brother of Simon casting a net in the sea: for they were fishers.	1 Now it came to pass, while the multitude pressed upon him, and heard the word of God, that he was standing by the lake of Gennesaret;

* Nazareth was never the Saviour's residence during his public ministry. After the wedding at Cana he lived a short time at *Capernaum* (§ 20), and henceforth that city will be his abode, till he leaves Galilee 6 months before the crucifixion—most of the time, however, being actually spent in several journeys throughout Galilee, together with a trip to Jerusalem (§ 37), and retirement to districts around Galilee (§ 57–67).

Matt. 4:18-22.	Mark 1:16-20.	Luke 5:1-11.
for they were fishers. 19 And he saith unto them, Come ye after me, and I will make you fishers of men. 20 And they straightway left the nets, and 21 followed him. And going on from thence he saw other two brethren, [1]James the *son* of Zebedee, and John his brother, in the boat with Zebedee their father, mending their nets; and he called them. 22 And they straightway left the boat and their father, and followed him.*	17 And Jesus said unto them, Come ye after me, and I will make you to become fishers of men. And straightway they left the nets, and 19 followed him. And going on a little further, he saw James the *son* of Zebedee, and John his brother, who were also in the boat mending 20 the nets. And straightway he called them: and they left their father Zebedee in the boat with the hired servants, and went after him.	2 and he saw two boats standing by the lake: but the fishermen had gone out of them, and were washing their nets. 3 And he entered into one of the boats, which was Simon's, and asked him to put out a little from the land. And he sat down and taught the multitudes out of 4 the boat. And when he had left speaking, he said unto Simon, Put out into the deep, and let down your nets for a 5 draught. And Simon answered and said, Master, we toiled all night, and

6 took nothing: but at thy word I will let down the nets. And when they had this done, they inclosed a great multitude of fishes; and 7 their nets were breaking; and they beckoned unto their partners in the other boat, that they should come and help them. And they 8 came, and filled both the boats, so that they began to sink. But Simon Peter, when he saw it, fell down at Jesus' knees, saying, Depart 9 from me; for I am a sinful man, O Lord. For he was amazed, and all that were with him, at the draught of the fishes which they 10 had taken; and so were also James and John, sons of Zebedee, which were partners with Simon. And Jesus said unto Simon, Fear 11 not; from henceforth thou shalt [2]catch men. And when they had brought their boats to land, they left all, and followed him.

1. Or, *Jacob:* and so elsewhere.   2. Gr. *take alive.*

§ 28. HE HEALS A DEMONIAC IN THE SYNAGOGUE AT CAPERNAUM.

Mark 1:21-28.	Luke 4:31-37.
21 And they go into Capernaum; and straightway on the sabbath day he entered into the synagogue and taught. And they were astonished at his teaching:	31 [And he came down to Capernaum, a city of Galilee.] And he was teaching them on the sabbath day: and they were astonished at his teaching; for his

*Three of these became his disciples at the beginning (§ 18), and James probably soon after, and they were doubtless among the "disciples" who attended his early ministry (§ 19, 20, 21, 22, 23). After the return to Galilee they may have seen no occasion to follow him still, for we find no mention of them in § 25 and § 26, and here he calls them to leave everything else, and follow him continually.

Mark 1:21-28.	Luke 4:31-37.
for he taught them as having authority, and not as the scribes. 23 And straightway there was in their synagogue a man with an unclean spirit, and he cried out, 24 saying, What have we to do with thee, thou Jesus of Nazareth? art thou come to destroy us? I know thee who thou art, the 25 Holy One of God. And Jesus rebuked ¹him, saying, hold thy peace, and come out of him. 26 And the unclean spirit, ²tearing him and crying with a loud voice, 27 came out of him. And they were all amazed, insomuch that they questioned among themselves, saying, What is this? a new teaching! with authority he commandeth even the unclean spirits, and 28 they obey him. And the report of him went out straightway everywhere into all the region of Galilee round about.	33 word was with authority. And in the synagogue there was a man, which had a spirit of an unclean ³devil; and he cried out 34 with a loud voice, ⁴Ah! what have we to do with thee, thou Jesus of Nazareth? art thou come to destroy us? I know thee who thou 35 art, the Holy One of God. And Jesus rebuked him, saying, Hold thy peace, and come out of him. And when the ³devil had thrown him down in the midst, he came out of him, having done him no 36 hurt. And amazement came upon all, and they spake together, one with another, saying, What is ⁵this word? for with authority and power he commandeth the unclean spirits, and they come 37 out. And there went forth a rumour concerning him into every place of the region round about.

1. Or, *it.* 2. Or, *convulsing.* 3. Gr. *demon.* 4. Or, *let alone.* 5. Or, *this word, that with authority—come out?*

§ 29. He Heals Peter's Mother-in-law and Many Others.

Capernaum.

Matt. 8:14-17.	Mark 1:29-34.	Luke 4:38-41.
	29 And straightway ³when they were come out of the synagogue, they came into the house of Simon and Andrew, with James and 30 John. Now Simon's wife's mother lay sick of a fever; and straightway they 31 tell him of her: and he came and took her by the hand, and raised her up; and the fever left her, and she ministered unto them.	
14 And when Jesus was come into Peter's house, he saw his wife's mother lying sick of a fever. 15 And he touched her hand, and the fever left her; and she arose, and ministered unto him.		38 And he rose up from the synagogue and entered into the house of Simon. And Simon's wife's mother was holden with a great fever; and they besought him for 39 her. And he stood over her, and rebuked the fever; and it left her: and immediately she rose up and ministered unto them.
16 And when even was	32 And at even, when	40 And when the sun

Matt. 8:14-17.	Mark 1:29-34.	Luke 4:38-41.
come, they brought unto him many ¹possessed with devils: and he cast out the spirits with a word, and healed all that 17 were sick: that it might be fulfilled which was spoken ²by Isaiah the prophet, saying, Himself took our infirmities, and bare our diseases.	the sun did set, they brought unto him all that were sick, and them that were ¹possessed 33 with devils. And all the city was gathered together at the 34 door. And he healed many that were sick with divers diseases, and cast out many ⁴devils; and he suffered not the ⁴devils to speak, because they knew him⁵.	was setting, all they that had any sick with divers diseases brought them unto him; and he laid his hands on every one of them, and healed 41 them. And ⁴devils also came out from many, crying out, and saying, Thou art the Son of God. And rebuking them, he suffered them not to speak, because they know that he was the Christ.

1. Or, *demoniacs*. 2. Or, *through*. 3. Some ancient authorities read *when he was come out of the synagogue, he came, &c.* 4. Gr. *demons*. 5. Many ancient authorities add *to be Christ*. See Luke 4:41.

In § 30-36 he makes a great journey about Galilee, teaching and healing, and afterwards performs several miracles at Capernaum, and calls Matthew.

§ 30. HE JOURNEYS ABOUT GALILEE, PREACHING AND HEALING.

Matt. 4:23-25.	Mark 1:35-39.	Luke 4:42-44.
	35 And in the morning, a great while before day, he rose up and went out, and departed into a desert place, and 36 there prayed. And Simon and they that were with him followed after him; and 37 they found him, and say unto him, All are seeking thee. 38 And he saith unto them, Let us go elsewhere into the next towns, that I may preach there also; for to this end came 23 And ¹Jesus went 39 I forth. And he went	42 And when it was day, he came out and went into a desert place: and the multitudes sought after him, and came unto him, and would have stayed him, that he should not go from 43 them. But he said unto them, I must preach the ⁵good tidings of the kingdom of God to the other cities also: for therefore was I sent.

MINISTRY IN GALILEE.

Matt. 4:23-25.	Mark 1:35-39.	Luke 4:42-44.
about in all Galilee,* teaching in their synagogues, and preaching the ²gospel of the kingdom, and healing all manner of disease and all manner of sickness 24 among the people.	into their synagogues throughout all Galilee, preaching and casting out ⁴devils.	44 And he was preaching in the synagogues of ⁶Galilee.

And the report of him went forth into all Syria: and they brought unto him all that were sick, holden with divers diseases and torments, ³possessed with devils, and epileptic, and 25 palsied: and he healed them. And there followed him great multitudes from Galilee and Decapolis and Jerusalem and Judea and *from beyond Jordan.*

1. Some ancient authorities read *he.* 2. Or, *good tidings:* and so elsewhere. 3. Or, *demoniacs.* 4. Gr. *demons.* 5. Or, *Gospel.* 6. Very many ancient authorities read *Judea.*

§ 31. A LEPER HEALED, AND MUCH POPULAR EXCITEMENT.

Matt. 8:2-4.	Mark 1:40-45.	Luke 5:12-16.
2 And behold, there came to him a leper and worshipped him, saying, Lord, if thou wilt thou canst make me clean,	40 And there cometh to him a leper, beseeching him, ¹and kneeling down to him, and saying unto him, If thou wilt, thou canst make me 41 clean.	12 And it came to pass, while he was in one of the cities, behold, a man full of leprosy: and when he saw Jesus, he fell on his face, and besought him, saying, Lord, if thou wilt, thou canst make me
3 And he stretched forth his hand, and touched him, saying, I will; be thou made clean. And straightway his leprosy was cleansed.	And being moved with compassion, he stretched forth his hand, and touched him, and saith unto him, I will: be thou made 42 clean. And straightway the leprosy departed from him, and he was made	13 clean. And he stretched forth his hand, and touched him, saying, I will; be thou made clean. And straightway the leprosy departed from him.
4 And Jesus saith unto him, See thou tell no man; but go thy way, shew thyself to the priest, and offer the gift that Moses com-	43 clean. And he²strictly charged him, and straightway sent 44 him out, and saith unto him, See thou say nothing to any man: but go thy way,	14 And he charged him to tell no man: but go thy way, and shew thyself to the priest, and offer for thy

*This journey about all Galilee included a *great mass* of teaching and healing (dwell on Matt. 4:23-25), of which only a few specimens are recorded (§ 31-36), and these apparently occurred at Capernaum, his headquarters. The journey in § 47 (given by Luke only) is probably distinct from this of § 30, and if so it would be a *second*, while that of § 55, which is quite certainly distinct, would then be a *third* journey about Galilee. The reader ought to expand his imagination and take in these extended labors.

Matt. 8:2-4.	Mark 1:40-45.	Luke 5:12-16.
manded, for a testimony unto them.	shew thyself to the priest, and offer for thy cleansing the things which Moses commanded, for a testimony unto them. 45 But he went out, and began to publish it much, and to spread abroad the ²matter, insomuch that ⁴Jesus could no more openly enter into ⁵a city, but was without in desert places: and they came to him from every quarter.	cleansing, according as Moses commanded, for a testimony unto them. 15 But so much the more went abroad the report concerning him: and great multitudes came together to hear, and to be healed of their 16 infirmities. But he withdrew himself in the deserts, and prayed.

1. Some ancient authorities omit *and kneeling down to him*. 2. Or, *sternly*. 3. Gr. *word*. 4. Gr. *he*. 5. Or, *the city*.

§ 32. Thronged in Capernaum, he heals a Paralytic lowered through the Roof.

Matt. 9:2-8.	Mark 2:1-12.	Luke 5:17-26.
	1 And when he entered again into Capernaum after some days, it was noised that he was 2 ⁴in the house. And many were gathered together, so that there was no longer room *for them*, no, not even about the door: and he spake the word unto them.	17 And it came to pass on one of those days, that he was teaching; and there were Pharisees and doctors of the law sitting by, which were come out of every village of Galilee and Judea and Jerusalem: and the power of the Lord was with him ⁶to
2 And behold they brought to him a man sick of the palsy, lying on a bed;	3 And they come bringing unto him a man sick of the palsy, borne of four. 4 And when they could not ⁵come nigh unto him for the crowd, they uncovered the roof where he was: and when they had broken it up, they let down the bed whereon the	18 heal. And behold, men bring on a bed a man that was palsied: and they sought to bring him in, and to lay him before 19 him. And not finding by what *way* they might bring him in because of the multitude, they went up to the housetop, and let him down through

MINISTRY IN GALILEE.

Matt. 9:2-8.	Mark 2:1-12.	Luke 5:17-26.
and Jesus seeing their faith said unto the sick of the palsy, ¹Son, be of good cheer; thy sins are 3 forgiven. And behold, certain of the scribes said within themselves, This man blasphemeth.	sick of the palsy lay. 5 And Jesus seeing their faith saith unto the sick of the 6 palsy, ¹Son, thy sins are forgiven. But there were certain of the scribes sitting there, and reasoning in their 7 hearts, Why doth this man thus speak? he blasphemeth: who can forgive sins but one,	the tiles with his couch into the midst 20 before Jesus. And seeing their faith, he said, Man, thy sins are forgiven thee. 21 And the scribes and the Pharisees began to reason, saying, Who is this that speaketh blasphemies? Who can forgive sins but God alone?
4 And Jesus ²knowing their thoughts said, Wherefore think ye evil in your hearts? 5 For whether is easier, to say, Thy sins are forgiven; or to say, Arise and walk?	8 even God? And straightway Jesus, perceiving in his spirit that they so reasoned within themselves, saith unto them, Why reason ye these things in your 9 hearts? Whether is easier, to say to the sick of the palsy, Thy sins are forgiven; or to say, Arise, and take up thy bed, and walk?	22 But Jesus perceiving their reasonings, answered and said unto them, ⁷What reason ye in your hearts? 23 Whether is easier to say, Thy sins are forgiven thee; or to say, Arise and walk?
6 But that ye may know that the Son of man hath ³power on earth to forgive sins (then saith he to the sick of the palsy), Arise, and take up thy bed, and go unto 7 thy house. And he arose, and departed to his house.	10 But that ye may know that the Son of man hath ³power on earth to forgive sins (he saith to the sick of the palsy), I 11 say unto thee, Arise, take up thy bed, and go unto thy house. 12 And he arose, and straightway took up the bed, and went forth before them all; insomuch that they were all amazed, and glorified God, saying, We never saw it on this fashion.	24 But that ye may know that the Son of man hath ³power on earth to forgive sins (he said unto him that was palsied), I say unto thee, Arise, and take up thy couch, and go 25 unto thy house. And immediately he rose up before them, and took up that whereon he lay, and departed to his house, 26 glorifying God. And amazement took hold on all, and they glorified God; and they
8 But when the multitudes saw it, they were afraid, and glorified God, which had giv-		

Matt. 9:2-8.	Luke 5:17-26.
en such ²power unto men.	were filled with fear, saying, We have seen strange things to-day.

1. Gr. *Child*. 2. Many ancient authorities read *seeing*. 3. Or, *authority*. 4. Or, *at home*. 5. Many ancient authorities read *bring him unto him*. 6. Gr. *that he should heal*. Many ancient authorities read *that he should heal them*. 7. Or, *Why*.

§ 33. THE CALL OF MATTHEW, WHO MAKES HIM A GREAT ENTERTAINMENT.

Capernaum.

Matt. 9:9-13.	Mark 2:13-17.	Luke 5:27-32.
9 And as Jesus passed by from thence, he saw a man, called Matthew, sitting at the place of toll: and he saith unto him, Follow me. And he arose, and followed him.	13 And he went forth again by the sea side; and all the multitude resorted unto him, and he taught them. 14 And as he passed by, he saw Levi the *son* of Alphæus sitting at the place of toll, and he saith unto him, Follow me. And he arose and	27 And after these things he went forth, and beheld a publican, named Levi, sitting at the place of toll, and said unto him, Follow me. 28 And he forsook all, and rose up and followed him.
10 And it came to pass, as he ¹sat at meat in the house, behold, many publicans and sinners came and sat down with Jesus and his disciples.	15 followed him. And it came to pass, that he was sitting at meat in his house, and many ⁴publicans and sinners sat down with Jesus and his disciples: for there were many, and they	29 And Levi made him a great feast in his house: and there was a great multitude of publicans and of others that were sitting at meat with them.
11 And when the Pharisees saw it, they said unto his disciples, Why eateth your ²Master with the publicans and sinners?	16 followed him. And the scribes⁵ of the Pharisees, when they saw that he was eating with the sinners and publicans, said unto his disciples, ⁶He eateth ⁷and drinketh with publicans and sinners.	30 And ⁸the Pharisees and their scribes murmured against his disciples, saying, Why do ye eat and drink with the publicans and sinners?
12 But when he heard it, he said, They that are ³whole have no need of a physician, but they that	17 And when Jesus heard it, he saith unto them, They that are ³whole have no need of a physi-	31 And Jesus answering said unto them, They that are ³whole have no need of a physician; but

MINISTRY IN GALILEE.

Matt. 9:9-13.	Mark 2:13-17.	Luke 5:27-32.
13 are sick. But go ye and learn what *this* meaneth, I desire mercy, and not sacrifice: for I came not to call the righteous, but sinners.	cian, but they that are sick: I came not to call the righteous, but sinners.	they that are sick. 32 I am not come to call the righteous but sinners to repentance.

1. Gr. *reclined:* and so always. 2. Or, *Teacher.* 3. Gr. *strong.* 4. That is, *collectors or renters of Roman taxes;* and so elsewhere. 5. Some ancient authorities read *and the Pharisees.* 6. Or, *how is it that he cateth....sinners?* 7. Some ancient authorities omit *and drinketh.* 8. Or, *the Pharisees and the scribes among them.*

§ 34. JESUS DISCOURSES ON FASTING.

Matt. 9:14-17.	Mark 2:18-22.	Luke 5:33-39.
14 Then come to him the disciples of John, saying, Why do we and the Pharisees fast ¹oft, but thy disciples fast not. And 15 Jesus said unto them, Can the sons of the bride-chamber mourn, as long as the bride-groom is with them? But the days will come, when the bride-groom shall be taken away from them, and then will they fast.	18 And John's disciples and the Pharisees were fasting: and they come and say unto him, Why do John's disciples and the disciples of the Pharisees fast, but thy disciples fast 19 not? And Jesus said unto them, Can the sons of the bride-chamber fast, while the bride-groom is with them? as long as they have the bride-groom with them they cannot 20 fast. But the days will come, when the bride-groom shall be taken away from them, and then they will fast in that day.	33 And they said unto him, The disciples of John fast often, and make supplications; likewise also the *disciples* of the Pharisees: but thine 34 eat and drink. And Jesus said unto them, Can ye make the sons of the bride-chamber fast while the bride-groom is with them? 35 But the days will come; and when the bride-groom shall be taken away from them, then will they fast in those days. 36 And he spake also a parable unto them; No man rendeth a piece from a new garment and putteth it upon an old garment; else he will rend the new, and also the piece from the new will not agree with the
16 And no man putteth a piece of undressed cloth upon an old garment; for that which should fill it up taketh from the garment, and a worse 17 rent is made. Neith-	21 No man seweth a piece of undressed cloth on an old garment; else that which should fill it up taketh from it, the new from the old, and a worse rent is made.	

Matt. 9:14-17.	Mark 2:18-22.	Luke 5:33-39.
er do *men* put new wine into old ²wineskins: else the skins burst and the wine is spilled, and the skins perish; but they put new wine into fresh wineskins, and both are preserved.	22 And no man putteth new wine into old ²wine-skins: else the wine will burst the skins, and the wine perisheth, and the skins: but *they put* new wine into fresh wine-skins.	37 old. And no man putteth new wine into old ²wine-skins; else the new wine will burst the skins, and itself will be spilled, and the skins will perish. 38 But new wine must be put into fresh 39 wine-skins. And no man having drunk old *wine* desireth new: for he saith, The old is ³good.

1. Some ancient authorities omit *oft*. 2. That is, *skins used as bottles*. 3. Many ancient authorities read *better*.

§ 35. HE RAISES JAIRUS' DAUGHTER, AND HEALS A WOMAN WHO ONLY TOUCHED HIS GARMENT.

Matt. 9:18-26.	Mark 5:22-43.	Luke 8:41-56.
18 While he spake these things unto them*, behold, there came ¹a ruler, and worshipped him, saying, My daughter is even now dead: but come and lay thy hand upon her, and she shall live. 19 And Jesus arose, and followed him, and *so did* his disciples.	22 And there cometh one of the rulers of the synagogue, Jairus by name; and seeing him, he falleth at his feet, and 23 beseecheth him much, saying, My little daughter is at the point of death: *I pray thee*, that thou come and lay thy hands on her, that she may be ²made 24 whole, and live. And he went with him; and a great multitude followed him, and they thronged him.	41 And behold there came a man named Jairus, and he was a ruler of the synagogue: and he fell down at Jesus' feet, and besought him to come into his 42 house; for he had an only daughter, about twelve years of age, and she lay a dying. But as he went the multitudes thronged him.
20 And behold, a woman, who had an issue of blood twelve years, came behind	25 And a woman, which had an issue 26 of blood twelve years, and had suffered	43 And a woman having an issue of blood twelve years, which ⁵had spent all her

*The express language of Matt. 9:18 compels us to place the incidents of § 35 directly after Matthew's entertainment. But Mark and Luke, who are usually chronological (while Matthew in this portion is not), give these incidents a good deal farther on. The question of position in the Harmony cannot be settled, and it makes no difference as to understanding the contents of the section.

Matt. 9:18–26.	Mark 5:22–43.	Luke 8:41–56.
him, and touched the border of his 21 garment: for she said within herself, If I do but touch his garment, I shall be ²made whole.	many things of many physicians, and had spent all that she had, and was nothing bettered, but rather 27 grew worse, having heard the things concerning Jesus, came in the crowd behind, and touched 28 his garment. For she said, If I touch but his garments, I shall be ²made whole. 29 And straightway the fountain of her blood was dried up; and she felt in her body that she was healed of her ⁵plague. 30 And straightway Jesus, perceiving in himself that the power *proceeding* from him had gone forth, turned him about in the crowd, and said, Who touched my gar- 31 ments? And his disciples said unto him, Thou seest the multitude thronging thee, and sayest thou, Who touched 32 me? And he looked round about to see her that had done 33 this thing. But the woman fearing and trembling, knowing what had been done to her, came and fell down before him, and told him all the 34 truth. And he said unto her, Daughter, thy faith hath ³made thee whole; go in peace, and be whole of thy ⁵plague.	living upon physicians, and could not be healed of any, 44 came behind him, and touched the border of his garment: and immediately the issue of her blood stanched. 45 And Jesus said, Who is it that touched me? And when all denied, Peter said, ⁹and they that were with him, Master, the multitudes press thee and crush *thee*. 46 But Jesus said, Some one did touch me; for I perceived that power had gone forth 47 from me. And when the woman saw that she was not hid, she came trembling, and falling down before him declared in the presence of all the people for what cause she touched him, and how she was healed immediately. 48 And he said unto her, Daughter, thy faith hath ³made thee whole; go in peace.

Matt. 9:18–26.	Mark 5:22–43.	Luke 8:41-56.
	35 While he yet spake, they come from the ruler of the synagogue's *house*, saying, Thy daughter is dead: why troublest thou the ⁶Master any further? But	49 While he yet spake, there cometh one from the ruler of the synagogue's *house*, saying, Thy daughter is dead; trouble not the ⁶Master. But Jesus hearing it, answered him, Fear not: only believe, and she shall be ²made whole.
22 But Jesus turning and seeing her said, Daughter, be of good cheer; thy faith hath ³made thee whole. And the woman was ²made whole from that 23 hour. And when Jesus came into the ruler's house, and saw the flute-players, and the crowd mak-24 ing a tumult, he said, Give place: for the damsel is not dead, but sleepeth. And they laughed 25 him to scorn. But when the crowd was put forth, he entered in, and took her by the hand; and the 26 damsel arose. And ⁴the fame hereof went forth into all that land.	36 Jesus, ʼnot heeding the word spoken, saith unto the ruler of the synagogue, Fear not, only be-37 lieve. And he suffered no man to follow with him, save Peter, and James, and John the brother 38 of James. And they come to the house of the ruler of the synagogue; and he beholdeth a tumult, and *many* weeping and wailing greatly. 39 And when he was entered in, he saith unto them, Why make ye a tumult and weep? the child is not dead, but 40 sleepeth. And they laughed him to scorn. But he, having put them all forth, taketh the father of the child and her mother and them that were with him, and goeth in where the child was. 41 And taking the child by the hand, he saith unto her, Talitha cumi; which is, being interpreted, Damsel, I say unto 42 thee, Arise. And straightway the damsel rose up, and walked; for she was twelve years old.	51 And when he came to the house, he suffered not any man to enter in with him, save Peter, and John, and James, and the father of the maiden and her mother 52 And all were weeping, and bewailing her: but he said, Weep not; for she is not dead, but sleep-53 eth. And they laughed him to scorn, knowing that 54 she was dead. But he, taking her by the hand, called, saying, Maiden, arise. 55 And her spirit returned, and she rose up immediately. and he commanded that *something* be given 56 her to eat. And her parents were amazed: but he charged them to tell no man what had been done.

MINISTRY IN GALILEE.

Mark 5:22-43.

43 · And they were amazed straightway with a great amazement. And he charged them much that no man should know this: and he commanded that *something* should be given her to eat.

1. Gr. *one ruler*. 2. Or, *saved*. 3. Or, *saved thee*. 4. Gr. *this fame*. 5. Gr. *scourge*. 6. Or, *Teacher*. 7. Or, *overhearing*. 8. Some ancient authorities omit *had spent all her living upon physicians, and*. 9. Some ancient authorities omit *and they that were with him*.

§ 36. HE HEALS TWO BLIND MEN, AND A DUMB DEMONIAC.

Matt. 9:27-34.

27 And as Jesus passed by from thence, two blind men followed him, cry-
28 ing out, and saying, Have mercy on us, thou son of David. And when he was come into the house, the blind men came to him: and Jesus saith unto them, Believe ye that I am able to do this? They say unto
29 him, Yea, Lord. Then touched he their eyes, saying, According to
30 your faith be it done unto you. And their eyes were opened. And
31 Jesus ¹strictly charged them, saying, See that no man know it. But they went forth, and spread abroad his fame in all that land.
32 And as they went forth, behold, there was brought to him a dumb
33 man possessed with a ²devil. And when the ²devil was cast out, the dumb man spake: and the multitudes marvelled, saying, It was never
34 so seen in Israel. But the Pharisees said, ³By the prince of the ⁴devils casteth he out ⁴devils.

1. Or, *sternly*. 2. Gr. *demon*. 3. Or, *In*. 4. Gr. *demons*.

In § 37-39 the Saviour seems to the Jews to break the Sabbath, and hence a great hostility, with design to kill him. He defends himself and his disciples (§ 38) by various arguments and personal claims.

§ 37. ATTENDING A FEAST IN JERUSALEM (PROBABLY THE PASSOVER), JESUS HEALS A MAN ON THE SABBATH, AND DEFENDS THIS ACTION.

John 5:1-47.

1 After these things there was ¹a feast* of the Jews; and Jesus went up to Jerusalem.

* This feast of John 5:1 was *most probably* a Passover (see note at end of volume, on § 37). If so, we should know that our Lord's public ministry lasted three years and a fraction, and that the great ministry in Galilee lasted some 18 to 20 months. Otherwise, we should know of only two years and a fraction for the former, and 6 to 8 months for the latter; as John gives three passovers beyond question (John 2:13; 6:4; 12:1), and our Lord's ministry began some time before the first of these (§ 15-20). If the feast of 5:1 was not a passover, it is quite impossible to determine what other feast it was. While one would be glad to settle these questions, if it were possible, yet it really does not matter as regards understanding our Lord's *recorded* history and teachings during the great ministry in Galilee, the only point of difference being that if this feast was a Passover we should conceive of the three journeys about Galilee as occupying a longer time, and including more extensive *unrecorded* labors in preaching and healing.

John 5:1-47.

2 Now there is in Jerusalem by the sheep *gate* a pool, which is called
3 in Hebrew ²Bethesda, having five porches. In these lay a multitude
5 of them that were sick, blind, halt, withered³. And a certain man
was there, which had been thirty and eight years in his infirmity.
6 When Jesus saw him lying, and knew that he had been now a long
time *in that case*, he saith unto him, Wouldst thou be made whole?
7 The sick man answered him, ⁴Sir, I have no man, when the water is
troubled, to put me into the pool: but while I am coming, another
8 steppeth down before me. Jesus saith unto him, Arise, take up thy
9 bed, and walk. And straightway the man was made whole, and took
up his bed and walked.
10 Now it was the sabbath on that day. So the Jews said unto him
that was cured, It is the sabbath, and it is not lawful for thee to take
11 up thy bed. But he answered them, He that made me whole, the
12 same said unto me, Take up thy bed, and walk. They asked him,
13 Who is the man that said unto thee, Take up *thy bed*, and walk? But
he that was healed wist not who it was: for Jesus had conveyed him-
14 self away, a multitude being in the place. Afterward Jesus findeth
him in the temple, and said unto him, Behold, thou art made whole:
15 sin no more, lest a worse thing befall thee. The man went away, and
16 told the Jews that it was Jesus which had made him whole. And for
this cause did the Jews persecute Jesus, because he did these things
17 on the sabbath. But Jesus answered them, My Father worketh even
18 until now, and I work. For this cause therefore the Jews sought the
more to kill him, because he not only brake the sabbath, but also
called God his own Father, making himself equal with God.
19 Jesus therefore answered and said unto them,

Verily, verily, I say unto you, The Son can do nothing of himself,
but what he seeth the Father doing: for what things soever he doeth,
20 these the Son also doeth in like manner. For the Father loveth the
Son, and sheweth him all things that himself doeth; and greater
21 works than these will he shew him, that ye may marvel. For as the
Father raiseth the dead and quickeneth them, even so the Son also
22 quickeneth whom he will. For neither doth the Father judge any
man, but he hath given all judgement unto the Son; that all may
23 honour the Son, even as they honour the Father. He that honoureth
24 not the Son honoureth not the Father which sent him. Verily, verily,
I say unto you, He that heareth my word, and believeth him that sent
me, hath eternal life, and cometh not into judgement, but hath passed
25 out of death into life. Verily, verily, I say unto you, The hour
cometh, and now is, when the dead shall hear the voice of the Son of
26 God; and they that hear shall live. For as the Father hath life
in himself, even so gave he to the Son also to have life in himself:
27 and he gave him authority to execute judgement, because he is ⁵the
28 Son of man. Marvel not at this: for the hour cometh, in which all
29 that are in the tombs shall hear his voice, and shall come forth; they
that have done good, unto the resurrection of life; and they that have
⁶done ill, unto the resurrection of judgement.
30 I can of myself do nothing: as I hear, I judge: and my judgement is
righteous; because I seek not mine own will, but the will of him that
31 sent me. If I bear witness of myself, my witness is not true. It is
32 another that beareth witness of me; and I know that the witness

John 5:1-47.

33 which he witnesseth of me is true. Ye have sent unto John, and he
34 hath borne witness unto the truth. But the witness which I receive
is not from man: howbeit I say these things, that ye may be saved.
35 He was the lamp that burneth and shineth: and ye were willing to
36 rejoice for a season in his light. But the witness which I have is
greater than *that of* John: for the works which the Father hath given
me to accomplish, the very works that I do, bear witness of me, that
37 the Father hath sent me. And the Father which sent me, he hath
borne witness of me. Ye have neither heard his voice at any time,
38 nor seen his form. And ye have not his word abiding in you: for
39 whom he sent, him ye believe not. ⁷Ye search the scriptures, because
ye think that in them ye have eternal life; and these are they which
40 bear witness of me; and ye will not come to me, that ye may have life.
41 I receive not glory from men. But I know you, that ye have not the
42 love of God in yourselves. I am come in my Father's name, and ye
43 receive me not; if another shall come in his own name, him ye will
44 receive. How can ye believe, which receive glory one of another, and
45 the glory that *cometh* from *the only God ye seek not? Think not that
I will accuse you to the Father: there is one that accuseth you, *even*
46 Moses, on whom ye have set your hope. For if ye believed Moses, ye
47 would believe me: for he wrote of me. But if ye believe not his
writings, how shall ye believe my words?*

1. Many ancient authorities read *the feast.* 2. Some ancient authorities read *Bethsaida*, others *Bethzatha.* 3. Many ancient authorities insert, wholly or in part, *waiting for the moving of the water:* 4. *for an angel went down at certain seasons into the pool, and troubled the water: whosoever then first after the troubling of the water stepped in was made whole, with whatsoever disease he was holden.* 4. Or, *Lord.* 5. Or, *a son of man.* 6. Or, *practised.* 7. Or, *Search the scriptures.* 8. Some ancient authorities read *the only one.*

§ 38. THE DISCIPLES OF JESUS PLUCK EARS OF GRAIN ON THE
SABBATH, AND HE DEFENDS THEM.†

Matt. 12:1-8.	Mark 2:23-28.	Luke 6:1-5.
1 At that season Jesus went on the sabbath-day through the corn-fields: and his disciples were an hungred, and began to pluck ears of corn, 2 and to eat. But the	23 And it came to pass, that he was going on the sabbath day through the cornfields; and his disciples ³began, as they went, to pluck the ears of corn.	1 Now it came to pass, on a ⁵sabbath, that he was going through the corn-fields: and his disciples plucked the ears of corn, and did eat, rubbing them in

*Observe that here more than a year before the crucifixion, and probably two years (i. e. if the feast of 5:1 was a passover), the hostility of the Jews *at Jerusalem* (comp. John 4:1) has reached the point of a desire to kill him, as a sabbath-breaker and a blasphemer (5:16-18). So we shall find him staying away from Jerusalem at the passover of John 6:4, and until the Tabernacles six months before the crucifixion (John 7:1-10, ¿ 73, 74). Meantime, the hostility will go on increasing in other parts of the country (¿ 39, Mark 3:6; ¿ 48, etc.).— Notice also that in this discourse at Jerusalem our Lord repeatedly declares himself in a high sense the Son of God (compare in ¿40), and the appointed judge of mankind (ver. 27), and says that Moses wrote concerning him (ver. 46). All this indicated that he was the Messiah, but he did not expressly assert it. That would have precipitated the collision, for to claim to be the Messiah would in the view of the Jewish rulers involve *political* consequences (since they expected the Messiah to be a *king*), and many of the rulers cared far more for politics than for religion. Comp. John 11:48.

†The important events and discourses of ¿ 38 and 39 doubtless occurred on the way back from Jerusalem, or in Galilee, as in ¿ 40 he withdraws to the sea of Galilee.

Matt. 12:1-8.	Mark 2:23-28.	Luke 6:1-5.
Pharisees, when they saw it, said unto him, Behold, thy disciples do that which it is not lawful to do upon the 3 sabbath. But he said unto them, Have ye not read what David did, when he was an hungred, and they that were with him; 4 how he entered into the house of God, and ¹did eat the shewbread, which it was not lawful for him to eat, neither for them that were with them, but only 5 for the priests? Or have ye not read in the law, how that on the sabbath day the priests in the temple profane the sabbath, and are guiltless? 6 But I say unto you, that ²one greater than the temple is 7 here. But if ye had known what this meaneth, I desire mercy, and not sacrifice, ye would not have condemned 8 the guiltless. For the Son of man is lord of the sabbath.	24 And the Pharisees said unto him, Behold, why do they on the sabbath day that which is not lawful? 25 And he said unto them, Did ye never read what David did, when he had need, and was an hungred, he, and they that were with 26 him? How he entered into the house of God ⁴when Abiathar was high priest, and did eat the shewbread, which is not lawful to eat, save for the priests, and gave also to them that were with him? 27 And he said unto them, The sabbath was made for man, and not man for 28 the sabbath: so that the Son of man is lord even of the sabbath.	2 their hands. But certain of the Pharisees said, Why do ye that which it is not lawful to do on the 3 sabbath day? And Jesus answering them said, Have ye not read even this, what David did, when he was an hungred, he, and they that were with him; 4 how he entered into the house of God, and did take and eat the shewbread, and gave also to them that were with him; which it is not lawful to eat save for the priests alone? 5 And he said unto them, The Son of man is lord of the sabbath.

1. Some ancient authorities read *they did eat.* 2. Gr. *a greater thing.* 3. Gr. *began to make* their *way plucking.* 4. Some ancient authorities read *in the days of Abiathar the high priest.* 5. Many ancient authorities insert *second-first.*

§ 39. JESUS HEALS A WITHERED HAND ON THE SABBATH, AND DEFENDS IT.

(Compare § 87.)

Matt. 12:9-14.	Mark 3:1-6.	Luke 6:6-11.
9 And he departed	1 And he entered a-	6 And it came to

Matt. 12:9-14.	Mark 3:1-6.	Luke 6:6-11.
thence, and went into their syna- 10 gogue; and behold, a man having a withered hand. And they asked him, saying, Is it lawful to heal on the sabbath day? that they might accuse him. 11 And he said unto them, What man shall there be of you, that shall have one sheep, and if this fall into a pit on the sabbath day, will he not lay hold on it, and lift 12 it out? How much then is a man of more value than a sheep! Wherefore it is lawful to do good on the sabbath day. 13 Then saith he to the man, Stretch forth thy hand. And he stretched it forth; and it was restored whole, as the other. 14 But the Pharisees went out, and took counsel against him, how they might destroy him.	gain into the synagogue; and there was a man there which had his hand withered. 2 And they watched him, whether he would heal him on the sabbath day; that they might accuse him. 3 And he saith unto the man that had his hand withered, ¹Stand 4 forth. And he saith unto them, Is it lawful on the sabbath day to do good, or to do harm? to save a life, or to kill? But they held their 5 peace. And when he had looked round about on them with anger, being grieved at the hardening of their hearts, he saith unto the man, Stretch forth thy hand. And he stretched it forth; and his hand was restored. 6 And the Pharisees went out and straightway with the Herodians took counsel against him, how they might destroy him.*	pass on another sabbath, that he entered into the synagogue and taught: and there was a man there, and his right hand was withered. 7 And the scribes and the Pharisees watched him, whether he would heal on the sabbath; that they might find how to 8 accuse him. But he knew their thoughts: and he said to the man that had his hand withered, Rise up, and stand forth in the midst. And he arose and stood 9 forth. And Jesus said unto them, I ask you, Is it lawful on the sabbath to do good, or to do harm? to save a life, or to 10 destroy it? And he looked round about on them all, and said unto him, Stretch forth thy hand. And he did *so:* and his hand was restored. 11 But they were filled with ²madness; and communed one with another what they might do to Jesus.

1. Gr. *Arise into the midst.* 2. Or, *foolishness.*

*Here at some point near the sea of Galilee, there is already a plot to kill him, as some had wished to do in Jerusalem (comp. on § 37).

In § 40-42 great throngs attend his ministry, and he selects twelve disciples to be his helpers, giving to them and the multitudes the Sermon on the Mount.

§ 40. GREAT MULTITUDES ATTEND HIM BESIDE THE SEA OF GALILEE.

Matt 12:15-21.

15 And Jesus perceiving *it*, withdrew from thence: and many followed him;

16 and he healed them all,

and charged them that they should
17 not make him known: that it might be fulfilled which was spoken [1]by Isaiah, the prophet, saying,
18 Behold, my servant whom I have chosen;
My beloved in whom my soul is well pleased:
I will put my Spirit upon him,
And he shall declare judgement to the Gentiles.
19 He shall not strive, nor cry aloud;
Neither shall any one hear his voice in the streets.
20 A bruised reed shall he not break,
And smoking flax shall he not quench,
Till he send forth judgement unto victory.
21 And in his name shall the Gentiles hope.

Mark 3:7-12.

7 And Jesus with his disciples withdrew to the sea: and a great multitude from Galilee followed:
8 and from Judea, and from Jerusalem, and from Idumæa, and beyond Jordan, and about Tyre and Sidon, a great multitude, hearing [2]what great things he
9 did, came unto him. And he spake to his disciples, that a little boat should wait on him because of the crowd, lest they
10 should throng him, for he had healed many; insomuch that as many as had [3]plagues [4]pressed upon him that they might touch
11 him. And the unclean spirits, whensoever they beheld him, fell down before him, and cried, saying, Thou art the Son of God.
12 And he charged them much that they should not make him known.

1. Or, *through.* 2. Or, *all the things that he did.* 3. Gr. *scourges.* 4. Gr. *fell.*

§ 41. AFTER A NIGHT OF PRAYER, JESUS SELECTS TWELVE APOSTLES.

Mark 3:13-19.

13 And he goeth up into the mountain, and calleth unto him whom

Luke 6:12-16.

12 And it came to pass in these days, that he went out into the

MINISTRY IN GALILEE.

Mark 3:13-19.	Luke 6:12-16.
he himself would: and they went 14 unto him. And he appointed twelve¹, that they might be with him, and that he might send 15 them forth to preach, and to have 16 authority to cast out ²devils; ³and 17 Simon he surnamed Peter; and James the *son* of Zebedee, and John the brother of James; and them he surnamed Boanerges, 18 which is, Sons of thunder: and Andrew, and Philip, and Bartholomew, and Matthew, and Thomas, and James the *son* of Alphæus, and Thaddæus, and Simon the ⁴Cananæan, 19 and Judas Iscariot, which also betrayed him.	mountain to pray; and he continued all night in prayer to 13 God. And when it was day, he called his disciples: and he chose from them twelve, whom also he named Apostles;* 14 Simon, whom he also named Peter, and Andrew his brother, and James and John, and Philip and Bartholomew, 15 and Matthew and Thomas, and James *the son* of Alphæus, and Simon which was 16 called the Zealot, and Judas, *the son* of ⁵James, and Judas Iscariot, which was the traitor.

1. Some ancient authorities add *whom also he named apostles*. See Luke 6:13. 2. Gr. *demons*. 3. Some ancient authorities insert *and he appointed twelve*. 4. Or, *Zealot*. See Luke 6:15; Acts 1:13. 5. Or, *brother*. See Jude 1.

§ 42. THE SERMON ON THE MOUNT. PRIVILEGES AND REQUIREMENTS OF THE MESSIANIC REIGN.

Matthew, chapters 5-7. Luke 6:17-49.†

A level place on a mountain, not far from Capernaum.

Introductory statements.

Matt. 5:1, 2.	Luke 6:17-19.
1 And seeing the multitudes, he went up into the mountain: and when he had sat down, his disci- 2 ples came unto him: and he opened his mouth and taught them, saying,	17 And he came down with them, and stood on a level place, and a great multitude of his disciples, and a great number of the people from all Judea and Jerusalem, and the sea coast of Tyre and Sidon, which came to hear him, and to be healed of their diseases; 18 and they that were troubled with unclean spirits were healed. 19 And all the multitude sought to touch him: for power came forth from him, and healed *them* all.

*Matthew postpones giving the names of the Twelve till they are sent out to preach in Galilee (§ 55). There is a fourth list in Acts 1:13. See the four compared in note at the end of this volume, on § 41.

†There is little doubt that the discourses given by Matthew and Luke are the same. Matthew locating it on "the mountain," and Luke "on a level place," which might easily be a level spot on a mountain. (See note at end of this book, on § 42.) Observe that they begin and end alike, and pursue the same general order. Luke omits various matters of special interest to Matthew's Jewish readers (e. g. Matt. 5:17-42), and other matters that he himself will give elsewhere (e. g. Luke 11:1-4; 12:22-31); while Luke has a few sentences (as ver. 24-26, 38-40), which are not given by Matthew.

(a) The Beatitudes. Privileges of the Messiah's subjects.

Matt. 5:3-12.	Luke 6:20-26.
3 Blessed are the poor in spirit: for theirs is the kingdom of hea 4 ven. ¹Blessed are they that mourn: for they shall be com 5 forted. Blessed are the meek: for they shall inherit the earth. 6 Blessed are they that hunger and thirst after righteousness: 7 for they shall be filled. Blessed are the merciful: for they shall 8 obtain mercy. Blessed are the pure in heart: for they shall see 9 God. Blessed are the peacemakers: for they shall be called 10 sons of God. Blessed are they that have been persecuted for righteousness' sake: for theirs is 11 the kingdom of heaven. Blessed are ye when *men* shall reproach you, and persecute you, and say all manner of evil against you 12 falsely, for my sake. Rejoice, and be exceeding glad: for great is your reward in heaven: for so persecuted they the prophets which were before you.	20 And he lifted up his eyes on his disciples, and said, Blessed *are* ye poor: for yours is the 21 kingdom of God. Blessed *are* ye that hunger now: for ye shall be filled. Blessed *are* ye that weep now: for ye shall laugh. 22 Blessed are ye, when men shall hate you, and when they shall separate you *from their company*, and reproach you, and cast out your name as evil, for the Son of 23 man's sake. Rejoice in that day, and leap *for joy:* for behold, your reward is great in heaven: for in the same manner did their fath 24 ers unto the prophets. But woe unto you that are rich! for ye have received your consolation. 25 Woe unto you, ye that are full now! for ye shall hunger. Woe *unto you*, ye that laugh now! for 26 ye shall mourn and weep. Woe *unto you*, when all men shall speak well of you! for in the same manner did their fathers to the false prophets.

1. Some ancient authorities transpose ver. 4 and 5.

(b) Influence and Responsibility of the Messiah's Subjects.

Matt. 5:13-16.

13 Ye are the salt of the earth: but if the salt have lost its savour, wherewith shall it be salted? it is thenceforth good for nothing, but
14 to be cast out and trodden under foot of men. Ye are the light
15 of the world. A city set on a hill cannot be hid. Neither do *men* light a lamp, and put it under the bushel, but on the stand; and it
16 shineth unto all that are in the house. Even so let your light shine before men, that they may see your good works, and glorify your Father which is in heaven.

(c) Relation of the Messianic teaching to the Law, and to the current teaching.

Matt. 5:17-48; Luke 6:27-36.

17 Think not that I came to destroy the law or the prophets: I came
18 not to destroy but to fulfil. For verily I say unto you, Till heaven and earth pass away, one jot or one tittle shall in no wise pass away from
19 the law, till all things be accomplished. Whosoever therefore shall

MINISTRY IN GALILEE.

Matt. 5:17–48; Luke 6:27–36.

break one of these least commandments, and shall teach men so, shall be called least in the kingdom of heaven: but whosoever shall do and
20 teach them, he shall be called great in the kingdom of heaven. For I say unto you, that except your righteousness shall exceed *the righteousness* of the scribes and Pharisees, ye shall in no wise enter into the kingdom of heaven.
21 Ye have heard that it was said to them of old time, Thou shalt not
22 kill; and whosoever shall kill shall be in danger of the judgement: but I say unto you, that every one who is angry with his brother ¹shall be in danger of the judgement, and whosoever shall say to his brother ²Raca, shall be in danger of the council; and whosoever shall
23 say, ³Thou fool, shall be in danger ⁴of the ⁵hell of fire. If therefore thou art offering thy gift at the altar, and there rememberest that
24 thy brother hath aught against thee, leave there thy gift before the altar, and go thy way, first be reconciled to thy brother, and then
25 come and offer thy gift. Agree with thine adversary quickly, whiles thou art with him in the way; lest haply the adversary deliver thee to the judge, and the judge ⁶deliver thee to the officer, and thou be
26 cast into prison. Verily I say unto thee, Thou shalt by no means come out thence, till thou have paid the last farthing.
27 Ye have heard that it was said, Thou shalt not commit adultery:
28 but I say unto you, that every one that looketh on a woman to lust after her hath committed adultery with her already in his heart.
29 And if thy right eye causeth thee to stumble, pluck it out, and cast it from thee; for it is profitable for thee that one of thy members should
30 perish, and not thy whole body be cast into ⁷hell. And if thy right hand causeth thee to stumble, cut it off, and cast it from thee: for it is profitable for thee that one of thy members should perish, and not thy
31 whole body go into ⁷hell. It was said also, Whosoever shall put
32 away his wife, let him give her a writing of divorcement: but I say unto you, that every one that putteth away his wife, saving for the cause of fornication, maketh her an adulteress: and whosoever shall marry her when she is put away committeth adultery.
33 Again, ye have heard that it was said to them of old time, Thou shalt not forswear thyself, but shalt perform unto the Lord thine
34 oaths: but I say unto you, Swear not at all; neither by the heaven, for
35 it is the throne of God; nor by the earth, for it is the footstool of his
36 feet: nor ⁸by Jerusalem, for it is the city of the great King. Neither shalt thou swear by thy head, for thou canst not make one hair white
37 or black. ⁹But let your speech be, Yea, yea; Nay, nay: and whatsoever is more than these is of ¹⁰the evil one.
38 Ye have heard that it was said, An eye for an eye, and a tooth for a
39 tooth: but I say unto you, Resist not ¹¹him that is evil; but whosoever
40 smiteth thee on thy right cheek, turn to him the other also. And if any man would go to law with thee, and take away thy coat, let him
41 have thy cloke also. And whosoever shall ¹²compel thee to go one
42 mile, go with him twain. Give to him that asketh thee, and from him that would borrow of thee turn not thou away.
43 Ye have heard that it was said, Thou shalt love thy neighbour,

Matt. 5:17-48.

44 and hate thine enemy: But I say unto you, Love your enemies, and pray for them that persecute
45 you; that ye may be sons of your Father which is in heaven: for he maketh his sun to rise on the evil and the good, and sendeth rain on the just and the unjust.

46 For if ye love them that love you, what reward have ye? do not even the [13]publicans the
47 same? And if you salute your brethren only, what do ye more *than others?* do not even the
48 Gentiles the same? Ye therefore shall be perfect, as your heavenly Father is perfect.

Luke 6:27-36.

27 But I say unto you which hear, Love your enemies, do good to them that
28 hate you, bless them that curse you, pray for them that despite-
29 fully use you. To him that smiteth thee on the *one* cheek offer also the other; and from him that taketh away thy cloke withhold not thy coat also.
30 Give to every one that asketh thee; and of him that taketh away thy goods ask them not
32 again. And if ye love them that love you, what thank have ye? for even sinners love
33 those that love them. And if ye do good to them that do good to you, what thank have ye? for
34 even sinners do the same. And if ye lend to them of whom ye hope to receive, what thank have ye? even sinners lend to sinners,
35 to receive again as much. But love your enemies, and do *them* good, and lend, [14]never despairing; and your reward shall be great, and ye shall be sons of the Most High: for he is kind toward
36 the unthankful and evil. Be ye merciful, even as your Father is merciful.

1. Many ancient authorities insert *without cause*. 2. An expression of contempt. 3. Or, *Moreh*, a Hebrew expression of condemnation. 4. Gr. *unto* or *into*. 5. Gr. *Gehenna of fire*. 6. Some ancient authorities omit *deliver thee*. 7. Gr. *Gehenna*. 8. Or, *toward*. 9. Some ancient authorities read *But your speech* shall be. 10. Or, *evil:* as in ver. 39; 6:13. 11. Or, *evil*. 12. Gr. *impress*. 13. That is, *collectors* or *renters of Roman taxes:* and so elsewhere. 14. Some ancient authorities read, *despairing of no man*.

(d) Good works must not be performed ostentatiously. For example, alms-giving, prayer, fasting.

Matt. 6:1-18.

1 Take heed that ye do not your righteousness before men, to be seen of them: else ye have no reward with your Father which is in heaven.
2 When therefore thou doest alms, sound not a trumpet before thee, as the hypocrites do in the synagogues and in the streets, that they may have glory of men. Verily I say unto you, They have received
3 their reward. But when thou doest alms, let not thy left hand know
4 what thy right hand doeth: that thine alms may be in secret: and thy Father which seeth in secret shall recompense thee.

Matt. 6:1-18.

5 And when ye pray, ye shall not be as the hypocrites: for they love to stand and pray in the synagogues and in the corners of the streets, that they may be seen of men. Verily I say unto you, They have re-
6 ceived their reward. But thou, when thou prayest, enter into thine inner chamber, and having shut thy door, pray to thy Father which is in secret, and thy Father which seeth in secret shall recompense
7 thee. And in praying use not vain repetitions, as the Gentiles do: for
8 they think that they shall be heard for their much speaking. Be not therefore like unto them: for ¹your Father knoweth what things
9 ye have need of, before ye ask him. After this manner therefore
10 pray ye: Our Father which art in heaven, Hallowed be thy name.
11 Thy kingdom come. Thy will be done, as in heaven, so on earth.
12 Give us this day ²our daily bread. And forgive us our debts, as we
13 also have forgiven our debtors. And bring us not into temptation,
14 but deliver us from ³the evil *one*. ⁴For if ye forgive men their tres-
15 passes, your heavenly Father will also forgive you. But if ye forgive not men their trespasses, neither will your Father forgive your trespasses.
16 Moreover when ye fast, be not, as the hypocrites, of a sad countenance: for they disfigure their faces, that they may be seen of men to
17 fast. Verily I say unto you, They have received their reward. But
18 thou, when thou fastest, anoint thy head, and wash thy face; that thou be not seen of men to fast, but of thy Father which is in secret: and thy Father, which seeth in secret, shall recompense thee.

1. Some ancient authorities read *God your Father*. 2. Gr. *our bread for the coming day*. 3. Or, *evil*. 4. Many authorities, some ancient, but with variations, add *For thine is the kingdom, and the power, and the glory, for ever, Amen*.

(e) Single-hearted devotion to God, as opposed to worldly aims and anxieties.

Matt. 6:19-34.

19 Lay not up for yourselves treasures upon the earth, where moth and
20 rust doth consume, and where thieves ¹break through and steal: but lay up for yourselves treasures in heaven, where neither moth nor
21 rust doth consume, and where thieves do not ¹break through nor
22 steal: for where thy treasure is, there will thy heart be also. The lamp of the body is the eye: if therefore thine eye be single, thy
23 whole body shall be full of light. But if thine eye be evil, thy whole body shall be full of darkness. If therefore the light that is in thee
24 be darkness, how great is the darkness! No man can serve two masters: for either he will hate the one, and love the other; or else he will hold to one, and despise the other. Ye cannot serve God and
25 mammon. Therefore I say unto you, Be not anxious for your life, what ye shall eat, or what ye shall drink; nor yet for your body, what ye shall put on. Is not the life more than the food, and the body
26 than the raiment? Behold, the birds of the heaven, that they sow not, neither do they reap, nor gather into barns; and your heavenly Father feedeth them. Are not ye of much more value than they?
27 And which of you by being anxious can add one cubit unto his ²stat-
28 ure? And why are ye anxious concerning raiment? Consider the

Matt. 6:19-34.

29 lilies of the field, how they grow; they toil not, neither do they spin: yet I say unto you, that even Solomon in all his glory was not arrayed
30 like one of these. But if God doth so clothe the grass of the field, which to-day is, and to-morrow is cast into the oven, *shall he* not much
31 more *clothe* you, O ye of little faith? Be not therefore anxious, saying, What shall we eat? or, What shall we drink? or, Wherewithal
32 shall we be clothed? For after all these things do the Gentiles seek; for your heavenly Father knoweth that ye have need of all these
33 things. But seek ye first his kingdom, and his righteousness; and all
34 these things shall be added unto you. Be not therefore anxious for the morrow: for the morrow will be anxious for itself. Sufficient unto the day is the evil thereof.

1. Gr. *dig through.*   2. Or, *age.*

(f) About judging others.

Matt. 7:1-6.

1 Judge not, that ye be not judg-
2 ed. For with what judgement ye judge, ye shall be judged: and with what measure ye mete, it shall be measured unto you.

3 And why beholdest thou the mote that is in thy brother's eye, but considerest not the beam that
4 is in thine own eye? Or how wilt thou say to thy brother, Let me cast out the mote out of thine eye; and lo, the beam is in thine
5 own eye? Thou hypocrite, cast out first the beam out of thine own eye; and then shalt thou see clearly to cast out the mote out of thy brother's eye.
6 Give not that which is holy unto the dogs, neither cast your pearls before the swine, lest hap-

Luke 6:37-42.

37 And judge not, and ye shall not be judged: and condemn not, and ye shall not be condemned: release, and ye shall be released:
38 give, and it shall be given unto you; good measure, pressed down, shaken together, running over, shall they give into your bosom. For with what measure ye mete it shall be measured to you again.
39 And he spake also a parable unto them, Can the blind guide the blind? shall they not both
40 fall into a pit? The disciple is not above his ¹master: but every one when he is perfected shall
41 be as his ¹master. And why beholdest thou the mote that is in thy brother's eye, but considerest not the beam that is in thine
42 own eye? Or how canst thou say to thy brother, Brother, let me cast out the mote that is in thine eye, when thou thyself beholdest not the beam that is in thine own eye? Thou hypocrite, cast out first the beam out of thine own eye, and then shalt thou see clearly to cast out the mote that is in thy brother's eye.

Matt. 7:1-6.
ly they trample them under their feet, and turn and rend you.

1. Or, *teacher*.

(g) Prayer, and the Golden Rule.

Matt. 7:7-12.

7 Ask, and it shall be given you; seek, and ye shall find; knock, and it shall be opened unto you:
8 for every one that asketh receiveth: and he that seeketh findeth; and to him that knocketh it shall
9 be opened. Or what man is there of you, who, if his son shall ask him for a loaf, will give him a
10 stone; or if he shall ask for a fish,
11 will give him a serpent? If ye then, being evil, know how to give good gifts unto your children, how much more shall your Father which is in heaven give good things to them that ask
12 him? All things therefore whatsoever ye would that men should do unto you, even so do ye also unto them: for this is the law and the prophets.

Luke 6:31.

31 And as ye would that men should do to you, do ye also to them likewise.

(h) The way of salvation hard to find and follow.

Matt. 7:13-23.

13 Enter ye in by the narrow gate: for wide [1]is the gate, and broad is the way, that leadeth to destruction, and many be they that enter in
14 thereby. [2]For narrow is the gate, and straitened the way, that leadeth unto life, and few be they that find it.
15 Beware of false prophets, which come to you in sheep's clothing,
16 but inwardly are ravening wolves. By their fruits ye shall know
17 them. Do men gather grapes of thorns, or figs of thistles? Even so every good tree bringeth forth good fruit: but the corrupt tree
18 bringeth forth evil fruit. A good tree cannot bring forth evil fruit,
19 neither can a corrupt tree bring forth good fruit. Every tree that bringeth not forth good fruit is hewn down, and cast into the fire.
20 Therefore by their fruits ye shall know them. Not every one that
21 saith unto me, Lord, Lord, shall enter the kingdom of heaven: but he
22 that doeth the will of my Father which is in heaven. Many will say to me in that day, Lord, Lord, did we not prophesy by thy name, and by thy name cast out [3]devils, and by thy name do many [4]mighty
23 works? And then will I profess unto them, I never knew you: depart from me, ye that work iniquity.

1. Some ancient authorities omit *is the gate*. 2. Many ancient authorities read *How narrow is the gate*, &c. 3. Gr. *demons*. 4. Gr. *powers*.

(i) Conclusion. The Two Builders.

Matt. 7:24-29.	Luke 6:47-49.
24 Every one therefore which heareth these words of mine, and doeth them, shall be likened unto a wise man, which built his 25 house upon the rock: and the rain descended, and the floods came, and the winds blew, and beat upon that house; and it fell not: for it was founded upon 26 the rock. And every one that heareth these words of mine, and doeth them not, shall be likened unto a foolish man, which built his house upon the 27 sand: and the rain descended, and the floods came, and the winds blew, and smote upon that house; and it fell: and great was the fall thereof. 28 And it came to pass, when Jesus ended these words, the multitudes were astonished at his 29 teaching: for he taught them as *one* having authority, and not as their scribes.	47 Every one that cometh unto me, and heareth my words, and doeth them, I will shew you to 48 whom he is like: he is like a man building a house, who digged and went deep, and laid a foundation upon the rock: and when a flood arose, the stream brake against that house, and could not shake it: ¹because it had been well 49 builded. But he that heareth, and doeth not, is like a man that built a house upon the earth without a foundation; against which the stream brake, and straightway it fell in; and the ruin of that house was great.

1. Many ancient authorities read *for it had been founded upon the rock:* as in Matt. 7:25.

§ 43. JESUS HEALS A CENTURION'S SERVANT AT CAPERNAUM.

Matt. 8:1,5-13.	Luke 7:1-10.
1 And when he was come down from the mountain, great multitudes followed him. 5 And when he was entered into Capernaum, there came unto him a centurion, 6 beseeching him, and saying, Lord, my ¹servant lieth in the house sick of the palsy, grievously tormented. 7 And he saith unto him, I will come and heal him.	1 After he had ended all his sayings in the ears of the people, he entered into Capernaum. 2 And a certain centurion's ⁵servant, who was ⁶dear unto him, was sick and at the point of 3 death. And when he heard concerning Jesus, he sent unto him elders of the Jews, asking him that he would come and 4 save his ⁶servant. And they, when they came to Jesus, besought him earnestly, saying, He is worthy that thou shouldst 5 do this for him: for he loveth our nation, and himself built us 6 our synagogue. And Jesus went with them. And when he was now not far from the house, the

Matt. 8:1,5-13.

8 And the centurion answered and said, Lord, I am not ²worthy that thou shouldest come under my roof: but only ³say the word, and my ¹servant shall be healed.

9 For I also am a man⁴under authority, having under myself soldiers: and I say to this one, Go, and he goeth; and to another, Come, and he cometh; and to my ⁵servant, Do this, and he doeth it.
10 And when Jesus heard it, he marvelled, and said to them that followed, Verily I say unto you, ⁶I have not found so great
11 faith, no, not in Israel. And I say unto you, that many shall come from the east and the west, and shall ⁷sit down with Abraham, and Isaac, and Jacob, in
12 the kingdom of heaven: but the sons of the kingdom shall be cast forth into the outer darkness: there shall be weeping and
13 gnashing of teeth. And Jesus said unto the centurion, Go thy way; as thou hast believed so be it done unto thee. And the ¹servant was healed in that hour.

Luke 7:1-10.

centurion sent friends to him, saying unto him, Lord, trouble not thyself: for I am not ²worthy that thou shouldest come under
7 my roof: wherefore neither thought I myself worthy to come unto thee: but ³say the word, and my ¹servant shall be healed.
8 For I also am a man set under authority, having under myself soldiers: and I say to this one, Go, and he goeth; and to another, Come, and he cometh; and to my ⁵servant, Do this, and he doeth
9 it. And when Jesus heard these things, he marvelled at him, and turned and said unto the multitude that followed him, I say unto you, I have not found so great faith, no, not in Israel.

10 And they that were sent, returning to the house, found the ⁵servant whole.

1. Or, *boy.* 2. Gr. *sufficient.* 3. Gr. *say with a word.* 4. Some ancient authorities insert *set: as* in Luke 7:8. 5. Gr. *bondservant.* 6. Many ancient authorities read *With no man in Israel have I found so great faith.* 7. Gr. *recline.* 8. Or, *precious to him* Or, *honourable with him.*

§ 44. He Raises a Widow's Son at Nain.

Luke 7:11-17.

11 And it came to pass ¹soon afterwards, that he went to a city called
12 Nain; and his disciples went with him, and a great multitude. Now when he drew near to the gate of the city, behold, there was carried out one that was dead, the only son of his mother, and she was a
13 widow: and much people of the city was with her. And when the Lord saw her, he had compassion on her, and said unto her, Weep
14 not. And he came nigh and touched the bier: and the bearers stood
15 still. And he said, Young man, I say unto thee, Arise. And he that was dead sat up, and began to speak. And he gave him to his mother.
16 And fear took hold on all: and they glorified God, saying, A great

Luke 7:11-17.

17 prophet is arisen among us: and, God hath visited his people. And this report went forth concerning him in the whole of Judea, and the region round about.*

1. Many ancient authorities read *on the next day*.

§ 45. A Message Comes from John the Baptist, and our Lord Discourses as to John, and Various Other Matters Suggested.

Galilee.

Matt. 11:2-30.	Luke 7:18-35.
2 Now when John heard in the prison† the works of the Christ, he sent by his disciples, and said 3 unto him, Art thou he that cometh, or look we for another?	18 And the disciples of John told 19 him all of these things. And John calling unto him ¹⁴two of his disciples sent them to the Lord, saying, Art thou he that cometh, or look we for another? 20 And when the men were come unto him, they said, John the Baptist hath sent us unto thee, saying, Art thou he that cometh, 21 or look we for another? In that hour he cured many of diseases and ¹⁵plagues and evil spirits; and on many that were blind he
4 And Jesus answered and said unto them, Go your way and tell John the things which ye do 5 hear and see: the blind receive their sight, and the lame walk, the lepers are cleansed, and the deaf hear, and the dead are raised up, and the poor have ¹good tidings preached to them. 6 And blessed is he, whosoever shall find none occasion of stumbling in me. 7 And as these went their way, Jesus began to say unto the multitudes concerning John, What went ye out into the wilderness to behold? a reed shaken with 8 the wind? But what went ye out for to see? a man clothed in soft *raiment?* Behold, they that wear soft *raiment* are in 9 kings' houses. ²But wherefore	22 bestowed sight. And he answered and said unto them, Go your way, and tell John what things ye have seen and heard; the blind receive their sight, the lame walk, the lepers are cleansed, and the deaf hear, the dead are raised up, the poor have ¹good 23 tidings preached to them. And blessed is he, whosoever shall find none occasion of stumbling in me. 24 And when the messengers of John were departed, he began to say unto the multitudes concerning John, What went ye out into the wilderness to behold? a 25 reed shaken with the wind? But what went ye out to see? a man clothed in soft raiment? Behold, they which are gorgeously apparelled, and live delicately, are

*Observe that his fame as having raised the dead, and as being "a great prophet," spread widely, and reaching John, led to his message of inquiry (connect Luke 7:17 and 18).

†John's prison was at Machaerus, east of the Dead Sea. Jesus was somewhere in Galilee, probably near Nain (§ 44), which was in the southern part of Galilee.

Matt. 11:2-30.	Luke 7:18-35.

went ye out? to see a prophet? Yea, I say unto you, and much 10 more than a prophet. This is he, of whom it is written,
  Behold, I send my messenger
    before thy face,
  Who shall prepare thy way before thee.
11 Verily I say unto you, Among them that are born of women there hath not arisen a greater than John the Baptist: yet he that is ³but little in the kingdom of heaven is greater than he.
12 And from the days of John the Baptist until now the kingdom of heaven suffereth violence, and men of violence take it by force.
13 For all the prophets and the law
14 prophesied until John. And if ye are willing to receive ⁴it, this is
15 Elijah, which is to come. He that hath ears ⁵to hear, let him hear.
	26 in kings' courts. But what went ye out to see? a prophet? Yea, I say unto you, and much more
	27 than a prophet. This is he of whom it is written,
	  Behold, I send my messenger
	    before thy face,
	  Who shall prepare thy way
	    before thee.
	28 I say unto you, Among them that are born of women there is none greater than John: yet he that is ³but little in the kingdom of God is greater than he.

16 But whereunto shall I liken this generation? It is like unto children sitting in the marketplaces, which call un- 17 to their fellows, and say, We piped unto you, and ye did not dance; we wailed, and ye did not ⁶mourn. 18 For John came neither eating nor drinking, and 19 they say, He hath a ⁷devil. The Son of man came eating and drinking, and they say, Behold, a gluttonous man, and a winebibber, a friend of publicans and sinners! And wisdom ⁸is justified by her ⁹works. 20 Then began he to upbraid the cities wherein most of his ¹⁰mighty works were done, be-	29 And all the people when they heard, and the publicans, justified God, ¹⁵being baptized with the baptism of 30 John. But the Pharisees and the lawyers rejected for themselves the counsel of God, ¹⁷being 31 not baptized of him. Whereunto then shall I liken the men of this generation, and to what are 32 they like? They are like unto children that sit in the marketplace, and call one to another; which say, We piped unto you, and ye did not dance; we wailed, 33 and ye did not weep. For John the Baptist is come eating no bread nor drinking wine; and ye 34 say, He hath a ⁷devil. The Son of man is come eating and drinking; and ye say, Behold, a gluttonous man, and a winebibber, a friend of publicans and sinners! 35 And wisdom ⁸is justified of all her children.

OUR LORD'S GREAT

Matt. 11:2-30.

21 cause they repented not. Woe unto thee, Chorazin! woe unto thee, Bethsaida! for if the ^{10}mighty works had been done in Tyre and Sidon which were done in you, they would have repented long ago in sack-
22 cloth and ashes. Howbeit I say unto you, it shall be more tolerable
23 for Tyre and Sidon in the day of judgement, than for you. And thou, Capernaum, shalt thou be exalted unto heaven? thou shalt ^{11}go down unto Hades: for if the ^{10}mighty works had been done in Sodom which
24 were done in thee, it would have remained until this day. Howbeit I say unto you, that it shall be more tolerable for the land of Sodom in the day of judgement, than for thee.
25 At that season Jesus answered and said, I ^{12}thank thee, O Father, Lord of heaven and earth, that thou didst hide these things from the
26 wise and understanding, and didst reveal them unto babes: yea, Fath-
27 er, ^{13}for so it was well-pleasing in thy sight. All things have been delivered unto me of my Father: and no one knoweth the Son, save the Father: neither doth any know the Father, save the Son, and he
28 to whomsoever the Son willeth to reveal *him*. Come unto me, all ye
29 that labour and are heavy laden, and I will give you rest. Take my yoke upon you, and learn of me; for I am meek and lowly in heart:
30 and ye shall find rest unto your souls. For my yoke is easy, and my burden is light.

1. Or, *the gospel*. 2. Many ancient authorities read *But what went ye out to see? a prophet?* 3. Gr. *lesser*. 4. Or, *him*. 5. Some ancient authorities omit *to hear*. 6. Gr. *beat the breast*. 7. Gr. *demon*. 8. Or, *was*. 9. Many ancient authorities read *children*: as in Luke vii. 35. 10. Gr. *powers*. 11. Many ancient authorities read *be brought down*. 12. Or, *praise*. 13. Or, *that*. 14. Gr. *certain two*. 15. Gr. *scourges*. 16. Or, *having been*. 17. Or, *not having been*.

§ 46. THE WOMAN THAT WAS A SINNER *ANOINTED THE SAVIOUR'S FEET. (Compare § 117.)

Galilee.

Luke 7:36-50.

36 And one of the Pharisees desired him that he would eat with him.
37 And he entered into the Pharisee's house, and sat down to meat. And behold, a woman which was in the city, a sinner; and when she knew that he was sitting at meat in the Pharisee's house, she brought ^{1}an
38 alabaster cruse of ointment, and standing behind at his feet, weeping, she began to wet his feet with her tears, and wiped them with the hair of her head, and ^{2}kissed his feet, and anointed them with the
39 ointment. Now when the Pharisee which had bidden him saw it, he spake within himself, saying, This man, if he were ^{3}a prophet, would have perceived who and what manner of woman this is which
40 toucheth him, that she is a sinner. And Jesus answering said unto him, Simon, I have somewhat to say unto thee. And he saith, ^{4}Mas-
41 ter, say on. A certain lender had two debtors: the one owed five

*This anointing in Galilee must be distinct from the anointing at Bethany, near Jerusalem, more than a year later. See §117. This sinful and penitent woman is represented by a very late tradition as being Mary Magdalene, and hence all the popular uses of the term Magdalen. But that notion has no historical support whatever, and it becomes violently improbable when we find that in the very next paragraph (§47) Luke introduces Mary Magdalene as a new figure in the history.

Luke 7:36-50.
42 hundred ²pence, and the other fifty. When they had not *wherewith* to
pay, he forgave them both. Which of them therefore will love him
43 most? Simon answered and said, He, I suppose, to whom he forgave
44 the most. And he said unto him, Thou hast rightly judged. And
turning to the woman, he said unto Simon, Seest thou this woman?
I entered into thine house, thou gavest me no water for my feet: but
she hath wetted my feet with her tears, and wiped them with her hair.
45 Thou gavest me no kiss: but she, since the time I came in, hath not
46 ceased to ⁶kiss my feet. My head with oil thou didst not anoint: but
47 she hath anointed my feet with ointment. Wherefore I say unto thee,
Her sins, which are many, are forgiven: for she loved much: but to
48 whom little is forgiven, *the same* loveth little. And he said unto her,
49 Thy sins are forgiven. And they that sat at meat with him began to
50 say ⁷within themselves, Who is this that even forgiveth sins? And he
said unto the woman, Thy faith hath saved thee; go in peace.

1. Or, *a flask*. 2. Gr. *kissed much*. 3. Some ancient authorities read *the prophet*. See John 1:21, 25. 4. Or, *Teacher*. 5. The word in the Greek denotes a coin worth about seventeen cents. 6. Gr. *kiss much*. 7. Or, *among*.

§ 47. FURTHER JOURNEYING ABOUT GALILEE.* (Comp. § 30.)

Luke 8:1-3.

1 And it came to pass soon afterwards, that he went about through
cities and villages, preaching and bringing the ¹good tidings of the
2 kingdom of God, and with him the twelve, and certain women which
had been healed of evil spirits and infirmities, Mary that was called
3 Magdalene, from whom seven ²devils had gone out, and Joanna the
wife of Chuza Herod's steward, and Susanna, and many others, which
ministered unto ³them of their substance.

1. Or, *gospel*. 2. Gr. *demons*. 3. Many ancient authorities read *him*.

Notice that the events of § 48-53 all occurred on the same day.

§ 48. BLASPHEMOUS ACCUSATION OF LEAGUE WITH BEELZEBUB.
(Compare § 84.)

Galilee.

Matt. 12:22-37.	Mark 3:19-30.
	19 And he cometh into a house.
	20 And the multitude cometh together again, so that they could
	21 not so much as eat bread. And when his friends heard it, they went out to lay hold on him: for they said, He is beside himself.
22 Then was brought unto him ¹one possessed with a devil, blind	

*This journey about Galilee is probably distinct from those of § 30 and § 55, making *three* such journeys in all. See on § 30.

Matt. 12:22-37.

and dumb: and he healed him, insomuch that the dumb man
23 spake and saw. And all the multitudes were amazed, and said,
24 Is this the son of David? But when the Pharisees heard it, they said, *This man doth not cast out ²devils, but ³by Beelzebub the prince of the ²devils.
25 And knowing their thoughts he said unto them, Every kingdom divided against itself is brought to desolation; and every city or house divided against itself shall
26 not stand: and if Satan casteth out Satan, he is divided against himself; how then shall his
27 kingdom stand? And if I ³by Beelzebub cast out ²devils, ³by whom do your sons cast them out? therefore shall they
28 be your judges. But if I ³by the Spirit of God cast out ²devils, then is the kingdom of God come
29 upon you. Or how can one enter into the house of the strong *man*, and spoil his goods, except he first bind the strong *man*? and then
30 he will spoil his house. He that is not with me is against me; and he that gathereth not with
31 me scattereth. Therefore I say unto you, every sin and blasphemy shall be forgiven ⁴unto men; but the blasphemy against the Spirit shall not be forgiven.
32 And whosoever shall speak a word against the Son of man, it shall be forgiven him; but whosoever shall speak against the Holy Spirit it shall not be forgiven him, neither in this ⁵world, nor
33 in that which is to come. Either make the tree good, and its fruit good; or make the tree corrupt, and its fruit corrupt: for the tree is
34 known by its fruit. Ye offspring of vipers, how can ye, being evil,

Mark 3:19-30.

22 And the scribes which came down from Jerusalem said, he hath Beelzebub, and, ³By the prince of the ²devils casteth he
23 out the ²devils. And he called them unto him, and said unto them in parables, How can Satan
24 cast out Satan? And if a kingdom be divided against itself,
25 that kingdom cannot stand. And if a house be divided against itself, that house will not be able
26 to stand. And if Satan hath risen up against himself, and is divided, he cannot stand, but hath an end.

27 But no one can enter into the house of the strong *man*, and spoil his goods, except he first bind the strong *man*; and then he will spoil his house.

28 Verily I say unto you, All their sins shall be forgiven unto the sons of men, and their blasphemies wherewith
29 soever they shall blaspheme: but whosoever shall blaspheme against the Holy Spirit hath never forgiveness, but is guilty
30 of an eternal sin: because they said, He hath an unclean spirit.

*See a similar accusation described hereafter in § 84; and allusion made to such accusation heretofore, § 36.——Observe here a very *busy day:* in the *forenoon* teaching a crowded audience (Mark 3:19), some of whom insult and blaspheme him, and others demand a sign (§ 49), and at length his mother and brother try to carry him off as insane (§ 50, comp. Mark 3:21); in the *afternoon* giving a group of most remarkable parables, several of which he interprets (§ 51); towards night crossing the Lake in a boat, so tired and worn that he sleeps soundly amid the alarming storm (§ 52); then healing the Gadarene demoniacs, and returning by boat, apparently the same evening (§ 53). What a day of toil and trial.

MINISTRY IN GALILEE.   59

Matt. 12:22–37.

speak good things? for out of the abundance of the heart the mouth
35 speaketh. The good man out of his own good treasure bringeth forth
good things: and the evil man out of his evil treasure bringeth forth
36 evil things. And I say unto you, that every idle word that men shall
37 speak, they shall give account thereof in the day of judgement. For
by thy words thou shalt be justified, and by thy words thou shalt be
condemned.

1. Or, *a demoniac*. 2. Gr. *demons*. 3. Or, *in*. 4. Some ancient authorities read *unto you men*. 5. Or, *age*.

§ 49. SCRIBES AND PHARISEES DEMAND A SIGN.
Same day. Galilee.
Matt. 12:38–45.

38 Then certain of the scribes and Pharisees answered him, saying,
39 ¹Master, we would see a sign from thee. But he answered and said
unto them, An evil and adulterous generation seeketh after a sign;
and there shall no sign be given to it but the sign of Jonah the
40 prophet: for as Jonah was three days and three nights in the belly of
the ²whale; so shall the Son of man be three days and three nights in
41 the heart of the earth. The men of Nineveh shall stand up in the
judgement with this generation, and shall condemn it: for they repented at the preaching of Jonah; and behold, ³a greater than Jonah
42 is here. The queen of the south shall rise up in the judgement with
this generation, and shall condemn it: for she came from the ends of
the earth to hear the wisdom of Solomon; and behold, ³a greater than
43 Solomon is here. But the unclean spirit, when ⁴he is gone out of the
man, passeth through waterless places, seeking rest, and findeth it
44 not. Then ⁴he saith, I will return into my house whence I came out;
and when ⁴he is come, ⁴he findeth it empty, swept, and garnished.
45 Then goeth ⁴he, and taketh with ⁵himself seven other spirits more
evil than ⁵himself, and they enter in and dwell there: and the last
state of that man becometh worse than the first. Even so shall it be
also unto this evil generation.

1. Or, *Teacher*. 2. Gr. *sea-monster*. 3. Gr. *more than*. 4. Or, *it*. 5. Or, *itself*.

§ 50. CHRIST'S MOTHER AND BRETHREN.
Same day. Galilee.

Matt. 12:46–50.	Mark 3:31–35.	Luke 8:19–21.
46 While he was yet speaking to the multitudes, behold, his mother and his brethren stood without, seeking to speak to 47 him. ¹And one said unto him, Behold,	31 And there come his mother and his brethren; and, standing without, they sent unto him, call-32 ing him. And a multitude was sitting	19 And there came to him his mother and brethren, and they could not come at him for the crowd. 20 And it was told him, Thy mother and thy

Matt. 12:46-50.	Mark 3:31-35.	Luke 8:19-21.
thy mother and thy brethren stand without, seeking to speak to thee.	about him; and they say unto him, Behold, thy mother and thy brethren without seek for thee. And he answereth them, and saith, Who is my mother and my brethren?	brethren stand without, desiring to see thee.
48 But he answered and said unto him that told him, Who is my mother? and who are my brethren? And he stretched forth his hand towards his disciples, and said, Behold, my mother and my brethren!	33	21 But he answered and said unto them,
49		
	34 And looking round on them which sat round about him, he saith, Behold, my mother and my brethren!	
50 For whosoever shall do the will of my Father which is in heaven, he is my brother, and sister, and mother.	35 For whosoever shall do the will of God, the same is my brother, and sister, and mother.	My mother and my brethren are these which hear the word of God, and do it.

1. Some ancient authorities omit ver. 47.

§ 51. THE FIRST GREAT GROUP OF PARABLES.*

Same day. Beside the Sea of Galilee.

Matt. 13:1-3.	Mark 4:1,2.	Luke 8:4.
1 On that day went Jesus out of the house, and sat by the sea side. And there were gathered unto him great multitudes, so that he entered into a boat, and sat; and all the multitude stood on the beach. And he spake to them many things in parables, saying,	1 And again he began to teach by the sea side. And there is gathered unto him a very great multitude, so that he entered into a boat, and sat in the sea; and all the multitude were by the sea on the land. 2 And he taught them many things in parables, and said unto them in his teaching, Hearken:	4 And when a great multitude came together, and they of every city resorted unto him, he spake by a parable:
2		
3		

*We have met various *separate* parables heretofore, but here is a *group* of eight. Two other great groups will occur hereafter, one group given in Luke only, §81—93, and the last group during the last week of our Lord's public ministry, §109.

MINISTRY IN GALILEE.

(a) Parable of the Sower.

Matt. 13:3-23.	Mark 4:3-25.	Luke 8:5-18.
3 Behold, the sower went forth to sow; 4 and as he sowed, some *seeds* fell by the way side, and the birds came and devoured 5 them; and others fell upon the rocky places, where they had not much earth: and straightway they sprang up, because they had no deepness of earth: 6 and when the sun was risen, they were scorched; and because they had no root, they withered 7 away. And others fell upon the thorns; and the thorns grew up, and choked them: 8 and others fell upon the good ground, and yielded fruit, some a hundredfold, some sixty, some thirty.	3 Behold, the sower went forth to sow; 4 and it came to pass, as he sowed, some *seed* fell by the way side, and the birds came and devoured 5 it. And other fell on the rocky *ground*, where it had not much earth: and straightway it sprang up, because it had no deepness 6 of earth: and when the sun was risen, it was scorched; and because it had no root, it withered away. 7 And other fell among the thorns, and the thorns grew up, and choked it, and it yielded no 8 fruit. And others fell into the good ground, and yielded fruit, growing up and increasing; and brought forth, thirtyfold, and sixtyfold, and a hundredfold.	5 The sower went forth to sow his seed: and as he sowed, some fell by the way side; and it was trodden under foot, and the birds of the hea-6 ven devoured it. And other fell on the rock; and as soon as it grew, it withered away, because it had no moisture. 7 And other fell amidst the thorns; and the thorns grew with it, 8 and choked it. And other fell into the good ground, and grew, and brought forth fruit a hundredfold. As he said these things, he cried,
9 He that hath ears, let him hear.	9 And he said, Who hath ears to hear, let him hear.	He that hath ears to hear, let him hear.
10 And the disciples came, and said unto him, Why speakest thou unto them in parables?	10 And when he was alone, they that were about him with the twelve asked of him the parables.	9 And his disciples asked him what this parable might be.
11 And he answered and said unto them, Unto you it is given to know the mysteries of the kingdom of heaven, but to them it is not 12 given. For whoso-	11 And he said unto them, Unto you is given the mystery of the kingdom of God: but unto them that are without, all things are done in parables:	10 And he said, Unto you it is given to know the mysteries of the kingdom of God: but to the rest in parables;

Matt. 13:3-23.	Mark 4:3-25.	Luke 8:5-18.
ever hath, to him shall be given, and he shall have abundance; but whosoever hath not, from him shall be taken away even that which he 13 hath. Therefore speak I to them in parables; because seeing they see not, and hearing they hear not, neither do they understand.	12 that seeing they may see, and not perceive; and hearing they may hear, and not understand; lest haply they should turn again, and it should be forgiven them.*	that seeing they may not see, and hearing they may not understand.

14 And unto them is fulfilled the prophecy of Isaiah, which saith,
By hearing ye shall hear, and shall in no wise understand;
And seeing ye shall see, and shall in no wise perceive:
15 For this people's heart is waxed gross,
And their ears are dull of hearing,
And their eyes they have closed;
Lest haply they should perceive with their eyes,
And hear with their ears,
And understand with their heart,
And should turn again,
And I should heal them.
16 But blessed are your eyes, for they see; and your ears, for they hear.
17 For verily I say unto you, that many prophets and righteous men desired to see the things which ye see, and saw them not; and to hear the things which ye hear, and heard them not.

	13 And he saith unto them, Know ye not	
18 Hear then ye the parable of the 19 sower. When any one heareth the word of the kingdom, and understandeth it not,	this parable? and how shall ye know all the parables? 14 The sower soweth 15 the word. And these are they by the way side, where the word is sown; and when they have heard,	11 Now the parable is this: The seed is the 12 word of God. And those by the way side are they that have heard;
then cometh the evil *one*, and snatcheth away that which hath been sown in his heart. This is he that was sown by the	straightway cometh Satan, and taketh away the word which hath been sown in 16 them. And these in like manner are they	then cometh the devil, and taketh away the word from their heart, that they may not believe and be saved.

*Observe that this was said just after the blasphemous accusation of league with Beelzebub (§ 48), on the same day (Matt. 13:1).

Matt. 13:3-23.	Mark 4:3-25.	Luke 8:5-18.
20 way side. And he that was sown upon the rocky places, this is he that heareth the word, and straightway with joy receiv- 21 eth it; yet hath he not root in himself, but endureth for a while: and when tribulation or persecution ariseth because of the word, straightway he stumbleth. 22 And he that was sown among the thorns, this is he that heareth the word; and the care of the ²world, and the deceitfulness of riches, choke the word, and he becom- 23 eth unfruitful. And he that was sown upon the good ground, this is he that heareth the word, and understandeth it: who verily beareth fruit, and bringeth forth, some a hundredfold, some sixty, some thirty.	that are sown upon the rocky *places*, who, when they have heard the word, straightway receive 17 it with joy; and they have no root in themselves, but endure for a while; then, when tribulation or persecution ariseth because of the word, straightway they stumble. 18 And others are they that are sown among the thorns; these are they that have heard 19 the word, and the cares of the ³world, and the deceitfulness of riches, and the lusts of other things entering in, choke the word, and it becometh unfruitful. 20 And those are they that were sown upon the good ground; such as hear the word, and accept it, and bear fruit, thirtyfold, and sixtyfold, and a hundredfold.	13 And those on the rock *are* they which, when they have heard, receive the word with joy; and these have no root, which for a while believe, and in time of temptation fall away. 14 And that which fell among the thorns, these are they that have heard, and as they go on their way they are choked with cares and riches and pleasures of *this* life, and bring no fruit to perfection. 15 And that in the good ground, these are such as in an honest and good heart, having heard the word, hold it fast, and bring forth fruit with patience.

Mark 4:21-25.	Luke 8:16-18.
21 And he said unto them, Is the lamp brought to be put under the bushel, or under the bed, *and* not to be put on the stand? 22 For there is nothing hid, save that it should be manifested; neither was *anything* made secret, but that it 23 should come to light. If any man hath ears to hear, let him hear. 24 And he said unto them, Take heed what ye hear: with what measure ye mete it shall be measured unto you: and more	16 And no man, when he hath lighted a lamp, covereth it with a vessel, or putteth it under a bed; but putteth it on a stand, that they which enter in may see 17 the light. For nothing is hid, that shall not be made manifest; nor *anything* secret, that shall not be known and come to light. 18 Take heed therefore how ye hear:

Mark 4:21-25.

25 shall be given unto you. For he that hath, to him shall be given: and he that hath not, from him shall be taken away even that which he hath.

Luke 8:16-18.

for whosoever hath, to him shall be given, and whosoever hath not, from him shall be taken away even that which he [3]thinketh he hath.

1. Some ancient authorities add here, and in ver. 43, *to hear:* as in Mark 4:9; Luke 8:8. 2. Or, *age.* 3. Or, *seemeth to have.*

(b) Parable of the Seed growing of itself.

Mark 4:26-29.

26 And he said, So is the kingdom of God, as if a man should cast seed
27 upon the earth; and should sleep and rise night and day, and the seed
28 should spring up and grow, he knoweth not how. The earth [1]beareth fruit of herself; first the blade, then the ear, then the full corn in the
29 ear. But when the fruit [2]is ripe, straightway he [3]putteth forth the sickle, because the harvest is come.

1. Or, *yieldeth.* 2. Or, *alloweth.* 3. Or, *sendeth forth.*

(c) Parable of the Tares.

Matt. 13:24-30.

24 Another parable set he before them, saying, The kingdom of hea-
25 ven is likened unto a man that sowed good seed in his field: but while men slept, his enemy came and sowed [1]tares also among the wheat,
26 and went away. But when the blade sprang up, and brought forth
27 fruit, then appeared the tares also. And the [2]servants of the householder came and said unto him, Sir, didst thou not sow good seed in
28 thy field? whence then hath it tares? And he said unto them, [3]An enemy hath done this. And the [2]servants say unto him, Wilt thou
29 then that we go and gather them up? But he saith, Nay; lest haply
30 while ye gather up the tares, ye root up the wheat with them. Let both grow together until the harvest: and in the time of the harvest I will say to the reapers, Gather up first the tares, and bind them in bundles to burn them: but gather the wheat into my barn.

1. Or, *darnel.* 2. Gr. *bondservants.* 3. Gr. *A man* that is *an enemy.*

(d) Parables of the Mustard Seed and the Leaven. (Comp. § 88.)

Matt 13:31-35.

31 Another parable set he before them, saying, The kingdom of heaven is like unto a grain of

Mark 4:30-34.

30 And he said, How shall we liken the kingdom of God? or in what
31 parable shall we set it forth? [1]It

MINISTRY IN GALILEE.

Matt. 13:31-35.	Mark 4:30-34.

mustard seed, which a man took, 32 and sowed in his field: which indeed is less than all seeds: but when it is grown, it is greater than the herbs, and becometh a tree, so that the birds of the heaven come and lodge in the branches thereof.

is like a grain of mustard seed, which, when it is sown upon the earth, though it be less than all the seeds that are upon the earth, 32 yet when it is sown, groweth up, and becometh greater than all the herbs, and putteth out great branches; so that the birds of the heaven can lodge under the shadow thereof.

33 Another parable spake he unto them; The kingdom of heaven is like unto leaven, which a woman took, and hid in three ¹measures of meal, till it was all leavened.
34 All these things spake Jesus in parables unto the multitudes; and without a parable spake he 35 nothing unto them: that it might be fulfilled which was spoken ²by the prophet, saying,
  I will open my mouth in parables;
  I will utter things hidden from the foundation ³of the world.

33 And with many such parables spake he the word unto them, as 34 they were able to hear it: and without a parable spake he not unto them: but privately to his disciples he expounded all things.

1. The word in the Greek denotes the Hebrew seah. a measure containing nearly a peck and a half. 2. Or, *through*. 3. Many ancient authorities omit *of the world*. 4. Gr. *As unto*.

(c) Parable of the Tares explained, and similar Parable of the Net added. Parables of the Hid Treasure, and the Pearl of Great Price.

Matt. 13:36-53.

36 Then he left the multitudes, and went into the house: and his disciples came unto him, saying, Explain unto us the parable of the tares 37 of the field. And he answered and said, He that soweth the good seed 38 is the Son of man; and the field is the world; and the good seed, these 39 are the sons of the kingdom; and the tares are the sons of the evil *one;* and the enemy that sowed them is the devil: and the harvest is ¹the 40 end of the world; and the reapers are angels. As therefore the tares are gathered up and burned with fire; so shall it be in the end of the 41 world. The Son of man shall send forth his angels, and they shall gather out of his kingdom all things that cause stumbling, and them 42 that do iniquity, and shall cast them into the furnace of fire: there 43 shall be the weeping and gnashing of teeth. Then shall the righteous shine forth as the sun in the kingdom of their Father. He that hath ears, let him hear.
44 The kingdom of heaven is like unto a treasure hidden in the field; which a man found, and hid; and ²in his joy he goeth and selleth all that he hath, and buyeth that field.

Matt. 13:36-53.

45 Again, the kingdom of heaven is like unto a man that is a merchant
46 seeking goodly pearls: and having found one pearl of great price, he
went and sold all that he had, and bought it.
47 Again, the kingdom of heaven is like unto a ³net, that was cast into
48 the sea, and gathered of every kind: which, when it was filled, they
drew up on the beach; and they sat down, and gathered the good into
49 vessels, but the bad they cast away. So shall it be in ¹the end of the
world: the angels shall come forth, and sever the wicked from among
50 the righteous, and shall cast them into the furnace of fire: there shall
be the weeping and gnashing of teeth.
51 Have ye understood all these things? They say unto him, Yea.
52 And he said unto them, Therefore every scribe who hath been made
a disciple to the kingdom of heaven is like unto a man that is a householder, which bringeth forth out of his treasure things new and old.
53 And it came to pass, when Jesus had finished these parables, he
departed thence.

1. Or, *the consummation of the age.* 2. Or, *for joy thereof.* 3. Gr. *drag-net.*

§ 52. IN CROSSING THE LAKE, JESUS STILLS THE TEMPEST.

Same day. Sea of Galilee.

Matt. 8:18,23-27.	Mark 4:35-41.	Luke 8:22-25.
18 Now when Jesus saw great multitudes about him, he gave commandment to depart unto the other side.	35 And on that day, when even was come, he saith unto them, Let us go over unto the other side.	
23 And when he was entered into a boat, his disciples followed him.	36 And leaving the multitude, they take him with them, even as he was, in the boat. And other boats were with him.	22 Now it came to pass on one of those days, that he entered into a boat, himself and his disciples; and he said unto them, Let us go over to the other side of the lake: and they
24 And behold, there arose a great tempest in the sea, insomuch that the boat was covered with the waves: but 25 he was asleep. And they came to him,	37 And there ariseth a great storm of wind, and the waves beat into the boat, insomuch that the boat was now filling. 38 And he himself was in the stern, asleep	23 launched forth. But as they sailed he fell asleep: and there came down a storm of wind on the lake: and they were filling *with water*, and were in jeopardy.

MINISTRY IN GALILEE.

Matt. 8:18, 23-27.	Mark 4:35-41.	Luke 8:22-25.
and awoke him, saying, Save, Lord; we perish.	on the cushion: and they awake him, and say unto him, ²Master, carest thou not 39 that we perish? And he awoke, and rebuked the wind, and said unto the sea, Peace, be still. And the wind ceased, and there was a great 40 calm. And he said unto them, Why are ye fearful? have ye not yet faith?	24 And they came to him, and awoke him, saying, Master, master, we perish, And he awoke, and rebuked the wind and the raging of the water: and they ceased, and there was a calm.
26 And he saith unto them, Why are ye fearful, O ye of little faith? Then he arose, and rebuked the winds and the sea; and there was a great calm.		25 And he said unto them, Where is your faith?
27 And the men marvelled, saying, What manner of man is this, that even the winds and the sea obey him?	41 And they feared exceedingly, and said one to another, Who then is this, that even the wind and the sea obey him?	And being afraid they marvelled, saying one to another, Who then is this, that he commandeth even the winds and the water, and they obey him?

§ 53. BEYOND THE LAKE, HE HEALS TWO GADARENE *DEMONIACS.

Gerasa (Khersa).

Matt. 8:28-34.	Mark 5:1-20.	Luke 8:26-39.
28 And when he was come to the other side into the country of the Gadarenes, there met him two ¹possessed with devils, coming forth out of the tombs, exceeding fierce, so that no man could pass by that way.	1 And they came to the other side of the sea, into the country 2 of the Gerasenes. And when he was come out of the boat, straightway there met him out of the tombs a man with an unclean 3 spirit, who had his dwelling in the tombs: and no man	26 And they arrived at the country of the 'Gerasenes, which is over against Galilee. 27 And when he was come forth upon the land, there met him a certain man out of the city, who had ²devils: and for a long time he had worn no clothes, and abode not in any house, but

*The long famous instance of "discrepancy" as to the *place* in this narrative has been cleared up in recent years by the decision of textual critics that the correct text in Luke is Gerasenes, as well as in Mark, and by Dr. Thomson's discovery of a ruin on the lake shore, named Khersa (Gerasa). If this village was included (a very natural supposition) in the district belonging to the city of Gadara, some miles south-eastward, then the locality could be described as either in the country of the Gadarenes, or in the country of the Gerasenes. The narratives cannot be said to contradict each other and thus lack credibility, when the apparent contradiction can be explained by a thoroughly natural and reasonable supposition. We do not need to prove, in any such case, that the supposition is certainly true.—Matthew mentions two demoniacs, Mark and Luke describe one, who was probably the prominent and leading one. They do not say there was *only* one. So in § 102.

Matt. 8:28–34.	Mark 5:1–20.	Luke 8:26–39.
	could any more bind him, no, not with a 4 chain; because that he had been often bound with fetters and chains, and the chains had been rent asunder by him, and the fetters broken in pieces: and no man had strength to tame 5 him. And always, night and day, in the tombs and in the mountains, he was crying out, and cutting himself with 6 stones. And when he saw Jesus from afar, he ran and worshipped him; and 7 crying out with a loud voice, he saith, What have I to do with thee, Jesus, thou Son of the Most High God? I adjure thee by God, torment 8 me not. For he said unto him, Come forth, thou unclean spirit, out of the man.	in the tombs.
29 And behold, they cried out, saying, What have we to do with thee, thou Son of God? art thou come hither to torment us before the time?		28 And when he saw Jesus, he cried out, and fell down before him, and with a loud voice said, What have I to do with thee, Jesus, thou Son of the Most High God? I beseech thee, torment 29 me not. For he commanded the unclean spirit to come out of the man. For ⁵oftentimes it had seized him: and he was kept under guard, and bound with chains and fetters; and breaking the bands asunder, he was driven of the ⁶devil into the deserts.
	9 And he asked him, What is thy name? And he saith unto him, My name is Legion; for we are 10 many. And he besought him much that he would not send them away out 11 of the country. Now there was there on the mountain side a	30 And Jesus asked him, What is thy name? And he said, Legion; for many ²devils were entered into him. 31 And they intreated him that he would not command them to depart into the 32 abyss. Now there was there a herd of
30 Now there was afar off from them a herd of many		

Matt. 8:28-34.	Mark 5:1-20.	Luke 8:26-39.
31 swine feeding. And the ²devils besought him, saying, If thou cast us out, send us away into the herd 32 of swine. And he said unto them, Go. And they came out, and went into the swine: and behold, the whole herd rushed down the steep into the sea, and perished in the waters. 33 And they that fed them fled, and went away into the city, and told everything, and what was befallen to them that were ¹possessed with 34 devils. And behold, all the city came out to meet Jesus: and when they saw him, they besought *him* that he would depart from their borders.	great herd of swine 12 feeding. And they besought him, saying, Send us into the swine, that we may enter into them. 13 And he gave them leave. And the unclean spirits came out, and entered into the swine: and the herd rushed down the steep into the sea, *in number* about two thousand; and they were choked in 14 the sea. And they that fed them fled, and told it in the city, and in the country. And they came to see what it was that had come to 15 pass. And they come to Jesus, and behold ³him that was possessed with devils sitting, clothed and in his right mind, *even* he that had the legion: and they 16 were afraid. And they that saw it declared unto them how it befell ³him that was possessed with devils, and concerning the swine. 17 And they began to beseech them to depart from their bor- 18 ders. And as he was entering into the boat, he that had been possessed with ²devils besought him that he might be 19 with him. And he suffered him not, but saith unto him, Go to thy house unto thy friends, and	swine feeding on the mountain: and they intreated him that he would give them leave to enter into them. And he gave them leave. 33 And the ²devils came out from the man, and entered into the swine: and the herd rushed down the steep into the lake and were 34 choked. And when they that fed them saw what had come to pass, they fled, and told it in the city and in the country. And they went out to see what had come to pass: and they came to Jesus, and found the man, from whom the ²devils were gone out, sitting, clothed and in his right mind, at the feet of Jesus: and they were afraid. 36 And they that saw it told them how he that was possessed with ²devils was 37 ⁷made whole. And all the people of the country of the ⁴Gerasenes round about asked him to depart from them: for they were holden with great fear: and he entered into a boat, 38 and returned. But the man from whom the ²devils were gone out prayed him that he might be with him: but he sent him 39 away, saying, Return to thy house, and

	Mark 5:1-20.	Luke 8:26-39.
	tell them how great things the Lord hath done for thee, and *how* he had mercy on thee. And he went his way, and began to publish in Decapolis how great things Jesus had done for him: and all men did marvel.	declare how great things God hath done for thee. And he went his way, publishing throughout the whole city how great things Jesus had done for him.
20		

1. Or, *demoniacs.* 2. Gr. *demons.* 3. Or, *the demoniac.* 4. Many ancient authorities read *Gergesenes;* others *Gadarenes.* 5. Or, *of a long time.* 6. Gr. *demon.* 7. Or, *saved.*

§ 54. RETURNING, HE VISITS NAZARETH,* AND IS AGAIN REJECTED.

(Compare § 26.)

Matt. 9:1; 13:54-58.	Mark 5:21; 6:1-6.	Luke 8:40.
1 And he entered into a boat, and crossed over and came into his own city.	21 And when Jesus had crossed over again in the boat unto the other side, a great multitude was gathered unto him: and he was by the sea.	40 And as Jesus returned, the multitude welcomed him; for they were all waiting for him.
13:54-58.	6:1-6.	
54 And coming into his own country he taught them in their synagogue, insomuch that they were astonished, and said, Whence hath this man this wisdom, and these ¹mighty works?	1 And he went out from thence; and he cometh into his own country; and his disciples follow him. 2 And when the sabbath was come, he began to teach in the synagogue: and ³many hearing him were astonished, saying, Whence hath this man these things? and, What is the wisdom that is given unto this man, and *what mean* such ¹mighty works wrought by his hands?	
55 Is not this the carpenter's son? is not his mother called Mary? and his brethren, James, and Joseph,	3 Is not this the carpenter, the son of Mary, and brother of James, and Joses, and Judas, and Simon? and are not his sisters here with	

*There is no sufficient occasion to identify this visit to Nazareth with that described by Luke in § 26. That was at the very beginning of the great ministry in Galilee, and this is near its close. The details are quite different. It is perfectly natural that after a long interval he should give the Nazarenes another opportunity to hear his teaching, and to witness miracles, which he would not work for them when demanded (§ 26), but now voluntarily works in a few cases, so far as their now *wonderful* unbelief left it appropriate.

MINISTRY IN GALILEE.

Matt. 13:54-58.	Mark 6:1-6.
56 and Simon, and Judas? And his sisters, are they not all with us? 57 Whence then hath this man all these things? And they were ²offended in him. But Jesus said unto them, a prophet is not without honour, save in his own country, and in his own house. 58 And he did not many ¹mighty works there because of their unbelief.	us? And they were ²offended in 4 him. And Jesus said unto them, A prophet is not without honour, save in his own country, and among his own kin, and in 5 his own house. And he could there do no ⁴mighty work, save that he laid his hands upon a few 6 sick folk, and healed them. And he marvelled because of their unbelief.

1. Gr. *powers*.   2. Gr. *caused to stumble*.   3. Some ancient authorities insert *the*. 4. Gr. *power*.

§ 55. JESUS YET AGAIN JOURNEYS ABOUT GALILEE (COMP. § 30 AND 47), AND NOW SENDS THE TWELVE BEFORE HIM (COMP. § 80), AFTER INSTRUCTING THEM.

Matt. 9:35 to 11:1.	Mark 6:6-13.
35 And Jesus went about all the cities and the villages* teaching in their synagogues, and preaching the gospel of the kingdom, and healing all manner of disease 36 and all manner of sickness. But when he saw the multitudes, he was moved with compassion for them, because they were distressed and scattered, as sheep not 37 having a shepherd. Then saith he unto his disciples, the harvest truly is plenteous, but the 38 labourers are few. Pray ye therefore the Lord of the harvest, that he send forth labourers into his harvest.	6 And he went round about the villages teaching.

Matt. 10:1-42.	Mark 6:7-13.	Luke 9:1-6.
1 And he called unto him his twelve disciples, and gave them authority over unclean spirits, to cast them out, and to heal all manner of disease and all manner of sickness.	7 And he called unto him the twelve, and began to send them forth by two and two; and he gave them authority over the unclean spirits; 8 and he charged them	1 And he called the twelve together, and gave them power and authority over all ²devils, and to cure diseases. 2 And he sent them forth to preach the kingdom of God, and

* This is certainly a *second*, and probably a *third* journey about Galilee. See on §30. Dwell on Matt. 9:35 and 11:1 (end of this section), and try to realize the extent of the Saviour's work in teaching and healing. He "crowded into three short years actions and labours of love that might have adorned a century." (Ro. Hall).

Matt. 10:1-42.

2 Now the names of the twelve apostles are these: The first, Simon, who is called Peter, and Andrew his brother; James the *son* of Zebedee, and John his broth-
3 er; Philip, and Bartholomew; Thomas, and Matthew the publican; James the *son* of Alphæus, and
4 Thaddæus; Simon the ¹Cananæan, and Judas Iscariot, who also ²betrayed him.
5 These twelve Jesus sent forth, and charged them, saying, Go not into *any* way of the Gentiles, and enter not into any city of the Sama-
6 ritans: but go rather to the lost sheep of the house of Israel.
7 And as ye go, preach, saying, The kingdom of heaven is at
8 hand. Heal the sick, raise the dead, cleanse the lepers, cast out ³devils: freely ye received, freely
9 give. Get you no gold, nor silver, nor brass in your ⁴purses;
10 no wallet for *your* journey, neither two coats, nor shoes, nor staff: for the labourer is worthy of his
11 food. And into whatsoever city or village ye shall enter, search out who in it is worthy; and there abide till ye go
12 forth. And as ye enter into the house,
13 salute it. And if

Mark 6:7-13.

that they should take nothing for *their* journey, save a staff only; no bread, no wallet, no ¹⁷money in their
9 ¹⁸purse; but *to go* shod with sandals: and, *said he*, put not on two coats.

10 And he said unto them, Wheresoever ye enter into a house, there abide

Luke 9:1-6.

to heal ¹⁹the sick.
3 And he said unto them,

Take nothing for your journey, neither staff, nor wallet, nor bread, nor money; neither have two coats.

4 And into whatsoever house ye enter, there abide, and thence de-
5 part. And as many

Matt. 10:1-42.	Mark 6:7-13.	Luke 9:1-6.
the house be worthy, let your peace come upon it: but if it be not worthy, let your peace return to you.	till ye depart thence. 11 And whatsoever place	
14 And whosoever shall not receive you, nor hear your words, as ye go forth out of that house or that city, shake off the dust of your feet.	shall not receive you, and they hear you not, as ye go forth thence, shake off the dust that is under your feet for a testimony unto them.	as receive you not, when ye depart from that city, shake off the dust from your feet for a testimony against them.
15 Verily, I say unto you, It shall be more tolerable for the land of Sodom and Gomorrah in the day of judgement, than for that city.		

16 Behold, I send you forth as sheep in the midst of wolves: be ye
17 therefore wise as serpents, and ⁵harmless as doves. But beware of men: for they will deliver you up to councils, and in their synagogues
18 they will scourge you; yea and before governors and kings shall ye be brought for my sake, for a testimony to them and to the Gentiles.
19 But when they deliver you up, be not anxious how or what ye shall speak: for it shall be given you in that hour what ye shall speak.
20 For it is not ye that speak, but the Spirit of your Father that speak-
21 eth in you. And brother shall deliver up brother to death, and the father his child: and children shall rise up against parents, and ⁶cause
22 them to be put to death. And ye shall be hated of all men for my name's sake: but he that endureth to the end, the same shall be saved.
23 But when they persecute you in this city, flee into the next: for verily I say unto you, Ye shall not have gone through the cities of Israel, till the Son of man be come.
24 A disciple is not above his ⁷master, nor a ⁸servant above his lord.
25 It is enough for the disciple that he be as his ⁷master, and the ⁸servant as his lord. If they have called the master of the house ⁹Beelzebub,
26 how much more *shall they call* them of his household! Fear them not therefore: for there is nothing covered, that shall not be revealed;
27 and hid, that shall not be known. What I tell you in the darkness, speak ye in the light: and what ye hear in the ear, proclaim upon the
28 housetops. And be not afraid of them which kill the body, but are not able to kill the soul: but rather fear him which is able to destroy
29 both soul and body in ¹⁰hell. Are not two sparrows sold for a farthing? and not one of them shall fall on the ground without your Father;
30 but the very hairs of your head are all numbered. Fear not, there-
31 fore; ye are of more value than many sparrows. Every one therefore
32 who shall confess ¹¹me before men, ¹²him will I also confess before my
33 Father which is in heaven. But whosoever shall deny me before men, him will I also deny before my Father which is in heaven.
34 Think not that I came to ¹³send peace on the earth: I came not to
35 ¹³send peace, but a sword. For I came to set a man at variance against

Matt. 10:1-42.

his father, and the daughter against her mother, and the daughter in
36 law against her mother in law: and a man's foes *shall be* they of his
37 own household. He that loveth father or mother more than me is
not worthy of me: and he that loveth son or daughter more than me is
38 not worthy of me. And he that doth not take his cross and follow
39 after me, is not worthy of me. He that ¹⁴findeth his ¹⁵life shall lose
it; and he that ¹⁶loseth his ¹⁵life for my sake shall find it.
40 He that receiveth you receiveth me, and he that receiveth me re-
41 ceiveth him that sent me. He that receiveth a prophet in the name
of a prophet shall receive a prophet's reward; and he that receiveth a
righteous man in the name of a righteous man shall receive a right-
42 eous man's reward. And whosoever shall give to drink unto one of
these little ones a cup of cold water only, in the name of a disciple,
verily I say unto you, he shall in no wise lose his reward.

Matt. 11:1.	Mark 6:12,13.	Luke 9:6.
1 And it came to pass, when Jesus had made an end of commanding his twelve disciples, he departed thence to teach and preach in their cities.	12 And they went out, and preached that *men* should re- 13 pent. And they cast out many ³devils, and anointed with oil many that were sick, and healed them.	6 And they departed, and went throughout the villages, preaching the gospel, and healing everywhere.

1. Or, *Zealot.* See Luke 6:15; Acts 1:13. 2. Or, *delivered him up,* and so always.
3. Gr. *demons.*   4. Gr. *girdles.*   5. Or, *simple.*   6. Or, *put them to death.*   7. Or, *teacher.*   8. Gr. *bondservant.*   9. Gr. *Beelzebul:* and so elsewhere.   10. Gr. *Gehenna.*
11. Gr. *in me.*   12. Gr. *in him.*   13. Gr. *cast.*   14. Or, *found.*   15. Or, *soul.*   16. Or, *lost.*
17. Gr. *brass.*   18. Gr. *girdle.*   19. Some ancient authorities omit *the sick.*

§ 56. HEROD ANTIPAS SUPPOSES JESUS TO BE JOHN THE BAPTIST
RISEN, WHOM HE HAD BEHEADED.

Matt. 14:1-12.	Mark 6:14-29.	Luke 9:7-9.
1 At that season Herod the tetrarch heard the report con- 2 cerning Jesus, and said unto his servants, This is John the Baptist: he is risen from the dead; and therefore do these powers work in him.	14 And king Herod heard* *thereof;* for his name had become known: and ¹he said, John ²the Baptist is risen from the dead, and therefore do 15 these powers work in him. But others said, It is Elijah. And others said, *It is* a prophet, *even* as	7 Now Herod the tetrarch heard of all that was done: and he was much perplexed, because that it was said by some, that John was risen 8 from the dead; and by some, that Elijah had appeared; and by others, that one of the old prophets

* Mark's connection shows that Herod Antipas was impressed by the account of miracles which the disciples had wrought, as well as by those of Jesus himself.

MINISTRY IN GALILEE.

Matt. 14:1-12.	Mark 6:14-29.	Luke 9:7-9.
	one of the prophets.	was risen again.
	16 But Herod, when he heard *thereof*, said, John, whom I beheaded, he is risen.	9 And Herod said, John I beheaded: but who is this, about whom I hear such things? And he sought to see him.
3 For Herod had laid hold on John, and bound him, and put him in prison for the sake of Herodias, his brother Philip's wife.	17 For Herod himself had sent forth and laid hold upon John, and bound him in prison for the sake of Herodias, his brother Philip's wife: for he	
4 For John said unto him, It is not lawful for thee to have her.	18 had married her. For John said unto Herod, It is not lawful for thee to have thy brother's	
5 And when he would have put him to death, he feared the multitude, because they counted him as a prophet.	19 wife. And Herodias set herself against him, 20 and desired to kill him; and she could not; for Herod feared John, knowing that he was a righteous man and a holy, and kept him safe. And when he heard him, he ²was much perplexed; and he heard him gladly.	
6 But when Herod's birthday came, the daughter of Herodias danced in the midst, and pleased Herod.	21 And when a convenient day was come, that Herod on his birthday made a supper to his lords, and the ⁴high captains, and the chief 22 men of Galilee: and when ⁵the daughter of Herodias herself came in and danced, ⁶she pleased Herod and them that sat at meat with him: and the king said unto the damsel, Ask of me whatsoever thou wilt, and I will give it	
7 Whereupon he promised with an oath to give her whatsoever		
8 she should ask. And she, being put forward by her mother, saith, Give me here in a charger the head of John the Baptist.	23 thee. And he sware unto her, Whatsoever thou shalt ask of me, I will give it thee, unto 24 the half of my kingdom. And she went out, and said unto her mother, What shall I ask? And she said, The head of John the Baptist.	
9 And the king was grieved: but for the sake of his oaths, and of them which sat at meat with him, he commanded it to be	25 And she came in straightway with haste unto the king, and asked, saying, I will that thou forthwith give me in a charger the head of 26 John the Baptist. And the king was exceeding sorry: but for the sake of his oaths, and of them that sat at meat, he would not reject her.	
10 given: and he sent, and beheaded John	27 And straightway the king sent forth a soldier of his guard, and commanded to bring his head: and he went and beheaded him in	
11 in the prison. And his head was brought in a charger, and given to the damsel: and she brought it to	28 the prison, and brought his head in a charger, and gave it to the damsel; and the damsel gave it to her mother. And when his	
12 her mother. And his disciples came,	29 disciples heard *thereof*, they came and took up his corpse, and laid it in a tomb.	

and took up the corpse, and buried him; and they went and told Jesus.

1. Some ancient authorities read *they*. 2. Gr. *the Baptizer*. 3. Many ancient authorities read *did many things*. 4. Or. *military tribunes*. Gr. *chiliarch*. 5. Some ancient authorities read *his daughter Herodias*. 6. Or, *it*.

PART V.

SEASON OF RETIREMENT INTO DISTRICTS AROUND GALILEE.

Six months, beginning* a year before the Crucifixion, and thus probably from spring to autumn of A.D. 29 (or 28).

Four separate withdrawals from Galilee are given, in §57, 61, 62, 63-67. Notice that in every case he keeps out of Herod's territory, and in every case he goes to the mountains.

§ 57. THE TWELVE RETURN, AND JESUS RETIRES WITH THEM BEYOND THE LAKE TO REST. FEEDING OF THE FIVE THOUSAND.

Matt. 14:13-21.	Mark 6:30-44.	Luke 9:10-17.	John 6:1-14.
	30 And the apostles gather themselves together unto Jesus; and they told him all things, whatsoever they had done, and whatsoever they had taught. 31 And he saith unto them, Come ye yourselves apart into a desert place, and rest a while. For there were many coming and going, and they had no leisure so much as to eat. And they went away in the boat to a desert place apart.	10 And the apostles, when they were returned, declared unto him what things they had done. And he took them, and withdrew apart to a city called Bethsaida.†	
13 Now when Jesus heard it, he withdrew from thence in a boat, to a desert place apart.	32		1 After these things Jesus went away to the other side of the sea of Galilee, which is *the sea* of Tiberias.

*This period begins just before the Passover (John 6:4), and extends to the Feast of Tabernacles (§73). He withdraws from the jealousy of Herod Antipas (§56), from the fanaticism of would be followers in Galilee (John 6:15), and the hostility of the Jewish rulers (§60). Leaving the hot shores of the Lake of Galilee, he spent the summer in mountain districts around, resting, and *instructing the Twelve*.

†The Bethsaida of Luke 9:10 was evidently the eastern Bethsaida, which the Tetrarch Philip had named Bethsaida Julias, while that of Mark 6:45 was the western Bethsaida, near Capernaum. The territory belonging to Bethsaida Julias would naturally extend some distance down the lake.

DISTRICTS AROUND GALILEE.

Matt. 14:13-21.	Mark 6:30-44.	Luke 9:10-17.	John 6:1-14.
13 And when the multitudes heard *thereof*, they followed him ¹on foot from the cities. 14 And he came forth, and saw a great multitude, and he had compassion on them, and healed their sick.	33 And *the people* saw them going, and many knew *them*, and they ran there together ¹on foot from all the cities, and outwent them. 34 And he came forth and saw a great multitude, and he had compassion on them, because they were as sheep not having a shepherd, and he began to teach them many things.	11 But the multitudes perceiving it followed him: and he welcomed them, and spake to them of the kingdom of God, and them that had need of healing he healed.	2 And a great multitude followed him, because they beheld the signs ⁸which he did on them that 3 were sick. And Jesus went up into the mountain, and there he sat with his disciples.
15 And when even was come, the disciples came to him, saying, The place is desert, and the time is already past; send the multitudes away, that they may go into the villages, and buy themselves food. 16 But Jesus said unto them, They have no need to go away; give ye them to eat.	35 And when the day was now far spent, his disciples came unto him, and said, The place is desert, and the day is now 36 far spent; send them away that they may go into the country and villages round about, and buy themselves somewhat to 37 eat. But he answered and said unto them, Give ye them to eat. And they say unto him, Shall we go and buy two hundred ³pennyworth of bread, and give them to eat? 38 And he saith	12 And the day began to wear away; and the twelve came and said unto him, Send the multitude away, that they may go into the villages and country round about, and lodge, and get victuals: for we are here in a desert 13 place. But he said unto them, Give ye them to eat.	4 Now the passover, the feast of the Jews, was at hand. 5 Jesus therefore lifting up his eyes, and seeing that a great multitude cometh unto him, saith unto Philip, Whence are we to buy ⁴bread, that these may eat? 6 And this he said to prove him: for he himself knew what he would 7 do. Philip answered him, Two hundred ³pennyworth of ⁴bread is not sufficient for them, that every one may take a little.

Matt. 14:13-21.	Mark 6:30-44.	Luke 9:10-17.	John 6:1-14.
	unto them, How many loaves have ye? go and see. And when they knew, they say, Five, and two fishes.	And they said, We have no more than five loaves and two fishes; except we should go and buy food for all this people. And he said unto his disciples, Make them sit down in companies, about fifty each. And they did so, and made them all sit down. And he took the five loaves and the two fishes, and looking up to heaven, he blessed them, and brake; and gave to the disciples to set before the multitude. And they did eat, and were all filled: and there was taken up that which remained over to them of broken pieces, twelve baskets.	8 One of his disciples, Andrew, Simon Peter's brother, saith unto him,
17 And they say unto him, We have here but five loaves, and			9 There is a lad here, which hath five barley loaves, and two fishes: but what are these among so
18 two fishes. And he said, Bring them hither			
19 to me. And he commanded the multitudes to ²sit down on the grass;	39 he commanded them that all should ²sit down by companies upon the green grass.	14	10 many? Jesus said, Make the people sit down. Now there was much grass in the place. So the men sat down, in number about five
	40 And they sat down in ranks, by hundreds, and by fifties.	15	
		16	
and he took the five loaves, and the two fishes, and looking up to heaven, he blessed, and brake and gave the loaves to the disciples, and the disciples to the mul-	41 And he took the five loaves and the two fishes, and looking up to heaven, he blessed, and brake the loaves; and he gave to the disciples to set before them; and the two fishes divided he among them all.	17	11 thousand. Jesus therefore took the loaves: and having given thanks, distributed to them that were set down; likewise also of the fishes as much as they would.
20 titudes. And they did all eat, and were filled: and they took up that which remained over of the broken pieces, twelve baskets	42 And they did all eat, and were filled.		12 And when they were filled, he saith unto his disciples, Gather up the broken pieces which remain over, that noth-
	43 And they took up broken pieces, twelve basketfuls, and also of the fishes. And they that ate the loaves were five thousand men.		13 ing be lost. So they gathered them up, and filled twelve baskets with broken pieces from the five barley loaves, which remained over unto them that had
21 full. And they that did eat were about five thousand men, beside women and children.	44	14 For they were about five thousand men.	

John 6:1-14.

14 eaten. When therefore the people saw the ⁵sign which he did, they said, This is of a truth the prophet that cometh into the world.

1. Or, *by land.* 2. Gr. *recline.* 3. The word in the Greek denotes a coin worth about seventeen cents. 4. Gr. *loaves.* 5. Some ancient authorities read *signs.*

§ 58. THE TWELVE TRY TO ROW BACK, AND JESUS COMES WALKING ON THE WATER.

Matt. 14:22-36.	Mark 6:45-56.	John 6:15-21.
22 And straightway he constrained the disciples to enter into the boat, and to go before him unto the other side, till he should send the multitudes away. 23 And after he had sent the multitudes away, he went up into the mountain apart to pray: and when even was come, he was there alone. 24 But the boat was now in the midst of the sea, distressed by the waves; for the wind was contrary. 25 And in the fourth watch of the night he came unto them, walking upon the sea. 26 And when the disciples saw him walking on the sea, they were troubled, saying, It is an appa-	45 And straightway he constrained his disciples to enter into the boat, and to go before *him* unto the other side to Bethsaida, while he himself sendeth the multitude away. 46 And after he had taken leave of them, he departed into the mountain to pray. 47 And when even was come, the boat was in the midst of the sea, and he alone on 48 the land. And seeing them distressed in rowing, for the wind was contrary unto them, about the fourth watch of the night he cometh unto them, walking on the sea; and he would have passed 49 by them: but they, when they saw him walking on the sea, supposed that it was an apparition, and	15 Jesus therefore perceiving that they were about to come and take him by force, to make him king, withdrew again into the mountain himself alone. 16 And when evening came, his disciples went down unto the 17 sea; and they entered into a boat, and were going over the sea unto Capernaum. And it was now dark, and Jesus had not yet come to them. 18 And the sea was rising by reason of a great wind that 19 blew. When therefore they had rowed about five and twenty or thirty furlongs, they behold Jesus walking on the sea,

Matt. 14:22-36.	Mark 6:45-56.	John 6:15-21.
rition; and they cried out for fear.	50 cried out: for they all saw him, and were troubled. But he straightway spake with them, and saith unto them, Be of good cheer: it is I; be not afraid.	and drawing nigh unto the boat: and they were afraid.
27 But straightway Jesus spake unto them, saying, Be of good cheer; it is I; be not 28 afraid. And Peter answered him, and said, Lord, if it be thou, bid me come unto thee upon the 29 waters. And he said, Come. And Peter went down from the boat, and walked upon the waters, ²to come to 30 Jesus. But when he saw the wind³, he was afraid, and beginning to sink, he cried out, saying, 31 Lord, save me. And immediately Jesus stretched forth his hand, and took hold of him, and saith unto him, O thou of little faith, wherefore didst thou doubt?		20 But he saith unto them, It is I; be not afraid.
32 And when they were gone up into the boat, the wind ceased. 33 And they that were in the boat worshipped him, saying, Of a truth thou art the Son of God.	51 And he went up unto them into the boat; and the wind ceased: and they were sore amazed in 52 themselves; for they understood not concerning the loaves, but their heart was hardened.	21 They were willing therefore to receive him into the boat:
34 And when they crossed over, they came to the land, unto Gennesaret.	53 And when they had ⁴crossed over, they came to the land unto Gennesaret, and moored to 54 the shore. And when they were come out of the boat, straightway *the peo-* 55 *ple* knew him, and ran about that whole	and straightway the boat was at the land whither they were going.

DISTRICTS AROUND GALILEE.

Matt. 14:22-36.	Mark 6:45-56.
35 And when the men of that place knew him, they sent unto all that region round about, and brought unto him all that were 36 sick; and they besought him that they might only touch the border of his garment: and as many as touched were made whole.	region, and began to carry about on their beds those that were sick, where they 56 heard he was. And wheresoever he entered, into villages, or into cities, or into the country, they laid the sick in the marketplaces, and besought him that they might touch if it were but the border of his garment: and as many as touched ⁵him were made whole.

1. Some ancient authorities read *was many furlongs distant from the land.* 2. Some ancient authorities read *and came.* 3. Many ancient authorities add *strong.* 4. Or, *crossed over to the land, they came unto Gennesaret.* 5. Or, *it.*

§ 59. HE DISCOURSES IN THE CROWDED SYNAGOGUE AT CAPERNAUM, ON EATING SPIRITUAL FOOD, AND ON THE NECESSITY OF A DIVINE TEACHING AND DRAWING IN ORDER TO TRUE DISCIPLESHIP. (COMP. § 92.)

John 6:22-71.

22 On the morrow the multitude which stood on the other side of the sea saw that there was none other ¹boat there, save one, and that Jesus entered not with his disciples into the boat, but *that* his disciples went 23 away alone (howbeit there came ²boats from Tiberias nigh unto the place where they ate the bread after the Lord had given thanks): 24 when the multitude therefore saw that Jesus was not there, neither his disciples, they themselves got into the ²boats, and came to Caper-25 naum, seeking Jesus. And when they found him on the other side of 26 the sea, they said unto him, Rabbi, when camest thou hither? Jesus answered them and said, Verily, verily, I say unto you, Ye seek me, not because ye saw signs, but because ye ate of the loaves and were 27 filled. Work not for the meat which perisheth, but for the meat which abideth unto eternal life, which the Son of man shall give unto 28 you: for him the Father, *even* God, hath sealed. They said therefore unto him, What must we do, that we may work the works of God? 29 Jesus answered and said unto them, This is the work of God, that ye 30 believe on him whom ³he hath sent. They said therefore unto him, What then doest thou for a sign, that we may see, and believe thee? 31 what workest thou? Our fathers ate the manna in the wilderness; as 32 it is written, He gave them bread out of heaven to eat. Jesus therefore said unto them, Verily, verily, I say unto you, It was not Moses

John 6:22-71.

that gave you the bread out of heaven: but my Father giveth you the
33 true bread out of heaven. For the bread of God is that which cometh
34 down out of heaven, and giveth life unto the world. They said there-
35 fore unto him, Lord, evermore give us this bread. Jesus said unto
them, I am the bread of life: he that cometh to me shall not hunger,
36 and he that believeth on me shall never thirst. But I said unto you,
37 that ye have seen me, and yet believe not. All that which the
Father giveth me shall come unto me: and him that cometh to me I will
38 in no wise cast out. For I am come down from heaven, not to do
39 mine own will, but the will of him that sent me. And this is the will
of him that sent me, that of all that which he hath given me I should
40 lose nothing, but should raise it up at the last day. For this is the
will of my Father, that every one that beholdeth the Son, and believeth on him, should have eternal life; and ⁴I will raise him up at
the last day.
41 The Jews therefore murmured concerning him, because he said, I
42 am the bread which came down out of heaven. And they said, Is not
this Jesus, the son of Joseph, whose father and mother we know? how
43 doth he now say, I am come down out of heaven? Jesus answered
44 and said unto them, Murmur not among yourselves. No man can
come to me, except the Father which sent me draw him: and I will
45 raise him up in the last day. It is written in the prophets, And they
shall all be taught of God. Every one that hath heard from the
46 Father, and hath learned, cometh unto me. Not that any man hath
seen the Father, save he which is from God, he hath seen the Father.
47 Verily, verily, I say unto you, He that believeth hath eternal life. I
48 am the bread of life. Your fathers did eat the manna in the wilder-
49 ness, and they died. This is the bread which cometh down out of
50 heaven, that a man may eat thereof, and not die. I am the living
51 bread which came down out of heaven: if any man eat of this bread,
he shall live for ever: yea and the bread which I will give is my flesh,
for the life of the world.
52 The Jews therefore strove one with another, saying, How can this
53 man give us his flesh to eat? Jesus therefore said unto them, Verily,
verily, I say unto you, Except ye eat the flesh of the Son of man and
54 drink his blood, ye have not life in yourselves. He that eateth my
55 flesh and drinketh my blood hath eternal life; and I will raise him up
at the last day. For my flesh is ⁵meat indeed, and my blood is ⁶drink
56 indeed. He that eateth my flesh and drinketh my blood abideth in
57 me, and I in him. As the living Father sent me, and I live because
of the Father; so he that eateth me, he also shall live because of me.
58 This is the bread which came down out of heaven: not as the fathers
59 did eat, and died: he that eateth this bread shall live for ever. These
things said he in ⁷the synagogue, as he taught in Capernaum.
60 Many therefore of his disciples, when they heard *this*, said, This is
61 a hard saying; who can hear ⁸it? But Jesus knowing in himself that
his disciples murmured at this, said unto them, Doth this cause you
62 to stumble? *What* then if ye should behold the Son of man ascending
63 where he was before? It is the spirit that quickeneth; the flesh
64 profiteth nothing: the words that I have spoken unto you are spirit,
and are life. But there are some of you that believe not. For Jesus
knew from the beginning who they were that believed not, and who it

John 6:22-71.

65 was that should betray him. And he said, For this cause have I said unto you, that no man can come unto me, except it be given unto him of the Father.
66 Upon this many of his disciples went back, and walked no more with
67 him. Jesus said therefore unto the twelve, Would ye also go away?
68 Simon Peter answered him, Lord, to whom shall we go? thou ⁹hast
69 the words of eternal life. And we have believed and know that thou
70 art the Holy One of God. Jesus answered them, Did not I choose you
71 the twelve, and one of you is a devil? Now he spake of Judas *the son* of Simon Iscariot, for he it was that should betray him, *being* one of the twelve.

1. Gr. *little boat.*   2. Gr. *little boats.*   3. Or, *he sent.*   4. Or, *that I should raise him up.*
5. Gr. *true meat.*   6. Gr. *true drink.*   7. Or, *a synagogue.*   8. Or, *him.*   9. Or, *hast words.*

§ 60. EMISSARIES FROM JERUSALEM REPROACH HIM FOR DISREGARDING TRADITION.

In Galilee, probably at Capernaum.

Matt. 15:1-20.	Mark 7:1-23.	John 7:1.
1 Then there come to Jesus from Jerusalem Pharisees and scribes,	1 And there are gathered together unto him the Pharisees, and certain of the scribes, which had come from 2 Jerusalem, and had seen that some of his disciples ate their bread with ⁶defiled, that is un- 3 washen, hands. For the Pharisees, and all the Jews, except they wash their hands ⁷diligently, eat not, holding the tra- 4 dition of the elders: and *when they come* from the marketplace, except they ⁸wash themselves, they eat not: and many other things there be, which they have received to hold, ⁹washings of cups, and pots, and brasen 5 vessels¹⁰. And the Pharisees and the scribes ask him, Why walk not thy disciples according to the tradition of the elders, but eat their bread with ⁶defiled	1 And after these things Jesus walked in Galilee: for he would not walk in Judea, because the Jews sought to kill him.
2 saying, Why do thy disciples transgress the tradition of the elders? for they wash not their 3 hands when they eat bread. And		

Matt. 15:1-20.	Mark 7:1-23.
he answered and said unto them,	6 hands? And he said unto them,
7 Ye hypocrites, well did Isaiah prophesy of you, saying,	Well did Isaiah prophesy of you hypocrites, as it is written,
8 This people honoureth me with their lips;	This people honoureth me with their lips,
But their heart is far from me.	But their heart is far from me.
But in vain do they worship me,	7 But in vain do they worship me,
Teaching *as their* doctrines the precepts of men.	Teaching *as their* doctrines the precepts of men.
3 Why do ye also transgress the commandment of God, because of your tradition?	8 Ye leave the commandment of God, and hold fast the tradition
	9 of men. And he said unto them, Full well do ye reject the commandment of God, that ye
4 For God said, Honour thy father and thy mother: and, He that speaketh evil of father or mother, let him	10 may keep your tradition. For Moses said, Honour thy father and thy mother; and, He that speaketh evil of father or moth-
5 ¹die the death. But ye say, Whosoever shall say to his father or his mother, That wherewith thou mightest have been profited	11 er, let him ¹die the death; but ye say, If a man shall say to his father or his mother, That wherewith thou mightest have been profited by me is Corban,
6 by me is given *to God;* he shall not honour his father². And ye	12 that is to say, Given *to God;* ye no longer suffer him to do aught for his father or his mother;
have made void the ²word of God because of your tradition.	13 making void the word of God by your tradition, which ye have delivered: and many such like
10 And he called to him the multitude, and said unto them, Hear, and under-	14 things ye do. And he called to him the multitude again, and said unto them, Hear me all of
11 stand: Not that which entereth into the mouth defileth the man, but that which proceedeth out of the mouth, this defileth the man.	15 you, and understand: there is nothing from without the man, that going into him can defile him: but the things which proceed out of the man are those
	17 that defile the man.¹¹ And when he was entered into the house from the multitude, his disciples asked of him the parable.
12 Then came the disciples, and said unto him, Knowest thou that the Pharisees were ⁴offended, when	
13 they heard this saying? But he answered and said, Every ⁵plant which my heavenly Father plant-	
14 ed not, shall be rooted up. Let them alone: they are blind guides. And if the blind guide the blind,	
15 both shall fall into a pit. And Peter answered and said unto	

DISTRICTS AROUND GALILEE.

Matt. 15:1-20.	Mark 7:1-23.
him. Declare unto us the parable. 16 And he said, Are ye also even yet 17 without understanding? Perceive ye not, that whatsoever goeth into the mouth passeth into the belly, and is cast out into 18 the draught? But the things which proceed out of the mouth come forth out of the heart; and 19 they defile the man. For out of the heart come forth evil thoughts, murders, adulteries, fornications, thefts, false witness, railings: 20 these are the things which defile the man: but to eat with unwashen hands defileth not the man.	18 And he saith unto them, Are ye so without understanding also? Perceive ye not, that whatsoever from without goeth into the 19 man, it cannot defile him; because it goeth not into his heart, but into his belly, and goeth out into the draught? *This he said*, 20 making all meats clean. And he said, That which proceedeth out of the man, that defileth the 21 man. For from within, out of the heart of men, [12]evil thoughts 22 proceed, fornications, thefts, murders, adulteries, covetings, wickednesses, deceit, lasciviousness, an evil eye, railing, pride, 23 foolishness: all these evil things proceed from within, and defile the man.

1. Or, *surely die*. 2. Some ancient authorities add *or his mother*. 3. Some ancient authorities read *law*. 4. Gr. *caused to stumble*. 5. Gr. *planting*. 6. Or, *common*. 7. Or, *up to the elbow*. Gr. *with the fist*. 8. Gr. *baptize*. Some ancient authorities read *sprinkle themselves*. 9. Gr. *baptizings*. 10. Many ancient authorities add *and couches*. 11. Many ancient authorities insert ver. 16, *If any man hath ears to hear, let him hear*. 12. Gr. *thoughts that are evil*.

§ 61. HE RETIRES TO THE REGION OF TYRE AND SIDON, AND HEALS A PHOENICIAN WOMAN'S DAUGHTER.

Matt. 15:21-28.	Mark 7:24-30.
21 And Jesus went out thence, and withdrew into the parts of Tyre and Sidon.* 22 And behold, a Canaanitish woman came out from those borders, and cried, saying, Have mercy on me, O Lord, thou son of David, my daughter is grievously vexed 23 with a [1]devil. But he answered her not a word. And his disciples came and besought him, saying, Send her away; for she 24 crieth after us. But he answered	24 And from thence he arose, and went away into the borders of Tyre [3]and Sidon. And he entered into a house, and would have no man know it: and he could 25 not be hid. But straightway a woman, whose little daughter had an unclean spirit, having heard of him, came and fell down 26 at his feet. Now the woman was a [4]Greek, a Syrophœnician by race. And she besought him that he would cast forth the [1]devil out of her daughter.

*It used to be questioned whether he actually left the land of Israel. Matthew's expression ought to have settled the question, and the corrected text of Mark 7:31 (?62) leaves no doubt.

Matt. 15:21-28.

and said, I was not sent but unto the lost sheep of the house of Is-
25 rael. But she came and worshipped him, saying, Lord, help
26 me. And he answered and said, It is not meet to take the children's ²bread and cast it to the
27 dogs. But she said, Yea, Lord: for even the dogs eat of the crumbs which fall from their masters'
28 table. Then Jesus answered and said unto her, O woman, great is thy faith; be it done unto thee even as thou wilt.

And her daughter was healed from that hour.

Mark 7:24-30.

27 And he said unto her, Let the children first be filled: for it is not meet to take the children's ²bread and cast it to the dogs.
28 But she answered and saith unto him, Yea, Lord: even the dogs under the table eat of the children's crumbs.
29 And he said unto her, For this saying go thy way: the ¹devil is gone out of thy
30 daughter. And she went away unto her house, and found the child laid upon the bed, and the ¹devil gone out.

1. Gr. *demon.* 2. Or, *loaf.* 3. Some ancient authorities omit *and Sidon.* 4. Or, *Gentile.*

§ 62. HE GOES FARTHER NORTH, AND THEN EAST AND SOUTH INTO DECAPOLIS*—HEALS MULTITUDES, AND FEEDS THE FOUR THOUSAND.

Matt. 15:29-38.

29 And Jesus departed thence, and came nigh unto the sea of Galilee; and he went up into the mountain, and sat there.

30 And there came unto him great multitudes, having with

Mark 7:31 to 8:9.

31 And again he went out from the borders of Tyre, and came through Sidon unto the sea of Galilee, through the midst of the bor-
32 ders of Decapolis. And they bring unto him one that was deaf, and had an impediment in his speech; and they beseech him to lay
33 his hand upon him. And he took him aside from the multitude privately, and put his fingers into his ears, and he spat, and
34 touched his tongue; and looking up to heaven, he sighed, and saith unto him, Ephpha-
35 tha, that is, Be opened. And his ears were opened, and the bond of his tongue was
36 loosed, and he spake plain. And he charged them that they should tell no man: but the more he charged them, so much the more a
37 great deal they published it. And they were beyond measure astonished, saying, He hath done all things well: he maketh even the

*Observe how carefully he keeps away from the territory ruled by Herod Antipas. The tetrarch Philip, who governed the districts east of the Lake of Galilee and of the upper Jordan, was a better man than Antipas, and moreover had no cause to feel uneasy about Jesus.

Matt. 15:29-38.	Mark 7:31 to 8:9.
them the lame, blind, dumb, maimed, and many others, and	deaf to hear, and the dumb to speak.

31 they cast them down at his feet; and he healed them: insomuch that the multitude wondered, when they saw the dumb speaking, the maimed whole, and the lame walking, and the blind seeing: and they glorified the God of Israel.

	1 In those days, when there was again a great multitude, and they had nothing to eat, he called unto him his disciples, and
32 And Jesus called unto him his disciples, and said, I have compassion on the multitude, because they continue with me now three days and have nothing to eat: and I would not send them away fasting, lest haply they faint in the way.	2 saith unto them, I have compassion on the multitude, because they continue with me now three days, and have nothing to eat; 3 and if I send them away fasting to their home, they will faint in the way; and some of them are
33 And the disciples say unto him, Whence should we have so many loaves in a desert place, as to fill so great a multi-	4 come from far. And his disciples answered him, Whence shall one be able to fill these men with ¹bread here in a desert
34 tude? And Jesus saith unto them, How many loaves have ye? And they said, Seven, and a few small	5 place? And he asked them, How many loaves have ye? And they
35 fishes. And he commanded the multitude to sit down on the	6 said, Seven. And he commanded the multitude to sit down on
36 ground: and he took the seven loaves and the fishes; and he gave thanks and brake, and gave to the disciples, and the disciples to the multitudes.	the ground: and he took the seven loaves, and having given thanks, he brake, and gave to his disciples, to set before them; and they set them before the
	7 multitude. And they had a few small fishes: and having blessed them, he commanded to set these
37 And they did all eat, and were filled: and they took up that which remained over of the broken pieces,	8 also before them. And they did eat, and were filled: and they took up, of broken pieces that remained over, seven baskets.
38 seven baskets full. And they that did eat were four thousand men, beside women and children.	9 And they were about four thousand: and he sent them away.

1. Gr. *loaves*.

§ 63. AFTER CROSSING TO GALILEE, HE AGAIN RETIRES INTO THE TETRARCHY OF PHILIP. A BLIND MAN HEALED.

Magadan and Bethsaida.*

Matt. 15:39 to 16:12.

39 And he sent away the multitudes, and entered into the boat, and came into the borders of Magadan.
1 And the Pharisees and Sadducees came, and tempting him† asked him to shew them a sign
2 from heaven. But he answered and said unto them, ¹When it is evening, ye say, *It will be* fair
3 weather: for the heaven is red. And in the morning, *It will be* foul weather to-day: for the heaven is red and lowring. Ye know how to discern the face of the heaven; but ye cannot *discern* the signs of
4 the times. An evil and adulterous generation seeketh after a sign; and there shall no sign be given unto it, but the sign of Jonah. And he left them, and departed.
5 And the disciples came to the other side and forgot to take
6 ²bread. And Jesus said unto them, Take heed and beware of the leaven of the Pharisees and
7 Sadducees. And they reasoned among themselves, saying, ³We
8 took no ²bread. And Jesus perceiving it said, O ye of little faith, why reason ye among yourselves because ye have no ²bread?
9 Do ye not yet perceive, neither remember the five loaves of the five thousand, and how many
10 ⁴baskets ye took up? Neither the seven loaves of the four thousand, and how many ⁴baskets ye
11 took up? How is it that ye do not perceive that I spake not to

Mark 8:10–26.

10 And straightway he entered into the boat with his disciples, and came into the parts of Dalmanutha.
11 And the Pharisees came forth, and began to question with him, seeking of him a sign from heaven, tempting him.

12 And he sighed deeply in his spirit, and saith, Why doth this generation seek a sign? verily I say unto you, There shall no sign be giv-
13 en unto this generation. And he left them, and again entering into *the boat* departed to the other side.
14 And they forgot to take bread; and they had not in the boat with them more than one loaf.
15 And he charged them, saying, Take heed, beware of the leaven of the Pharisees and the leaven
16 of Herod. And they reasoned one with another, ⁵saying. ⁶We
17 have no bread. And Jesus perceiving it saith unto them, Why reason ye, because ye have no bread? do ye not yet perceive, neither understand? have ye
18 your heart hardened? having eyes, see ye not? and having ears, hear ye not? and do ye not
19 remember? When I brake the five loaves among the five thousand, how many ⁷baskets full of

---

*This means the Bethsaida east of the Jordan (comp. on §57). The situation of Magadan was unknown to some early students or copyists, as it is to us, and so they changed it to the familiar Magdala, found in our common texts.

†The moment he returns to Galilee, the Jewish leaders begin again to attack him, as in §60. So he immediately withdraws again to the region of Caesarea Philippi, where no hostility had been aroused, and he could quietly instruct the Twelve. He probably remained in that vicinity several months, as this whole period of retirement lasted six months (see on §57).

Matt. 15:39 to 16:12.	Mark 8:10-26.
you concerning ²bread? But beware of the leaven of the Pharisees and Sadducees. Then they understood how that he bade them not beware of the leaven of ²bread, but of the teaching of the Pharisees and Sadducees.	20 broken pieces took ye up? They say unto him, Twelve. And when the seven among the four thousand, how many ⁴basketfuls of broken pieces took ye up? 21 And they say unto him, Seven. And he said unto them, Do ye not yet understand? 22 And they come unto Bethsaida. And they bring to him a blind man, and beseech him to touch 23 him. And he took hold of the blind man by the hand, and brought him out of the village; and when he had spit on his eyes, and laid his hands upon him, he asked him, Seest thou aught? 24 And he looked up, and said, I see men; for I behold *them* as trees, 25 walking. Then again he laid his hands upon his eyes; and he looked stedfastly, and was restored, and saw all things clear-26 ly. And he sent him away to his home, saying, Do not even enter into the village.

1. The following words, to the end of ver. 3, are omitted by some of the most ancient and other important authorities. 2. Gr. *loaves*. 3. Or, It is *because we took no bread*. 4. *Basket* in ver. 9 and 10 represents different Greek words. 5. Some ancient authorities read *because they had no bread*. 6. Or, It is *because we have no bread*. 7. *Basket* in ver. 19 and 20 represents different Greek words.

§ 64. In the Neighborhood of Cæsarea-Philippi, the Twelve Avow (through Peter) Their Belief that He is the Messiah.

Matt. 16:13-20.	Mark 8:27-30.	Luke 9:18-21.
13 Now when Jesus came into the parts of Cæsarea Philippi, he asked his disciples, saying, Who do men say ¹that the 14 Son of man is? And they said, Some say John the Baptist; some, Elijah; and others, Jeremiah, or one of the prophets. 15 He saith unto them,	27 And Jesus went forth, and his disciples, into the villages of Cæsarea Philippi: and in the way he asked his disciples, saying unto them, Who do men say 28 that I am? And they told him, saying, John the Baptist: and others, Elijah: but others, One	18 And it came to pass, as he was praying alone, the disciples were with him: and he asked them, saying, Who do the multitudes say that I am? 19 And they answering said, John the Baptist; but others *say*, Elijah; and others, that one of the old prophets is risen a-

SEASON OF RETIREMENT INTO

Matt. 16:13–20.	Mark 8:27–30.	Luke 9:18–21.
But who say ye that 16 I am? And Simon Peter answered and said, Thou art the Christ,* the Son of 17 the living God. And Jesus answered and said unto him, Blessed art thou, Simon Bar-Jonah: for flesh and blood hath not revealed it unto thee, but my Father which 18 is in heaven. And I also say unto thee, that thou art ²Peter, and upon this ³rock I will build my church; and the gates of Hades shall not prevail against 19 it. I will give unto thee the keys of the kingdom of heaven: and whatsoever thou shalt bind on earth shall be bound in heaven: and whatsoever thou shalt loose on earth shall be loosed in heaven. 20 Then charged he the disciples that they should tell no man that he was the Christ.	of the prophets. 29 And he asked them, But who say ye that I am? Peter answereth and saith unto him, Thou art the Christ. 30 And he charged them that they should tell no man of him.	20 gain. And he said unto them, But who say ye that I am? And Peter answering said, The Christ of God. 21 But he charged them, and commanded *them* to tell this to no man;

1. Many ancient authorities read *that I the Son of man am.* See Mark 8:27; Luke 9:18. 2. Gr. *Petros.* 3. Gr. *petra.*

*Some understand ver. 16f. as showing that they had never before believed him to be the Messiah, and so hold that the other Gospels here utterly conflict with John, who represents the first disciples (§ 18) as believing Jesus to be the Messiah. But it is easy to suppose that their early faith in his Messiahship was shaken by his continued failure to gather armies and set up the expected temporal kingdom, and while still believing him to have a divine mission they had questioned whether he was the Messiah, as John the Baptist did in prison (§ 45). Compare on § 23, (c), and observe that in Matthew and Luke he long before this time distinctly *implied* that he was the Messiah, in response to the Forerunner's inquiries (§ 45).

§ 65. JESUS DISTINCTLY FORETELLS THAT HE, THE MESSIAH, WILL BE REJECTED AND KILLED, AND WILL RISE THE THIRD DAY.

Matt. 16:21-28.	Mark 8:31-38; 9:1.	Luke 9:22-27.
21 From that time began ¹Jesus to shew unto his disciples, how that he must go unto Jerusalem, and suffer many things of the elders and chief priests and scribes, and be killed, and the third day be raised up. 22 And Peter took him, and began to rebuke him, saying, ²Be it far from thee, Lord: this shall never be unto 23 thee. But he turned, and said unto Peter, Get thee behind me, Satan: thou art a stumbling-block unto me: for thou mindest not the things of God, but the things 24 of men. Then said Jesus unto his disciples, If any man would come after me, let him deny himself, and take up his cross, and follow me. 25 For whosoever would save his ³life shall lose it: and whosoever shall lose his ³life for my sake shall 26 find it. For what shall a man be profited, if he shall gain the whole world, and forfeit his ³life? or what shall a man give in exchange for his ³life?	31 And he began to teach them, that the Son of man must suffer many things, and be rejected by the elders, and the chief priests, and the scribes, and be killed, and after three days rise again. 32 And he spake the saying openly. And Peter took him, and began to rebuke him. 33 But he turning about, and seeing his disciples, rebuked Peter, and saith, Get thee behind me, Satan: for thou mindest not the things of God, but the things of men. 34 And he called unto him the multitude with his disciples, and said unto them, If any man would come after me, let him deny himself, and take up his cross, 35 and follow me. For whosoever would save his ³life shall lose it: and whosoever shall lose his ³life for my sake and the gospel's shall 36 save it. For what doth it profit a man, to gain the whole world, and forfeit his 37 ³life? For what should a man give in exchange for his ³life?	22 saying, The Son of man must suffer many things, and be rejected of the elders and chief priests and scribes, and be killed, and the third day be raised up. 23 And he said unto all, If any man would come after me, let him deny himself, and take up his cross daily, and 24 follow me. For whosoever would save his ³life shall lose it: but whosoever shall lose his ³life for my sake, the same shall 25 save it. For what is a man profited, if he gain the whole world, and lose or forfeit his own self?

SEASON OF RETIREMENT INTO

Matt. 16:21-28.	Mark 8:31-38; 9:1.	Luke 9:22-27.
27 For the Son of man shall come in the glory of his Father with his angels; and then shall he render unto every man according 28 to his ⁴deeds. Verily I say unto you, There be some of them that stand here, which shall in no wise taste of death, till they see the Son of man coming in his kingdom.	38 For whosoever shall be ashamed of me and of my words in this adulterous and sinful generation, the Son of man also shall be ashamed of him, when he cometh in the glory of his Father with the holy angels. 1 And he said unto them, Verily I say unto you, There be some here of them that stand *by*, which shall in no wise taste of death, till they see the kingdom of God come with power.	26 For whosoever shall be ashamed of me and of my words, of him shall the Son of man be ashamed, when he cometh in his own glory, and *the glory* of the Father, and of the holy an- 27 gels. But I tell you of a truth, There be some of them that stand here, which shall in no wise taste of death, till they see the kingdom of God.

1. Some ancient authorities read *Jesus Christ*. 2. Or, God *have mercy on thee*. 3. Or, *soul*. 4. Gr. *doing*.

§ 66. THE TRANSFIGURATION, AND DISCOURSE IN DESCENDING.

On a mountain, in the region of Caesarea-Philippi.*

Matt. 17:1-13.	Mark 9:2-13.	Luke 9:28-36.
1 And after six days Jesus taketh with him Peter, and James, and John his brother, and bringeth them up into a high mountain apart: 2 and he was transfigured before them; and his face did shine as the sun, and his garments became white as the light. 3 And behold, there appeared unto them Moses and Elijah talking with him.	2 And after six days Jesus taketh with him Peter, and James, and John, and bringeth them up into a high mountain apart by themselves: and he was transfigured be- 3 fore them: and his garments became glistering, exceeding white; so as no fuller on earth can 4 whiten them. And there appeared unto them Elijah with Moses: and they were talking with Jesus.	28 And it came to pass, about eight days after these sayings, he took with him Peter and John and James, and went up into the mountain to pray. 29 And as he was praying, the fashion of his countenance was altered, and his raiment *became* white 30 *and* dazzling. And behold, there talked with him two men, which were Moses 31 and Elijah; who appeared in glory, and spake of his ³decease which he was

*The tradition which places the Transfiguration on Mount Tabor is beyond question false.

Matt. 17:1-13.	Mark 9:2-13.	Luke 9:28-36.
		about to accomplish 32 at Jerusalem. Now Peter and they that were with him, were heavy with sleep: but ⁴when they were fully awake, they saw his glory, and the two men that 33 stood with him. And it came to pass, as they were parting from him, Peter said unto Jesus, Master, it is good for us to be here: and let us make three ¹tabernacles; one for thee, and one for Moses, and one for Elijah: not knowing what he 34 said. And while he said these things, there came a cloud, and overshadowed them: and they feared as they entered 35 into the cloud. And a voice came out of the cloud, saying, This is ⁵my Son, my chosen: hear ye him.
4 And Peter answered, and said unto Jesus, Lord, it is good for us to be here: if thou wilt, I will make here three ¹tabernacles; one for thee, and one for Moses, and one for Elijah. 5 While he was yet speaking, behold, a bright cloud overshadowed them: and behold, a voice out of the cloud, saying, This is my beloved Son, in whom I am well pleased; hear ye him. 6 And when the disciples heard it, they fell on their face, and 7 were sore afraid. And Jesus came and touched them and said, Arise, and be 8 not afraid. And lifting up their eyes, they saw no one, save Jesus only. 9 And as they were coming down from the mountain, Jesus commanded them, saying, Tell the vision to no man, until the Son of man be risen from the dead.	5 And Peter answereth and saith unto Jesus, Rabbi, it is good for us to be here: and let us make three ¹tabernacles: one for thee, and one for Moses, and one for Elijah. 6 For he wist not what to answer; for they became sore afraid. 7 And there came a cloud overshadowing them: and there came a voice out of the cloud, This is my beloved Son: hear ye him. 8 And suddenly looking round about, they saw no one any more, save Jesus only with themselves. 9 And as they were coming down from the mountain, he charged them that they should tell no man what things they had seen, save when the Son of man should have risen again from 10 the dead. And they kept the saying, questioning among themselves what the rising again	36 And when the voice ⁶came, Jesus was found alone. And they held their peace, and told no man in those days any of the things which they had seen.

Matt. 17:1-13.	Mark 9:2-13.
10 And his disciples asked him, saying, Why then say the scribes that Elijah must first come? 11 And he answered and said, Elijah indeed cometh, and shall restore all 12 things: but I say unto you, that Elijah is come already, and they knew him not, but did unto him whatsoever they listed. Even so shall the Son of man also suffer of them. 13 Then understood the disciples that he spake unto them of John the Baptist.	11 from the dead should mean. And they asked him, saying, ²The scribes say that Elijah 12 must first come. And he said unto them, Elijah indeed cometh first, and restoreth all things: and how is it written of the Son of man, that he should suffer many things and be 13 set at naught? But I say unto you, that Elijah is come, and they have also done unto him whatsoever they listed, even as it is written of him.

1. Or, *booths*. 2. Or, How is it *that the scribes say..come!* 3. Or, *departure*. 4. Or, *having remained awake*. 5. Many ancient authorities read *my beloved Son*. See Matt. 17:5; Mark 9:7. 6. Or, *was past*.

§ 67. THE DEMONIAC BOY, WHOM THE DISCIPLES COULD NOT HEAL.

In the region of Cæsarea Philippi.

Matt. 17:14-20.	Mark 9:14-29.	Luke 9:37-43.
	14 And when they came to the disciples, they saw a great multitude about them, and scribes questioning	
	15 with them. And straightway all the multitude, when they saw him, were greatly amazed, and running to him sa-	37 And it came to pass, on the next day, when they were come down from the mountain, a great multitude met him.
14 And when they were come to the multitude, there came to him a man, kneeling to him, and saying, 15 Lord, have mercy on	16 luted him. And he asked them, What question ye with 17 them? And one of the multitude answered him, ³Mas-	38 And behold, a man from the multitude cried, saying, ³Mas-

Matt. 17:14-20.	Mark 9:14-29.	Luke 9:37-43.
my son: for he is epileptic, and suffereth grievously: for ofttimes he falleth into the fire, and ofttimes into the water. 16 And I brought him to thy disciples, and they could not cure him. 17 And Jesus answered and said, O faithless and perverse generation, how long shall I bear with you? bring him hither to me.	ter, I brought unto thee my son, which hath a dumb spirit; 18 and wheresoever it taketh him, it ⁴dasheth him down: and he foameth, and grindeth his teeth, and pineth away: and I spake to thy disciples that they should cast it out: and they were not 19 able. And he answereth them and saith, O faithless generation, how long shall I be with you? how long shall I bear with you? bring him unto me. 20 And they brought him unto him: and when he saw him, straightway the spirit ⁵tare him grievously; and he fell on the ground, and wallowed foam- 21 ing. And he asked his father, How long time is it since this hath come unto him? And he said, 22 From a child. And ofttimes it hath cast him both into the fire and into the waters, to destroy him: but if thou canst do anything, have compassion on 23 us, and help us. And Jesus said unto him, If thou canst! All things are possible to him that believ- 24 eth. Straightway the father of the child cried out, and said⁶, I believe: help thou mine unbelief.	ter, I beseech thee to look upon my son; for he is mine only 39 child: and behold, a spirit taketh him, and he suddenly crieth out; and it ⁹teareth him that he foameth, and it hardly departeth from him, bruising him 40 sorely. And I besought thy disciples to cast it out; and 41 they could not. And Jesus answered and said, O faithless and perverse generation, how long shall I be with you, and bear with you? bring 42 hither thy son. And as he was yet a coming, the ¹devil ¹⁰dashed him down, and ⁵tare *him* grievously.

Matt. 17:14-20.	Mark 9:14-29.	Luke 9:37-43.
	25 And when Jesus saw that a multitude came running together, he rebuked the unclean spirit, saying unto him, Thou dumb and deaf spirit, I command thee, come out of him, and enter no more into 26 him. And having cried out, and [6]torn him much, he came out: and *the child* became as one dead; insomuch that the more part said, He 27 is dead. But Jesus took him by the hand, and raised him up; and he 28 arose. And when he was come into the house, his disciples asked him privately, [7]*saying*, We could not cast it out. 29 And he said unto them, This kind can come out by nothing, save by prayer[8].	But Jesus rebuked the unclean spirit, and healed the boy, and gave him back 43 to his father. And they were all astonished at the majesty of God.
18 And Jesus rebuked him; and the [1]devil went out from him: and the boy was cured from that hour.		
19 Then came the disciples to Jesus apart, and said, Why could not we cast it out? 20 And he said unto them, Because of your little faith: for verily I say unto you, If ye have faith as a grain of mustard seed, ye shall say unto this mountain, Remove hence to yonder place; and it shall remove; and nothing shall be impossible unto you[2].		

1. Gr. *demon*. 2. Many authorities, some ancient, insert ver. 21 *But this kind goeth not out save by prayer and fasting*. See Mark 9:29. 3. Or, *Teacher*. 4. Or, *rendeth him*. 5. Or, *convulsed*. 6. Many ancient authorities add *with tears*. 7. Or, How is it *that we could not cast it out?* 8. Many ancient authorities add *and fasting*. 9. Or, *convulseth*. 10. Or, *rent him*.

§ 68. Returning Privately Through Galilee, He Again Foretells His Death and Resurrection.

(Comp. §65 and 66, and 101).

Matt. 17:22,23.	Mark 9:30-32.	Luke 9:43-45.
22 And while they ¹abode in Galilee, Jesus said unto them, The Son of man shall be delivered up into the hands of men; 23 and they shall kill him, and the third day he shall be raised up. And they were exceeding sorry.	30 And they went forth from thence, and passed through Galilee: and he would not that any man should know it. 31 For he taught his disciples, and said unto them, The Son of man is delivered up into the hands of men, and they shall kill him; and when he is killed, after three days he shall rise again. 32 But they understood not the saying, and were afraid to ask him.	43 But while all were marvelling at all the things which he did, he said unto his disciples, Let these words sink into your ears: for the Son of man shall be delivered up into the hands of men. 45 But they understood not this saying, and it was concealed from them, that they should not perceive it: and they were afraid to ask him about this saying.

1. Some ancient authorities read *were gathering themselves together*.

The season of retirement from Galilee is now ended (§ 57-68). The remaining events at this time (§ 69-74) probably occupied only a few days.

§ 69. Jesus, The Messiah, Pays The Half-Shekel For The Temple.

Capernaum.

Matt. 17:24-27.

24 And when they were come to Capernaum, they that received the ¹half-shekel came to Peter, and said, Doth not your ²master pay the 25 ¹half-shekel? He saith, Yea. And when he came into the house, Jesus spake first to him, saying, What thinkest thou, Simon? the kings of the earth, from whom do they receive toll or tribute? from 26 their sons, or from strangers? And when he said, From strangers, 27 Jesus said unto him, Therefore the sons are free. But, lest we cause them to stumble, go thou to the sea and cast a hook, and take up the fish that first cometh up; and when thou hast opened his mouth, thou shalt find a ³shekel: that take, and give unto them for me and thee.

1. Gr. *didrachma*. 2. Or, *teacher*. 3. Gr. *stater*.

§ 70. THE TWELVE CONTEND AS TO WHO SHALL BE THE GREATEST UNDER THE MESSIAH'S REIGN. HIS SUBJECTS MUST BE CHILDLIKE. (COMP. § 99.)

Capernaum.

Matt. 18:1-14.	Mark 9:33-50.	Luke 9:46-50.
1 In that hour came the disciples unto Jesus, saying, who then is ¹greatest in the kingdom of heaven?	33 And they came to Capernaum: and when he was in the house he asked them, What were ye reasoning in the 34 way? But they held their peace: for they had disputed one with another in the way, who *was* the	46 And there arose a reasoning among them, which of them should be ¹greatest.
2 And he called to him a little child, and set him in the midst of 3 them, and said, Verily I say unto you, Except ye turn, and become as little children, ye shall in no wise enter into the kingdom of heaven. 4 Whosoever therefore shall humble himself as this little child, the same is the ¹greatest in the king- 5 dom of heaven. And whoso shall receive one such little child in my name receiveth me:	35 ¹greatest. And he sat down, and called the twelve; and he saith unto them, If any man would be first, he shall be last of all, and minister 36 of all. And he took a little child, and set him in the midst of them: and taking him in his arms, he said unto them, 37 Whosoever shall receive one of such little children in my name, receiveth me: and whosoever receiveth me, receiveth not me, but him that sent me.	47 But when Jesus saw the reasoning of their heart, he took a little child, and set him by his side, and said unto them, 48 Whosoever shall receive this little child in my name receiveth me: and whosoever shall receive me receiveth him that sent me: for he that is ¹⁵least among you all, the same is great.
	38 John said unto him, ⁷Master, we saw one casting out ⁶devils in thy name: and we forbade him, because he followed not us. 39 But Jesus said, Forbid him not: for there is no man	49 And John answered and said, Master, we saw one casting out ⁶devils in thy name; and we forbade him, because he followeth not with 50 us. But Jesus said unto him, Forbid

Matt. 18:1-14.	Mark 9:33-50.	Luke 9:46-50.
	which shall do a ⁹mighty work in my name, and be able quickly to speak 40 evil of me. For he that is not against 41 us is for us. For whosoever shall give you a cup of water to drink ¹⁰because ye are Christ's, verily I say unto you, he shall in no wise lose his reward.	him not: for he that is not against you is for you.
6 but whoso shall cause one of these little ones which believe on me to stumble, it is profitable for him that ²a great millstone should be hanged about his neck, and *that* he should be sunk in the depth of 7 the sea. Woe unto the world because of occasions of stumbling! for it must needs be that the occasions come; but woe to that man through whom the occasion cometh!	42 And whosoever shall cause one of these little ones that believe ¹¹on me to stumble, it were better for him if ²a great millstone were hanged about his neck, and he were cast into the sea.	
8 And if thy hand or thy foot causeth thee to stumble, cut it off, and cast it from thee: it is good for thee to enter into life maimed or halt, rather than having two hands or two feet to be cast into the eternal fire.	43 And if thy hand cause thee to stumble, cut it off: it is good for thee to enter into life maimed, rather than having thy two hands to go into ¹²hell, into the unquenchable fire¹³. 45 And if thy foot cause thee to stumble, cut it off: it is good for thee to enter into life halt, rather than having thy two feet to be	
9 And if thine	47 cast into ¹²hell. And	

Matt. 18:1-14.	Mark 9:33-50.
eye causeth thee to stumble, pluck it out, and cast it from thee: it is good for thee to enter into life with one eye, rather than having two eyes to be cast into the ³hell of fire. 10 See that ye despise not one of these little ones; for I say unto you, that in heaven their angels do always behold the face of my Father which 12 is in heaven⁴. How think ye? if any man have a hundred sheep, and one of them be gone astray, doth he not leave the ninety and nine, and go unto the mountains, and seek that	if thine eye cause thee to stumble, cast it out: it is good for thee to enter into the kingdom of God with one eye, rather than having two eyes to 48 be cast into ¹²hell; where their worm dieth not, and the fire is not quenched. 49 For every one shall be salted with fire¹⁴. 50 Salt is good: but if the salt have lost its saltness, wherewith will ye season it? Have salt in yourselves, and be at peace one with another.

13 which goeth astray? And if so be that he find it, verily I say unto you, he rejoiceth over it more than over the ninety and nine which
14 have not gone astray. Even so it is not ⁵the will of ⁶your Father which is in heaven, that one of these little ones should perish.

1. Gr. *greater.* 2. Gr. *a millstone turned by an ass.* 3. Gr. *Gehenna of fire.* 4. Many authorities, some ancient, insert ver. 11 *For the Son of man came to save that which was lost.* See Luke 19:10. 5. Gr. *a thing willed before your father.* 6. Some ancient authorities read *my.* 7. Or, *teacher.* 8. Gr. *demons.* 9. Gr. *power.* 10. Gr. *in name that ye are.* 11. Many ancient authorities omit *on me.* 12. Gr. *Gehenna.* 13. Ver. 44 and 46 (which are identical with ver. 48) are omitted by the best ancient authorities. 14. Many ancient authorities add *and every sacrifice shall be salted with salt.* See Lev. 2:13. 15. Gr. *lesser.*

§ 71. RIGHT TREATMENT OF A BROTHER WHO HAS SINNED AGAINST ONE, AND DUTY OF PATIENTLY FORGIVING A BROTHER.

Matt. 18:15-35.

15 And if thy brother sin ¹against thee, go, shew him his fault between
16 thee and him alone: if he hear thee, thou hast gained thy brother. But if he hear *thee* not, take with thee one or two more, that at the
17 mouth of two witnesses or three every word may be established. And if he refuse to hear them, tell it unto the ²church: and if he refuse to hear the ²church also, let him be unto thee as the Gentile and the
18 publican. Verily I say unto you, What things soever ye shall bind on earth shall be bound in heaven: and what things soever ye shall loose
19 on earth shall be loosed in heaven. Again I say unto you, that if two

Matt. 18:15–35.

of you shall agree on earth as touching anything that they shall ask,
20 it shall be done for them of my Father which is in heaven. For where two or three are gathered together in my name, there am I in the midst of them.
21 Then came Peter, and said to him, Lord, how oft shall my brother
22 sin against me, and I forgive him? until seven times? Jesus saith unto him, I say not unto thee, Until seven times; but, Until ³seventy
23 times seven. Therefore is the kingdom of heaven likened unto a cer-
24 tain king, which would make a reckoning with his ⁴servants. And when he had begun to reckon, one was brought unto him, which owed
25 him ten thousand ⁵talents. But forasmuch as he had not *wherewith* to pay, his lord commanded him to be sold, and his wife, and children,
26 and all that he had, and payment to be made. The ⁶servant there-
fore fell down and worshipped him, saying, Lord, have patience with
27 me, and I will pay thee all. And the lord of that ⁶servant, being
28 moved with compassion, released him, and forgave him the debt. But that ⁶servant went out, and found one of his fellow-servants, which owed him a hundred ⁸pence: and he laid hold on him, and took *him* by
29 the throat, saying, Pay what thou owest. So his fellow-servant fell down and besought him, saying, Have patience with me, and I will
30 pay thee. And he would not: but went and cast him into prison, till
31 he should pay that which was due. So when his fellow-servants saw what was done, they were exceeding sorry, and came and told unto
32 their lord all that was done. Then his lord called him unto him, and saith unto him, Thou wicked ⁶servant, I forgave thee all that debt,⁷
33 because thou besoughtest me: shouldest not thou also have had mercy
34 on thy fellow-servant, even as I had mercy on thee?* And his lord was wroth, and delivered him to the tormentors, till he should pay
35 all that was due. So shall also my heavenly Father do unto you, if ye forgive not every one his brother from your hearts.

1. Some ancient authorities omit *against thee*. 2. Or, *congregation*. 3. Or, *seventy times and seven*. 4. Gr. *bond-servants*. 5. This talent was probably worth about $1200. 6. Gr. *bond-servant*. 7. Or, *loan*. 8. The word in the Greek denotes a coin worth about seventeen cents.

§ 72. THE MESSIAH'S FOLLOWERS MUST GIVE UP EVERYTHING FOR HIS SERVICE.

Matt. 8:19–22.	Luke 9:57–62.
19 And there came ¹a scribe, and said unto him, ²Master, I will follow thee whithersoever thou go- 20 est. And Jesus saith unto him, the foxes have holes, and the birds of the heaven *have* ³nests: but the Son of man hath not 21 where to lay his head. And another of the disciples saith unto	57 And as they went in the way, a certain man said unto him, I will follow thee whithersoever thou 58 goest. And Jesus said unto him, the foxes have holes, and the birds of the heaven *have* ¹nests: but the Son of man hath not 59 where to lay his head. And he said unto another, Follow me.

*The king forgave the servant $1,200,000; the servant refused to forgive $17. We might say in round numbers, a million, and ten dollars.

Matt. 8:19-22.	Luke 9:57-62.
him, Lord, suffer me first to go 22 and bury my father. But Jesus saith unto him, Follow me; and leave the dead to bury their own dead.	But he said, Lord, suffer me first 60 to go and bury my father. But he said unto him, Leave the dead to bury their own dead; but go thou and publish abroad the 61 kingdom of God. And another also said, I will follow thee, Lord; but first suffer me to bid farewell to them that are at my 62 house. But Jesus said unto him, No man, having put his hand to the plough, and looking back, is fit for the kingdom of God.

1. Gr. *one scribe.* 2. Or, *Teacher.* 3. Gr. *lodging-places.*

§ 73. THE UNBELIEVING BROTHERS OF JESUS COUNSEL HIM TO EXHIBIT HIMSELF IN JUDEA, AND HE REJECTS THE ADVICE.

John 7:2-9.

2 Now the feast of the Jews, the feast of tabernacles, was at hand.
3 His brethren therefore said unto him, Depart hence, and go into Judea, that thy disciples also may behold thy works which thou doest.
4 For no man doeth anything in secret, [1]and himself seeketh to be
5 known openly. If thou doest these things, manifest thyself to the
6 world. For even his brethren did not believe on him. Jesus therefore saith unto them, My time is not yet come; but your time is alway
7 ready. The world cannot hate you; but me it hateth, because I testify
8 of it, that its works are evil. Go ye up unto the feast: I go not up [2]yet
9 unto this feast; because my time is not yet fulfilled. And having said these things unto them, he abode *still* in Galilee.

1. Some ancient authorities read *and seeketh it to be known openly.* 2. Many ancient authorities omit *yet.*

§ 74. HE GOES PRIVATELY TO JERUSALEM THROUGH SAMARIA.

Luke 9:51-56.	John 7:10.
51 And it came to pass, when the days [1]were well-nigh come that he should be received up, he stedfastly set his face to go to Je- 52 rusalem, and sent messengers before his face: and they went, and entered into a village of the Samaritans, to make ready for him. 53 And they did not receive him, because his face was as *though he*	10 But when his brethren were gone up unto the feast, then went he also up, not publicly, but as it were in secret.

Luke 9:51-56.

54 *were* going to Jerusalem. And when his disciples James and John saw *this*, they said, Lord, wilt thou that we bid fire to come down from heaven, and consume
55 them?[2] But he turned, and re-
56 buked them.[3] And they went to another village.

1. Gr. *were being fulfilled.* 2. Many ancient authorities add, *even as Elijah did.*
3. Some ancient authorities add *and said, Ye know not what manner of spirit ye are of.* Some, but fewer, add also *For the Son of man came not to destroy men's lives, but to save them.*

PART VI.

CLOSING MINISTRY, IN ALL PARTS OF THE HOLY LAND. SIX MONTHS PRECEDING THE CRUCIFIXION (NOT INCLUDING THE LAST WEEK).*

Time probably from autumn of A. D. 29 to spring of A. D. 30 (or a year earlier.)

This comprises §75-103, of which §75-79 contain discourses at the Feast of Tabernacles, given by John only.

§75. AT THE FEAST OF TABERNACLES JESUS TEACHES IN THE TEMPLE, AND PEOPLE WONDER WHETHER HE IS THE MESSIAH. ATTEMPT OF THE RULERS TO ARREST HIM.

John 7:11-52.

11 The Jews therefore sought him at the feast, and said, Where is he?
12 And there was much murmuring among the multitudes concerning him. Some said, He is a good man: others said, Nay, but he leads the multitude
13 astray. Yet no one spoke openly concerning him, for fear of the Jews.
14 But when it was now the midst of the feast Jesus went up into the
15 temple, and taught. The Jews therefore marvelled, saying, How
16 knoweth this man letters, having never learned? Jesus therefore answered them, and said, My teaching is not mine, but his that sent
17 me. If any man willeth to do his will, he shall know of the teaching,
18 whether it be of God, or *whether* I speak from myself. He that speaketh from himself seeketh his own glory: but he that seeketh the glory of him that sent him, the same is true, and no unrighteousness is in
19 him. Did not Moses give you the law, and *yet* none of you doeth the
20 law? Why seek ye to kill me? The multitude answered, Thou hast a
21 ¹devil: who seeketh to kill thee? Jesus answered and said unto them,
22 I did one work, and ye all ²marvel. For this cause hath Moses given you circumcision (not that it is of Moses, but of the fathers); and on
23 the sabbath ye circumcise a man. If a man receiveth circumcision on the sabbath, that the law of Moses may not be broken; are ye wroth with me, because I made a man every whit whole on the sabbath?
24 Judge not according to appearance, but judge righteous judgement.
25 Some therefore of them of Jerusalem said, Is not this he whom they
26 seek to kill? And lo, he speaketh openly, and they say nothing unto him. Can it be that the rulers indeed know that this is the Christ?
27 Howbeit we know this man whence he is: but when the Christ cometh,
28 no one knoweth whence he is. Jesus therefore cried in the temple, teaching and saying, Ye both know me, and know whence I am; and I am not come of myself, but he that sent me is true, whom ye
29 know not. I know him; because I am from him, and he sent me.
30 They sought therefore to take him: and no man laid his hands on him,
31 because his hour was not yet come. But of the multitude many believed on him; and they said, When the Christ shall come, will he do
32 more signs than those, which this man hath done? The Pharisees

---

*The Feast of Tabernacles was six months before the Passover, and this period of six months was divided into two nearly equal parts by the Feast of the Dedication (§ 89).—As to the combination of Luke and John for this portion of the history, see the end of this volume, Note on § 75.

John 7:14–52.

heard the multitude murmuring these things concerning him; and
33 the chief priests and the Pharisees sent officers to take him. Jesus
therefore said, Yet a little while am I with you, and I go unto him
34 that sent me. Ye shall seek me, and shall not find me: and where I
35 am, ye cannot come. The Jews therefore said among themselves,
Whither will this man go that we shall not find him? will he go unto
36 the Dispersion ²among the Greeks, and teach the Greeks? What is
this word that he said, Ye shall seek me, and shall not find me: and
where I am, ye cannot come?
37 Now on the last day, the great *day* of the feast, Jesus stood and
cried, saying, If any man thirst, let him come unto me, and drink.
38 He that believeth on me, as the scripture hath said, out of his belly
39 shall flow rivers of living water. But this spake he of the Spirit,
which they that believed on him were to receive: ⁴for the Spirit was
40 not yet *given;* because Jesus was not yet glorified. Some of the multitude
therefore, when they heard these words, said, This is of a truth
41 the prophet. Others said, This is the Christ. But some said, What,
42 doth the Christ come out of Galilee? Hath not the scripture said
that the Christ cometh of the seed of David, and from Bethlehem, the
43 village where David was? So there arose a division in the multitude
44 because of him. And some of them would have taken him; but no
man laid hands on him.
45 The officers therefore came to the chief priests and Pharisees; and
46 they said unto them, Why did ye not bring him? The officers an-
47 swered, Never man so spake. The Pharisees therefore answered
48 them, Are ye also led astray? Hath any of the rulers believed on
49 him, or of the Pharisees? But this multitude which knoweth not the
50 law are accursed. Nicodemus saith unto them (he that came to him
51 before, being one of them), Doth our law judge a man, except it first
52 hear from himself and know what he doeth? They answered and said
unto him, Art thou also of Galilee? Search, and ⁵see that out of Galilee
ariseth no prophet.

1. Gr. *demon.*   2. Or, *marvel because of this.*   *Moses hath given you circumcision.*
3. Gr. *of.*   4. Some ancient authorities read *for the Holy Spirit was not yet given.*
5. Or, *see: for out of Galilee, etc.*

[§ 76. STORY OF AN ADULTERESS BROUGHT TO JESUS FOR JUDGMENT.

John 7:53 to 8:11.]*

53, 1 [¹And they went every man unto his own house: but Jesus went unto
2 the mount of Olives. And early in the morning he came again into
the temple, and all the people came unto him; and he sat down, and
3 taught them. And the scribes and the Pharisees bring a woman
4 taken in adultery; and having set her in the midst, they say unto him,
²Master, this woman hath been taken in adultery, in the very act.
5 Now in the law Moses commanded us to stone such: what then sayest
6 thou of her? And this they said, ³tempting him, that they might

*This paragraph can no longer be considered a part of the Gospel of John, but it is in all
probability a true story of Jesus, very likely drawn by early students from the collection of
Papias, published about A.D. 140. See Hovey on John (American Comm. on N. T.) Observe
that without it § 77 goes right on after § 75.

CLOSING MINISTRY,

John 7:53 to 8:11.

have *whereof* to accuse him. But Jesus stooped down, and with his
7 finger wrote on the ground. But when they continued asking him,
he lifted up himself, and said unto them, He that is without sin
8 among you, let him first cast a stone at her. And again he stooped
9 down, and with his finger wrote on the ground. And they, when they
heard it, went out one by one, beginning from the eldest, *even* unto
the last: and Jesus was left alone, and the woman, where she was, in
10 the midst. And Jesus lifted up himself, and said unto her, Woman,
11 where are they? did no man condemn thee? And she said, No man,
Lord. And Jesus said, Neither do I condemn thee: go thy way; from
henceforth sin no more.]

1. Most of the ancient authorities omit John 7:53—8:11. Those which contain it vary much from each other. 2. Or, *Teacher*. 3. Or, *trying*.

§ 77. JESUS CLAIMS TO BE THE SON OF GOD, AND TO HAVE EXISTED BEFORE ABRAHAM. ATTEMPT OF THE PEOPLE TO STONE HIM.

Jerusalem.

John 8:12-59.

12 Again therefore Jesus spake unto them, saying, I am the light of
the world: he that followeth me shall not walk in the darkness, but
13 shall have the light of life. The Pharisees therefore said unto him,
14 Thou bearest witness of thyself; thy witness is not true. Jesus answered and said unto them, Even if I bear witness of myself, my witness is true; for I know whence I came, and whither I go; but ye
15 know not whence I come, or whither I go. Ye judge after the flesh;
16 I judge no man. Yea and if I judge, my judgement is true; for I am
17 not alone, but I and the Father that sent me. Yea and in your law it
18 is written, that the witness of two men is true. I am he that beareth
witness of myself, and the Father that sent me beareth witness of me.
19 They said therefore unto him, Where is thy Father? Jesus answered,
Ye know neither me, nor my Father: if ye knew me, ye would know
20 my Father also. These words spake he in the treasury, as he taught
in the temple: and no man took him; because his hour was not yet
come.
21 He said therefore again unto them, I go away, and ye shall seek
22 me, and shall die in your sin: whither I go, ye cannot come. The
Jews therefore said, Will he kill himself, that he saith, Whither I
23 go, ye cannot come? And he said unto them, Ye are from beneath; I
24 am from above: ye are of this world; I am not of this world. I said
therefore unto you, that ye shall die in your sins: for except ye be-
25 lieve that ¹I am *he*, ye shall die in your sins. They said therefore unto
him, Who art thou? Jesus said unto them, ²Even that which I have
26 also spoken unto you from the beginning. I have many things to
speak and to judge concerning you: howbeit he that sent me is true;
and the things which I heard from him, these speak I ³unto the
27 world. They perceived not that he spake to them of the Father.

John 8:12-59.

28 Jesus therefore said, When ye have lifted up the Son of man, then
shall ye know that 'I am *he*, and *that* I do nothing of myself, but as the
29 Father taught me, I speak these things. And he that sent me is with
me: he hath not left me alone; for I do always the things that are
30 pleasing to him. As he spake these things, many believed on him.
31 Jesus therefore said to those Jews which had believed him, If ye
32 abide in my word, *then* are ye truly my disciples; and ye shall know
33 the truth, and the truth shall make you free. They answered unto
him, We be Abraham's seed, and have never yet been in bondage to
34 any man: how sayest thou, Ye shall be made free? Jesus answered
them, Verily, verily, I say unto you, Every one that committeth sin
35 is the bondservant of sin. And the bondservant abideth not in the
36 house for ever: the son abideth for ever. If therefore the Son shall
37 make you free, ye shall be free indeed. I know that ye are Abraham's seed; yet ye seek to kill me, because my word *b*hath not free
38 course in you. I speak the things which I have seen with *c*my Father;
and ye also do the things which ye heard from *your* father. They an-
39 swered and said unto him, Our Father is Abraham. Jesus saith unto
them, If ye *f*were Abraham's children, *g*ye would do the works of
40 Abraham. But now ye seek to kill me, a man that hath told you the
41 truth, which I heard from God: this did not Abraham. Ye do the
works of your father. They said unto him, We were not born of for-
42 nication; we have one Father, *even* God. Jesus said unto them, If
God were your Father, ye would love me: for I came forth and am
come from God: for neither have I come of myself, but he sent me.
43 Why do ye not *understand my speech? *Even* because ye cannot hear
44 my word. Ye are of *your* father, the devil, and the lusts of your
father it is your will to do. He was a murderer from the beginning,
*i*and stood not in the truth, because there is no truth in him. *k*When
he speaketh a lie, he speaketh of his own: for he is a liar, and the
45 father thereof. But because I say the truth, ye believe me not.
46 Which of you convicteth me of sin? If I say truth, why do ye not
47 believe me? He that is of God heareth the words of God: for this
48 cause ye hear *them* not, because ye are not of God. The Jews answered
and said unto him, Say we not well that thou art a Samaritan, and
49 hast a *l*devil? Jesus answered, I have not a *l*devil; but I honour my
50 Father, and ye dishonour me. But I seek not mine own glory: there
51 is one that seeketh and judgeth. Verily, verily, I say unto you, If a
52 man keep my word, he shall never see death. The Jews said unto
him, Now we know that thou hast a *l*devil. Abraham is dead, and
the prophets; and thou sayest, If a man keep my word, he shall never
53 taste of death. Art thou greater than our father Abraham, which is
54 dead? and the prophets are dead: whom makest thou thyself? Jesus
answered, If I glorify myself, my glory is nothing: it is my Father
55 that glorifieth me; of whom ye say, that he is your God: and ye have
not known him: but I know him: and if I should say, I know him not,
I shall be like unto you, a liar: but I know him, and keep his word.
56 Your father Abraham rejoiced *n*to see my day; and he saw it, and was
57 glad. The Jews therefore said unto him, Thou art not yet fifty years
58 old, and hast thou seen Abraham? Jesus said unto them, Verily,
59 verily, I say unto you, Before Abraham *o*was, I am. They took up

John 8:12–59.

stones therefore to cast at him: but Jesus [15]hid himself, and went out of the temple[16].

1. Or, *I am*. 2. Or, *How is it that I even speak to you at all?* 3. Gr. *into.* 4. Or, *I am* Or, *I am he: and I do*. 5. Or, *hath no place in you*. 6. Or, *the Father: do ye also therefore the things which ye heard from the Father*. 7. Gr. *are*. 8. Some ancient authorities read *ye do the works of Abraham*. 9. Or, *know*. 10. Some ancient authorities read *standeth*. 11. Or, *When one speaketh a lie, he speaketh of his own; for his father also is a liar*. 12. Gr. *demon*. 13. Or, *that he should see*. 14. Gr. *was born*. 15. Or, *was hidden, and went, etc*. 16. Many ancient authorities add *and going through the midst of them went his way, and so passed by*.

§78. JESUS HEALS A MAN BORN BLIND. THE RULERS FORBID HIS BEING RECOGNIZED AS THE MESSIAH.

Jerusalem.

John 9:1–41.

1, 2 And as he passed by, he saw a man blind from his birth. And his disciples asked him, saying, Rabbi, who did sin, this man, or his
3 parents, that he should be born blind? Jesus answered, Neither did this man sin, nor his parents: but that the works of God should be
4 made manifest in him. We must work the works of him that sent
5 me, while it is day: the night cometh, when no man can work. When
6 I am in the world, I am the light of the world. When he had thus spoken, he spat on the ground, and made clay of the spittle, and
7 ¹anointed his eyes with the clay, and said unto him, Go, wash in the
8 pool of Siloam (which is by interpretation, Sent). He went away therefore, and washed, and came seeing. The neighbours therefore, and they which saw him aforetime, that he was a beggar, said, Is not
9 this he that sat and begged? Others said, It is he: others said, No,
10 but he is like him. He said, I am *he*. They said therefore unto him,
11 How then were thine eyes opened? He answered, the man that is called Jesus made clay, and anointed mine eyes, and said unto me, Go to Siloam, and wash: so I went away and washed, and I received sight.
12 And they said unto him, Where is he? He saith, I know not.
13, 14 They bring to the Pharisees him that aforetime was blind. Now it was the sabbath on the day when Jesus made the clay, and opened
15 his eyes. Again therefore the Pharisees also asked him how he received his sight. And he said unto them, He put clay upon mine
16 eyes, and I washed, and do see. Some therefore of the Pharisees said, This man is not from God, because he keepeth not the sabbath. But
17 others said, How can a man that is a sinner do such signs? And there was a division among them. They say therefore unto the blind man again, What sayest thou of him, in that he opened thine eyes? And
18 he said, He is a prophet. The Jews therefore did not believe concerning him, that he had been blind, and had received his sight, until they called the parents of him that had received his sight, and asked
19 them, saying, Is this your son, who ye say was born blind? how then
20 doth he now see? His parents answered and said, We know that this
21 is our son, and that he was born blind: but how he now seeth, we know not; or who opened his eyes, we know not: ask him; he is of age;

John 9:1-41.

22 he shall speak for himself. These things said his parents, because they feared the Jews: for the Jews had agreed already, that if any man should confess him to be Christ, he should be put out of the 23 synagogue. Therefore said his parents, He is of age; ask him. 24 So they called the second time the man that was blind, and said unto 25 him, Give glory to God: we know that this man is a sinner. He therefore answered, Whether he be a sinner, I know not: one thing I know, 26 that, whereas I was blind, now I see. They said therefore unto him, 27 What did he to thee? how opened he thine eyes? He answered them, I told you even now, and ye did not hear: wherefore would ye hear it 28 again? would ye also become his disciples? And they reviled him, 29 and said, Thou art his disciple, but we are disciples of Moses. We know that God hath spoken unto Moses: but as for this man, we know 30 not whence he is. The man answered and said unto them, Why, herein is the marvel, that ye know not whence he is, and yet he opened 31 mine eyes. We know that God heareth not sinners: but if any man 32 be a worshipper of God, and do his will, him he heareth. Since the world began it was never heard that any one opened the eyes of a man 33 born blind. If this man were not from God, he could do nothing. 34 They answered and said unto him, Thou wast altogether born in sins, and dost thou teach us? And they cast him out.
35 Jesus heard that they had cast him out; and finding him, he said, 36 Dost thou believe on ²the Son of God? He answered and said, And 37 who is he, Lord, that I may believe on him? Jesus said unto him, 38 Thou hast both seen him, and he it is that speaketh with thee. And 39 he said, Lord, I believe. And he worshipped him. And Jesus said, For judgement came I into this world, that they which see not may 40 see; and that they which see may become blind. Those of the Pharisees which were with him heard these things, and said unto him, Are we 41 also blind? Jesus said unto them, If ye were blind, ye would have no sin: but now ye say, We see: your sin remaineth.

1. Or, *and with the clay thereof anointed his eyes.* 2. Many ancient authorities read *the Son of man.*

§ 79. JESUS INTIMATES THAT HE IS GOING TO DIE FOR HIS FLOCK, AND COME TO LIFE AGAIN.

Jerusalem.

John 10:1-21.

1 Verily, verily, I say unto you, He that entereth not by the door into the fold of the sheep, but climbeth up some other way, the same is a 2 thief and a robber. But he that entereth in by the door is ¹the shep- 3 herd of the sheep. To him the porter openeth; and the sheep hear his voice: and he calleth his own sheep by name, and leadeth them 4 out. When he hath put forth all his own, he goeth before them, and 5 the sheep follow him: for they know his voice. And a stranger will they not follow, but will flee from him: for they know not the voice of 6 strangers. This ²parable spake Jesus unto them: but they understood not what things they were which he spake unto them.

John 10:1-21.

7 Jesus therefore said unto them again, Verily, verily, I say unto you,
8 I am the door of the sheep. All that came before me are thieves and
9 robbers: but the sheep did not hear them. I am the door: by me if
any man enter in, he shall be saved, and shall go in and go out, and
10 shall find pasture. The thief cometh not, but that he may steal, and
kill, and destroy: I came that they may have life, and may ³have *it*
11 abundantly. I am the good shepherd: the good shepherd layeth
12 down his life for the sheep. He that is a hireling, and not a shepherd, whose own the sheep are not, beholdeth the wolf coming, and
leaveth the sheep, and fleeth, and the wolf snatcheth them, and scat-
13 tereth *them: he fleeth* because he is a hireling, and careth not for the
14 sheep. I am the good shepherd; and I know mine own, and mine own
15 know me, even as the Father knoweth me, and I know the Father;
16 and I lay down my life for the sheep. And other sheep I have, which
are not of this fold: them also I must ⁴bring, and they shall hear my
17 voice; and ⁵they shall become one flock, one shepherd. Therefore
doth the Father love me, because I lay down my life, that I may take
18 it again. No one ⁶taketh it away from me, but I lay it down of myself. I have ⁷power to lay it down, and I have ⁷power to take it again.
This commandment received I from my Father.
19 There arose a division again among the Jews because of these
20 words. And many of them said, He hath a ⁸devil, and is mad; why
21 hear ye him? Others said, These are not the sayings of one possessed
with a ⁸devil. Can a ⁸devil open the eyes of the blind?

1. Or, *a shepherd.* 2. Or, *proverb.* 3. Or, *have abundance.* 4. Or, *lead.* 5. Or, *there shall be one flock.* 6. Some ancient authorities read *took it away.* 7. Or, *right.* 8. Gr. *demon.*

In § 80-88 we have matters given by Luke only, which probably occurred in Judea. Several of them are similar to events and discourses of the ministry in Galilee, given by Matthew and Mark.

§ 80. MISSION OF THE SEVENTY, AND THEIR RETURN.

(Compare Mission of the Twelve in § 55.)

Probably in Judea.

Luke 10:1-24.

1 Now after these things the Lord appointed seventy¹ others, and
sent them two and two before his face into every city and place,
2 whither he himself was about to come. And he said unto them, The
harvest is plenteous, but the labourers are few: pray ye therefore the
Lord of the harvest, that he send forth labourers into his harvest.
3 Go your ways: behold, I send you forth as lambs in the midst of
4 wolves. Carry no purse, no wallet, no shoes; and salute no man on
5 the way. And into whatsoever house ye shall ²enter, first say, Peace

*These sections are all we have for about three months; from the Tabernacles to the Dedication (see on § 75). Observe that here, as in previous portions of the history, we possess only a few specimens from what must have been the great mass of our Lord's doings and sayings.

IN ALL PARTS OF THE HOLY LAND.

Luke 10:1-24.

6 *be* to this house. And if a son of peace be there, your peace shall rest
7 upon ³him: but if not, it shall turn to you again. And in that same
house remain, eating and drinking such things as they give: for the
8 labourer is worthy of his hire. Go not from house to house. And
into whatsoever city ye enter, and they receive you, eat such things
9 as are set before you: and heal the sick that are therein, and say unto
10 them, The kingdom of God is come nigh unto you. But into whatsoever city ye shall enter, and they receive you not, go out into the
11 streets thereof and say, Even the dust from your city, that cleaveth
to our feet, we do wipe off against you: howbeit know this, that the
12 kingdom of God is come nigh. I say unto you, It shall be more toler-
13 able in that day for Sodom, than for that city. Woe unto thee,
Chorazin! woe unto thee, Bethsaida! for if the 'mighty works had been
done in Tyre and Sidon, which were done in you, they would have
14 repented long ago, sitting in sackcloth and ashes. Howbeit it shall
be more tolerable for Tyre and Sidon in the judgement, than for you.
15 And thou, Capernaum, shalt thou be exalted unto heaven? thou shalt
16 be brought down unto Hades. He that heareth you heareth me; and
he that rejecteth me; and he that rejecteth me rejecteth
him that sent me.
17 And the seventy returned with joy, saying, Lord, even the ⁵devils
18 are subject unto us in thy name. And he said unto them, I beheld
19 Satan fallen as lightning from heaven. Behold, I have given you
authority to tread upon serpents and scorpions, and over all the power
20 of the enemy: and nothing shall in any wise hurt you. Howbeit in
this rejoice not, that the spirits are subject unto you; but rejoice that
your names are written in heaven.
21 In that same hour he rejoiced ⁶in the Holy Spirit, and said, I 'thank
thee, O Father, Lord of heaven and earth, that thou didst hide these
things from the wise and understanding, and didst reveal them unto
22 babes: yea, Father; ⁸for so it was well-pleasing in thy sight. All
things have been delivered unto me of my Father: and no one knoweth
who the Son is, save the Father; and who the Father is, save the Son,
23 and he to whomsoever the Son willeth to reveal *him*. And turning to
the disciples, he said privately, Blessed are the eyes which see the
24 things that ye see: for I say unto you, that many prophets and kings
desired to see the things which ye see, and saw them not: and to hear
the things which ye hear, and heard them not.

1. Many ancient authorities add *and two:* and so in verse 17. 2. Or, *enter first, say*.
3. Or, *it*. 4. Gr. *powers*. 5. Gr. *demons*. 6. Or, *by*. 7. Or, *praise*. 8. Or, *that*.

§ 81. JESUS ANSWERS A LAWYER'S QUESTION AS TO ETERNAL LIFE, GIVING THE PARABLE OF THE GOOD SAMARITAN.

Probably in Judea.

Luke 10:25-37.

25 And behold, a certain lawyer stood up and tempted him, saying,
26 ¹Master, what shall I do to inherit eternal life? And he said unto
27 him, What is written in the law? how readest thou? And he answer-

Luke 10:25-37.

ing said, Thou shalt love the Lord thy God ²with all thy heart, and with all thy soul, and with all thy strength, and with all thy mind; 28 and thy neighbour as thyself. And he said unto him, Thou hast 29 answered right: do this, and thou shalt live. But he, desiring to 30 justify himself, said unto Jesus, And who is my neighbour? Jesus made answer and said, A certain man was going down from Jerusalem to Jericho; and he fell among robbers, which both stripped him and 31 beat him, and departed, leaving him half dead. And by chance a certain priest was going down that way: and when he saw him, he 32 passed by on the other side. And in like manner a Levite also, when 33 he came to the place, and saw him, passed by on the other side. But a certain Samaritan, as he journeyed, came where he was: and when 34 he saw him, he was moved with compassion, and came to him, and bound up his wounds, pouring on *them* oil and wine; and he set him on his own beast, and brought him to an inn, and took care of him. 35 And on the morrow he took out two ³pence, and gave them to the host, and said, Take care of him; and whatsoever thou spendest more, I, 36 when I come back again, will repay thee. Which of these three, thinkest thou, proved neighbour to him that fell among the robbers? 37 And he said, He that shewed mercy on him. And Jesus said unto him, Go, and do thou likewise.

1. Or, *Teacher.* 2. Gr. *from.* 3. The word in the Greek denotes a coin worth about seventeen cents.

§ 82. JESUS THE GUEST OF MARTHA AND MARY.

Bethany, near Jerusalem.*

Luke 10:38-42.

38 Now as they went on their way, he entered into a certain village: and a certain woman named Martha received him into her house. 39 And she had a sister called Mary, which also sat at the Lord's feet, 40 and heard his word. But Martha was ¹cumbered about much serving; and she came up to him, and said, Lord, dost thou not care that my sister did leave me to serve alone? bid her therefore that she help me. 41 But the Lord answered and said unto her, ²Martha, Martha, thou art 42 anxious and troubled about many things: ³but one thing is needful: for Mary hath chosen the good part, which shall not be taken away from her.

1. Gr. *distracted.* 2. A few ancient authorities read, *Martha, Martha, thou art troubled; Mary hath chosen, etc.* 3. Many ancient authorities read *but few things are needful, or one.*

§ 83. JESUS AGAIN GIVES A MODEL OF PRAYER (COMP. §42,D), AND ENCOURAGES HIS DISCIPLES TO PRAY.

Probably in Judea.

Luke 11:1-13.

1 And it came to pass, as he was praying in a certain place, that when he ceased, one of his disciples said unto him, Lord, teach us to pray,

*There was another Bethany beyond Jordan (§17, 18, 89). The present Bethany, near Jerusalem, we shall visit again in §94, 104, and 117.

Luke 11:1-13.

2 even as John also taught his disciples. And he said unto them, When
3 ye pray, say, ¹Father, Hallowed be thy Name. Thy kingdom come.²
4 Give us day by day ³our daily bread. And forgive us our sins; for we
ourselves also forgive every one that is indebted to us. And bring us
not into temptation⁴.*
5 And he said unto them, Which of you shall have a friend, and shall
go unto him at midnight, and say to him, Friend, lend me three
6 loaves; for a friend of mine is come to me from a journey, and I have
7 nothing to set before him; and he from within shall answer and say,
Trouble me not: the door is now shut, and my children are with me
8 in bed; I cannot rise and give thee? I say unto you, Though he will
not rise and give him, because he is his friend, yet because of his im-
9 portunity he will arise and give him ⁵as many as he needeth. And I
say unto you, Ask, and it shall be given you; seek, and ye shall find;
10 knock, and it shall be opened unto you. For every one that asketh
receiveth; and he that seeketh findeth; and to him that knocketh it
11 shall be opened. And of which of you that is a father shall his son
ask a ⁶loaf, and he give him a stone? or a fish, and he for a fish give
12 him a serpent? Or *if* he shall ask an egg, will he give him a scorpion?
13 If ye then, being evil, know how to give good gifts unto your children,
how much more shall *your* heavenly Father give the Holy Spirit to
them that ask him?

1. Many ancient authorities read *Our Father, which art in heaven.* See Matt. 6:9.
2. Many ancient authorities add *Thy will be done, as in heaven, so on earth.* See Matt. 6:10. 3. Gr. *our bread for the coming day.* 4. Many ancient authorities add *but deliver us from the evil one* (or, *from evil*). See Matt. 6:13. 5. Or, *whatsoever things.* 6. Some ancient authorities omit *a loaf, and he gave him a stone?* or.

§ 84. BLASPHEMOUS ACCUSATION OF LEAGUE WITH BEELZEBUB.

(Compare § 48.)†

Probably in Judea.

Luke 11:14-36.

14 And he was casting out a ¹devil which was dumb. And it came to
pass, when the ²devil was gone out, the dumb man spake; and the
15 multitudes marvelled. But some of them said, ³By Beelzebub the
16 prince of the ²devils casteth he out devils. And others, tempting
17 him, sought of him a sign from heaven. But he, knowing their
thoughts, said unto them, Every kingdom divided against itself is

*Observe that while the phraseology is here quite different from that of the prayer as given in § 12,d, the ideas are the same.

†It is perfectly natural that the blasphemous accusation made in Galilee (§ 48), and probably more than once (§ 39, Matt. 9:34), should be repeated a year or so afterward in Judea or Perea, and that Jesus should make substantially the same argument in reply. This sort of thing occurs to every travelling religious teacher. Our Lord does not here give the solemn warning that such an accusation is really blaspheming against the Holy Spirit, and is unpardonable. (See § 86, Luke 12:10.) And the subsequent occurrences are quite different in the two cases. In § 48f, he afterwards goes out by the lake-side and gives the great group of parables, presently explaining some of them to the disciples in a house, and then crosses the lake to Gerasa, etc. Here in § 84, he breakfasts with a Pharisee, and utters such solemn woes against the Pharisees as are found only in the closing months of his ministry, and then gives to vast multitudes a series of instructions wholly unlike the great group of parables. So it is quite unsuitable to identify this occurrence with that of § 48.

Luke 11:14-36.

brought to desolation; ⁴and a house divided against a house falleth.
18 And if Satan also is divided against himself, how shall his kingdom
19 stand? because ye say that I cast out ³devils ²by Beelzebub. And if I
²by Beelzebub cast out ³devils, by whom do your sons cast them out?
20 therefore shall they be your judges. But if I by the finger of God
21 cast out ³devils, then is the kingdom of God come upon you. When
the strong *man* fully armed guardeth his own court, his goods are in
22 peace: but when a stronger than he shall come upon him, and overcome him, he taketh from him his whole armour wherein he trusted,
23 and divideth his spoils. He that is not with me is against me; and
24 he that gathereth not with me scattereth. The unclean spirit when
⁵he is gone out of the man, passeth through waterless places, seeking
rest; and finding none, ⁵he saith, I will turn back unto my house
25 whence I came out. And when he is come, ⁵he findeth it swept and
26 garnished. Then goeth ⁶he, and taketh *to him* seven other spirits
more evil than ⁶himself; and they enter in and dwell there: and the
last state of that man becometh worse than the first.
27 And it came to pass, as he said these things, a certain woman out
of the multitude lifted up her voice, and said unto him, Blessed is the
28 womb that bare thee, and the breasts which thou didst suck. But he
said, Yea rather, blessed are they that hear the word of God, and
keep it.
29 And when the multitudes were gathering together unto him, he
began to say, This generation is an evil generation: it seeketh after a
sign; and there shall no sign be given to it but the sign of Jonah.
30 For even as Jonah became a sign unto the Ninevites, so shall also the
31 Son of man be to this generation. The queen of the south shall rise
up in the judgement with the men of this generation, and shall condemn them: for she came from the ends of the earth to hear the wis-
32 dom of Solomon; and behold, ⁷a greater than Solomon is here. The
men of Nineveh shall stand up in the judgement with this generation
and shall condemn it: for they repented at the preaching of Jonah;
and behold, ⁷a greater than Jonah is here.
33 No man, when he hath lighted a lamp, putteth it in a cellar, neither
under the bushel, but on the stand, that they which enter in may see
34 the light. The lamp of thy body is thine eye: when thine eye is single, thy whole body also is full of light; but when it is evil, thy body
35 also is full of darkness. Look therefore whether the light that is in
36 thee be not darkness. If therefore thy whole body be full of light,
having no part dark, it shall be wholly full of light, as when the
lamp with its bright shining doth give the light.

1. Gr. *demon*. 2. Or, *in*. 3. Gr. *demons*. 4. Or, *and house falleth upon house*. 5. Or, *it*. 6. Or, *itself*. 7. Gr. *more than*.

§ 85. WHILE BREAKFASTING WITH A PHARISEE, JESUS SEVERELY
DENOUNCES THE PHARISEES AND LAWYERS, AND
EXCITES THEIR ENMITY.

Probably in Judea.

Luke 11:37-54.

37 Now as he spake, a Pharisee asketh him to ¹dine with him: and he

Luke 11:37-54.

38 went in, and sat down to meat. And when the Pharisee saw it, he
39 marvelled that he had not washed before ¹dinner. And the Lord said
unto him, Now do ye Pharisees cleanse the outside of the cup and of
the platter; but your inward part is full of extortion and wickedness.
40 Ye foolish ones, did not he that made the outside make the inside
41 also? Howbeit give for alms those things which ²are within; and behold,
all things are clean unto you.
42 But woe unto you Pharisees! for ye tithe mint and rue and every
herb, and pass over judgement and the love of God: but these ought
43 ye to have done, and not to leave the other undone. Woe unto you
Pharisees! for ye love the chief seats in the synagogues, and the salu-
44 tations in the marketplaces. Woe unto you! for ye are as the tombs
which appear not, and the men that walk over *them* know it not.
45 And one of the lawyers answering saith unto him, ³Master, in say-
46 ing this thou reproachest us also. And he said, Woe unto you lawyers also! for ye lade men with burdens grievous to be borne, and ye
47 yourselves touch not the burdens with one of your fingers. Woe unto
you! for ye build the tombs of the prophets, and your fathers killed
48 them. So ye are witnesses and consent unto the works of your fathers:
49 for they killed them, and ye build *their tombs*. Therefore also said
the wisdom of God, I will send unto them prophets and apostles; and
50 *some* of them they shall kill and persecute; that the blood of all the
prophets, which was shed from the foundation of the world, may be
51 required of this generation; from the blood of Abel unto the blood of
Zachariah, who perished between the altar and the ⁴sanctuary: yea, I
52 say unto you, it shall be required of this generation. Woe unto you
lawyers! for ye took away the key of knowledge: ye entered not in
yourselves, and them that were entering in ye hindered.
53 And when he was come out from thence, the scribes and the Pharisees began to ⁵press upon *him* vehemently, and to provoke him to
54 speak of ⁶many things; laying wait for him, to catch something out of
his mouth.

1. Gr. *breakfast*. 2. Or, *ye can*. 3. Or, *Teacher*. 4. Gr. *house*. 5. Or, *set themselves vehemently against him*. 6. Or, *more*.

§ 86. He Speaks to His Disciples and a Vast Throng, about Hypocrisy, Worldly Anxieties (Comp. §42, E), Watchfulness, and His Own Approaching Passion.

Probably in Judea.

Luke 12.

1 In the mean time, when ¹the many thousands of the multitude were
gathered together, insomuch that they trode one upon another, he
began to ²say unto his disciples first of all, Beware ye of the leaven of
2 the Pharisees, which is hypocrisy. But there is nothing covered up;
3 that shall not be revealed: and hid, that shall not be known. Wherefore
whatsoever ye have said in the darkness shall be heard in the
light; and what ye have spoken in the ear in the inner chambers shall

Luke 12.

4 be proclaimed upon the housetops. And I say unto you my friends, Be not afraid of them which kill the body, and after that have no
5 more that they can do. But I will warn you whom ye shall fear: Fear him, which after he hath killed hath ²power to cast into ⁴hell; yea, I
6 say unto you, Fear him. Are not five sparrows sold for two farthings?
7 and not one of them is forgotten in the sight of God. But the very hairs of your head are all numbered. Fear not: ye are of more value
8 than many sparrows. And I say unto you, Every one who shall confess ⁵me before men, ⁶him shall the Son of man also confess before the
9 angels of God: but he that denieth me in the presence of men shall be
10 denied in the presence of the angels of God. And every one who shall speak a word against the Son of man, it shall be forgiven him: but unto him that blasphemeth against the Holy Spirit it shall not be
11 forgiven. And when they bring you before the synagogues, and the rulers, and the authorities, be not anxious how or what ye shall an-
12 swer, or what ye shall say: for the Holy Spirit shall teach you in that very hour what ye ought to say.
13 And one out of the multitude said unto him, ⁷Master, bid my brother
14 divide the inheritance with me. But he said unto him, Man, who
15 made me a judge or a divider over you? And he said unto them, Take heed, and keep yourselves from all covetousness: ⁸for a man's life consisteth not in the abundance of the things which he possesseth.
16 And he spake a parable unto them, saying, The ground of a certain
17 rich man brought forth plentifully: and he reasoned within himself, saying, What shall I do, because I have not where to bestow my
18 fruits? And he said, This will I do: I will pull down my barns, and build greater; and there will I bestow all my corn and my goods.
19 And I will say to my ⁹soul, ⁹Soul, thou hast much goods laid up for
20 many years; take thine ease, eat, drink, be merry. But God said unto him, Thou foolish one, this night ¹⁰is thy ⁹soul required of thee;
21 and the things which thou hast prepared, whose shall they be? So is he that layeth up treasure for himself, and is not rich toward God.
22 And he said unto his disciples, Therefore I say unto you, Be not anxious for *your* ¹¹life, what ye shall eat; nor yet for your body, what ye shall put
23 on. For the ¹¹life is more than the food, and the body than the rai-
24 ment. Consider the ravens, that they sow not, neither reap; which have no store-chamber nor barn: and God feedeth them: of how much
25 more value are ye than the birds! And which of you by being anx-
26 ious can add a cubit unto his ¹²stature? If then ye are not able to do even that which is least, why are ye anxious concerning the rest?
27 Consider the lilies, how they grow: they toil not, neither do they spin; yet I say unto you, Even Solomon in all his glory was not array-
28 ed like one of these. But if God doth so clothe the grass in the field, which to-day is, and to-morrow is cast into the oven; how much more
29 *shall he clothe* you, O ye of little faith? And seek not ye what ye shall
30 eat, and what ye shall drink, neither be ye of doubtful mind. For all these things do the nations of the world seek after: but your Father
31 knoweth that ye have need of these things. Howbeit seek ye ¹³his
32 kingdom, and these things shall be added unto you. Fear not, little flock; for it is your Father's good pleasure to give you the kingdom.
33 Sell that ye have, and give alms; make for yourselves purses which wax not old, a treasure in the heavens that faileth not, where no thief

Luke 12.

34 draweth near, neither moth destroyeth. For where your treasure is, there will your heart be also.

35, 36 Let your loins be girded about, and your lamps burning; and be ye yourselves like unto men looking for their lord, when he shall return from the marriage feast; that, when he cometh and knocketh,

37 they may straightway open unto him. Blessed are those ¹⁴servants, whom the lord when he cometh shall find watching: verily I say unto you, that he shall gird himself, and make them sit down to meat, and

38 shall come and serve them. And if he shall come in the second watch, and if in the third, and find *them* so, blessed are those *servants*.

39 ¹⁵But know this, that if the master of the house had known in what hour the thief was coming, he would have watched, and not have left

40 his house to be ¹⁶broken through. Be ye also ready: for in an hour that ye think not the Son of man cometh.

41 And Peter said, Lord, speakest thou this parable unto us, or even

42 unto all? And the Lord said, Who then is ¹⁷the faithful and wise steward, whom his lord shall set over his household, to give them

43 their portion of food in due season? Blessed is that ¹⁸servant, whom

44 his lord when he cometh shall find so doing. Of a truth I say unto

45 you, that he will set him over all that he hath. But if that ¹⁸servant shall say in his heart, My lord delayeth his coming; and shall begin to beat the menservants and the maidservants, and to eat and drink,

46 and to be drunken; the lord of that ¹⁸servant shall come in a day when he expecteth not, and in an hour when he knoweth not, and shall

47 ¹⁹cut him asunder, and appoint his portion with the unfaithful. And that ¹⁸servant, which knew his lord's will, and made not ready, nor

48 did according to his will, shall be beaten with many *stripes;* but he that knew not, and did things worthy of stripes, shall be beaten with few *stripes*. And to whomsoever much is given, of him shall much be required: and to whom they commit much, of him will they ask the more.

49 I came to cast fire upon the earth; and what will I, if it is already

50 kindled? But I have a baptism to be baptized with; and how am I

51 straitened till it be accomplished! Think ye that I am come to give

52 peace in the earth? I tell you, Nay; but rather division: for there shall be from henceforth five in one house divided, three against two,

53 and two against three. They shall be divided, father against son, and son against father; mother against daughter, and daughter against her mother; mother in law against her daughter in law, and daughter in law against her mother in law.

54 And he said to the multitudes also, When ye see a cloud rising in the west, straightway ye say, There cometh a shower; and so it com-

55 eth to pass. And when *ye see* a south wind blowing, ye say, There

56 will be a ²⁰scorching heat; and it cometh to pass. Ye hypocrites, ye know how to ²¹interpret the face of the earth and the heaven; but how

57 is it that ye know not how to ²¹interpret this time? And why even of

58 yourselves judge ye not what is right? For as thou art going with thine adversary before the magistrate, on the way give diligence to be quit of him; lest haply he hale thee unto the judge, and the judge shall deliver thee to the ²²officer, and the ²²officer shall cast thee into

Luke 12.

59 prison. I say unto thee, Thou shalt by no means come out thence, till thou have paid the very last mite.

1. Gr. *the myriads of.* 2. Or, *say unto his disciples, First of all beware ye.* 3. Or, *authority.* 4. Gr. *Gehenna.* 5. Gr. *in me.* 6. Gr. *in him.* 7. Or, *Teacher.* 8. Gr. *for not in a man's abundance consisteth his life, from the things which he possesseth.* 9. Or, *life.* 10. Gr. *they require thy soul.* 11. Or, *soul.* 12. Or, *age.* 13. Many ancient authorities read *the kingdom of God.* 14. Gr. *bond-servants.* 15. Or, *But this ye know.* 16. Or, *digged through.* 17. Or, *the faithful steward, the wise* man *whom, etc.* 18. Gr. *bond-servant.* 19. Or, *severely scourge him.* 20. Or, *hot wind.* 21. Gr. *prove.* 22. Gr. *exactor.*

§ 87. ALL MUST REPENT OR PERISH; PARABLE OF THE BARREN FIG TREE.

Probably in Judea.

Luke 13: 1-9.

1 Now there were some present at that very season which told him of the Galileans, whose blood Pilate had mingled with their sacrifices.
2 And he answered and said unto them, Think ye that these Galileans were sinners above all the Galileans, because they have suffered these
3 things? I tell you, Nay: but, except ye repent, ye shall all in like
4 manner perish. Or those eighteen, upon whom the tower in Siloam fell, and killed them, think ye that they were ¹offenders above all the
5 men that dwell in Jerusalem? I tell you, Nay: but, except ye repent, ye shall all likewise perish.
6 And he spake this parable; A certain man had a fig tree planted in his vineyard; and he came seeking fruit thereon, and found none.
7 And he said unto the vinedresser, Behold, these three years I come seeking fruit on this fig tree, and find none: cut it down; why doth it
8 also cumber the ground? And he answering saith unto him, Lord,
9 let it alone this year also, till I shall dig about it, and dung it: and if it bear fruit thenceforth, *well;* but if not, thou shalt cut it down.

1. Gr. *debtors.*

§ 88. JESUS HEALS ON THE SABBATH, AND DEFENDS HIMSELF (COMP. § 37-39 AND § 91). PARABLES OF THE MUSTARD SEED AND THE LEAVEN (COMP. § 51 D).

Probably in Judea.

Luke 13:10-21.

10 And he was teaching in one of the synagogues on the sabbath day.
11 And behold, a woman which had a spirit of infirmity eighteen years:
12 and she was bowed together, and could in no wise lift herself up. And when Jesus saw her, he called her, and said to her, Woman, thou art
13 loosed from thine infirmity. And he laid his hands upon her: and
14 immediately she was made straight, and glorified God. And the ruler of the synagogue, being moved with indignation because Jesus had healed on the sabbath, answered and said to the multitude, There

Luke 13:10-21.

are six days in which men ought to work: in them therefore come and
15 be healed, and not on the day of the sabbath. But the Lord answered
him, and said, Ye hypocrites, doth not each one of you on the sabbath
loose his ox or his ass from the ¹stall, and lead him away to watering?
16 And ought not this woman, being a daughter of Abraham, whom
Satan had bound, lo, *these* eighteen years, to have been loosed from
17 this bond on the day of the sabbath? And as he said these things,
all his adversaries were put to shame: and all the multitude rejoiced
for all the glorious things that were done by him.
18 He said therefore, Unto what is the kingdom of God like? and
19 whereunto shall I liken it? It is like unto a grain of mustard seed,
which a man took, and cast into his own garden; and it grew, and became a tree: and the birds of the heaven lodged in the branches
20 thereof. And again he said, Whereunto shall I liken the kingdom of
21 God? It is like unto leaven, which a woman took and hid in three
²measures of meal, till it was all leavened.

1. Gr. *manger*. 2. The word in the Gr. denotes the Hebrew seah, a measure containing nearly a peck and a half (cf. on Matt. 13:33).

Here again the Gospel of John takes us up, and carries us to Jerusalem, and then to Perea.

§ 89. AT THE FEAST OF DEDICATION, JESUS WILL NOT YET OPENLY
SAY THAT HE IS THE MESSIAH. THEY TRY TO STONE
HIM, AND HE RETIRES TO PEREA.

Jerusalem, and Bethany beyond the Jordan.

John 10:22-42.

22 ¹And it was the feast of the dedication at Jerusalem: it was win-
23 ter; and Jesus was walking in the temple in Solomon's porch.
24 The Jews therefore came round about him, and said unto him, How
25 long dost thou hold us in suspense? If thou art the Christ, tell us
plainly. Jesus answered them, I told you, and ye believe not: the
26 works that I do in my Father's name, these bear witness of me. But
27 ye believe not, because ye are not of my sheep. My sheep hear my
28 voice, and I know them, and they follow me: and I give unto them
eternal life; and they shall never perish, and no one shall snatch them
29 out of my hand. ²My Father, which hath given *them* unto me, is
greater than all; and no one is able to snatch ²*them* out of the Father's
30, 31 hand. I and the Father are one. The Jews took up stones again
32 to stone him. Jesus answered them, Many good works have I showed
33 you from the Father; for which of those works do ye stone me? The
Jews answered him, For a good work we stone thee not, but for blasphemy; and because that thou, being a man, makest thyself God.
34 Jesus answered them, Is it not written in your law, I said, ye are gods?
35 If he called them gods, unto whom the word of God came (and the
36 scripture cannot be broken), say ye of him, whom the Father ³sanctified and sent into the world, Thou blasphemest; because I said, I am

John 10:22-42.

37 the Son of God? If I do not the works of my Father, believe me not.
38 But if I do them, though you believe not me, believe the works: that ye may know and understand that the Father is in me, and I in the
39 Father. They sought again to take him: and he went forth out of their hand.
40 And he went away again beyond Jordan into the place where John
41 was at the first baptizing; and there he abode. And many came unto him; and they said, John indeed did no sign: but all things whatsoever
42 John spake of this man were true. And many believed on him there.

1. Some ancient authorities read *At that time was the feast.* 2. Some ancient authorities read *That which my Father hath given unto me.* 3. Or, aught. 4. Or, *consecrated.*

Notice that §§ 90-93 are from Luke alone, and the matters seem to have occurred in Perea.

§ 90. TEACHING IN PEREA, ON A JOURNEY TOWARD JERUSALEM. WARNED AGAINST HEROD ANTIPAS.

Luke 13:22-35.

22 And he went on his way through cities and villages, teaching, and
23 journeying on unto Jerusalem.* And one said unto him, Lord, are
24 they few that be saved? And he said unto them, Strive to enter in by the narrow door: for many, I say unto you, shall seek to enter in, and
25 shall not be ¹able. When once the master of the house is risen up, and hath shut to the door, and ye begin to stand without, and to knock at the door, saying, Lord, open to us; and he shall answer and
26 say to you, I know you not whence ye are; then shall ye begin to say, We did eat and drink in thy presence, and thou didst teach in our
27 streets; and he shall say, I tell you, I know not whence ye are; depart
28 from me, all ye workers of iniquity. There shall be weeping and gnashing of teeth, when ye shall see Abraham, and Isaac, and Jacob, and all the prophets, in the kingdom of God, and yourselves cast forth
29 without. And they shall come from the east and west, and from the north and south, and shall ²sit down in the kingdom of God.
30 And behold, there are last which shall be first, and there are first which shall be last.
31 In that very hour there came certain Pharisees, saying to him, Get
32 thee out, and go hence: for Herod would fain kill thee. And he said unto them, Go and say to that fox, Behold, I cast out ³devils and perform cures to-day and to-morrow, and the third *day* I am perfected.
33 Howbeit I must go on my way to-day and to-morrow and the *day* fol-
34 lowing: for it cannot be that a prophet perish out of Jerusalem. O Jerusalem, Jerusalem, which killeth the prophets, and stoneth them that are sent unto her! how often would I have gathered thy children together, even as a hen *gathereth* her own brood under her wings, and

*The period of three to four months from the Dedication to the final Passover is divided by another visit to Jerusalem (§ 94). We cannot tell how many weeks preceded this event. All along here we have only a few specimens of the Saviour's teaching and works.

35 ye would not! Behold, your house is left unto you *desolate:* and I say unto you, Ye shall not see me, until ye shall say, Blessed *is* he that cometh in the name of the Lord.

1. Or, *able, when once.* 2. Gr. *recline.* 3. Gr. *demons.*

§ 91. WHILE DINING (BREAKFASTING) WITH A CHIEF PHARISEE, HE AGAIN HEALS ON THE SABBATH, AND DEFENDS HIMSELF (COMP. § 88, AND § 37–39). THREE LESSONS SUGGESTED BY THE OCCASION.

Probably in Perea.
Luke 14:1–24.

1 And it came to pass, when he went into the house of one of the rulers of the Pharisees on a sabbath to eat bread, that they were
2 watching him. And behold, there was before him a certain man
3 which had the dropsy. And Jesus answering spake unto the lawyers and Pharisees, saying, Is it lawful to heal on the sabbath, or not?
4 But they held their peace. And he took him, and healed him, and
5 let him go. And he said unto them, Which of you shall have ¹an ass or an ox fallen into a well, and will not straightway draw him up on a
6 sabbath day? And they could not answer again unto these things.
7 And he spake a parable unto those which were bidden, when he
8 marked how they chose out the chief seats; saying unto them, When thou art bidden of any man to a marriage feast, ²sit not down in the chief seat; lest haply a more honourable man than thou be bidden of
9 him, and he that bade thee and him shall come and say to thee, Give this man place; and then thou shalt begin with shame to take the
10 lowest place. But when thou art bidden, go and sit down in the lowest place; that when he that hath bidden thee cometh, he may say to thee, Friend, go up higher: then shalt thou have glory in the pres-
11 ence of all that sit at meat with thee. For every one that exalteth himself shall be humbled; and he that humbleth himself shall be exalted.
12 And he said to him also that had bidden him, When thou makest a dinner or a supper,* call not thy friends, nor thy brethren, nor thy kinsmen, nor rich neighbours: lest haply they also bid thee again,
13 and a recompense be made thee. But when thou makest a feast, bid the poor, the maimed, the lame, and the blind: and thou shalt be blessed;
14 because they have not *wherewith* to recompense thee: for thou shalt be recompensed in the resurrection of the just.
15 And when one of them that sat at meat with him heard these things, he said unto him, Blessed is he that shall eat bread in the
16 kingdom of God. But he said unto him, A certain man made a great
17 supper; and he bade many: and he sent forth his ³servant at supper

*More exactly, "a breakfast or a dinner" (comp. § 85 and § 140). The two principal meals of the Jews answered to the present English breakfast (in the forenoon and often near noon), and dinner (at or after dark); and so in our cities. In the time of King James, as in many of our country homes now, the meal towards noon answered to dinner, and the night meal to supper. Hence a certain confusion in the older and more recent English versions.— In ver. 16, 17 the right word would be dinner, according to city usage, and so elsewhere.

Luke 14:1-24.

time to say to them that were bidden, Come, for *all* things are now
18 ready. And they all with one *consent* began to make excuse. The
first said unto him, I have bought a field, and I must needs go out and
19 see it: I pray thee have me excused. And another said, I have bought
five yoke of oxen, and I go to prove them: I pray thee have me ex-
20 cused. And another said, I have married a wife, and therefore I can-
21 not come. And the ³servant came, and told his lord these things.
Then the master of the house being angry said to his ³servant, Go out
quickly into the streets and lanes of the city, and bring in hither the
22 poor and maimed and blind and lame. And the ³servant said, Lord,
23 what thou didst command is done, and yet there is room. And the
Lord said unto the ³servant, Go out into the highways and hedges,
24 and constrain *them* to come in, that my house may be filled. For I say
unto you, that none of those men which were bidden shall taste of my
supper.

1. Many ancient authorities read *a son*. See ch. 13:15. 2. Gr. *recline not*. 3. Gr. *bond-servant*.

§ 92. GREAT CROWDS FOLLOW HIM, AND HE WARNS THEM TO COUNT THE COST OF DISCIPLESHIP TO HIM (COMP. §59).

Probably in Perea.

Luke 14:25-35.

25 Now there went with him great multitudes: and he turned, and said
26 unto them, If any man cometh unto me, and hateth not his own father,
and mother, and wife, and children, and brethren, and sisters, yea,
27 and his own life also, he cannot be my disciple. Whosoever doth not
28 bear his own cross, and come after me, cannot be my disciple. For
which of you, desiring to build a tower, doth not first sit down and
29 count the cost, whether he have *wherewith* to complete it? Lest haply,
when he hath laid a foundation, and is not able to finish, all that be-
30 hold begin to mock him, saying, This man began to build, and was not
31 able to finish. Or what king, as he goeth to encounter another king
in war, will not sit down first and take counsel whether he is able with
ten thousand to meet him that cometh against him with twenty thou-
32 sand? Or else, while the other is yet a great way off, he sendeth an
33 ambassage, and asketh conditions of peace. So therefore whosoever
he be of you that renounceth not all that he hath, he cannot be my
34 disciple. Salt therefore is good: but if even the salt have lost its
35 savour, wherewith shall it be seasoned? It is fit neither for the land
nor for the dunghill: *men* cast it out. He that hath ears to hear, let
him hear.

§ 93. FIVE GREAT PARABLES—THE LOST SHEEP, THE LOST COIN, THE LOST SON—THE UNRIGHTEOUS STEWARD—THE RICH MAN AND LAZARUS. SOME OTHER BRIEF LESSONS.

Probably in Perea.

Luke 15:1 to 17:10.

1 Now all the publicans and sinners were drawing near unto him for
2 to hear him. And both the Pharisees and the scribes murmured, saying, This man receiveth sinners, and eateth with them.
3, 4 And he spake unto them this parable, saying, What man of you, having a hundred sheep, and having lost one of them, doth not leave the ninety and nine in the wilderness, and go after that which is lost,
5 until he find it? And when he hath found it, he layeth it on his
6 shoulders, rejoicing. And when he cometh home, he calleth together his friends and his neighbours, saying unto them, Rejoice with me,
7 for I have found my sheep which was lost. I say unto you, that even so there shall be joy in heaven over one sinner that repenteth, *more* than over ninety and nine righteous persons, which need no repentance.
8 Or what woman having ten ¹pieces of silver, if she lose one piece, doth not light a lamp, and sweep the house, and seek diligently until
9 she find it? And when she hath found it, she calleth together her friends and neighbours, saying, Rejoice with me, for I have found the
10 piece which I had lost. Even so, I say unto you, there is joy in the presence of the angels of God over one sinner that repenteth.
11, 12 And he said, A certain man had two sons: and the younger of them said to his father, Father, give me the portion of ²*thy* substance
13 that falleth to me. And he divided unto them his living. And not many days after the younger son gathered all together, and took his journey into a far country; and there he wasted his substance with
14 riotous living. And when he had spent all, there arose a mighty
15 famine in that country: and he began to be in want. And he went and joined himself to one of the citizens of that country; and he sent
16 him into his fields to feed swine. And he would fain have been filled with ³the husks that the swine did eat: and no man gave unto him.
17 But when he came to himself he said, How many hired servants of my father's have bread enough and to spare, and I perish here with
18 hunger! I will arise and go to my father, and will say unto him,
19 Father, I have sinned against heaven, and in thy sight; I am no more worthy to be called thy son: make me as one of thy hired servants.
20 And he arose, and came to his father. But while he was yet afar off, his father saw him, and was moved with compassion, and ran, and fell
21 on his neck, and ⁴kissed him. And the son said unto him, Father, I have sinned against heaven, and in thy sight; I am no more worthy
22 to be called thy son.⁵ But the father said to his ⁶servants, Bring forth quickly the best robe, and put it on him: and put a ring on his
23 hand, and shoes on his feet: and bring the fatted calf, *and* kill it, and
24 let us eat, and make merry: for this my son was dead, and is alive
25 again; he was lost, and is found. And they began to be merry. Now his elder son was in the field: and as he came and drew nigh to the
26 house, he heard music and dancing. And he called to him one of the

CLOSING MINISTRY,

Luke 15:1 to 17:10.

27 ⁶servants, and inquired what these things might be. And he said unto him, Thy brother is come; and thy father hath killed the fatted
28 calf, because he hath received him safe and sound. But he was angry, and would not go in: and his father came out, and entreated him.
29 But he answered and said to his father, Lo, these many years do I serve thee, and I never transgressed a commandment of thine: and yet thou never gavest me a kid, that I might make merry with my
30 friends: but when this thy son came, which hath devoured thy living
31 with harlots, thou killedst for him the fatted calf. And he said unto
32 him, ⁷Son, thou art ever with me, and all that is mine is thine. But it was meet to make merry and be glad: for this thy brother was dead, and is alive *again;* and *was* lost, and is found.

16 And he said unto the disciples, There was a certain rich man, which had a steward; and the same was accused unto him that he was wast-
2 ing his goods. And he called him, and said unto him, What is this that I hear of thee? render the account of thy stewardship; for thou
3 canst be no longer steward. And the steward said within himself, What shall I do, seeing that my lord taketh away the stewardship
4 from me? I have not strength to dig; to beg I am ashamed. I am resolved what to do, that, when I am put out of the stewardship, they
5 may receive me into their houses. And calling to him each one of his lord's debtors, he said to the first, How much owest thou unto my
6 lord? And he said, A hundred ⁸measures of oil. And he said unto
7 him, Take thy ⁹bond, and sit down quickly and write fifty. Then said he to another, And how much owest thou? And he said, A hundred ¹⁰measures of wheat. He saith unto him, Take thy ⁹bond, and
8 write fourscore. And his lord commended ¹¹the unrighteous steward because he had done wisely: for the sons of this ¹²world are for their
9 own generation wiser than the sons of the light. And I say unto you, make to yourselves friends ¹³by means of the mammon of unrighteousness; that, when it shall fail, they may receive you into the eternal
10 tabernacles. He that is faithful in a very little is faithful also in
11 much. If therefore ye have not been faithful in the unrighteous
12 mammon, who will commit to your trust the true *riches?*. And if ye have not been faithful in that which is another's, who will give you
13 that which is ¹⁴your own? No ¹⁵servant can serve two masters: for either he will hate the one, and love the other; or else he will hold to one, and despise the other. Ye cannot serve God and mammon.
14 And the Pharisees, who were lovers of money, heard all these
15 things; and they scoffed at him. And he said unto them, Ye are they that justify yourselves in the sight of men; but God knoweth your hearts: for that which is exalted among men is an abomination in the
16 sight of God. The law and the prophets *were* until John: from that time the gospel of the kingdom of God is preached, and every man
17 entereth violently into it. But it is easier for heaven and earth to
18 pass away, than for one tittle of the law to fall. Every one that putteth away his wife, and marrieth another, committeth adultery: and he that marrieth one that is put away from a husband committeth adultery.
19 Now there was a certain rich man, and he was clothed in purple and
20 fine linen, ¹⁶faring sumptuously every day: and a certain beggar named
21 Lazarus was laid at his gate, full of sores, and desiring to be fed with

Luke 15:1 to 17:10.

the *crumbs* that fell from the rich man's table: yea, even the dogs
22 came and licked his sores. And it came to pass, that the beggar
died, and that he was carried away by the angels into Abraham's
23 bosom: and the rich man also died, and was buried. And in Hades
he lifted up his eyes, being in torments, and seeth Abraham afar off,
24 and Lazarus in his bosom. And he cried and said, Father Abraham,
have mercy on me, and send Lazarus, that he may dip the tip of his
finger in water, and cool my tongue; for I am in anguish in this flame.
25 But Abraham said, "Son, remember that thou in thy lifetime receiv-
edst thy good things, and Lazarus in like manner evil things: but now
26 here he is comforted, and thou art in anguish. And ¹⁸beside all this,
between us and you there is a great gulf fixed, that they which would
pass from hence to you may not be able, and that none may cross over
27 from thence to us. And he said, I pray thee therefore, father, that
28 thou wouldest send him to my father's house: for I have five brethren;
that he may testify unto them; lest they also come into this place of
29 torment. But Abraham saith, They have Moses and the prophets;
30 let them hear them. And he said, Nay, father Abraham: but if one
31 go to them from the dead, they will repent. And he said unto him,
If they hear not Moses and the prophets, neither will they be per-
suaded, if one rise from the dead.

17 And he said unto his disciples, It is impossible but that occasions of
stumbling should come: but woe unto him, through whom they come!
2 It were well for him if a millstone were hanged about his neck, and
he were thrown into the sea, rather than that he should cause one of
3 these little ones to stumble. Take heed to yourselves: if thy brother
4 sin, rebuke him; and if he repent, forgive him. And if he sin against
thee seven times in the day, and seven times turn again to thee, saying, I repent; thou shalt forgive him.
5, 6 And the apostles said unto the Lord, Increase our faith. And the
Lord said, If ye have faith as a grain of mustard seed, ye would say
unto this sycamine tree, Be thou rooted up, and be thou planted in
7 the sea; and it would have obeyed you. But who is there of you, having a ¹⁹servant plowing or keeping sheep, that will say unto him, when
he is come in from the field, Come straightway and sit down to meat;
8 and will not rather say unto him, Make ready wherewith I may sup, and
gird thyself, and serve me, till I have eaten and drunken; and after-
9 ward thou shalt eat and drink? Doth he thank the ¹⁹servant because
10 he did the things that were commanded? Even so ye also, when ye
shall have done all the things that are commanded you, say, We are
unprofitable ²⁰servants; we have done that which it was our duty to
do.

1. Gr. *drachma*, a coin worth about sixteen cents. 2. Gr. *the*. 3. Gr. *the pods of the carob-tree*. 4. Gr. *kissed him much*. 5. Some ancient authorities add *make me as one of thy hired servants*. See ver. 19. 6. Gr. *bond-servants*. 7. Gr. *Child*. 8. Gr. *baths*, the bath being a Hebrew measure. See Ezek. 45:10, 11, 14. 9. Gr. *writings*. 10. Gr. *cors*, the cor being a Hebrew measure. See Ezek. 45:14. 11. Gr. *the steward of unright-eousness*. 12. Or, *age*. 13. Gr. *out of*. 14. Some ancient authorities read, *our own*. 15. Gr. *household-servant*. 16. Or, *living in mirth and splendor every day*. 17. Gr. *Child*. 18. Or, *in all these things*. 19. Gr. *bond-servant*. 20. Gr. *bond-servants*.

§ 94. JESUS RAISES LAZARUS FROM THE DEAD.

From Perea* to Bethany near Jerusalem.

John 11:1–46.

1 Now a certain man was sick, Lazarus of Bethany, of the village of
2 Mary and her sister Martha. And it was that Mary, which anointed
the Lord with ointment, and wiped his feet with her hair, whose
3 brother Lazarus was sick. The sisters therefore sent unto him, say-
4 ing, Lord, behold, he whom thou lovest is sick. But when Jesus
heard it, he said, this sickness is not unto death, but for the glory of
5 God, that the Son of God may be glorified thereby. Now Jesus loved
6 Martha, and her sister, and Lazarus. When therefore he heard that
he was sick, he abode at that time two days in the place where he was.
7 Then after this he saith to the disciples, Let us go into Judea again.
8 The disciples say unto him, Rabbi, the Jews were but now seeking to
9 stone thee; and goest thou thither again? Jesus answered, Are there
not twelve hours in the day? If a man walk in the day, he stumbleth
10 not, because he seeth the light of this world. But if a man walk in
11 the night, he stumbleth, because the light is not in him. These things
spake he: and after this he saith unto them, Our friend Lazarus is
12 fallen asleep; but I go, that I may awake him out of sleep. The disciples therefore said unto him, Lord, if he is fallen asleep, he will
13 ¹recover. Now Jesus had spoken of his death: but they thought that
14 he spake of taking rest in sleep. Then Jesus therefore said unto
15 them plainly, Lazarus is dead. And I am glad for your sakes that I
was not there, to the intent ye may believe; nevertheless let us go
16 unto him. Thomas therefore, who is called ²Didymus, said unto his
fellow-disciples, Let us also go, that we may die with him.
17 So when Jesus came, he found that he had been in the tomb four
18 days already. Now Bethany was nigh unto Jerusalem, about fifteen
19 furlongs off; and many of the Jews had come to Martha and Mary, to
20 console them concerning their brother. Martha therefore, when she
heard that Jesus was coming, went and met him: but Mary still sat in
21 the house. Martha therefore said unto Jesus, Lord, if thou hadst
22 been here, my brother had not died. And even now I know that
23 whatsoever thou shalt ask of God, God will give thee. Jesus saith
24 unto her, Thy brother shall rise again. Martha saith unto him, I
know that he shall rise again in the resurrection at the last day.
25 Jesus said unto her, I am the resurrection, and the life: he that be-
26 lieveth on me, though he die, yet shall he live: and whosoever liveth
27 and believeth on me shall never die. Believest thou this? She saith
unto him, Yea, Lord: I have believed that thou art the Christ, the
28 Son of God, *even* he that cometh into the world. And when she
had said this, she went away, and called Mary ³her sister secretly,
29 saying, The ⁴Master is here, and calleth thee. And she, when she
30 heard it, arose quickly, and went unto him. (Now Jesus was not yet
come into the village, but was still in the place where Martha met
31 him.) The Jews then which were with her in the house, and were
comforting her, when they saw Mary, that she rose up quickly and
went out, followed her, supposing that she was going unto the tomb

---

*Our Lord was apparently at a distance of two or three days' journey (ver. 6,17) from Beth-
any; and by comparing §§ 89, 90 we see that he was probably in Perea. This visit to Bethany,
a suburb of Jerusalem, may be that to which Luke pointed in 13:22 (§ 90).

John 11:1-46.

32 to ⁴weep there. Mary therefore, when she came where Jesus was, and saw him, fell down at his feet, saying unto him, Lord, if thou
33 hadst been here, my brother had not died. When Jesus therefore saw her ⁵weeping, and the Jews *also* ⁵weeping which came with her, he
34 ⁷groaned in the spirit, and ⁸was troubled, and said, Where have
35 ye laid him? They say unto him, Lord, come and see. Jesus wept.
36, 37 The Jews therefore said, Behold how he loved him! But some of them said, Could not this man, which opened the eyes of him that
38 was blind, have caused that this man also should not die? Jesus therefore again ⁹groaning in himself cometh to the tomb. Now it was
39 a cave, and a stone lay ¹⁰against it. Jesus saith, Take ye away the stone. Martha, the sister of him that was dead, saith unto him, Lord, by this time he stinketh: for he hath been *dead* four days.
40 Jesus saith unto her, Said I not unto thee, that, if thou believedst,
41 thou shouldest see the glory of God? So they took away the stone. And Jesus lifted up his eyes, and said, Father, I thank thee that thou
42 heardest me. And I know that thou hearest me always: but because of the multitude which standeth around I said it, that they may be-
43 lieve that thou didst send me. And when he had thus spoken, he
44 cried with a loud voice, Lazarus, come forth. He that was dead came forth, bound hand and foot with ¹¹grave-clothes; and his face was bound about with a napkin. Jesus saith unto them, Loose him, and let him go.
45 Many therefore of the Jews, which came to Mary and beheld ¹²that
46 which he did, believed on him. But some of them went away to the Pharisees, and told them the thing which Jesus had done.

1. Gr. *be saved*. 2. That is, *Twin*. 3. Or, *her sister, saying secretly*. 4. Or, *Teacher*. 5. Gr. *wail*. 6. Gr. *wailing*. 7. Or, *was moved with indignation in the spirit*. 8. Gr. *troubled himself*. 9. Or, *being moved with indignation in himself*. 10. Or, *upon*. 11. Or, *grave-bands*. 12. Many ancient authorities read *the things which he did*.

§ 95. THE SANHEDRIN PLOT HIS DEATH, AND HE RETIRES AGAIN.

Jerusalem, and Ephraim in Judea.

John 11:47-54.

47 The chief priests therefore and the Pharisees gathered a council,
48 and said, What do we? for this man doeth many signs. If we let him thus alone, all men will believe on him: and the Romans will come
49 and take away both our place and our nation. But a certain one of them, Caiaphas, being high priest that year, said unto them, Ye
50 know nothing at all, nor do ye take account that it is expedient for you that one man should die for the people, and that the whole nation
51 perish not. Now this he said not of himself: but being high priest
52 that year, he prophesied that Jesus should die for the nation; and not for the nation only, but that he might also gather together into one
53 the children of God that are scattered abroad. So from that day forth they took counsel that they might put him to death.
54 Jesus therefore walked no more openly among the Jews, but departed thence into the country near to the wilderness, into a city called Ephraim; and there he tarried with the disciples.

§ 96. JOURNEYING THROUGH SAMARIA AND GALILEE TOWARD JERUSALEM, HE TEACHES THAT THE MESSIANIC REIGN WILL COME UNEXPECTEDLY.

In Samaria or Galilee.

Luke 17:11–37.

11 And it came to pass, ¹as they were on the way to Jerusalem, that he
12 was passing ²through the midst of Samaria and Galilee.* And as he entered into a certain village, there met him ten men that were
13 lepers, which stood afar off: and they lifted up their voices, saying,
14 Jesus, Master, have mercy on us. And when he saw them, he said unto them, Go and shew yourselves unto the priests. And it came to
15 pass, as they went, they were cleansed. And one of them, when he saw that he was healed, turned back, with a loud voice glorifying
16 God; and he fell upon his face at his feet, giving him thanks: and he
17 was a Samaritan. And Jesus answering said, Were not the ten
18 cleansed? but where are the nine? ³Were there none found that re-
19 turned to give glory to God, save this ⁴stranger? And he said unto him, Arise, and go thy way: thy faith hath ⁶made thee whole.
20 And being asked by the Pharisees, when the kingdom of God cometh, he answered them and said, the kingdom of God cometh not with
21 observation: neither shall they say, Lo, here! or, There! for lo, the kingdom of God is ⁶within you.
22 And he said unto the disciples, The days will come, when ye shall desire to see one of the days of the Son of man, and ye shall not see
23 it. And they shall say to you, Lo, there! Lo, here! go not away, nor
24 follow after *them*: for as the lightning, when it lighteneth out of the one part under the heaven, shineth unto the other part under heaven:
25 so shall the Son of man be ⁷in his day. But first must he suffer many
26 things and be rejected of this generation. And as it came to pass in the days of Noah, even so shall it be also in the days of the Son of
27 man. They ate, they drank, they married, they were given in marriage, until the day that Noah entered the ark, and the flood came,
28 and destroyed them all. Likewise even as it came to pass in the days of Lot; they ate, they drank, they bought, they sold, they planted,
29 they builded: but in the day that Lot went out from Sodom it rained
30 fire and brimstone from heaven, and destroyed them all: after the same manner shall it be in the day that the Son of man is revealed.
31 In that day, he which shall be on the housetop, and his goods in the house, let him not go down to take them away: and let him that is in
32, 33 the field likewise not return back. Remember Lot's wife. Whosoever shall seek to gain his ⁸life shall lose it: but whosoever shall
34 lose *his life* shall ⁹preserve it. I say unto you, In that night there shall be two men on one bed; the one shall be taken and the other
35 shall be left. There shall be two women grinding together; the one

*As Ephraim (§ 95) was pretty certainly in the northern part of Judea, it has been reasonably supposed (Wieseler, Clark, and others) that, when the Passover was approaching, Jesus went from that region northward through Samaria into the southern or southeastern part of Galilee, so as to fall in with the pilgrims going from Galilee through Perea to Jerusalem. We thus again combine Luke's account with that of John in easy agreement. And this explains Luke's mention of Samaria first, which would be strange in describing a journey from Galilee through Samaria to Jerusalem, while the marginal translation, "between Samaria and Galilee," would be obscure and hard to account for.—From this point he is making his final journey to Jerusalem, for the Passover of the crucifixion.

Luke 17:11-37.

37 shall be taken, and the other shall be left¹⁰. And they answering say unto him, Where, Lord? And he said unto them, Where the body is, thither will the ¹¹eagles also be gathered together.

1. Or, *as he was*. 2. Or, *between*. 3. Or, *There were none found..save this stranger*. 4. Or, *alien*. 5. Or, *saved thee*. 6. Or, *in the midst of you*. 7. Some ancient authorities omit *in his day*. 8. Or, *soul*. 9. Or, *save it alive*. 10. Some ancient authorities add ver. 36 *There shall be two men in the field; the one shall be taken, and the other shall be left*. 11. Or, *vultures*.

§ 97. PARABLES OF THE IMPORTUNATE WIDOW, AND OF THE PHARISEE AND THE PUBLICAN.

Luke 18:1-14.

1 And he spake a parable unto them to the end that they ought always
2 to pray, and not to faint; saying, There was in a city a judge, which
3 feared not God, and regarded not man: and there was a widow in that city; and she came oft unto him, saying, ¹Avenge me of mine adver-
4 sary. And he would not for a while: but afterward he said within
5 himself, Though I fear not God, nor regard man: yet because this widow troubleth me, I will avenge her, lest she ²wear me out by her con-
6 tinual coming. And the Lord said, Hear what ³the unrighteous judge
7 saith. And shall not God avenge his elect, which cry to him day and
8 night, and he is longsuffering over them? I say unto you, that he will avenge them speedily. Howbeit when the Son of man cometh, shall he find ⁴faith on the earth?
9 And he spake also this parable unto certain which trusted in them-
10 selves that they were righteous, and set ⁵all others at nought: Two men went up into the temple to pray; the one a Pharisee, and the other
11 a publican. The Pharisee stood and prayed thus with himself, God, I thank thee, that I am not as the rest of men, extortioners, unjust,
12 adulterers, or even as this publican. I fast twice in the week; I give
13 tithes of all that I get. But the publican, standing afar off, would not lift up so much as his eyes unto heaven, but smote his breast, saying,
14 God, ⁶be merciful to me ⁷a sinner. I say unto you, This man went down to his house justified rather than the other: for every one that exalteth himself shall be humbled; but he that humbleth himself shall be exalted.

1. Or, *Do me justice of*: and so in ver. 5, 7, 8. 2. Gr. *bruise*. 3. Gr. *the judge of unrighteousness*. 4. Or, *the faith*. 5. Gr. *the rest*. 6. Or, *he propitiated*. 7. Or, *the sinner*.

§ 98. GOING FROM GALILEE THROUGH PEREA,* HE TEACHES CONCERNING DIVORCE.

Perea.

Matt. 19:1-12.	Mark 10:1-12.
1 And it came to pass, when Jesus	1 And he arose from thence, and

*Matthew expressly states that he went from Galilee through Perea, and soon afterwards carries him forward to Jericho and Jerusalem. (Comp. Mark also.) Yet he says that Jesus did this when he had finished the parable of the unforgiving servant, which we have placed nearly 6 months earlier (§71). Luke here presently agrees with Matthew and Mark, and they go on together to the end, while heretofore Matthew and Mark have given us nothing since Jesus went to the Feast of Tabernacles. In one way or another we must suppose quite a break in their narrative. See the author's commentary on Matthew 19:1, and compare note on §75.

Matt. 19:1-12.

had finished these words, he departed from Galilee, and came into the borders of Judea beyond
2 Jordan; and great multitudes followed him; and he healed them there.
3 And there came unto him ¹Pharisees, tempting him, and saying, Is it lawful *for a man* to put away his wife for every
4 cause? And he answered and said, Have ye not read, that he which ²made *them* from the beginning
5 made them male and female, and said, For this cause shall a man leave his father and mother, and shall cleave to his wife; and the twain shall become one flesh?
6 So that they are no more twain, but one flesh. What therefore God hath joined together, let not man put asunder.
7 They say unto him, Why then did Moses command to give a bill of divorce-
8 ment, and to put *her* away? He saith unto them, Moses for your hardness of heart suffered you to put away your wives: but from the beginning it hath not been
9 so. And I say unto you, Whosoever shall put away his wife, ³except for fornication, and shall marry another, committeth adultery: ⁴and he that marrieth her when she is put away committeth
10 adultery. The disciples say unto him, If the case of the man is so with his wife, it is not expedient
11 to marry. But he said unto them, All men cannot receive this saying, but they to whom
12 it is given. For there are eunuchs which were so born from their mother's womb: and there are eunuchs, which were made eunuchs by men: and there are

Mark 10:1-12.

cometh into the borders of Judea and beyond Jordan: and multitudes come together unto him again; and, as he was wont, he taught them again.
2 And there came unto him Pharisees, and asked him, Is it lawful for a man to put away *his*
3 wife? tempting him. And he answered and said unto them, What did Moses command you?
4 And they said, Moses suffered to write a bill of divorcement, and
5 to put her away. But Jesus said unto them, For your hardness of heart he wrote you this com-
6 mandment. But from the beginning of the creation, Male and
7 female made he them. For this cause shall a man leave his father and mother, ⁵and shall cleave to
8 his wife; and the twain shall become one flesh: so that they are no more twain, but one flesh.
9 What therefore God hath joined together, let not man put asunder.
10 And in the house the disciples asked him again of this matter.

11 And he saith unto them, Whosoever shall put away his wife, and marry another, committeth
12 adultery against her: and if she herself shall put away her husband, and marry another, she committeth adultery.

Matt. 19:1-12.

eunuchs, which made themselves eunuchs for the kingdom of heaven's sake. He that is able to receive it, let him receive it.

1. Many authorities, some ancient, insert *the*. 2. Some ancient authorities read *created*. 3. Some ancient authorities read *saving for the cause of fornication, maketh her an adulteress;* as in ch. 5:32, § 43. 4. The following words, to the end of the verse, are omitted by some ancient authorities. 5. Some ancient authorities omit *and shall cleave to his wife*.

§ 99. He Blesses Some Infant Children, and Teaches that Subjects of the Messianic Reign Must be Childlike. (Comp. § 70.)

Perea.

Matt. 19:13-15.	Mark 10:13-16.	Luke 18:15-17.*
13 Then were there brought unto him little children, that he should lay his hands on them, and pray: and the disciples rebuked them.	13 And they brought unto him little children, that he should touch them: and the disciples rebuked 14 them. But when Jesus saw it, he was moved with indignation, and said unto them, Suffer the little children to come unto me; forbid them not: for of such is the kingdom 15 of God. Verily I say unto you, Whosoever shall not receive the kingdom of God as a little child, he shall in no wise en-16 ter therein. And he took them in his arms, and blessed them, laying his hands upon them.	15 And they brought unto him also their babes, that he should touch them: but when the disciples saw it, they rebuked them. 16 But Jesus called them unto him, saying, Suffer the little children to come unto me, and forbid them not: for of such is the kingdom of God. 17 Verily I say unto you, Whosoever shall not receive the kingdom of God as a little child, he shall in no wise enter therein.
14 But Jesus said, Suffer the little children, and forbid them not, to come unto me: for of such is the kingdom of heaven.		
15 And he laid his hands on them, and departed thence.		

*From this point Matthew, Mark and Luke will be parallel more frequently than they were even during the great ministry in Galilee.

§100. THE RICH YOUNG RULER, AND THE PERILS OF RICHES. THE REWARDS OF FORSAKING ALL TO FOLLOW THE MESSIAH (COMP. §72) WILL BE GREAT, BUT WILL BE SOVEREIGN. (PARABLE OF THE LABORERS IN THE VINEYARD.)

In Perea.

Matt. 19:16 to 20:16.	Mark 10:17-31.	Luke 18:18-30.
	17 And as he was going forth *into the way, there ran one to him, and kneeled to him, and asked him, Good ²Master, what shall I do that I may inherit eternal life? And Jesus said unto him, Why callest thou me good? none is good save one, *even* God.	18 And a certain ruler asked him, saying, Good ²Master, what shall I do to inherit eternal life?
16 And behold, one came to him and said, ¹Master², what good thing shall I do that I may have eternal 17 life? And he said unto him, ³Why askest thou me concerning that which is good? One there is who is good: but if thou wouldest enter into life, keep the 18 commandments. He saith unto him, Which? And Jesus said, Thou shalt not kill, Thou shalt not commit adultery, Thou shalt not steal, Thou shalt not bear 19 false witness, Honour thy father and thy mother: and, Thou shalt love thy neigh-20 bour as thyself. The young man saith unto him, All these things have I observed: what lack I 21 yet? Jesus said unto him, If thou wouldest be perfect, go, sell that thou hast, and give to the poor, and thou shalt have treasure in heaven: and come, follow me. 22 But when the young man		19 And Jesus said unto him, Why callest thou me good? none is good save one, God.
	19 Thou knowest the commandments,	20 Thou knowest the commandments,
	Do not kill, Do not commit adultery, Do not steal, Do not bear false witness, Do not defraud, Honour thy father and mother.	Do not commit adultery, Do not kill, Do not steal, Do not bear false witness, Honour thy father and mother.
	20 And he said unto him, ²Master, all these things have I observed 21 from my youth. And Jesus looking upon him loved him, and said unto him, One thing thou lackest: go, sell whatsoever thou hast, and give to the poor, and thou shalt have treasure in heaven: and come, 22 follow me. But his countenance fell at	21 And he said, All these things have I observed from my 22 youth up. And when Jesus heard it, he said unto him, One thing thou lackest yet: sell all that thou hast, and distribute unto the poor, and thou shalt have treasure in heaven: and come, follow me. 23 But when he heard these things, he be-

Matt. 19:16 to 20:16.	Mark 10:17-31.	Luke 18:18-30.
heard the saying, he went away sorrowful: for he was one that had great possessions. 23 And Jesus said unto his disciples, Verily I say unto you, It is hard for a rich man to enter into the kingdom of heaven. 24 And again I say unto you, It is easier for a camel to go through a needle's eye, than for a rich man to enter into the kingdom 25 of God. And when the disciples heard it, they were astonished exceedingly, saying, Who then 26 can be saved? And Jesus looking upon *them* said to them, With men this is impossible; but with God all things are 27 possible. Then answered Peter and said unto him, Lo, we have left all, and followed thee; what then shall 28 we have? And Jesus said unto them, Verily I say unto you, that ye which have followed me, in the regeneration when the Son of man shall sit on the throne of	the saying, and he went away sorrowful: for he was one that had great possessions. 23 And Jesus looked round about, and saith unto his disciples, How hardly shall they that have riches enter into the kingdom of God! 24 And the disciples were amazed at his words. But Jesus answereth again, and saith unto them, Children, how hard is it ⁸for them that trust in riches to enter into the kingdom 25 of God! It is easier for a camel to go through a needle's eye, than for a rich man to enter into the kingdom of God. 26 And they were astonished exceedingly, saying ¹⁰unto him, Then who can 27 be saved? Jesus looking upon them saith, With men it is impossible, but not with God: for all things are possible with God. 28 Peter began to say unto him, Lo, we have left all, and followed thee. 29 Jesus said, Verily I say unto you,	came exceeding sorrowful; for he was very rich. 24 And Jesus seeing him said, How hardly shall they that have riches enter into the kingdom of God! 25 For it is easier for a camel to enter in through a needle's eye, than for a rich man to enter into the kingdom of God. 26 And they that heard it said, Then who can be saved? 27 But he said, The things that are impossible with men are possible with 28 God. And Peter said, Lo, we have left ¹²our own, and followed thee. 29 And he said unto them, Verily I say unto you,

Matt. 19:16 to 20:16.	Mark 10:17–31.	Luke 17:18–30.
his glory, ye also shall sit upon twelve thrones, judging the twelve tribes of Israel. 29 And every one that hath left houses, or brethren, or sisters, or father, or mother,⁴ or children, or lands, for my name's sake, shall receive ⁵a hundred fold,	There is no man that hath left house, or brethren, or sisters, or mother, or father, or children, or lands, for my sake, and for the gospel's 30 sake, but he shall receive a hundredfold now in this time, houses, and brethren, and sisters, and mothers, and children, and lands, with persecutions; and in the ¹¹world to come eternal life.	There is no man that hath left house, or wife, or brethren, or parents, or children, for the kingdom of God's sake, 30 who shall not receive manifold more in this time,
and shall inherit eternal life. 30 But many shall be last *that are* first; and first *that are* last.	31 But many *that are* first shall be last; and the last first.	and in the ¹¹world to come eternal life.

20 For the kingdom of heaven is like unto a man that is a householder, which went out early in the morning to hire labourers into his vine-
2 yard. And when he had agreed with the labourers for a ⁶penny a
3 day, he sent them into his vineyard. And he went out about the third
4 hour and saw others standing in the marketplace idle; and to them he said, Go ye also into the vineyard, and whatsoever is right I will give
5 you. And they went their way. Again he went out about the sixth
6 and the ninth hour, and did likewise. And about the eleventh *hour* he went out, and found others standing: and he saith unto them,
7 Why stand ye here all the day idle? They say unto him, Because no man hath hired us. He saith unto them, Go ye also into the vine-
8 yard. And when even was come, the lord of the vineyard saith unto his steward, Call the labourers, and pay them their hire, beginning
9 from the last unto the first. And when they came that *were hired*
10 about the eleventh hour, they received every man a ⁶penny. And when the first came, they supposed that they would receive more; and
11 they likewise received every man a ⁶penny. And when they received
12 it, they murmured against the householder, saying, These last have spent *but* one hour, and thou hast made them equal unto us, which
13 have borne the burden of the day and the ⁷scorching heat. But he answered and said to one of them, Friend, I do thee no wrong: didst
14 not thou agree with me for a ⁶penny? Take up that which is thine, and go thy way; it is my will to give unto this last, even as unto thee.
15 Is it not lawful for me to do what I will with mine own? or is thine

Matt. 20:16.

16 eye evil, because I am good? So the last shall be first, and the first last.

1. Some ancient authorities read *Good Master.* See Mark 10:17; Luke 18:18. 2. Or, *Teacher.* 3. Some ancient authorities read *Why callest thou me good? None is good save one, even God.* See Mark 10:18; Luke 18:19. 4. Many ancient authorities add or *wife:* as in Luke 18:29. 5. Some ancient authorities read *manifold.* 6. The Roman denarius, about seventeen cents of our money. 7. Or, *hot wind.* 8. Or, *on his way.* 9. Some ancient authorities omit *for them that trust in riches.* 10. Many ancient authorities read *among themselves.* 11. Or, *age.* 12. Or, *our own homes.*

§101. JESUS FORETELLS TO THE DISCIPLES HIS DEATH AND RESURRECTION (COMP. §65, 66, 67), AND REBUKES THE SELFISH AMBITION OF JAMES AND JOHN.

Probably in Perea.

Matt. 20:17-28.	Mark 10:32-45.	Luke 18:31-34.
17 And as Jesus was going up to Jerusalem,	32 And they were in the way, going up to Jerusalem*; and Jesus was going before them: and they were amazed: ⁸and they that followed were afraid. And	
he took the twelve disciples apart, and in the way he said unto them,	he took again the twelve, and began to tell them the things that were to happen unto him, *saying,*	31 And he took unto him the twelve, and said unto them, Behold, we go up to Jerusalem, and all the things that are written ⁶by the prophets shall be accomplished unto the Son of man.
18 Behold, we go up to Jerusalem: and the Son of man shall be delivered unto the chief priests and scribes; and they shall condemn him 19 to death, and shall deliver him unto the Gentiles to mock,	33 Behold, we go up to Jerusalem: and the Son of man shall be delivered unto the chief priests and the scribes; and they shall condemn him to death, and shall deliver him unto 34 the Gentiles: and they shall mock him,	32 For he shall be delivered up unto the Gentiles, and shall be mocked, and shamefully entreated, and spit upon:
and to scourge, and to crucify; and the third day he shall	and shall spit upon him, and shall scourge him, and shall kill him; and after three days he	33 and they shall scourge and kill him: and the third day he shall rise a-

* He left Galilee in §96, crossing the Jordan into Perea, probably in company with many Jews from Galilee (who regularly went this way to Jerusalem), and will now soon cross the river again and reach Jericho (§102).

Matt. 20:17-28.	Mark 10:32-45.	Luke 18:31-34.
be raised up.	shall rise again.	34 gain. And they understood none of these things; and this saying was hid from them, and they perceived not the things that were said.

20 Then came to him the mother of the sons of Zebedee with her sons, worshipping *him*, and asking a certain thing of him.

21 And he said unto her, What wouldest thou? She said unto him, Command that these my two sons may sit, one on thy right hand, and one on thy left hand, in thy king-

22 dom. But Jesus answered and said, Ye know not what ye ask. Are ye able to drink the cup that I am about to drink? They say unto him, We are able.

23 He saith unto them, My cup indeed ye shall drink: but to sit on my right hand, and on *my* left hand, is not mine to give, but *it is for them* for whom it hath been prepared of

24 my Father. And when the ten heard it, they were moved with indignation concerning the two

25 brethren. But Jesus called them unto him, and said, Ye know that the rulers of the Gentiles lord it over them, and their great ones exercise authority over them.

26 Not so shall it be among you; but whosoever would become great among you shall be your [1]minis-

27 ter; and whosoever would be first among you shall be your [2]ser-

28 vant: even as the Son of man came not to be ministered unto, but to minister, and to give his life a ransom for many.

35 And there come near unto him James and John, the sons of Zebedee, saying unto him, [4]Master, we would that thou shouldest do for us whatsoever we shall ask of

36 thee. And he said unto them, What would ye that I should do

37 for you? And they said unto him, Grant unto us that we may sit, one on thy right hand, and one on *thy* left hand, in thy glory.

38 But Jesus said unto them, Ye know not what ye ask. Are ye able to drink the cup that I drink? or to be baptized with the baptism that I am baptized with?

39 And they said unto him, We are able. And Jesus said unto them, The cup that I drink ye shall drink; and with the baptism that I am baptized withal shall ye be

40 baptized: but to sit on my right hand or on *my* left hand is not mine to give: but *it is for them* for whom it hath been prepared.

41 And when the ten heard it, they began to be moved with indignation concerning James and John.

42 And Jesus called them to him, and saith unto them, Ye know that they which are accounted to rule over the Gentiles lord it over them: and their great ones exercise authority over them. But it

43 is not so among you: but whosoever would become great among

44 you, shall be your [1]minister: and whosoever would be first among

45 you, shall be [2]servant of all. For verily the Son of man came not to be ministered unto, but to minister, and to give his life a ransom for many.

1. Or, *servant*. 2. Gr. *bond-servant*. 3. Or, *but some as they followed were afraid*. 4. Or, *Teacher*. 5. Or, *through*.

§102. BLIND BARTIMÆUS AND HIS COMPANION HEALED.
At Jericho.

Matt. 20:29-34.	Mark 10:46-52.	Luke 18:35-43.
29 And as they went out from Jericho, a great multitude followed him.	46 And they come to Jericho: and as he went out from Jericho, with his disciples and a great multitude, the son of Timæus, Bartimæus, a blind beggar, was sitting by the way side.	35 And it came to pass, as he drew nigh unto Jericho,
30 And behold, two *blind men sitting by the way side,		a certain blind man sat by the way side begging:
		36 and hearing a multitude going by, he inquired what
when they heard that Jesus was passing by, cried out, saying, Lord, have mercy on us, thou 31 Son of David. And the multitude rebuked them, that they should hold their peace: but they cried out the more, saying, Lord, have mercy on us, thou 32 son of David. And Jesus stood still, and called them,	47 And when he heard that it was Jesus of Nazareth, he began to cry out, and say, Jesus, thou son of David, have mercy 48 cy on me. And many rebuked him, that he should hold his peace: but he cried out the more a great deal, Thou son of David, have mercy on me. 49 And Jesus stood still, and said, call ye him. And they call the blind man, saying unto him, Be of good cheer: rise, he call- 50 eth thee. And he, casting away his garment, sprang up, and came to Jesus. 51 And Jesus answered him, and said, What wilt thou that I should do unto thee? And the blind man	37 this meant. And they told him, that Jesus of Nazareth 38 passeth by. And he cried, saying, Jesus, thou son of David, have mercy on me. 39 And they that went before rebuked him, that he should hold his peace: but he cried out the more a great deal, Thou son of David, have mercy 40 on me. And Jesus stood, and commanded him to be brought unto him:
and said, What will ye that I should do unto you? 33 They say unto him,		and when he was come near, he 41 asked him, What wilt thou that I should do unto thee? And he said, Lord,

*Matthew mentions two blind men, while Mark and Luke describe one, probably the more conspicuous one, comp. on §53.—The discrepancy as to place, "as he went out from Jericho," "as he drew nigh unto Jericho," is best explained by the recent suggestion that the healing occurred after he left the old Jericho, and as he was approaching the new Jericho which Herod the Great had built at some distance away. An older, and also possible explanation was that the blind men made application when he was approaching the city, but were not then healed, and only when he had left the city were they healed. (Comp. Matt. 15:22 ff., §61, and Mark 8:22 f., §65.)

Matt. 20:29-34.	Mark 10:46-52.	Luke 18:35-43.
Lord, that our eyes 34 may be opened. And Jesus being moved with compassion, touched their eyes: and straightway they received their sight, and followed him.	said unto him, ¹Rabboni, that I may re-52 ceive my sight. And Jesus said unto him, Go thy way; thy faith hath ²made thee whole. And straightway he received his sight, and followed him in the way.	that I may receive 42 my sight. And Jesus said unto him, Receive thy sight: thy faith hath ²made 43 thee whole. And immediately he received his sight, and followed him, glorifying God: and all the people, when they saw it, gave praise unto God.

1. See John 20:16.   2. Or, *saved thee*.

§103. JESUS VISITS ZACCHÆUS, AND SPEAKS THE PARABLE OF THE POUNDS,* AND SETS OUT FOR JERUSALEM.

Jericho.

Luke 19:1-28.

1, 2 And he entered and was passing through Jericho. And behold, a man called by name Zacchæus; and he was a chief publican, and he
3 was rich. And he sought to see Jesus who he was; and could not for
4 the crowd, because he was little of stature. And he ran on before, and climbed up into a sycomore tree to see him: for he was to pass
5 that way. And when Jesus came to the place, he looked up, and said unto him, Zacchæus, make haste, and come down; for to-day I must
6 abide at thy house. And he made haste, and came down, and received
7 him joyfully. And when they saw it, they all murmured, saying, He
8 is gone in to lodge with a man that is a sinner. And Zacchæus stood, and said unto the Lord, Behold, Lord, the half of my goods I give to the poor; and if I have wrongfully exacted aught of any man, I restore
9 fourfold. And Jesus said unto him, To-day is salvation come to this
10 house, forasmuch as he also is a son of Abraham. For the Son of man came to seek and to save that which was lost.
11 And as they heard these things, he added and spake a parable, because he was nigh to Jerusalem, and *because* they supposed that the
12 kingdom of God was immediately to appear. He said therefore, A certain nobleman went into a far country, to receive for himself a
13 kingdom, and to return. And he called ten ¹servants of his, and gave them ten ²pounds, and said unto them, Trade ye *herewith* till I come.
14 But his citizens hated him, and sent an ambassage after him, saying,
15 We will not that this man reign over us. And it came to pass, when he was come back again, having received the kingdom, that he commanded these ¹servants, unto whom he had given the money, to be called to him, that he might know what they had gained by trading.
16 And the first came before him, saying, Lord, thy pound hath made

*The similar parable of the Talents was given several days later. See §116. On this first occasion the illustration has a specific design (ver. 11 f.), which will not appear on the second.

Luke 19:1-28.

17 ten pounds more. And he said unto him, Well done, thou good [3]servant: because thou wast found faithful in a very little, have thou au-
18 thority over ten cities. And the second came, saying, Thy pound,
19 Lord, hath made five pounds. And he said unto him also, Be thou
20 also over five cities. And [4]another came, saying, Lord, behold, here
21 is thy pound, which I kept laid up in a napkin: for I feared thee, because thou art an austere man: thou takest up that thou layedst not
22 down, and reapest that thou didst not sow. He saith unto him, Out of thine own mouth will I judge thee, thou wicked [3]servant. Thou knewest that I am an austere man, taking up that I laid not down,
23 and reaping that I did not sow; then wherefore gavest thou not my money into the bank, and [5]I at my coming should have required it
24 with interest? And he said unto them that stood by, Take away from
25 him the pound, and give it unto him that hath the ten pounds. And
26 they said unto him, Lord, he hath ten pounds. I say unto you, that unto every one that hath shall be given: but from him that hath not,
27 even that which he hath shall be taken away from him. Howbeit these mine enemies, which would not that I should reign over them, bring hither, and slay them before me.
28 And when he had thus spoken, he went on before, going up to Jerusalem.

1. Gr. *bond-servants*. 2. *Mina*, here translated a pound, is equal to one hundred drachmas. See ch. 15:8. $103. 3. Gr. *bond-servant*. 4. Gr. *the other*. 5. Or, *I should have gone and required*.

PART VII.

LAST WEEK OF OUR LORD'S MINISTRY, AND HIS CRUCIFIXION.

Spring of A.D. 30 (or A.D 29).*

§104. JESUS ARRIVES AT BETHANY,† NEAR JERUSALEM.

Friday afternoon.

John 11:55 to 12:1, and 12:9-11.

55 Now the passover of the Jews was at hand: and many went up to Jerusalem out of the country before the passover, to purify them-
56 selves. They sought therefore for Jesus, and spake one with another, as they stood in the temple, What think ye? That he will not come
57 to the feast? Now the chief priests and the Pharisees had given commandment, that, if any man knew where he was, he should shew it, that they might take him.
1 Jesus therefore six days before the passover came to Bethany, where Lazarus was, whom Jesus raised from the dead.
9 The common people therefore of the Jews learned that he was there: and they came, not for Jesus' sake only, but that they might see Laz-
10 arus also, whom he raised from the dead. But the chief priests took
11 counsel that they might put Lazarus also to death: because that by reason of him many of the Jews went away, and believed on Jesus.

In §105–116 we have the Saviour's movements and teachings on Sunday, Monday and Tuesday—the close of his public ministry, except the little that he said during the Jewish and Roman trial. All of his teaching thereafter will be given to his disciples.

§105. HIS TRIUMPHAL ENTRY INTO JERUSALEM AS THE MESSIAH.

From Bethany to Jerusalem and back (*Sunday*).

Matt. 21:1-11 and 14-17.	Mark 11:1-11.	Luke 19:29-44.	John 12:12-19.
1 And when they drew nigh unto Jerusalem, and came unto Beth-	1 And when they draw nigh unto Jerusalem, unto Bethphage and	29 And it came to pass, when he drew nigh unto Bethphage and	

*If the feast of John 5:1 was a Passover, and so his ministry lasted over three years, then his death was pretty certainly in A.D. 30; otherwise in A.D. 29. (Comp. ou §7.)
†Compare former visits to this Bethany, §82, 94, and see also below, §117.

AND HIS CRUCIFIXION.

Matt. 21:1-11 and 14-17.	Mark 11:1-11.	Luke 19:29-44.	John 12:12-19.
phage, unto the mount of Olives, then Jesus sent two 2 disciples, saying unto them, Go into the village that is over against you, and straightway ye shall find an ass tied, and a colt with her: loose *them*, and bring *them* unto me.	Bethany, at the mount of Olives, he sendeth two of his 2 disciples, and saith unto them, Go your way into the village that is over against you, and straightway as ye enter into it, ye shall find a colt tied, whereon no man ever yet sat: loose him, and bring him.	Bethany, at the mount that is called *the mount* of Olives, he 30 sent two of the disciples, saying, Go your way into the village over against *you;* in the which as ye enter ye shall find a colt tied, whereon no man ever yet sat: loose him, and bring him.	
3 And if any one say aught unto you, ye shall say, The Lord hath need of them; and straightway he will send them.	3 And if any one say unto you, Why do ye this? say ye, The Lord hath need of him; and straightway ²he will send him ᵇback 4 hither. And	31 And if any one ask you, Why do ye loose him? thus shall ye say, The Lord hath need of him.	
6 And the disciples went, and did even as Jesus appointed them,	they went away, and found a colt tied at the door without in the open street: and they 5 loose him. And certain of them that stood there said unto them, What do ye, loosing the 6 colt? And they said unto them even as Jesus had said: and they let them	32 And they that were sent went away, and found even as he had said unto them. And 33 as they were loosing the colt, the owners thereof said unto them, Why loose ye the 34 colt? And they said, The Lord hath need of 35 him. And they brought	12 On the morrow ᵒa great multitude that had come to the feast, when they heard that Jesus was coming to Jerusalem, 13 took the branches of the palm trees, and went forth to meet him, and cried out, Hosanna: Blessed
7 and brought the ass and the colt, and put on them their	7 go. And they bring the colt unto Jesus, and cast on him their gar-	him to Jesus: and they throw their garments upon the colt, and set	*is* he that cometh in the name

Matt. 21:1-11 and 14-17.	Mark 11:1-11.	Luke 19:29-44.	John 12:12-19.
garments, and he sat thereon. 4 Now this is come to pass, that it might be fulfilled which was spoken ¹by the prophet, saying, 5 Tell ye the daughter of Zion, Behold, thy King cometh unto thee, Meek, and riding upon an ass, And upon a colt the foal of an ass. 8 And the most part of the multitude spread their garments in the way; and others cut branches from the trees, and spread them in 9 the way. And the multitudes that went before him, and that followed, cried, saying, Hosanna to the son of David: Blessed *is* he that cometh in the name of the Lord; Hosanna in the highest.	ments; and he sat upon him. 8 And many spread their garments upon the way; and others ⁴branches, which they had cut from 9 the fields. And they that went before, and they that followed, cried, Hosanna, Blessed *is* he that cometh in the name of the Lord: 10 Blessed *is* the kingdom that cometh, *the kingdom* of our father David: Hosanna in the highest.	Jesus thereon. 36 And as he went, they spread their garments in the 37 way. And as he was now drawing nigh, *even* at the descent of the mount of Olives the whole multitude of the disciples began to rejoice and praise God with a loud voice for all the ⁵mighty works which they had seen; 38 saying, Blessed *is* the King that cometh in the name of the Lord: peace in heaven, and glory in the highest.	of the Lord, even the King 14 of Israel. And Jesus, having found a young ass, sat thereon; as it is 15 written, Fear not, daughter of Zion: behold thy King cometh, sitting on an ass's colt. 16 These things understood not his disciples at the first: but when Jesus was glorified, then remembered they that these things were written of him, and that they had done these things unto him. The multitude therefore 17 that was with him when he called Lazarus out of the tomb, and raised him from the dead, bare witness. 18 For this cause also the multitude went and met him, for that they heard that he had done this sign. 19 The Pharisees therefore said among themselves, ¹⁰Behold how ye prevail nothing: lo, the world is gone after him.

Luke 19:39-44.

39 And some of the Pharisees from the multitude
40 said unto him, ⁶Master, rebuke thy disciples. And he answered and said, I tell you that, if these shall hold their peace, the stones will cry out.
41 And when he drew nigh, he saw the city and wept
42 over it, saying, ⁷If thou hadst known in this day, even thou, the things which belong unto peace! but
43 now they are hid from thine eyes. For the days shall come upon thee, when thine enemies shall cast up a ⁸bank about thee, and compass thee round, and
44 keep thee in on every side, and shall dash thee to the ground, and thy children within thee; and they shall not leave in thee one stone upon another; because thou knewest not the time of thy visitation.

Matt. 21:1-11 and 14-17.

10 And when he was come into Jerusalem, all the city was stirred,
11 saying, Who is this? And the multitudes said, This is the prophet, Jesus, from Nazareth
14 of Galilee. And the blind and the lame came to him in the temple: and he healed them.
15 But when the chief priests and the scribes saw the wonderful things that he did, and the children that were crying in the temple and saying, Hosanna to the son of David; they were
16 moved with indignation, and said unto him, Hearest thou what these are saying? And Jesus saith unto them, Yea: did ye never read, Out of the mouth of babes and sucklings thou hast
17 perfected praise? And he left them, and went forth out of the city to Bethany, and lodged there.

Mark 11:1-11.

11 And he entered into Jerusalem,

into the temple;

and when he had looked round about upon all things, it being now eventide, he went out unto Bethany with the twelve.

---

1. Or, *through.* 2. Gr. *sendeth.* 3. Or, *again.* 4. Gr. *layers of leaves.* 5. Gr. *powers.* 6. Or, *Teacher.* 7. Or, *O that thou hadst known.* 8. Gr. *palisade.* 9. Some ancient authorities read *the common people.* 10. Or, *Ye behold.*

§ 106. THE BARREN FIG TREE CURSED, AND THE SECOND CLEANSING OF THE TEMPLE. (COMP. §21, A.)

Bethany and Jerusalem (*Monday*).

Matt. 21:18,19, and 12,13.	Mark 11:12–18.	Luke 19:45–48.
18 Now in the morning as he returned to the city, he hungered. 19 And seeing a 'fig tree by the way side, he came to it and found nothing thereon, but leaves only; and he saith unto it, Let there be no fruit from thee henceforward for ever.	12 And on the morrow, when they were come out from Bethany, he hungered. 13 And seeing a fig tree afar off having leaves, he came, if haply he might find anything thereon: and when he came to it, he found nothing but leaves; for it was not the season of 14 figs. And he answered and said unto it, No man eat fruit from thee henceforward for ever. And his disciples heard it.	
12 And Jesus entered into the temple ²of God, and cast out all them that sold and bought in the temple, and overthrew the tables of the money-changers, and the seats of them that sold the doves;	15 And they come to Jerusalem: and he entered into the temple, and began to cast out them that sold and them that bought in the temple, and overthrew the tables of the money-changers, and the seats of them that sold the 16 doves; and he would not suffer that any man should carry a vessel through the 17 temple. And he taught, and said unto them, Is it not written, My house shall be called a house of prayer for all the nations? but ye have made it a den of	45 And he entered into the temple, and began to cast out them that sold, 46 saying unto them, It is written, And my house shall be a house of prayer: but ye have made it a den of robbers. 47 And he was teach-
13 and he saith unto them, It is written, My house shall be called a house of prayer: but ye make it a den of robbers.		

AND HIS CRUCIFIXION. 145

Mark 11:12-18.	Luke 19:45-48.
18 robbers. And the chief priests and the scribes heard it, and sought how they might destroy him: for they feared him, for all the multitude was astonished at his teaching.	ing daily in the temple. But the chief priests and the scribes and the principal men of the people sought to destroy 48 him: and they could not find what they might do; for the people all hung upon him, listening.

1. Or, *a single*. 2. Some ancient authorities omit *of God*.

§ 107. SOME GREEKS WISH TO SEE JESUS, AND HE FORETELLS THAT BY BEING "LIFTED UP" HE WILL DRAW ALL MEN TO HIM.

Jerusalem.

John 12:20-50.

20 Now there were certain Greeks among those that went up to worship
21 at the feast: these therefore came to Philip, which was of Bethsaida
22 of Galilee, and asked him saying, Sir, we would see Jesus. Philip cometh and telleth Andrew: Andrew cometh, and Philip, and they tell
23 Jesus. And Jesus answereth them, saying, The hour is come, that
24 the Son of man should be glorified. Verily, verily, I say unto you, Except a grain of wheat fall into the earth and die, it abideth by itself
25 alone; but if it die, it beareth much fruit. He that loveth his ¹life loseth it; and he that hateth his ¹life in this world shall keep it unto
26 life eternal. If any man serve me, let him follow me: and where I am, there shall also my servant be: if any man serve me, him will the
27 Father honour. Now is my soul troubled; and what shall I say? Father, save me from this ²hour. But for this cause came I unto this
28 hour. Father, glorify thy name. There came therefore a voice out of heaven, *saying*, I have both glorified it, and will glorify it again.
29 The multitude therefore, that stood by, and heard it, said that it had
30 thundered: others said, An angel hath spoken to him. Jesus answered and said, This voice hath not come for my sake, but for your sakes.
31 Now is ³the judgement of this world: now shall the prince of this
32 world be cast out. And I, if I be lifted up ⁴from the earth, will draw
33 all men unto myself. But this he said, signifying by what manner of
34 death he should die. The multitude therefore answered him, We have heard out of the law that the Christ abideth for ever: and how sayest thou, The Son of man must be lifted up? who is this Son of man?
35 Jesus therefore said unto them, Yet a little while is the light ⁵among you. Walk while ye have the light, that darkness overtake you not: and he that walketh in the darkness knoweth not whither he goeth.
36 While ye have the light, believe on the light, that ye may become sons of light.

These things spake Jesus, and he departed and ⁶hid himself from
37 them. But though he had done so many signs before them, yet they

John 12:20-50.

38 believed not on him: that the word of Isaiah the prophet might be fulfilled, which he spake,
Lord, who hath believed our report?
And to whom hath the arm of the Lord been revealed?
39 For this cause they could not believe, for that Isaiah said again,
40 He hath blinded their eyes, and he hardened their heart;
Lest they should see with their eyes, and perceive with their heart,
And should turn,
And I should heal them.
41 These things said Isaiah, because he saw his glory: and he spake of
42 him. Nevertheless even of the rulers many believed on him; but because of the Pharisees they did not confess ⁷it, lest they should be put
43 out of the synagogue; for they loved the glory of men more than the glory of God.
44 And Jesus cried and said, He that believeth on me, believeth not on
45 me, but on him that sent me. And he that beholdeth me beholdeth
46 him that sent me. I am come a light into the world, that whosoever
47 believeth on me may not abide in the darkness. And if any man hear my sayings, and keep them not, I judge him not: for I came not to
48 judge the world, but to save the world. He that rejecteth me, and receiveth not my sayings, hath one that judgeth him: the word that
49 I spake, the same shall judge him in the last day. For I spake not from myself; but the Father which sent me, he hath given me a com-
50 mandment, what I should say, and what I should speak. And I know that his commandment is life eternal: the things therefore which I speak, even as the Father hath said unto me, so I speak.

1. Or, *soul.* 2. Or, *hour?* 3. Or, *a judgement.* 4. Or, *out of.* 5. Or, *in.* 6. Or, *was hidden from them.* 7. Or, *him.*

§108. THE BARREN FIG-TREE FOUND TO HAVE WITHERED.

On the way from Bethany to Jerusalem. (*Tuesday.**)

Matt. 21:19-22.	Mark 11:19-25.	Luke 21:37, 38.
19 And immediately the fig tree withered 20 away. And when the disciples saw it, they marvelled, saying, How did the fig tree immediately 21 wither away? And Jesus answered and said unto them, Verily I say unto you, If ye have faith, and	19 And ¹every evening ²he went forth 20 out of the city. And as they passed by in the morning, they saw the fig tree withered away from 21 the roots. And Peter calling to remembrance saith unto him, Rabbi, behold, the fig tree which thou cursedst is withered away. 22 And Jesus answer-	37 And every day he was teaching in the temple; and every night he went out, and lodged in the mount that is called *the mount* of Olives. 38 And all the people came early in the morning to him in the temple, to hear him.

*We have a larger mass of our Lord's teaching for this day (§108—116) than for any other single day of his ministry. Another very busy day was §48—53.

Matt. 21:19-22.	Mark 11:19-26.
doubt not, ye shall not only do what is done to the fig tree, but even if ye shall say unto this mountain, Be thou taken up and cast into the sea, it shall be done. 22 And all things, whatsoever ye shall ask in prayer, believing, ye shall receive.	ing saith unto them, Have faith in God. 23 Verily I say unto you, Whosoever shall say unto this mountain, Be thou taken up and cast into the sea; and shall not doubt in his heart, but shall believe that what he saith cometh to pass; he shall have it. 24 Therefore I say unto you, All things whatsoever ye pray and ask for, believe that ye have received them, and ye shall 25 have them. And whensoever ye stand praying, forgive, if ye have aught against any one; that your Father also which is in heaven may forgive you your trespasses.[3]

1. Gr. *whenever evening came.* 2. Some ancient authorities read *they.* 3. Many ancient authorities add ver. 26 *But if ye do not forgive, neither will your Father which is in heaven forgive your trespasses.*

§ 109. THE RULERS QUESTION* THE AUTHORITY OF JESUS. HE REFUSES TO EXPLAIN, AND SETS FORTH THEIR WICKEDNESS BY THREE PARABLES. (a) PARABLE OF THE TWO SONS.
(b) PARABLE OF THE WICKED HUSBANDMEN.
(c) PARABLE OF THE MARRIAGE FEAST
OF THE KING'S SON.

In the court of the Temple. (*Tuesday.*

Matt. 21:23 to 22:14.	Mark 11:27 to 12:12.	Luke 20:1-19.
23 And when he was come into the tem-	27 And they come again to Jerusalem: and as he was walking in the temple,	1 And it came to pass, on one of the days, as he was teaching the people

*It was very common to test a Rabbi with hard questions. See this continued in § 110-112. In like manner the Fourth Gospel gave us much animated dialogue between Jesus and the Jews at Jerusalem in chap. 5, and chap. 7-10.

Matt. 21:23 to 22:14.	Mark 11:27 to 12:12.	Luke 20:1-19.
ple, the chief priests and the elders of the people came unto him as he was teaching, and said,	there come to him the chief priests, and the scribes, 28 and the elders; and they said unto him,	in the temple, and preaching the gospel, there came upon him the chief priests and the scribes with 2 the elders; and they spake, saying unto him, Tell us: By what authority doest thou these things? or who is he that gave thee 3 this authority? And he answered and said unto them, I also will ask you a ¹question; and tell 4 me: The baptism of John, was it from heaven, or from men?
By what authority doest thou these things? and who gave thee 24 this authority? And Jesus answered and said unto them, I also will ask you one ¹question, which if ye tell me, I likewise will tell you by what authority I do these 25 things. The baptism of John, whence was it? from heaven or from men? And they reasoned with themselves, saying, If we shall say, From heaven; he will say unto us, Why then did ye not believe him? 26 But if we shall say, From men; we fear the multitude; for all hold John as a 27 prophet. And they answered Jesus, and said, We know not.	By what authority doest thou these things? or who gave thee this authority to do 29 these things? And Jesus said unto them, I will ask of you one ¹question, and answer me, and I will tell you by what authority I do 30 these things. The baptism of John, was it from heaven, or from men? answer me. And they reasoned with themselves, saying, If we shall say, From heaven; he will say, Why then did ye not 32 believe him? 'But should we say, From men — they feared the people: ⁸for all verily held John to 33 be a prophet. And they answered Jesus and say, We know not. And Jesus saith unto them, Neither tell I you by what authority I do these things.	5 And they reasoned with themselves, saying, If we shall say, From heaven; he will say, Why did ye not be-6 lieve him? But if we shall say, From men; all the people will stone us: for they be persuaded that John was a 7 prophet. And they answered, that they knew not whence *it* 8 *was*. And Jesus said unto them, Neither tell I you by what authority I do these things.
He also said unto them, Neither tell I you by what authority I do these things.		
28 But what think ye? A man had two sons; And he came to the first, and said, ²Son, go work to-day in the 29 vineyard. And he answered and said, I will not: but afterward he repented		

Matt. 21:23 to 22:14.	Mark 11:27 to 12:12.	Luke 20:1-19.
himself, and went. 30 And he came to the second, and said likewise. And he answered and said, I *go*, sir: and went not. 31 Whether of the twain did the will of his father? They say, The first. Jesus saith unto them, Verily I say unto you, that the publicans and the harlots go into the kingdom of God before you. 32 For John came unto you in the way of righteousness, and ye believed him not: but the publicans and the harlots believed him: and ye, when ye saw it, did not even repent yourselves afterward, that ye might believe him. 33 Hear another parable: There was a man that was a householder, which planted a vineyard, and set a hedge about it, and digged a winepress in it, and built a tower, and let it out to husbandmen, and went into another country. 34 And when the season of the fruits drew near, he sent his ³servants to the husbandmen, to receive ⁴his fruits. 35 And the husbandmen took his ³servants, and beat one, and killed another, and stoned another. 36 Again, he sent oth-	12 And he began to speak unto them in parables. A man planted a vineyard, and set a hedge about it, and digged a pit for the winepress, and built a tower, and let it out to husbandmen, and went into another country. 2 And at the season he sent to the husbandmen a ⁹servant, that he might receive from the husbandmen of the fruits of the 3 vineyard. And they took him, and beat him, and sent him 4 away empty. And again he sent unto	9 And he began to speak unto the people this parable: A man planted a vineyard, and let it out to husbandmen, and went into another country for a 10 long time. And at the season he sent unto the husbandmen a ⁹servant, that they should give him of the fruit of the vineyard: but the husbandmen beat him, and sent him 11 away empty. And he sent yet another ⁹servant: and him al-

Matt. 21:23 to 22:14.	Mark 11:27 to 12:12.	Luke 20:1-19.
er ³servants more than the first: and they did unto them in like manner.	them another ⁹servant: and him they wounded in the head, and handled 5 shamefully. And he sent another; and him they killed: and many others; beating some, and killing some. He had 6 yet one, a beloved son: he sent him last unto them, saying, they will reverence my son.	so they beat, and handled him shamefully, and sent him 12 away empty. And he sent yet a third: and him also they wounded, and cast 13 him forth. And the Lord of the vineyard said, What shall I do? I will send my beloved son: it may be they will reverence him.
37 But afterward he sent unto them his son, saying, They will reverence my son. 38 But the husbandmen, when they saw the son, said among themselves, This is the heir; come, let us kill him and take his inheritance.	7 But those husbandmen said among themselves, This is the heir; come, let us kill him, and the inheritance shall be ours.	14 But when the husbandmen saw him, they reasoned one with another, saying, This is the heir: let us kill him, that the inheritance
39 And they took him, and cast him forth out of the vineyard, and 40 killed him. When therefore the lord of the vineyard shall come, what will he do unto those hus- 41 bandmen? They say unto him, He will miserably destroy those miserable men, and will let out the vineyard unto other husbandmen, which shall render him the fruits in their sea- 42 sons. Jesus saith unto them, Did ye never read in the scriptures,	8 And they took him, and killed him, and cast him forth out of the 9 vineyard. What therefore will the lord of the vineyard do? he will come and destroy the husbandmen, and will give the vineyard unto others.	15 may be ours. And they cast him forth out of the vineyard, and killed him. What therefore will the lord of the vineyard do unto them? 16 He will come and destroy those husbandmen, and will give the vineyard unto others. And when they heard it, they said, ¹⁰God forbid. 17 But he looked upon them, and said, What then is this that is written,
The stone which the builders rejected, The same was made the head of the corner: This was from the Lord,	10 Have ye not read even this scripture; The stone which the builders rejected, The same was made the head of the corner: 11 This was from the Lord,	The stone which the builders rejected, The same was made the head of the corner?

Matt. 21:23 to 22:14.	Mark 11:27 to 12:12.	Luke 20:1-19.
And it is marvellous in our eyes? 43 Therefore say I unto you, the kingdom of God shall be taken away from you, and shall be given to a nation bringing forth the fruits 44 thereof. ⁵And he that falleth on this stone shall be broken to pieces; but on whomsoever it shall fall, it will scatter 45 him as dust. And when the chief priests and the Pharisees heard his parables, they perceived that he spake of 46 them. And when they sought to lay hold on him, they feared the multitudes, because they took him for a prophet.	And it is marvellous in our eyes? 12 And they sought to lay hold on him; and they feared the multitude: for they perceived that he spake the parable against them: and they left him and went away.	18 Every one that falleth on that stone shall be broken to pieces; but on whomsoever it shall fall, it will scatter him as dust. 19 And the scribes and the chief priests sought to lay hands on him in that very hour; and they feared the people: for they perceived that he spake this parable against them.

22 And Jesus answered and spake again in parables unto
2 them, saying, The kingdom of heaven is likened unto a certain king,
3 which made a marriage feast for his son, and sent forth his ³servants to call them that were bidden to the marriage feast: and they would
4 not come. Again he sent forth other ⁸servants, saying, tell them that are bidden, Behold, I have made ready my dinner: my oxen and my fatlings are killed, and all things are ready; come to the marriage
5 feast. But they made light of it, and went their ways, one to his own
6 farm, another to his merchandise: and the rest laid hold on his ⁸ser-
7 vants, and entreated them shamefully, and killed them. But the king was wroth; and he sent his armies, and destroyed those murder-
8 ers, and burned their city. Then saith he to his ⁸servants, The wed-
9 ding is ready, but they that were bidden were not worthy. Go ye therefore unto the partings of the highways, and as many as ye shall
10 find, bid to the marriage feast. And those ⁸servants went out into the highways, and gathered together all as many as they found, both
11 bad and good: and the wedding was filled with guests. But when the king came in to behold the guests, he saw there a man which had not
12 on a wedding-garment: and he saith unto him, Friend, how camest

LAST WEEK OF OUR LORD'S MINISTRY,
Matt. 21:23 to 22:14.

13 thou in hither not having a wedding-garment? And he was speechless. Then the king said to the ⁶servants, Bind him hand and foot, and cast him out into the outer darkness; there shall be the weeping
14 and gnashing of teeth. For many are called, but few chosen.

1. Gr. *word*. 2. Gr. *Child*. 3. Gr. *bondservants*. 4. Or, *the fruits of it*. 5. Some ancient authorities omit ver. 44. 6. Or, *ministers*. 7. Or, *But shall we say, From men?* 8. Or, *for all held John to be a prophet indeed*. 9. Gr. *bondservant*. 10. Gr. *Be it not so*.

§110. THE PHARISEES AND THE HERODIANS TRY TO ENSNARE JESUS ABOUT PAYING TRIBUTE TO CÆSAR.

In the Court of the Temple. (*Tuesday*.)

Matt. 22:15–22.	Mark 12:13–17.	Luke 20:20–26.
15 Then went the Pharisees, and took counsel how they might ensnare him in *his* 16 talk. And they send to him their disciples, with the Herodians, saying, ¹Master, we know that thou art true, and teachest the way of God in truth, and carest not for any one: for thou regardest not the person of 17 men. Tell us therefore, What thinkest thou? Is it lawful to give tribute unto 18 Cæsar, or not? But Jesus perceived their wickedness, and said, Why tempt ye me, 19 ye hypocrites? Shew me the tribute money. And they brought unto him a 20 ²penny. And he saith unto them, Whose is this image and superscription? 21 They say unto him,	13 And they send unto him certain of the Pharisees and of the Herodians, that they might catch him in talk. 14 And when they were come, they say unto him, ¹Master, we know that thou art true, and carest not for any one; for thou regardest not the person of men, but of a truth teachest the way of God: Is it lawful to give tribute unto Cæsar, or not? Shall we give, or shall we not 15 give? But he, knowing their hypocrisy, said unto them, Why tempt ye me? bring me a ²penny, that I 16 may see it. And they brought it. And he saith unto them, Whose is this image and superscription? And they said unto	20 And they watched him, and sent forth spies, which feigned themselves to be righteous, that they might take hold of his speech, so as to deliver him up to the rule and to the authority of the gov-21 ernor. And they asked him, saying, ¹Master, we know that thou sayest and teachest rightly, and acceptest not the person *of any*, but of a truth teachest the 22 way of God: Is it lawful for us to give tribute unto Cæsar, or not? 23 But he perceived their craftiness, and said unto 24 them, Shew me a ²penny. Whose image and superscription hath it? And they

Matt. 22:15-22.	Mark 12:13-17.	Luke 20:20-26.
Cæsar's. Then saith he unto them, Render therefore unto Cæsar the things that are Cæsar's; and unto God the things that are God's. 22 And when they heard it, they marvelled, and left him, and went their way.	17 him, Cæsar's. And Jesus said unto them, Render unto Cæsar the things that are Cæsar's, and unto God the things that are God's. And they marvelled greatly at him.	25 said, Cæsar's. And he said unto them, Then render unto Cæsar the things that are Cæsar's, and unto God the things that are God's. 26 And they were not able to take hold of the saying before the people: and they marvelled at his answer, and held their peace.

1. Or, *Teacher*. 2. See marginal note on Matt. 18:28, ¶90,

§111. THE SADDUCEES ASK HIM A PUZZLING QUESTION ABOUT THE RESURRECTION.

In the Court of the Temple. (*Tuesday.*)

Matt. 22:23-33.	Mark 12:18-27.	Luke 20:27-40.
23 On that day there came to him Sadducees, ¹which say that there is no resurrec- 24 tion: and they asked him, saying, ²Master, Moses said, If a man die, having no children, his brother ³shall marry his wife, and raise up seed unto his brother. 25 Now there were with us seven brethren: and the first married and deceased, and having no seed left his wife 26 unto his brother: in like manner the second also, and the third, unto the ⁴sev- 27 enth. And after them all the woman 28 died. In the resur-	18 And there come unto him Sadducees, which say that there is no resurrection; and they asked him, 19 saying, ²Master, Moses wrote unto us, If a man's brother die, and leave a wife behind him, and leave no child, that his brother should take his wife, and raise up seed unto 20 his brother. There were seven brethren: and the first took a wife, and dying left 21 no seed; and the second took her, and died, leaving no seed behind him; and the 22 third likewise: and the seven left no seed. Last of all the woman also died. 23 In the resurrection	27 And there came to him certain of the Sadducees, they which say that there is no resurrection; and they asked him, 28 saying, ²Master, Moses wrote unto us, that if a man's brother die, having a wife, and he be childless, his brother should take the wife, and raise up seed unto 29 his brother. There were therefore seven brethren; and the 30 first took a wife, and died childless, and 31 the second; and the third took her; and likewise the seven also left no children; and died. 32 Afterward the woman also died. 33 In the resurrection

Matt. 22:23-33.	Mark 12:18-27.	Luke 20:27-40.
rection therefore whose wife shall she be of the seven? for 29 they all had her. But Jesus answered and said unto them, Ye do err, not knowing the scriptures, nor the power of God.	whose wife shall she be of them? for the seven had her to 24 wife. Jesus said unto them, Is it not for this cause that ye err, that ye know not the scriptures, nor the power of God?	therefore whose wife of them shall she be? for the seven had her 34 to wife. And Jesus said unto them,
		The sons of this [6]world marry, and are given 35 in marriage: but they that are accounted
30 For in the resurrection they neither marry, nor are given in marriage, but are	25 For when they shall rise from the dead, they neither marry, nor are given in marriage; but are	worthy to attain to that [6]world, and the resurrection from the dead, neither marry, nor are given in marriage: for neither can 36 they die any more: for they are equal unto the angels; and
as angels [5]in heaven.	as angels in heaven.	are sons of God, being sons of the resurrec- 37 tion. But that the dead are raised,
31 But as touching the resurrection of the dead, have ye not read that which was spoken unto you by God, saying, 32 I am the God of Abraham, and the God of Isaac, and the God of Jacob? God is not the God of 33 the dead, but of the living. And when the multitudes heard it, they were astonished at his teaching.	26 But as touching the dead, that they are raised; have ye not read in the book of Moses, in the place concerning the Bush, how God spake unto him, saying, I am the God of Abraham, and the God of Isaac, and the God of Jacob? 27 He is not the God of the dead, but of the living: ye do greatly err.	even Moses showed in the place concerning the Bush, when he calleth the Lord the God of Abraham, and the God of Isaac, and the 38 God of Jacob. Now he is not the God of the dead, but of the living: for all live un- 39 to him. And certain of the scribes answering said, [2]Master, thou hast well said. 40 For they durst not any more ask him any question.

1. Gr. saying. 2. Or, Teacher. 2. Gr. shall perform the duty of a husband's brother to his wife. Compare Deut. 25:5. 4. Gr. seven. 5. Many ancient authorities add of God. 6. Or. age.

§ 112. A PHARISEE WHO IS A LAWYER ASKS ANOTHER QUESTION, AND THEN JESUS ASKS THE PHARISEES A QUESTION ABOUT THE MESSIAH, WHICH THEY CANNOT ANSWER.

In the court of the Temple. (*Tuesday.*)

Matt. 22:34-46.	Mark 12:28-37.	Luke 20:41-44.
34 But the Pharisees, when they heard that he had put the Sadducees to silence, gathered themselves 35 together. And one of them, a lawyer, asked him a question, tempting him, 36 ¹Master, which is the great commandment in the law? And he said unto him, 37 Thou shalt love the Lord thy God with all thy heart, and with all thy soul, and with 38 all thy mind. This is the great and first 39 commandment. ²And a second like *unto it* is this, Thou shalt love thy neighbour 40 as thyself. On these two commandments hangeth the whole law, and the prophets.	28 And one of the scribes came, and heard them questioning together, and knowing that he had answered them well, asked him, What commandment is the 29 first of all? Jesus answered, The first is, Hear, O Israel; ³The Lord our God, 30 the Lord is one: and thou shalt love the Lord thy God ⁴with all thy heart, and ⁴with all thy soul, and ⁴with all thy mind, and ⁴with all 31 thy strength. The second is this, Thou shalt love thy neighbour as thyself. There is none other commandment greater than these. 32 And the scribe said unto him, Of a truth, ¹Master, thou hast well said that he is one; and there is none other but he: 33 and to love him with all the heart, and with all the understanding, and with all the strength, and to love his neighbour as himself, is much more than all whole burnt offerings and	

Matt. 22:34–46.	Mark 12:28–37.	Luke 20:41–44.
	34 sacrifices. And when Jesus saw that he answered discreetly, he said unto him, Thou art not far from the kingdom of God. And no man after that durst ask him any question.	
41 Now while the Pharisees were gathered together, Jesus asked them a question, 42 saying, What think ye of the Christ? whose son is he? They say unto him, *The son* of David.	35 And Jesus answered and said, as he taught in the temple, How say the scribes that the Christ is the son of David?	41 And he said unto them, How say they that the Christ is David's son?
43 He saith unto them, How then doth David in the Spirit call him Lord, saying,	36 David himself said in the Holy Spirit,	42 For David himself saith in the book of Psalms,
44 The Lord said unto my Lord, Sit thou on my right hand, Till I put thine enemies underneath thy feet?	The Lord said unto my Lord, Sit thou on my right hand, Till I make thine enemies ⁵the footstool of thy feet.	The Lord said unto my Lord, Sit thou on my right hand, 43 Till I make thine enemies the footstool of thy feet.
45 If David then calleth him Lord, how is he 46 his son? And no one was able to answer him a word, neither durst any man from that day forth ask him any more questions.	37 David himself calleth him Lord; and whence is he his son? And ⁶the common people heard him gladly.	44 David therefore calleth him Lord, and how is he his son?

1. Or, *Teacher*. 2. Or, *And a second is like unto it, Thou shalt love*, etc. 3. Or, *The Lord is our God; the Lord is one*. 4. Gr. *from*. 5. Some ancient authorities read, *underneath thy feet*. 6. Or, *the great multitude*.

§ 113. IN HIS LAST PUBLIC DISCOURSE, JESUS SOLEMNLY DENOUNCES THE SCRIBES AND PHARISEES (COMP. § 85).

In the courts of the Temple. (*Tuesday*.)

Matt. 23:1–39.	Mark 12:38–40.	Luke 20:45–47.
1 Then spake Jesus to the multitudes and to his disciples,	38 And in his teaching he said, Beware of	45 And in the hearing of all the people he said unto his disci-

Matt. 23:1-39.	Mark 12:38-40.	Luke 20:45-47.
2 saying, The scribes and the Pharisees sit on Moses' seat: 3 all things therefore whatsoever they bid you, *these* do and observe: but do not ye after their works; for they say, and do 4 not. Yea, they bind heavy burdens ¹and grievous to be borne, and lay them on men's shoulders; but they themselves will not move them with 5 their finger. But all their works they do for to be seen of men: for they make broad their phylacteries, and enlarge the borders *of their garments*, 6 and love the chief place at feasts, and the chief seats in the 7 synagogues, and the salutations in the marketplaces, and to be called of men, Rab- 8 bi. But be not ye called Rabbi: for one is your teacher, and all ye are brethren. 9 And call no man your father on the earth: for one is your Father,²which is in heav- 10 en. Neither be ye called masters: for one is your master, 11 *even* the Christ. But he that is ³greatest among you shall be 12 your ⁴servant. And whosoever shall exalt himself shall be humbled; and whosoever shall humble himself shall be exalted. 13 But woe unto you,	the scribes, which desire to walk in long robes, and *to have* salutations in the 39 marketplaces, and chief seats in the synagogues, and chief places at feasts:	46 ples, Beware of the scribes, which desire to walk in long robes, and love salutations in the marketplaces, and chief seats in the synagogues, and chief places at feasts;

Matt. 23:1-39.	Mark 12:38-40.	Luke 20:45-47.
scribes and Pharisees, hypocrites! because ye shut the kingdom of heaven ⁵against men: for ye enter not in yourselves, neither suffer ye them that are entering in to enter⁶.		
	40 they which devour widows' houses, ¹²and for a pretence make long prayers; these shall receive greater condemnation.	47 which devour widows' houses, and for a pretence make long prayers: these shall receive greater condemnation.

15 Woe unto you, scribes and Pharisees, hypocrites! for ye compass sea and land to make one proselyte; and when he is become so, ye make him twofold more a son of ⁷hell than yourselves.

16 Woe unto you, ye blind guides, which say, Whosoever shall swear by the ⁸temple, it is nothing; but whosoever shall swear by the gold
17 of the ⁸temple he is ⁹a debtor. Ye fools and blind: for whether is
18 greater, the gold, or the ⁸temple that hath sanctified the gold? And, Whosoever shall swear by the altar, it is nothing; but whosoever
19 shall swear by the gift that is upon it, he is ⁹a debtor. Ye blind: for whether is greater, the gift, or the altar that sanctifieth the gift?
20 He therefore that sweareth by the altar, sweareth by it, and by all
21 things thereon. And he that sweareth by the ⁸temple, sweareth by
22 it, and by him that dwelleth therein. And he that sweareth by the heaven, sweareth by the throne of God, and by him that sitteth thereon.

23 Woe unto you, scribes and Pharisees, hypocrites! for ye tithe mint and ¹⁰anise and cummin, and have left undone the weightier matters of the law, judgement, and mercy, and faith: but these ye ought to
24 have done, and not to have left the other undone. Ye blind guides, which strain out the gnat, and swallow the camel.

25 Woe unto you scribes and Pharisees, hypocrites! for ye cleanse the outside of the cup and of the platter, but within they are full from
26 extortion and excess. Thou blind Pharisee, cleanse first the inside of the cup and of the platter, that the outside thereof may become clean also.

27 Woe unto you, scribes and Pharisees, hypocrites! for ye are like unto whited sepulchres, which outwardly appear beautiful, but in-
28 wardly are full of dead men's bones, and of all uncleanness. Even so ye also outwardly appear righteous unto men, but inwardly ye are full of hypocrisy and iniquity.

29 Woe unto you, scribes and Pharisees, hypocrites! for ye build the sepulchres of the prophets, and garnish the tombs of the righteous,

Matt. 23:1-39.

30 and say, If we had been in the days of our fathers, we should not
31 have been partakers with them in the blood of the prophets. Wherefore ye witness to yourselves, that ye are sons of them that slew the
32, 33 prophets. Fill ye up then the measure of your fathers. Ye serpents, ye offspring of vipers, how shall ye escape the judgement of
34 ⁷hell? Therefore, behold, I send unto you prophets, and wise men, and scribes: some of them shall ye kill and crucify; and some of them shall ye scourge in your synagogues, and persecute from city to city:
35 that upon you may come all the righteous blood shed on the earth, from the blood of Abel the righteous unto the blood of Zachariah son of Barachiah, whom ye slew between the sanctuary and the altar.
36 Verily I say unto you, All these things shall come upon this generation.
37 O Jerusalem, Jerusalem, which killeth the prophets, and stoneth them that are sent unto her! how often would I have gathered thy children together, even as a hen gathereth her chickens under her
38 wings, and ye would not! Behold, your house is left unto you ¹¹desolate. For I say unto you, Ye shall not see me henceforth, till ye shall
39 say, blessed is he that cometh in the name of the Lord.

1. Many ancient authorities omit *and grievous to be borne.* 2. Gr. *the heavenly.* 3. Gr. *greater.* 4. Or, *minister.* 5. Gr. *before.* 6. Some authorities insert here or after ver. 12, ver. 14 *Woe unto you, scribes and Pharisees, hypocrites! for ye devour widows' houses, even while for a pretence ye make long prayers: therefore ye shall receive greater condemnation.* See Mark 12:40; Luke 20:47, above. 7. Gr. *Gehenna.* 8. Or, *sanctuary:* as in ver. 35. 9. Or, *bound by his oath.* 10. Or, *dill.* 11. Some ancient authorities omit *desolate.* 12. Or, *even while for a pretence they make.*

§ 114. JESUS CLOSELY OBSERVES* THE CONTRIBUTIONS IN THE TEMPLE, AND COMMENDS THE POOR WIDOW'S GIFT.

(*Tuesday.*)

Mark 12:41-44.

41 And he sat down over against the treasury, and beheld how the multitude cast ¹money into the treasury: and many that were
42 rich cast in much. And there came ²a poor widow, and she cast in two mites, which make a
43 farthing. And he called unto him his disciples, and said unto them, Verily I say unto you, This poor widow cast in more than all they which are casting into the
44 treasury: for they all did cast in of their superfluity; but she of her want did cast in all that she had, *even* all her living.

Luke 21:1-4.

1 And he looked up, ³and saw the rich men that were casting their
2 gifts into the treasury. And he saw a certain poor widow casting in thither two mites.

3 And he said, Of a truth I say unto you, This poor widow cast in more
4 than they all: for all these did of their superfluity cast in unto the gifts: but she of her want did cast in all the living that she had.

1. Gr. *brass.* 2. Gr. *one.* 3. Or, *and saw them that...treasury, and they were rich.*

* Notice that this was the last occurrence in the Saviour's public ministry, except the trial and the crucifixion.

§ 115. SITTING ON THE MOUNT OF OLIVES, JESUS SPEAKS TO HIS DISCIPLES ABOUT THE DESTRUCTION OF JERUSALEM, AND HIS OWN SECOND COMING.

(*Tuesday.*)

Matt. 24:1-51.	Mark 13:1-37.	Luke 21:5-36.
1 And Jesus went out from the temple, and was going on his way; and his disciples came to him to shew him the buildings of the temple. 2 But he answered and said unto them, See ye not all these things? verily I say unto you, There shall not be left here one stone upon another, that shall not be thrown down. 3 And as he sat on the mount of Olives, the disciples came unto him privately, saying, Tell us, when shall these things be? and what *shall be* the sign of thy ¹coming, and of ²the end of the 4 world? And Jesus answered and said unto them, Take heed that no man 5 lead you astray. For many shall come in my name, saying, I am the Christ; and shall lead many a- 6 stray. And ye shall hear of wars and rumours of wars: see that ye be not troubled: for *these things* must needs come to pass; but the end is 7 not yet. For nation shall rise against na-	1 And as he went forth out of the temple, one of his disciples saith unto him, ¹⁸Master, behold, what manner of stones and what manner of buildings! 2 And Jesus said unto him, Seest thou these great buildings? there shall not be left here one stone upon another, which shall not be thrown down. 3 And as he sat on the mount of Olives over against the temple, Peter and James and John and Andrew asked him pri- 4 vately, Tell us, when shall these things be? and what *shall be* the sign when these things are all about to be accom- 5 plished? And Jesus began to say unto them, Take heed that no man lead 6 you astray. Many shall come in my name, saying, I am *he;* and shall lead 7 many astray. And when ye shall hear of wars and rumours of wars, be not troubled: *these things* must needs come to pass; but the end is 8 not yet. For nation shall rise against na-	5 And as some spake of the temple, how it was adorned with goodly stones and of- 6 ferings, he said, As for these things which ye behold, the days will come, in which there shall not be left here one stone upon another, that shall not be thrown down. 7 And they asked him, saying, ¹⁸Master, when therefore shall these things be? and what *shall be* the sign when these things are about to come to pass? 8 And he said, Take heed that ye be not led astray: for many shall come in my name, saying, I am *he;* and, The time is at hand: go ye not 9 after them. And when ye shall hear of wars and tumults, be not terrified: for these things must needs come to pass first; but the end is not immediately. 10 Then said he unto

AND HIS CRUCIFIXION.

Matt. 24:1-51.	Mark 13:1-37.	Luke 21:5-36.

tion, and kingdom against kingdom: and there shall be famines and earthquakes in divers places.

tion, and kingdom against kingdom: there shall be earthquakes in divers places; there shall be famines:

them, Nation shall rise against nation, and kingdom against 11 kingdom: and there shall be great earthquakes, and in divers places famines and pestilences; and there shall be terrors and great signs from heaven.

8 But all these things are the beginning of travail.
9 Then shall they deliver you up unto tribulation, and shall kill you:

and ye shall be hated of all the nations for my name's sake.

these things are the beginning of travail.
9 But take ye heed to yourselves: for they shall deliver you up to councils: and in synagogues shall ye be beaten; and before governors and kings shall ye stand for my sake, for a testimony unto them.

10 And the gospel must first be preached unto all the nations.
11 And when they lead you *to judgement*, and deliver you up, be not anxious beforehand what ye shall speak: but whatsoever shall be given you in that hour, that speak ye: for it is not ye that speak, but the Holy Ghost.

10 And then shall many stumble, and shall deliver up one another, and shall hate one another.

12 And brother shall deliver up brother to death, and the father his child: and children shall rise up against parents, and ¹⁹cause them to be
13 put to death. And ye shall be hated of all men for my name's sake:

12 But before all these things, they shall lay their hands on you, and shall persecute you, delivering you up to the synagogues and prisons, ²²bringing you before kings and governors for my name's
13 sake. It shall turn unto you for a testimony.

14 Settle it therefore in your hearts, not to meditate beforehand how to an-
15 swer: for I will give you a mouth and wisdom, which all your adversaries shall not be able to withstand
16 or to gainsay. But ye shall be delivered up even by parents, and brethren, and kinsfolk, and friends; and *some* of you ²³shall they cause to be put
17 to death. And ye shall be hated of all men for my name's
18 sake. And not a hair of your head shall

11

Matt. 24:1-51.	Mark 13:1-37.	Luke 21:5-36.
		perish. In your patience ye shall win your [24]souls.
11 And many false prophets shall arise, and shall lead 12 many astray. And because iniquity shall be multiplied, the love of the many 13 shall wax cold. But he that endureth to the end, the same 14 shall be saved. And [3]this gospel of the kingdom shall be preached in the whole [4]world for a testimony unto all the nations; and then shall the end come. 15 When therefore ye see the abomination of desolation, which was spoken of [5]by Daniel the prophet, standing in [6]the holy place (let him that readeth understand),	but he that endureth to the end, the same shall be saved. 14 But when ye see the abomination of desolation standing where he ought not (let him that readeth understand),	20 But when ye see Jerusalem compassed with armies, then know that her desolation is at
16 then let them that are in Judea flee unto the mountains:	then let them that are in Judea flee unto the mountains:	[21 hand. Then let them that are in Judea flee unto the mountains; and let them that are in the midst of her depart out; and let not them that are in the country enter therein.
17 let him that is on the housetop not go down to take out the things that are in his 18 house: and let him that is in the field not return back to take his cloke.	15 and let him that is on the housetop not go down, nor enter in, to take anything 16 out of his house: and let him that is in the field return not back to take his cloke.	

Matt. 24:1-51.	Mark 13:1-37.	Luke 21:5-36.
		22 For these are days of vengeance, that all things which are written may be
19 But woe unto them that are with child and to them that give suck 20 in those days! And pray ye that your flight be not in the winter, neither on a 21 sabbath: for then shall be great tribulation, such as hath not been from the beginning of the world until now, no, nor ever shall be. 22 And except those days had been shortened, no flesh would have been saved: but for the elect's sake those days shall be shortened.	17 But woe unto them that are with child and to them that give suck in those 18 days! And pray ye that it be not in 19 the winter. For those days shall be tribulation, such as there hath not been the like from the beginning of the creation which God created until now, and never 20 shall be. And except the Lord had shortened the days no flesh would have been saved: but for the elect's sake, whom he chose, he shortened the days.	23 fulfilled. Woe unto them that are with child and to them that give suck in those days!
		for there shall be great distress upon the ²⁵land, and wrath unto this peo- 24 ple. And they shall fall by the edge of the sword, and shall be led captive into all the nations: and Jerusalem shall be trodden down of the Gentiles, until the times of the Gentiles be fulfilled.
23 Then if any man shall say unto you, Lo, here is the Christ, or, Here; 24 believe ⁷it not. For there shall arise false Christs, and false prophets, and shall shew great signs and wonders; so as to lead astray, if possible, even the elect.	21 And then if any man shall say unto you, Lo, here is the Christ; or, Lo, there; 22 believe ⁷it not: for there shall arise false Christs and false prophets, and shall shew signs and wonders, that they may lead astray, if possible, the elect.	

Matt. 24:1-51.	Mark 13:1-37.	Luke 21:5-36.
25 Behold, I have told you beforehand. If therefore they shall say unto you, Behold, he is in the wilderness; go not forth: Behold, he is in the inner chambers; be- 27 lieve *it not. For as the lightning cometh forth from the east, and is seen even unto the west; so shall be the ¹coming of the Son of man. 28 Wheresoever the carcase is, there will the ⁹eagles be gathered together. 29 But immediately, after the tribulation of those days, the sun shall be darkened, and the moon shall not give her light, and the stars shall fall from heaven, and the powers of the heavens shall be 30 shaken: and then shall appear the sign of the Son of man in heaven: and then shall all the tribes of the earth mourn, and they shall see the Son of man coming on the clouds of heaven with power 31 and great glory. And he shall send forth his angels ¹⁰with ¹¹a great sound of a trumpet, and they shall gather together his elect from the four winds, from one	23 But take ye heed: behold, I have told you all things beforehand. 24 But in those days, after that tribulation, the sun shall be darkened, and the moon shall not give 25 her light, and the stars shall be falling from heaven, and the powers that are in the heavens shall be shaken. 26 And then shall they see the Son of man coming in clouds with great power and glory. 27 And then shall he send forth the angels, and shall gather together his elect from the four winds, from the uttermost part of the earth to	25 And there shall be signs in sun and moon and stars; and upon the earth distress of nations, in perplexity for the roaring of the sea and 26 the billows; men ²⁶fainting for fear, and for expectation of the things which are coming on ²⁷the world: for the powers of the heavens shall be shaken. 27 And then shall they see the Son of man coming in a cloud with power and great glory.

Matt. 24:1-51.	Mark 13:1-37.	Luke 21:5-36.
end of heaven to the other.	the uttermost part of heaven.	

28 But when these things begin to come to pass, look up, and lift up your heads; because your redemption draweth nigh.

32 Now from the fig tree learn her parable: when her branch is now become tender, and putteth forth its leaves, ye know that the sum-
33 mer is nigh; even so ye also, when ye see all these things, know ye that ¹²he is nigh, even at the
34 doors. Verily I say unto you, This generation shall not pass away, till all these things be accom-
35 plished. Heaven and earth shall pass away, but my words shall not pass away.
36 But of that day and hour knoweth no one, not even the angels of heaven, ¹³neither the Son, but the Father only.
37 And as were the days of Noah, so shall be the ¹coming of the
38 Son of man. For as in those days which were before the flood they were eating and drinking, marrying and giving in marriage, until the day that Noah entered
39 into the ark, and they knew not until the flood came, and took them all away: so shall be the ¹coming

28 Now from the fig tree learn her parable: when her branch is now become tender, and putteth forth its leaves, ye know that the sum-
29 mer is nigh; even so ye also, when ye see these things coming to pass, know ye that ¹²he is nigh, even
30 at the doors. Verily I say unto you, This generation shall not pass away, until all these things be ac-
31 complished. Heaven and earth shall pass away: but my words shall not pass away.
32 But of that day or that hour knoweth no one, not even the angels in heaven, neither the Son, but the Father.

29 And he spake to them a parable: Behold the fig tree, and
30 all the trees: when they now shoot forth, ye see it and know of your own selves that the summer is now
31 nigh. Even so ye also, when ye see these things coming to pass, know ye that the kingdom of God
32 is nigh. Verily I say unto you, this generation shall not pass away, till all things be accomplished.
33 Heaven and earth shall pass away: but my words shall not pass away.

Matt. 24:1-51.	Mark 13:1-37.	Luke 21-5-36.
of the Son of man. 40 Then shall two men be in the field; one is taken, and one is left: 41 two women *shall be* grinding at the mill; one is taken, and one is left		
	33 Take ye heed, watch [20]and pray: for ye know not when the time 34 is. *It is* as *when* a man, sojourning in another country, having left his house, and given authority to his [21]servants, to each one his work, commanded also the porter to	34 But take heed to yourselves, lest haply your hearts be overcharged with surfeiting and drunkenness, and cares of this life, and that day come on you suddenly 35 as a snare: for *so* shall it come upon all them that dwell on the face of all the earth.
42 Watch therefore: for ye know not on what day your Lord cometh.	35 watch. Watch therefore: for ye know not when the lord of the house cometh, whether at even, or at midnight, or at cockcrowing, or in 36 the morning; lest coming suddenly he find you sleeping. 37 And what I say unto you I say unto all, Watch.	36 But watch ye at every season, making supplication, that ye may prevail to escape all these things that shall come to pass, and to stand before the Son of man.

43 [14]But know this, that if the master of the house had known in what
44 watch the thief was coming, he would have watched and would not have suffered his house to be [15]broken through. Therefore be ye also
45 ready: for in an hour that ye think not the Son of man cometh. Who then is the faithful and wise [16]servant, whom his lord hath set over
46 his household, to give them their food in due season? Blessed is that [16]servant, whom his lord when he cometh shall find so doing.
47 Verily I say unto you, that he will set him over all that he hath.
48 But if that evil [16]servant shall say in his heart, My lord tarrieth;
49 and shall begin to beat his fellow-servants, and shall eat and drink
50 with the drunken; the lord of that [16]servant shall come in a day when
51 he expecteth not, and in an hour when he knoweth not, and shall [17]cut him asunder, and appoint his portion with the hypocrites; there shall be the weeping and gnashing of teeth.

1. Gr. *presence*. 2. Or, *the consummation of the age*. 3. Or, *these good tidings*. 4. Gr. *inhabited earth*. 5. Or, *through*. 6. Or, *a holy place*. 7. Or, *him*. 8. Or, *them*. 9. Or, *vultures*. 10. Many ancient authorities read *with a great trumpet, and they shall gather, &c.* 11. Or, *a trumpet of great sound*. 12. Or, *it*. 13. Many authorities, some ancient, omit *neither the Son*. 14. Or, *But this ye know*. 15. Gr. *digged through*. 16. Gr. *bond-*

servant. 17. Or, severely scourge him. 18. Or, Teacher. 19. Or, put them to death. 20. Some ancient authorities omit and pray. 21, Gr. bondservants. 22, Gr. you being brought. 23. Or, shall they put to death. 24. Or, lives. 25. Or, earth. 26. Or, expiring. 27. Gr. the inhabited earth.

§116. CONCLUSION OF THIS DISCOURSE—AS TO THE SECOND COMING— PARABLE OF THE TEN VIRGINS, AND OF THE TALENTS— THE FINAL JUDGMENT.

On the Mount of Olives. (*Tuesday.*)

Matt. chap. 25.

1 Then shall the kingdom of heaven be likened unto ten virgins,
2 which took their ¹lamps, and went forth to meet the bridegroom. And
3 five of them were foolish, and five were wise. For the foolish, when
4 they took their ¹lamps, took no oil with them: but the wise took oil in
5 their vessels with their ¹lamps. Now while the bridegroom tarried,
6 they all slumbered and slept. But at midnight there is a cry, Behold,
7 the bridegroom! Come ye forth to meet him. Then all those virgins
8 arose, and trimmed their ¹lamps. And the foolish said unto the wise,
9 Give us of your oil; for our ¹lamps are going out. But the wise answered, saying, Peradventure there will not be enough for us and
10 you: go ye rather to them that sell, and buy for yourselves. And while they went away to buy, the bridegroom came; and they that were ready went in with him to the marriage feast: and the door was
11 shut. Afterward come also the other virgins, saying, Lord, Lord,
12 open to us. But he answered and said, Verily I say unto you, I know
13 you not. Watch therefore, for ye know not the day nor the hour.
14 For *it is* as *when* a man, going into another country, called his own
15 ²servants, and delivered unto them his goods. And unto one he gave five talents, to another two, to another one; to each according to his
16 several ability; and he went on his journey. Straightway he that received the five talents went and traded with them, and made other
17 five talents. In like manner he also that *received* the two gained other
18 two. But he that received the one went away and digged in the earth,
19 and hid his lord's money. Now after a long time the lord of those
20 ²servants cometh and maketh a reckoning with them. And he that received the five talents came and brought other five talents, saying, Lord, thou deliveredst unto me five talents: lo, I have gained other
21 five talents. His lord said unto him, Well done, good and faithful ³servant: thou hast been faithful over a few things, I will set thee over
22 many things: enter thou into the joy of thy lord. And he also that *received* the two talents came and said, Lord, thou deliveredst unto me
23 two talents: lo, I have gained other two talents. His lord said unto him, Well done, good and faithful ³servant; thou hast been faithful over a few things, I will set thee over many things: enter thou into the joy
24 of thy lord. And he also that had received the one talent came and said, Lord, I knew thee that thou art a hard man, reaping where thou
25 didst not sow, and gathering where thou didst not scatter: and I was afraid, and went away and hid thy talent in the earth: lo, thou hast
26 thine own. But his lord answered and said unto him, Thou wicked and slothful ³servant, thou knewest that I reap where I sowed not,

Matt. chap. 25.

27 and gather where I did not scatter; thou oughtest therefore to have put my money to the bankers, and at my coming I should have received
28 back mine own with interest. Take ye away therefore the talent
29 from him, and give it unto him that hath the ten talents. For unto every one that hath shall be given, and he shall have abundance: but from him that hath not, even that which he hath shall be taken
30 away. And cast ye out the unprofitable ²servant into the outer darkness: there shall be the weeping and gnashing of teeth.
31 But when the Son of man shall come in his glory, and all the angels
32 with him, then shall he sit on the throne of his glory: and before him shall be gathered all the nations: and he shall separate them one from
33 another, as the shepherd separateth the sheep from the ⁴goats; and he
34 shall set the sheep on his right hand, but the ⁴goats on the left. Then shall the King say unto them on his right hand, Come, ye blessed of my Father, inherit the kingdom prepared for you from the foundation
35 of the world: for I was an hungred, and ye gave me meat: I was thirsty, and ye gave me drink: I was a stranger, and ye took me in;
36 naked, and ye clothed me: I was sick, and ye visited me: I was in
37 prison, and ye came unto me. Then shall the righteous answer him, saying, Lord, when saw we thee an hungred, and fed thee? or athirst,
38 and gave thee drink? And when saw we thee a stranger, and took
39 thee in? or naked, and clothed thee? And when saw we thee sick, or
40 in prison, and came unto thee? And the King shall answer and say unto them, Verily I say unto you, Inasmuch as ye did it unto one of
41 these my brethren, *even* these least, ye did it unto me. Then shall he say also unto them on the left hand,⁵Depart from me, ye cursed, into the
42 eternal fire which is prepared for the devil and his angels: for I was an hungred, and ye gave me no meat: I was thirsty, and ye gave me
43 no drink: I was a stranger, and ye took me not in; naked, and ye
44 clothed me not; sick, and in prison, and ye visited me not. Then shall they also answer, saying, Lord, when saw we thee an hungred, or athirst, or a stranger, or naked, or sick, or in prison, and did not
45 minister unto thee? Then shall he answer them, saying, Verily, I say unto you, Inasmuch as ye did it not unto one of these least, ye did
46 it not unto me. And these shall go away into eternal punishment: but the righteous into eternal life.

1. Or, *torches.* 2. Gr. *bondservants.* 3. Gr. *bondservant.* 4. Gr. *kids.* 5. Or, *Depart from me under a curse.*

AND HIS CRUCIFIXION.

In §117-123 we have the successive steps by which our Lord prepared himself for his approaching death, and prepared his disciples for enduring the separation, and for afterwards carrying on his work.

§117. JESUS AGAIN PREDICTS, AND THE RULERS PLOT, HIS DEATH. MARY ANOINTS HIM BEFOREHAND FOR BURIAL (COMP. §46), AND JUDAS BARGAINS TO BETRAY HIM.

Bethany and Jerusalem.   Probably beginning of Wednesday (our Tuesday after sunset).

Matt. 26:1-16.	Mark 14:1-11.	Luke 22:1-6.	John 12:2-8.
1 And it came to pass, when Jesus had finished all these words, he said unto his disciples, 2 Ye know that after two days the passover cometh, and the Son of man is delivered up to be crucified. 3 Then were gathered together the chief priests, and the elders of the people, unto the court of the high priest, who was called Caiaphas: 4 and they took counsel together that they might take Jesus by subtilty, and kill him. 5 But they said, Not during the feast, lest a tumult arise among the people. 6 Now when Jesus was in	1 Now after two days was *the feast of* the passover and the unleavened bread: and the chief priests and the scribes sought how they might take him with subtilty, and kill 2 him: for they said, Not during the feast, lest haply there shall be a tumult of the people. 3 And while he was in Beth-	1 Now the feast of unleavened bread drew nigh, which is called the Passover. 2 And the chief priests and the scribes sought how they might put him to death; for they feared the people.	 2 So they made him a supper

Matt. 26:1-16.	Mark 14:1-11.	Luke 22:1-6.	John 12:2-8.
Bethany, in the house of Simon the leper, there came unto him a woman having an alabaster cruse of exceeding precious ointment, and she poured it upon his head as he sat at meat. 8 But when the disciples saw it, they had indignation, saying,	any in the house of Simon the leper, as he sat at meat, there came a woman having ¹an alabaster cruse of ointment of ²spikenard very costly, *and* she brake the cruse, and poured it over 4 his head. But there were some that had indignation among themselves, *saying*,		there: and Martha served; but Lazarus was one of them that sat at meat with 3 him. Mary* therefore took a pound of ointment of ²spikenard, very precious, and anointed the feet of Jesus, and wiped his feet with her hair: and the house was filled with the odour of the ointment. 4 But Judas Iscariot, one of his disciples, which should betray him,
To what purpose is this 9 waste? For this ointment might have been sold for much, and given to the poor.	To what purpose hath this waste of the ointment been 5 made? For this ointment might have been sold for above three hundred ³pence, and given to the poor. And they murmured against her.		5 saith, Why was not this ointment sold for three hundred ³pence, and given to the poor? 6 Now this he said, not because he cared for the poor; but because he was a thief, and having the ⁶bag ⁷took away what was put there-
10 But Jesus perceiving it said unto them, Why trouble ye the woman? for she hath wrought a good work up- 11 on me. For ye	6 But Jesus said, Let her alone, why trouble ye her? she hath wrought a good work on 7 me. For ye have the poor always with		7 in. Jesus therefore said, ⁸Suffer her to keep it against the

---

*This anointing has nothing in common with that given by Luke (§46), except the fact of a woman anointing the Saviour's feet, and the name Simon, which was common. The former was in Galilee, this is at Bethany near Jerusalem. There the host despised the woman who anointed, here her brother is one of the guests, and her sister an active attendant. There the woman was "a sinner," a notoriously bad woman, here it is the devout Mary who "sat at the Lord's feet and heard his word" months before (§82). There the host thought strange that Jesus allowed her to touch him, here the disciples complain of the waste. There the Saviour gave assurance of forgiveness, here of perpetual and world-wide honor. Especially notice that here the woman who anoints is anticipating his speedy death and burial, of which at the former time he had never distinctly spoken. In view of all these differences it is absurd to represent the two anointings as the same, and outrageous on such slender ground to cast reproach on Mary of Bethany.

Matt. 26:1-16.	Mark 14:1-11.	Luke 22:1-6.	John 12:2-8.
have the poor always with you; but me ye have not always. For in that she poured this ointment upon my body, she did it to prepare me for burial. Verily I say unto you, Wheresoever this gospel shall be preached in the whole world, that also which this woman hath done shall be spoken of for a memorial of her.	you, and whensoever ye will ye can do them good: but me ye have not always. She hath done what she could: she hath anointed my body aforehand for the burying. And verily I say unto you, Wheresoever the gospel shall be preached throughout the whole world, that also which this woman hath done shall be spoken of for a memorial of her.		day of my burying. For the poor ye have always with you; but me ye have not always.

12 ways. 13 ~~Verily~~

8 always. 9 burying.

8 ing.

| 14 Then one of the twelve, who was called Judas Iscariot, | 10 And Judas Iscariot, he that was one of the twelve, | 3 And Satan entered into Judas who was called Iscariot, being of the number of the twelve. And he went away, and communed with the chief priests and captains, how he might deliver him unto them. | |

4

| went unto the chief priests, | went away unto the chief priests, | | |
| | that he might deliver him unto them. | | |

15 and said, What are ye willing to give me, and I will deliver him unto you?

| | 11 And they, when they heard it, were glad, and promised to give him mon- | 5 And they were glad, and covenanted to give him mon- | |

AND HIS CRUCIFIXION. 171

172 LAST WEEK OF OUR LORD'S MINISTRY,

Matt. 26:1-16.	Mark 14:1-11.	Luke 22:1-6.
	ey.	6 ey. And he consented,
And they weighed unto him thirty pieces of silver. And from that time he sought opportunity to deliver him *unto them.*	And he sought how he might conveniently deliver him *unto them.*	and sought opportunity to deliver him unto them [5]in the absence of the multitude.

1. Or, *a flask*. 2. Gr. *pistic nard*, pistic being perhaps a local name. Others take it to mean *genuine;* others, *liquid.* 3. The word in the Greek denotes a coin worth about seventeen cents. 4. Gr. *the one of the twelve.* 5. Or, *without tumult.* 6. Or, *box.* 7. Or, *carried what was put therein.* 8. Or, *let her alone: it was that she might keep it.*

§ 118. PREPARATION FOR THE PASCHAL MEAL, AND CONTENTION AMONG THE TWELVE AS TO PRECEDENCE UNDER THE MESSIANIC REIGN.

Bethany to Jerusalem. Thursday afternoon and (after sunset) beginning of Friday.

Matt. 26:17-20.	Mark 14:12-17.	Luke 22:7-16 and 24-30.
17 Now on the first *day* of unleavened bread the disciples came to Jesus, saying, Where wilt thou that we make ready for thee to eat the 18 passover? And he said,	12 And on the first day of unleavened bread, when they sacrificed the passover, his disciples say unto him, Where wilt thou that we go and make ready that thou mayest eat the 13 passover? And he sendeth two of his disciples, and saith unto them,	7 And the day of unleavened bread came, on which the passover must be sacrificed. 8 And he sent Peter and John, saying, Go and make ready for us the passover, that we may 9 eat. And they said unto him, Where wilt thou that we make 10 ready? And he said unto them, Behold, when ye are entered into the city, there shall meet you a man bearing a pitcher of
Go into the city to such a man, and say unto him,	Go into the city, and there shall meet you a	

AND HIS CRUCIFIXION.

Matt. 26:17-20.	Mark 14:12-17.	Luke 22:7-16 and 24-30.
	man bearing a pitcher of water: follow 14 him; and wheresoever he shall enter in, say to the goodman of the house, The ¹Master saith, Where is my guest-chamber, where I shall eat the passover with my 15 disciples? And he will himself shew you a large upper room furnished *and* ready: and there make ready for us.	water; follow him into the house whereinto he goeth. And ye shall say unto the goodman of the house, The ¹Master saith unto thee, Where is the guest-chamber, where I shall eat the passover with my disciples? And he will shew you a large upper room furnished: there make ready.
The ¹Master saith, My time is at hand; I keep the passover at thy house with my disciples.		
19 And the disciples did as Jesus appointed them; and they made ready the passover. 20 Now when even was come he was sitting at meat with the twelve ²disciples;	16 And the disciples went forth, and came into the city, and found as he had said unto them: and they made ready the passover. 17 And when it was evening he cometh with the twelve.	13 And they went, and found as he had said unto them: and they made ready the passover.
		14 And when the hour was come, he sat down, and the apos-

15 tles with him. And he said unto them, With desire I have desired
16 to eat this passover* with you before I suffer: for I say unto you, I will not eat it, until it be fulfilled in the kingdom of God.
24 And there arose also a contention among them, which of them is
25 accounted to be ³greatest. And he said unto them, The kings of the Gentiles have lordship over them; and they that have authority over
26 them are called Benefactors. But ye *shall* not *be* so: but he that is the greater among you, let him become as the younger; and he that is
27 chief, as he that doth serve. For whether is greater, he that ⁴sitteth at meat, or he that serveth? is not he that ⁴sitteth at meat? but I am
28 in the midst of you as he that serveth. But ye are they which have
29 continued with me in my temptations; and ⁵I appoint unto you a kingdom, even as my Father appointed unto me, that ye may eat and drink
30 at my table in my kingdom; and ye shall sit on thrones judging the twelve tribes of Israel.

1. Or, *Teacher.* 2. Many authorities, some ancient, omit *disciples.* 3. Gr. *greater.* 4. Gr. *reclineth.* 5. Or, *I appoint unto you, even as my Father appointed unto me a kingdom, that ye may eat and drink, etc.*

*Some regard certain expressions in the Gospel of John as showing that Jesus did not eat the Paschal meal, and thus hopelessly contradicting the other Gospels. But no one of John's expressions shows what is supposed, and one of them really indicates the contrary. See note at end of the volume, on § 118. Matthew, Mark, and Luke clearly show that he did eat the regular Passover meal.

§ 119. During the Paschal Meal, Jesus Washes the Feet of His Disciples.

Evening before the Crucifixion.

John 13:1-20.

1 Now before the feast of the passover, Jesus knowing that his hour was come that he should depart out of this world unto the Father, having loved his own which were in the world, he loved them [1]unto
2 the end. And during supper, the devil having already put into the
3 heart of Judas Iscariot, Simon's *son*, to betray him, *Jesus*, knowing that the Father had given all things into his hands, and that he came forth
4 from God and goeth unto God, riseth from supper, and layeth aside his
5 garments; and he took a towel and girded himself. Then he poureth water into the bason, and began to wash the disciples' feet, and to
6 wipe them with the towel wherewith he was girded. So he cometh to Simon Peter. He saith unto him, Lord, dost thou wash my feet?
7 Jesus answered and said unto him, What I do thou knowest not now;
8 but thou shalt understand hereafter. Peter saith unto him, Thou shalt never wash my feet. Jesus answered him, If I wash thee not,
9 thou hast no part with me. Simon Peter saith unto him, Lord, not
10 my feet only, but also my hands and my head. Jesus saith to him, He that is bathed needeth not [2]save to wash his feet, but is clean every
11 whit: and ye are clean, but not all. For he knew him that should betray him; therefore said he, Ye are not all clean.
12 So when he had washed their feet, and taken his garments, and [3]sat
13 down again, he said unto them, Know ye what I have done to you? Ye
14 call me, [4]Master, and, Lord: and ye say well; for so I am. If I then, the Lord and the [4]Master, have washed your feet, ye also ought to
15 wash one another's feet. For I have given you an example, that ye
16 also should do as I have done to you. Verily, verily, I say unto you, A [5]servant is not greater than his lord; neither [6]one that is sent
17 greater than he that sent him. If ye know these things, blessed are
18 ye if ye do them. I speak not of you all: I know whom I [7]have chosen: but that the scripture may be fulfilled, He that eateth [8]my bread lifted
19 up his heel against me. From henceforth I tell you before it come to pass, that, when it is come to pass, ye may believe that [9]I am *he.*
20 Verily, verily, I say unto you, He that receiveth whomsoever I send receiveth me; and he that receiveth me receiveth him that sent me.

1. Or, *to the uttermost.* 2. Some ancient authorities omit *save,* and *his feet.* 3. Gr. *reclined.* 4. Or, *Teacher.* 5. Gr. *bondservant.* 6. Gr. *an apostle.* 7. Or, *chose.* 8. Many ancient authorities read *his bread with me.* 9. Or, *I am.*

§ 120. Jesus Foretells That Judas Will Betray Him, and Peter Will Deny Him.

Evening before the Crucifixion.

Matt. 26:21-25 and 31-35.	Mark 14:18-21 and 27-31.	Luke 22:21-23 and 31-38.	John 13:21-38.
21 and as they	18 And as they [2]sat and were	21 But behold, the hand of	21 When Jesus had thus said,

Matt. 26:21-25 and 31-35.	Mark 14:18-21 and 27-31.	Luke 22:21-23 and 31-38.	John 13:21-38.
were eating, he said, Verily I say unto you, that one of you shall betray me.	eating, Jesus said, Verily I say unto you, One of you shall betray me, *even* he that eateth with me.	him that betrayeth me is 22 with me on the table. For the Son of man indeed goeth, as it hath been determined: but woe unto that man through whom he is betrayed!	he was troubled in the spirit, and testified, and said, Verily, verily, I say unto you, that one of you shall betray me.
22 And they were exceeding sorrowful, and began to say unto him every one, Is it I, Lord? 23 And he answered and said, He that dipped his hand with me in the dish, the same shall 24 betray me. The Son of man goeth, even as it is written of him: but woe unto that man through whom the Son of man is betrayed! good were it ⁵for that man if he had not been born.	19 They began to be sorrowful, and to say unto him one by one, Is it I? 20 And he said unto them, *It is* one of the twelve, he that dippeth with me in the dish. 21 For the Son of man goeth, even as it is written of him: but woe unto that man through whom the Son of man is betrayed! good were it ⁵for that man if he had not been born.	23 And they began to question among themselves, which of them it was that should do this thing.	22 The disciples looked one on another, doubting of whom he spake.
			23 There was at the table reclining in Jesus' bosom one of his disciples, whom Jesus 24 loved. Simon Peter therefore beckoneth to him, and saith unto him, Tell

LAST WEEK OF OUR LORD'S MINISTRY,

Matt. 26:21-25 and 31-35.	Mark 14:18-21 and 27-31.	Luke 22:21-23 and 31-38.	John 13:21-38.
			us who it is of whom he 25 speaketh. He leaning back, as he was, on Jesus' breast saith un- 26 to him, Lord, who is it? Jesus therefore answereth, He it is, for whom I shall dip the sop, and give it him. So when he had dipped the sop, he taketh and giveth it to Judas, *the son* of Simon Iscariot.
25 And Judas, which betrayed him, answered and said, Is it I, Rabbi? He saith unto him, Thou hast said.			

27 And after the sop, then entered Satan into him. Jesus therefore saith unto him, That thou doest,
28 do quickly. Now no man at the table knew for what intent he spake
29 this unto them. For some thought, because Judas had the 'bag, that Jesus said unto him, Buy what things we have need of for the feast:
30 or, that he should give something to the poor. He then having received the sop went out straightway: and it was night.
31 When therefore he was gone out, Jesus saith, Now ⁸is the Son of
32 man glorified, and God ⁸is glorified in him; and God shall glorify him
33 in himself, and straightway shall he glorify him. Little children, yet a little while I am with you. Ye shall seek me: and as I said unto
34 the Jews, Whither I go, ye cannot come; so now I say unto you. A new commandment I give unto you, that ye love one another; ʳeven
35 as I have loved you, that ye also love one another. By this shall all men know that ye are my disciples, if ye have love one to another.

| 31 Then saith Jesus unto them, All ye shall be¹offend- ed in me this night: for it is written, I will smite the shep- herd, and the sheep of the flock shall be scattered a- 32 broad. But af- ter I am raised up, I will go be- fore you into | 27 And Jesus saith unto them, All ye shall be¹offend- ed: for it is written, I will smite the shep- herd, and the sheep shall be scattered a- 28 broad. How- beit, after I am raised up, I will go before you into Gali- lee. | 31 Simon, Si- mon, behold, Satan ⁴asked to have you, that he might sift you as wheat: 32 but I made sup- plication for thee, that thy faith fail not: and do thou, when once thou hast turn- ed again, stab- lish thy breth- ren. | 36 Simon Peter saith unto him, Lord, whither goest thou? Je- sus answered, Whither I go, thou canst not follow me now; but thou shalt follow after- wards. |

Matt. 26:21-25 and 31-35.	Mark 14:18-21 and 27-31.	Luke 22:21-23 and 31-38.	John 13:21-38.
33 Galilee. But Peter answered and said unto him, If all shall be ¹offended in thee, I will never be 34 ¹offended. Jesus said unto him, Verily I say unto thee, that this night, before the cock crow, thou shalt deny me 35 thrice. Peter saith unto him, Even if I must die with thee, yet will I not deny thee. Likewise also said all the disciples.	29 But Peter said unto him, Although all shall be ¹offended, yet will 30 not I. And Jesus saith unto him, Verily I say unto thee, that thou to-day, even this night, before the cock crow twice shalt deny me thrice. 31 But he spake exceeding vehemently, If I must die with thee, I will not deny thee. And in like manner also said they all.	33 And he said unto him, Lord, with thee I am ready to go both to prison and to 34 death. And he said, I tell thee, Peter, the cock shall not crow this day, until thou shalt thrice deny that thou knowest me.	37 Peter saith unto him, Lord, why cannot I follow thee even now? I will lay down my life for 38 thee. Jesus answereth, Wilt thou lay down thy life for me? Verily, verily, I say unto thee, The cock shall not crow, till thou hast denied me thrice.

35 And he said unto them, When I sent you forth without purse, and wallet, and shoes, lacked ye anything? And they said, Nothing.
36 And he said unto them, But now, he that hath a purse, let him take it, and likewise a wallet: ⁵and he that hath none, let him sell his
37 cloke, and buy a sword. For I say unto you, that this which is written must be fulfilled in me, And he was reckoned with transgressors: for that which concern-
38 eth me hath ⁶fulfilment. And they said, Lord, behold, here are two swords. And he said unto them, It is enough.

1. Gr. *caused to stumble.* 2. Gr. *reclined.* 3. Gr. *for him if that man.* 4. Or, *obtained you by asking.* 5. Or, *and he that hath no sword, let him sell his cloke and buy one.* 6. Gr. *end.* 7. Or, *box.* 8. Or, *was.* 9. Or, *even as I loved you, that ye also may love one another.*

§121. JESUS INSTITUTES THE MEMORIAL OF EATING BREAD AND DRINKING WINE.

Jerusalem. Evening before the Crucifixion.

Matt. 26:26-29	Mark 14:22-25.	Luke 22:17-20.	I Cor. 11:23-26.
		17 And he received a cup, and when he had given thanks he said, Take this, and divide it among yourselves: 18 for I say unto you, I will not drink from henceforth of the fruit of the vine until the kingdom of God shall come.	
26 And as they were eating, Jesus took ¹bread, and blessed, and brake it; and he gave to the disciples, and said, Take, eat; this is my body. 27 And he took ²a cup, and gave thanks, and gave to them, saying, Drink ye all of it; 28 for this is my blood of ³the ⁴covenant, which is shed for many unto remission 29 of sins. But I say unto you, I will not drink henceforth of	22 And as they were eating, he took ¹bread, and when he had blessed, he brake it, and gave to them, and said, Take ye: this is my body. 23 And he took a cup, and when he had given thanks, he gave to them, and they all drank of it. 24 And he said unto them, This is my blood of ³the ⁴covenant, which is shed for many. 25 Verily I say unto you, I will no more drink of the fruit of	19 And he took ¹bread, and when he had given thanks, he brake it, and gave to them, saying, This is my body ⁵which is given for you: this do in remembrance of me. 20 And the cup in like manner after supper, saying, This cup is the new ⁶covenant in my blood, even that which is poured out for you.	23 For I received of the Lord that which also I delivered unto you, how that the Lord Jesus in the night in which he was betrayed took bread; 24 and when he had given thanks, he brake it, and said, This is my body, which ⁷is for you: this do in remembrance of me. 25 In like manner also the cup, after supper, saying, This cup is the new ⁶covenant in my blood: this do, as oft as ye drink it, in re-

Matt. 26:26-29.	Mark 14:22-25.	I Cor. 11:23-26.
this fruit of the vine, until that day when I drink it new with you in my Father's kingdom.	the vine, until that day when I drink it new in the kingdom of God.	membrance of 26 me. For as often as ye eat this bread, and drink the cup, ye proclaim the Lord's death till he come.

1. Or, *a loaf*. 2. Some ancient authorities read *the cup*. 3. Or, *the testament*. 4. Many ancient authorities insert *new*. 5. Some ancient authorities omit *which is given for you..which is poured out for you*. 6. Or, *testament*. 7. Many ancient authorities read *is broken for you*.

§ 122. Farewell Discourse to His Disciples.

Jerusalem.

John, chap. 14 to chap. 17.

(a) chap. **14.**—1 Let not your heart be troubled: ¹ye believe in God,
2 believe also in me. In my Father's house are many ²mansions; if it were not so, I would have told you; for I go to prepare a place for you.
3 And if I go and prepare a place for you, I come again, and will receive
4 you unto myself; that where I am *there* ye may be also. ³And whither
5 I go, ye know the way. Thomas saith unto him, Lord, we know not
6 whither thou goest: how know we the way? Jesus saith unto him, I am the way, and the truth, and the life: no one cometh unto the
7 Father, but ⁴by me. If ye had known me, ye would have known my Father also: from henceforth ye know him, and have seen him.
8 Philip saith unto him, Lord, shew us the Father, and it sufficeth us.
9 Jesus saith unto him, Have I been so long time with you, and dost thou not know me, Philip? he that hath seen me hath seen the Father;
10 how sayest thou, Shew us the Father? Believest thou not that I am in the Father, and the Father in me? the words that I say unto you I speak not from myself: but the Father abiding in me doeth his works.
11 Believe me that I am in the Father and the Father in me: or else be-
12 lieve me for the very works' sake. Verily, verily, I say unto you, he that believeth on me, the works that I do shall he do also; and greater
13 *works* than these shall he do: because I go unto the Father. And whatsoever ye shall ask in my name, that will I do, that the Father
14 may be glorified in the Son. If ye shall ask ⁵me anything in my name,
15 that will I do. If ye love me, ye will keep my commandments.
16 And I will ⁶pray the Father, and he shall give you another ⁷Comforter,
17 that he may be with you for ever, *even* the Spirit of truth: whom the world cannot receive; for it beholdeth him not, neither knoweth him:
18 ye know him: for he abideth with you, and shall be in you. I will not
19 leave you ⁸desolate: I come unto you. Yet a little while, and the world beholdeth me no more; but ye behold me: because I live, ⁹ye
20 shall live also. In that day ye shall know that I am in my Father,
21 and ye in me, and I in you. He that hath my commandments, and keepeth them, he it is that loveth me: and he that loveth me shall

John, chap. 14 to chap. 17.

he loved of my Father, and I will love him, and will manifest myself
22 unto him. Judas (not Iscariot) saith unto him, Lord, what is come to
pass that thou wilt manifest thyself unto us, and not unto the world?
23 And Jesus answered and said unto him, If a man love me, he will
keep my word: and my Father will love him, and we will come unto
24 him, and make our abode with him. He that loveth me not keepeth
not my words: and the word which ye hear is not mine, but the
Father's who sent me.
25 These things have I spoken unto you, while yet abiding with you.
26 But the ⁷Comforter, *even* the Holy Spirit, whom the Father will send
in my name, he shall teach you all things, and bring to your remem-
27 brance all that I said unto you. Peace I leave with you; my peace I
give unto you: not as the world giveth, give I unto you. Let not your
28 heart be troubled, neither let it be fearful. Ye heard how I said
to you, I go away, and I come unto you. If ye loved me, ye would
have rejoiced, because I go unto the Father: for the Father is greater
29 than I. And now I have told you before it come to pass, that, when it
30 is come to pass, ye may believe. I will no more speak much with you,
31 for the prince of the world cometh: and he hath nothing in me; but
that the world may know that I love the Father, and as the Father
gave me commandment, even so I do. Arise, let us go hence.

1. Or, *believe in God.* 2. Or, *abiding-places.* 3. Many ancient authorities read *And whither I go, ye know, and the way ye know.* 4. Or, *through.* 5. Many ancient authorities omit *me.* 6. Gr. *make request of.* 7. Or, *Advocate,* Or, *Helper.* Gr. *Paraclete.* 8. Or, *orphans.* 9. Or, *and ye shall live.*

(b) chaps. 15 and 16.—**15.** I am the true vine, and my Father is the
2 husbandman. Every branch in me that beareth not fruit, he taketh
it away: and every *branch* that beareth fruit, he cleanseth it, that it
3 may bear more fruit. Already ye are clean because of the word which
4 I have spoken unto you. Abide in me, and I in you. As the branch
cannot bear fruit of itself, except it abide in the vine; so neither can
5 ye, except ye abide in me. I am the vine, ye are the branches: He
that abideth in me, and I in him, the same beareth much fruit: for
6 apart from me ye can do nothing. If a man abide not in me, he is
cast forth as a branch, and is withered; and they gather them, and
7 cast them into the fire, and they are burned. If ye abide in me, and
my words abide in you, ask whatsoever ye will, and it shall be done
8 unto you. Herein ¹is my Father glorified, ²that ye bear much fruit:
9 and *so* shall ye be my disciples. Even as the Father hath loved me,
10 I also have loved you: abide ye in my love. If ye keep my commandments, ye shall abide in my love; even as I have kept my Father's
11 commandments, and abide in his love. These things have I spoken
unto you, that my joy may be in you, and *that* your joy may be fulfilled.
12 This is my commandment, that ye love one another, even as I have
13 loved you. Greater love hath no man than this, that a man lay down
14 his life for his friends. Ye are my friends, if ye do the things which
15 I command you. No longer do I call you ³servants; for the ⁴servant
knoweth not what his lord doeth: but I have called you friends; for
all things that I heard from my Father I have made known unto you.
16 Ye did not choose me, but I chose you, and appointed you, that ye
should go and bear fruit, and *that* your fruit should abide: that what-

John, chap. 14 to chap. 17.

soever ye shall ask of the Father in my name, he may give it you.
17, 18 These things I command you, that ye may love one another. If the world hateth you, *ye know that it hath hated me before *it hated* you.
19 If ye were of the world, the world would love its own; but because ye are not of the world, but I chose you out of the world, therefore the
20 world hateth you. Remember the word that I said unto you, A *servant is not greater than his lord. If they persecuted me, they will also
21 persecute you: if they keep my word, they will keep yours also. But all these things will they do unto you for my name's sake, because
22 they know not him that sent me. If I had not come and spoken unto them, they had not had sin: but now they have no excuse for their
23, 24 sin. He that hateth me hateth my Father also. If I had not done among them the works which none other did, they had not had sin:
25 but now have they both seen and hated both me and my Father. But *this cometh to pass*, that the word may be fulfilled that is written in
26 their law, They hated me without a cause. But when the °Comforter is come, whom I will send unto you from the Father, *even* the Spirit of truth, which ⁷proceedeth from the Father, he shall bear witness of
27 me: *and ye also bear witness, because ye have been with me from the beginning.

16. 1. These things have I spoken unto you that ye should not be
2 made to stumble. They shall put you out of the synagogues: yea, the hour cometh, that whosoever killeth you shall think that he offereth
3 service unto God. And these things will they do, because they have
4 not known the Father, nor me. But these things have I spoken unto you, that when their hour is come, ye may remember them, how that I told you. And these things I said not unto you from the beginning,
5 because I was with you. But now I go unto him that sent me: and
6 none of you asketh me, Whither goest thou? But because I have
7 spoken these things unto you, sorrow hath filled your heart. Nevertheless I tell you the truth; It is expedient for you that I go away: for if I go not away, the °Comforter will not come unto you: but if I go, I
8 will send him unto you. And he, when he is come, will convict the
9 world in respect of sin, and of righteousness, and of judgement: of
10 sin, because they believe not on me: of righteousness, because I go to
11 the Father, and ye behold me no more; of judgement, because the
12 prince of this world hath been judged. I have yet many things to say
13 unto you, but ye cannot bear them now. Howbeit when he, the Spirit of truth, is come, he shall guide you into all the truth: for he shall not speak from himself; but what things soever he shall hear, *these* shall he speak: and he shall declare unto you the things that are to
14 come. He shall glorify me: for he shall take of mine, and shall
15 declare *it* unto you. All things whatsoever the Father hath are mine: therefore said I, that he taketh of mine, and shall declare *it* unto you.
16 A little while, and ye behold me no more: and again a little while,
17 and ye shall see me. *Some* of his disciples therefore said one to another, What is this that he saith unto us, A little while, and ye behold me not; and again a little while, and ye shall see me: and,
18 Because I go to the Father? They said therefore, What is this that
19 he saith, A little while? We know not what he saith. Jesus perceived that they were desirous to ask him, and he said unto them, Do

John, chap. 14 to chap. 17.

ye inquire among yourselves concerning this, that I said, A little while, and ye behold me not, and again a little while, and ye shall
20 see me? Verily, verily, I say unto you, that ye shall weep and lament, but the world shall rejoice: ye shall be sorrowful, but your sorrow
21 shall be turned into joy. A woman when she is in travail hath sorrow because her hour is come: but when she is delivered of the child, she remembereth no more the anguish, for the joy that a man is born
22 into the world. And ye therefore now have sorrow: but I will see you again, and your heart shall rejoice, and your joy no one taketh
23 away from you. And in that day ye shall ⁹ask me nothing. Verily, verily, I say unto you, If ye shall ask anything of the Father, he will
24 give it you in my name. Hitherto have ye asked nothing in my name: ask and ye shall receive, that your joy may be fulfilled.
25 These things have I spoken unto you in ¹⁰proverbs: the hour cometh, when I shall no more speak unto you in ¹⁰proverbs, but shall tell you
26 plainly of the Father. In that day ye shall ask in my name: and I say
27 not unto you, that I will ¹¹pray the Father for you; for the Father himself loveth you, because ye have loved me, and have believed that I
28 came forth from the Father. I came out from the Father, and am come into the world: again, I leave the world, and go unto the Father.
29 His disciples say, Lo, now speakest thou plainly, and speakest no
30 ¹²proverb. Now know we that thou knowest all things, and needest not that any man should ask thee: by this we believe that thou camest
31, 32 forth from God. Jesus answered them, Do ye now believe? Behold, the hour cometh, yea, is come, that ye shall be scattered, every man to his own, and shall leave me alone: and *yet* I am not alone, be-
33 cause the Father is with me. These things have I spoken unto you, that in me ye may have peace. In the world ye have tribulation: but be of good cheer; I have overcome the world.

1. Or, *was*. 2. Many ancient authorities read *that ye bear much fruit, and he my disciples*. 3. Gr. *bondservants*. 4. Gr. *bondservant*. 5. Or, *know ye*. 6. Or, *Advocate*. Or, *Helper*. Gr. *Paraclete*. 7. Or, *goeth forth from*. 8. Or, *and bear ye also witness*. 9. Or, *ask me no question*. 10. Or, *parables*. 11. Gr. *make request of*. 12. Or, *parable*.

(c) chap. 17. 1. These things spake Jesus; and lifting up his eyes to heaven, he said, Father, the hour is come; glorify thy Son, that the
2 Son may glorify thee: even as thou gavest him authority over all flesh, that whatsoever thou hast given him, to them he should give eternal
3 life. And this is life eternal, that they should know thee the only
4 true God, and him whom thou didst send, *even* Jesus Christ. I glorified thee on the earth, having accomplished the work which thou
5 hast given me to do. And now, O Father, glorify thou me with thine own self with the glory which I had with thee before the world was.
6 I manifested thy name unto the men whom thou gavest me out of the world: thine they were, and thou gavest them to me; and they have
7 kept thy word. Now they know that all things whatsoever thou hast
8 given me are from thee: for the words which thou hast given me I have given unto them; and they received *them*, and knew of a truth that I came forth from thee, and they believed that thou didst
9 send me. I ¹pray for them: I ¹pray not for the world, but for those
10 whom thou hast given me; for they are thine: and all things that are
11 mine are thine, and thine are mine; and I am glorified in them. And

AND HIS CRUCIFIXION.   183

John, chap. 14 to chap. 17.

I am no more in the world, and these are in the world, and I come to thee. Holy Father, keep them in thy name which thou hast given
12 me, that they may be one, even as we *are*. While I was with them, I kept them in thy name which thou hast given me: and I guarded them, and not one of them perished, but the son of perdition; that the
13 scripture might be fulfilled. But now I come to thee: and these things I speak in the world, that they may have my joy fulfilled in
14 themselves. I have given them my word; and the world hated them,
15 because they are not of the world, even as I am not of the world. I ¹pray not that thou shouldest take them ²from ³the evil *one*. They are not of the
16 thou shouldest keep them ²from ³the evil *one*. They are not of the
17 world, even as I am not of the world. ⁴Sanctify them in the truth: thy
18 word is truth. As thou didst send me into the world, even so sent I
19 them into the world. And for their sakes I ⁴sanctify myself, that they
20 themselves also may be sanctified in truth. Neither for these only do I ¹pray, but for them also that believe on me through their word;
21 that they may all be one; even as thou, Father, *art* in me, and I in thee, that they also may be in us: that the world may believe that thou
22 didst send me. And the glory which thou hast given me I have given
23 unto them; that they may be one, even as we *are* one; I in them, and thou in me, that they may be perfected into one; that the world may know that thou didst send me, and lovedst them, even as thou lovedst
24 me. Father, ⁵that which thou hast given me, I will that, where I am, they also may be with me; that they may behold my glory, which thou hast given me: for thou lovedst me before the foundation of the
25 world. O righteous Father, the world knew thee not, but I knew
26 thee; and these knew that thou didst send me: and I made known unto them thy name, and will make it known: that the love wherewith thou lovedst me may be in them, and I in them.

1. Gr. *make request.*   2. Gr. *out of.*   3. Or, *evil.*   4. Or, *Consecrate.*   5. Many ancient authorities read *those whom.*

§123. GOING FORTH TO GETHSEMANE, JESUS SUFFERS LONG IN AGONY.

In an open garden, between the brook Kedron and the foot of the Mount of Olives.

Late in the night introducing Friday.

Matt. 26:30, and 36–46.	Mark 14:26, and 32–42.	Luke 22:39–46.	John 18:1
30 And when they had sung a hymn, they went out unto the Mount of Olives.	26 And when they had sung a hymn, they went out unto the Mount of Olives.	39 And he came out, and went, as his custom was, unto the Mount of Olives; and the disciples also followed him.	1 When Jesus had spoken these words, he went forth with his disciples over the ⁴brook ⁵Kidron, where was a

Matt. 26:30, and 36–46.	Mark 14:26, and 32–42.	Luke 22:39-46.	John 18:1.
36 Then cometh Jesus with them unto ¹a place called Gethsemane, and saith unto his disciples, Sit ye here, while I go yonder 37 and pray. And he took with him Peter and the two sons of Zebedee, and began to be sorrowful and sore troubled. 38 Then saith he unto them, My soul is exceeding sorrowful, even unto death: abide ye here, and watch with 39 me. And he went forward a little, and fell on his face, and prayed, saying, O my Father, if it be possible, let this cup pass away from me: nevertheless, not as I will, but as thou wilt.	32 And they come unto ¹a place which was named Gethsemane: and he saith unto his disciples, Sit ye here, while I pray. 33 And he taketh with him Peter and James and John, and began to be greatly amazed, and sore troubled. 34 And he saith unto them, My soul is exceeding sorrowful even unto death: abide ye here, and watch. And 35 he went forward a little, and fell on the ground, and prayed that, if it were possible, the hour might pass away from him. 36 And he said, Abba, Father, all things are possible unto thee; remove this cup from me: howbeit not what I will, but what thou wilt.	40 And when he was at the place, he said unto them, Pray that ye enter not into temptation. 41 And he was parted from them about a stone's cast: and he kneeled down and prayed, 42 saying, Father, if thou be willing, remove this cup from me: nevertheless not my will, but thine, be done. 43 ³And there appeared unto him an angel from heaven,	garden, into the which he entered, himself and his disciples.

Matt. 26:30, and 36–46.	Mark 14:26, and 32–42.	Luke 22:39–46.
		strengthening him. And being in an agony he prayed more earnestly: and his sweat became as it were great drops of blood falling down upon the ground. And when he rose up from his prayer, he came unto the disciples, and found them sleeping for sorrow, and said unto them, Why sleep ye? rise and pray, that ye enter not into temptation.

(Luke verses: 44, 45, 46)

Matt.	Mark	
40 And he cometh unto the disciples, and findeth them sleeping, and saith unto Peter, What, could ye not watch with me one hour?	37 And he cometh, and findeth them sleeping, and saith unto Peter, Simon, sleepest thou? couldest thou not watch one hour?	
41 Watch and pray, that ye enter not into temptation: the spirit indeed is willing, but the flesh is weak.	38 Watch and pray, that ye enter not into temptation: the spirit indeed is willing, but the flesh is weak.	
42 Again a second time he went away, and prayed, saying, O my Father, if this cannot pass away, except I drink it, thy will be done.	39 And again he went away, and prayed, saying the same words.	
43 And he came again and found them sleeping, for their eyes were heavy.	40 And again he came, and found them sleeping, for their eyes were very heavy; and they wist not what to an-	
44 And he left them again, and went away,		

Matt. 26:30, and 36–46.	Mark 14:26, and 32–42.
and prayed a third time, saying again the same words.	swer him.
45 Then cometh he to the disciples, and saith unto them, Sleep on now, and take your rest: behold, the hour is at hand, and the Son of man is betrayed unto the hands of sinners.	41 And he cometh the third time, and saith unto them, Sleep on now, and take your rest: it is enough; the hour is come; behold, the Son of man is betrayed into the hands of sinners.
46 Arise, let us be going: behold, he is at hand that betrayeth me.	42 Arise, let us be going: behold, he that betrayeth me is at hand.

1. Gr. *an enclosed piece of ground*. 2. Or, *Watch ye, and pray that ye enter not*. 3. Many ancient authorities omit ver. 43, 44. 4. Or, *ravine*. Gr. *winter-torrent*. 5. Or, *of the Cedars*.

In §124–132 our Lord is arrested, tried, and sentenced to be crucified.

§124. JESUS IS BETRAYED, ARRESTED AND FORSAKEN.

Garden of Gethsemane. Friday, long before dawn.

Matt. 26:47–56.	Mark 14:43–52.	Luke 22:47–53.	John 18:2–12.
			2 Now Judas also, which betrayed him, knew the place: for Jesus ofttimes resorted thither with his disciples.
47 And while he yet spake, lo, Judas, one of the twelve, came, and with him a great multitude with	43 And straightway, while he yet spake, cometh Judas, one of the twelve, and with him a multitude	47 While he yet spake, behold, a multitude, and he that was called Judas, one of the twelve, went	3 Judas then, having received the ³band *of soldiers*, and officers from the chief priests and the Pharisees, com-

Matt. 26:47-56.	Mark 14:43-52.	Luke 22:47-53.	John 18:2-12.
swords and staves, from the chief priests and elders of the people.	with swords and staves, from the chief priests and the scribes and the elders.	before them;	eth thither with lanterns and torches and weapons. 4 Jesus therefore, knowing all the things that were coming upon him, went forth, and saith unto them, Whom 5 seek ye? They answered him, Jesus of Nazareth. Jesus saith unto them, I am *he*. And Judas also, which betrayed him, was standing with 6 them. When therefore he said unto them, I am *he*, they went backward, and fell to the 7 ground. Again therefore he asked them, Whom seek ye? And they said, Jesus of Naza-8 reth. Jesus answered, I told you that I am *he:* if therefore ye seek me, let these go their 9 way: that the word might be fulfilled which he spake, Of those whom thou hast given me I lost not one.
48 Now he that betrayed him gave them a sign, saying,	44 Now he that betrayed him had given them a token,		

Matt. 26:47-56.	Mark 14:43-52.	Luke 22:47-53.	John 18:2-12.
Whomsoever I shall kiss, that is he; take him.	saying, Whomsoever I shall kiss, that is he: take him, and lead him away 45 safely. And when he was come, straightway he came to him, and saith, Rabbi; and ¹kissed him.		
49 And straightway he came to Jesus, and said, Hail, Rabbi; and ¹kissed him.		and he drew near unto Jesus, to kiss 48 him. But Jesus said unto him, Judas, betrayest thou the Son of man with a kiss?	
50 And Jesus said unto him, Friend, do that for which thou art come. Then 46 they came and laid hands on Jesus, and took 51 him. And behold, one of them that were with Jesus stretched out his hand, and drew his sword, and smote the ²servant of the high priest, and struck off 52 his ear. Then saith Jesus unto him, Put up again thy sword into its place: for all they that take the sword shall perish with 53 the sword. Or thinkest thou that I cannot beseech my Father, and he shall even now send me more	And they laid hands on him, and took 47 him. But a certain one of them that stood by drew his sword, and smote the ²servant of the high priest, and struck off his ear.	49 And when they that were about him saw what would follow, they said, Lord, shall we smite with the sword? 50 And a certain one of them smote the ²servant of the high priest, and struck off his right ear. 51 But Jesus answered and said, Suffer ye thus far. And he touched his ear, and healed him.	12 So the ³band and the ⁴chief captain, and the officers of the Jews, seized Jesus and bound him. 10 Simon Peter therefore having a sword drew it, and struck the high priest's ²servant, and cut off his right ear. Now the ²servant's name was Malchus. 11 Jesus therefore said unto Peter, Put up the sword into the sheath: the cup which the Father hath given me, shall I not drink it?

Matt. 26:47-56.	Mark 14:43-52.	Luke 22:47-53.	John 18:2-12.
than twelve legions of angels? How then should the scriptures be fulfilled, that thus it must be? In that hour said Jesus to the multitudes, Are ye come out as against a robber with swords and staves to seize me? I sat daily in the temple teaching, and ye took me not. But all this is come to pass, that the scriptures of the prophets might be fulfilled. Then all the disciples left him and fled.	And Jesus answered and said unto them, Are ye come out as against a robber, with swords and staves to seize me? I was daily with you in the temple teaching, and ye took me not: but *this is done* that the scriptures might be fulfilled. And they all left him, and fled. And a certain young man followed with him, having a linen cloth cast about him, over *his* naked *body:* and they lay hold on him; but he left the linen cloth, and fled naked.	And Jesus said unto the chief priests, and captains of the temple, and elders, which were come against him, Are ye come out, as against a robber, with swords and staves? When I was daily with you in the temple, ye stretched not forth your hands against me: but this is your hour, and the power of darkness.	

Verse numbers: Matt 54, 55, 56; Mark 48, 49, 50, 51, 52; Luke 52, 53.

1. Gr. *kissed him much.* 2. Gr. *bondservant.* 3. Or, *cohort.* 4. Or, *military tribune.* Gr. *chiliarch.*

190 LAST WEEK OF OUR LORD'S MINISTRY,

The Jewish Trial and related occurrences, §125–9.

§125. JESUS FIRST* EXAMINED BY ANNAS, THE EX-HIGH-PRIEST.

Friday before dawn.

John 18:12–14, 19–23.

12 So the ¹band and the ²chief captain, and the officers of the Jews,
13 seized Jesus and bound him, and led him to Annas first; for he was
14 father in law to Caiaphas, which was high priest that year. Now Caiaphas was he which gave counsel to the Jews, that it was expedient that one man should die for the people.
19 The high priest therefore asked Jesus of his disciples, and of his
20 teaching. Jesus answered him, I have spoken openly to the world; I ever taught in ³synagogues, and in the temple, where all the Jews
21 come together; and in secret spake I nothing. Why askest thou me? ask them that have heard *me*, what I spake unto them: behold, these
22 know the things which I said. And when he had said this, one of the officers standing by struck Jesus ⁴with his hand, saying, Answer-
23 est thou the high priest so? Jesus answered him, If I have spoken evil, bear witness of the evil; but if well, why smitest thou me?

1. Or, *cohort.* 2. Or, *military tribune,* Gr. *chiliarch.* 3. Gr. *synagogue.* 4. Or, *with a rod.*

§126. TRIED AND CONDEMNED BY CAIAPHAS AND THE SANHEDRIN.

Residence of the High-priest Caiaphas. Before dawn on Friday.

Matt. 26:57,59–68.   Mark 14:53,55–65.   Luke 22:54,63–65.   John 18:24.

Matt. 26:57,59–68.	Mark 14:53,55–65.	Luke 22:54,63–65.	John 18:24.
57 And they that had taken Jesus led him away to *the house of* Caiaphas the high priest, where the scribes and the elders were gathered together.	53 And they led Jesus away to the high priest: and there come together with him all the chief priests and the elders and the scribes.	54 And they seized him, and led him away, and brought him into the high priest's house.	24 Annas therefore sent him bound unto Caiaphas the high priest.
59 Now the chief priests and the whole council sought false witness against Jesus, that they might put him	55 Now the chief priests and the whole council sought witness against Jesus to put him to death; and found it		

*The *Jewish trial* comprised three stages, the preliminary examination by Annas (§125), the informal trial by the Sanhedrin, probably before dawn (§126), and the formal trial after dawn (§128). With these are narrated two related matters, the denial by Peter (§127), and the suicide of Judas (§129).

Matt. 26:57,59-68. Mark 14:53,55-65. Luke 22:54,63-65.

Matt.	Mark
60 to death; and they found it not, though many false witnesses came.	56 not. For many bare false witness against him, and their witness agreed not together.
61 But afterward came two, and said,	57 And there stood up certain, and bare false witness against him,
This man said, I am able to destroy the ¹temple of God, and to build it in three days.	58 saying, We heard him say, I will destroy this ¹temple that is made with hands, and in three days I will build another made without hands.
	59 And not even so did their witness agree together.
62 And the high priest stood up, and said unto him, Answerest thou nothing? what is it which these witness against thee?	60 And the high priest stood up in the midst, and asked Jesus, saying, Answerest thou nothing? what is it which these witness against thee?
63 But Jesus held his peace.	61 But he held his peace, and answered ¹nothing. Again the high priest asked him, and saith unto him,
And the high priest said unto him, I adjure thee by the living God, that thou tell us whether thou be the Christ, the Son of God.	Art thou the Christ, the Son of the Blessed?
64 Jesus saith unto him, Thou hast	62 And Jesus said, I am:

Matt. 26:57,59–68. Mark 14:53,55–65. Luke 22:54,63–65.

Matt.	Mark	Luke
said: nevertheless I say unto you, Henceforth ye shall see the Son of man sitting at the right hand of power, and coming on the clouds of heaven. Then the high priest rent his garments, saying, He hath spoken blasphemy: what further need have we of witnesses? behold, now ye have heard the blasphemy: what think ye? They answered and said, He is ²worthy of death. Then did they spit in his face and buffet him: and some smote him ³with the palms of their hands, saying, Prophesy unto us, thou Christ, who is he that struck thee?	and ye shall see the Son of man sitting at the right hand of power, and coming with the clouds of heaven. And the high priest rent his clothes, and saith, What further need have we of witnesses? Ye have heard the blasphemy: what think ye? And they all condemned him to be ²worthy of death. And some began to spit on him, and to cover his face, and to buffet him, and to say unto him, Prophesy: and the officers received him with ⁴blows of their hands.	And the men that held ⁵Jesus mocked him and beat him. And they blindfolded him, and asked him, saying, Prophesy: who is he that struck thee? And many other things spake they against him, reviling him.

1. Or, *sanctuary*: as in chap. 23:35; 27:5. 2. Gr. *liable to*. 3. Or, *with rods*. 4. Or, *strokes of rods*. 5. Gr. *him*.

§ 127. PETER THRICE DENIES HIS LORD.

Court of the High-priest's residence, during the series of trials.

Friday before and about dawn.

Matt. 26:58, 69–75. Mark 14:54, 66–72. Luke 22:54–62. John 18:15–18, 25–27.

Matt.	Mark	Luke	John
58 But Peter followed him afar off,	54 And Peter had followed him afar off,	54 But Peter followed afar off.	15 And Simon Peter followed Jesus, and *so did* another disciple. Now that disciple was known unto the high priest, and entered in with Jesus into the court of the high priest;
			16 but Peter was standing at the door without. So the other disciple, which was known unto the high priest, went out and spake unto her that kept the door, and brought in Peter.
unto the court of the high priest, and entered in,	even within, into the court of the high priest;		17 The maid therefore that kept the door saith unto Peter, Art thou also *one* of this man's disciples? He saith,
			18 I am not. Now the [b]servants and the officers were standing *there*, having made [c]a fire of coals; for it was cold; and they
and sat with the officers, to see the end.	and he was sitting with the officers, and		were warming themselves: and Peter also was with them,

LAST WEEK OF OUR LORD'S MINISTRY,

~Matt. 26:58,69–75.　Mark 14:54,66–72.　Luke 22:54–62.　John 18:15–18, 25–27.

Matt.	Mark	Luke	John
	warming himself in the light *of the fire*.	55 And when they had kindled a fire in the midst of the court, and had sat down together, Peter sat in the midst of them.	standing and warming himself.
69 Now Peter was sitting without in the court: and a maid came unto him, saying, Thou also wast with Jesus the Galilæan.	66 And as Peter was beneath in the court, there cometh one of the maids of the high priest; 67 and seeing Peter warming himself, she looked upon him, and saith, Thou also wast with the Nazarene, *even* Jesus.	56 And a certain maid seeing him as he sat in the light *of the fire*, and looking stedfastly upon him, said, This man also was with him.	25 Now Simon Peter was standing and warming himself. They said therefore unto him, Art thou also one of his disciples?
70 But he denied before them all, saying, I know not what thou sayest.	68 But he denied, saying, ¹I neither know, nor understand what thou sayest: and he went out into the ²porch; ³and the cock crew.	57 But he denied, saying, Woman, I know him not.	He denied and said, I am not.
71 And when he was gone out into the porch, another *maid* saw him, and saith unto them that were there, This man also was with Jesus the Nazarene.	69 And the maid saw him, and began again to say to them that stood by, This is *one* of them.	58 And after a little while another saw him, and said, Thou also art *one* of them. But Peter said, Man, I am not.	
72 And again he denied with an oath, I know not the man.	70 But he again denied it.		
73 And after a little while they that stood by came and said to Peter,	And after a little while again they that stood by said to Peter,	59 And after the space of about one hour another confidently affirmed, saying,	26 One of the ⁵servants of the high priest, being a kinsman of him whose ear Peter cut

Matt. 26:58,69-75.	Mark 14:54,66-72.	Luke 22:54-62.	John 18:15-18, 25-27.
Of a truth thou also art *one* of them; for thy speech bewray- 74 eth thee. Then began he to curse and to swear, I know not the man. And straightway the cock crew.	Of a truth thou art *one* of them; for thou art a 71 Galilæan. But he began to curse, and to swear, I know not this man of whom ye speak. 72 And straightway the second time the cock crew.	Of a truth this man also was with him: for he is a Gali- 60 læan. But Peter said, Man, I know not what thou sayest. And immediately, while he yet spake, the cock crew. 61 And the Lord turned, and looked upon Peter. And Peter remembered the word of the Lord, how that he said unto him, Before the cock crow this day, thou shalt deny me 62 thrice. And he went out, and wept bitterly.	off, saith, Did not I see thee in the garden 27 with him? Peter therefore denied again: and straightway the cock crew.
75 And Peter remembered the word which Jesus had said, Before the cock crow, thou shalt deny me thrice.* And he went out, and wept bitterly.	And Peter called to mind the word, how that Jesus said unto him, Before the cock crow twice, thou shalt deny me thrice. 'And when he thought thereon, he wept.		

1. Or, *I neither know, nor understand: thou, what sayest thou?* 2. Gr. *forecourt.* 3. Many ancient authorities omit *and the cock crew.* 4. Or, *And he began to weep.* 5. Gr. *bondservants.* 6. Gr. *a fire of charcoal.*

§128. AFTER DAWN, JESUS IS FORMALLY CONDEMNED BY THE SANHEDRIN, AND LED AWAY TO PILATE.

(*Friday.*)

Matt. 27:1, 2.	Mark 15:1.	Luke 22:66-23:1.	John 18:28.
1 Now when morning was	1 And straightway in the	66 And as soon as it was day,	

*Each of the four Gospels records three denials; but the details differ considerably, as must always be the case where in each narrative a few facts are selected out of many sayings and doings. We have seen (footnote on §125) that there were *three stages* of the Jewish trial, (1) before Annas, (2) before Caiaphas and the Sanhedrin for informal examination, (3) before them in a formal trial. Now John gives only the first of the three stages, Luke only the last, Matthew and Mark give the second stage fully, and the third in brief mention. If Peter's denials ran through all three (and Luke says in ver. 59 that there was an hour between his second and third denials), then no one of the four Gospels could give each of the denials precisely at the time of its occurrence; and so each Gospel merely throws them together, as in another way we here bring them together in one section. There is no difficulty about the substantial fact of the denials; and we must be content with our inability to arrange all the circumstances into a complete programme.

Matt. 27:1, 2.	Mark 15:1.	Luke 22:66–23:1.	John 18:28.
come, all the chief priests and the elders of the people took counsel against Jesus to put him to death:	morning the chief priests with the elders and scribes, and the whole council, held a consultation,	the assembly of the elders of the people was gathered together, both chief priests and scribes, and they led him away into their council, 67 saying, If thou art the Christ, tell us. But he said unto them, If I tell you, ye will not 68 believe: and if I ask *you*, ye will not an-69 swer. But from henceforth shall the Son of man be seated on the right hand of the power of 70 God. And they all said, Art thou then the Son of God? And he said unto them, ¹Ye say that I am. 71 And they said, What further need have we of witness? for we ourselves have heard from his own mouth.	
2 and they bound him, and led him away, and delivered him up to Pilate the governor.	and bound Jesus, and carried him away, and delivered him up to Pilate.	1 And the whole company of them rose up, and brought him before Pilate.	28 They lead Jesus therefore from Caiaphas into the ²palace: and it was early;

1. Or, *Ye say it, because I am.*   2. Gr. *Prætorium.*

§129. REMORSE AND SUICIDE OF JUDAS THE BETRAYER.

In the Temple, and in a place without the walls of Jerusalem.

Friday morning.

Matt. 27:3-10.

3 Then Judas, which betrayed him, when he saw that he was condemned, repented himself, and brought back the thirty pieces of silver to the chief
4 priests and elders, saying, I have sinned in that I betrayed ¹inno-
5 cent blood. But they said, What is that to us? see thou *to it*. And he cast down the pieces of silver into the sanctuary, and departed; and he went away and hanged
6 himself. And the chief priests took the pieces of silver, and said, It is not lawful to put them into the ²treasury, since it is the
7 price of blood. And they took counsel, and bought with them the potter's field, to bury stran-
8 gers in. Wherefore that field was called, The field of blood,
9 unto this day. Then was fulfilled that which was spoken ³by Jeremiah the prophet, saying, And ⁴they took the thirty pieces of silver, the price of him that was priced, ⁵whom *certain* of the
10 children of Israel did price; and ⁶they gave them for the potter's field, as the Lord appointed me.

Acts 1:18, 19.

18 (Now this man obtained a field with the reward of his iniquity; and falling headlong, he burst asunder in the midst, and all his
19 bowels gushed out. And it became known to all the dwellers at Jerusalem; insomuch that in their language that field was called Akeldama, that is, The field of blood.)

1. Many ancient authorities read *righteous*. 2. Gr. *corbanas*, that is, *sacred treasury*. Comp. Mark 7:11. 3. Or, *through*. 4. Or, *I took*. 5. Or, *whom they priced on the part of the sons of Israel*. 6. Some ancient authorities read *I gave*.

The Roman Trial, §130-132.

§130. JESUS BEFORE PILATE THE FIRST* TIME.

Jerusalem. Friday, early morning.

Matt. 27:11-14.   Mark 15:2-5.   Luke 23:2-5.   John 18:28-38.

28 and they themselves entered not into the

*The Roman Trial also comprised three stages, (1) the first appearance before the Roman procurator Pilate (§130), (2) the appearance before Herod Antipas, the native ruler of Galilee appointed by the Romans (§131), and (3) the final appearance before Pilate (§132).

Matt. 27:11-14.	Mark 15:2-5.	Luke 23:2-5.	John 18:28-38.
			²palace, that they might not be defiled, but might eat the 29 passover. Pilate therefore went out unto them, and saith,
		2 And they began to accuse him, saying, We found this man perverting our nation, and forbidding to give tribute to Cæsar, and saying that he himself is ¹Christ a king.	What accusation bring ye against this 30 man? They answered and said unto him, If this man were not an evil-doer we should not have delivered him up unto thee.
			31 Pilate therefore said unto them, Take him yourselves, and judge him according to your law. The Jews said unto him, It is not lawful for us to put any man to 32 death: that the word of Jesus might be fulfilled, which he spake signifying by what manner of death he should die.
			33 Pilate therefore entered again into the ²palace, and
11 ¹Now Jesus stood before the governor: and the governor asked him, saying, Art thou the King of the	2 And Pilate asked him, Art thou the King	3 And Pilate asked him, saying, Art thou the King of the	called Jesus, and said unto him, Art thou the King of the

Matt. 27:11-14.	Mark 15:2-5.	Luke 23:2-5.	John 18:28-38.
Jews? And Jesus said unto him, Thou sayest.	of the Jews? And he answering saith unto him, Thou sayest.	Jews? And he answered him and said, Thou sayest.	Jews? Jesus answered, Sayest thou this of thyself, or did others tell it thee concerning me? 35 Pilate answered, Am I a Jew? Thine own nation and the chief priests delivered thee unto me: what hast thou done? 36 Jesus answered, My kingdom is not of this world: if my kingdom were of this world, then would my ³servants fight, that I should not be delivered to the Jews: but now is my kingdom not from hence. 37 Pilate therefore said unto him, Art thou a king then? Jesus answered, ⁴Thou sayest that I am a king. To this end have I been born, and to this end am I come into the world, that I should bear witness unto the truth. Every one that is of the truth heareth my voice. 38 Pilate saith unto him, What is truth?

Matt. 27:11-14.	Mark 15:2-5.	Luke 23:2-5.	John 18:28-38.
		4 And Pilate said unto the chief priests and the multitudes, I find no fault in in this man.	And when he had said this, he went out again unto the Jews, and saith unto them, I find no crime in him.
12 And when he was accused by the chief priests and elders, he answered noth-13 ing. Then saith Pilate unto him, Hearest thou not how many things they witness against 14 thee? And he gave him no answer, not even to one word: insomuch that the governor marvelled greatly.	3 And the chief priests accused him of many things. 4 And Pilate again asked him, saying, Answerest thou nothing? behold how many things they accuse 5 thee of. But Jesus no more answered anything; insomuch that Pilate marvelled.		
		5 But they were the more urgent, saying, He stirreth up the people, teaching throughout all Judea, and beginning from Galilee even unto this place.	

1. Or, *an anointed king*.   2. Gr. *Prætorium*.   3. Or, *officers*: as in ver. 3, 12, 18, 22.
4. Or, *Thou sayest it, because I am a king*.

§131. JESUS BEFORE HEROD ANTIPAS THE TETRARCH.

Jerusalem. Friday, early morning.

Luke 23:6-12.

6 But when Pilate heard it, he asked whether the man were a Gali-
7 læan. And when he knew that he was of Herod's jurisdiction, he sent
him unto Herod, who himself also was at Jerusalem in these days.

Luke 23:6–12.

8 Now when Herod saw Jesus, he was exceeding glad: for he was of a long time desirous to see him, because he had heard concerning him;*
9 and he hoped to see some ¹miracle done by him. And he questioned
10 him in many words; but he answered him nothing. And the chief
11 priests and the scribes stood, vehemently accusing him. And Herod with his soldiers set him at nought, and mocked him, and arraying
12 him in gorgeous apparel sent him back to Pilate. And Herod and Pilate became friends with each other that very day: for before they were at enmity between themselves.

1. Gr. *sign*.

§132. BROUGHT BACK TO PILATE, WHO SLOWLY AND RELUCTANTLY CONSENTS THAT HE SHALL BE CRUCIFIED.

Friday toward sunrise (John 19:14).

Matt. 27:15–30.	Mark 15:6–19.	Luke 23:13–25.	John 18:39–19:16.
15 Now at ¹the feast the governor was wont to release unto the multitude one prisoner, whom they 16 would. And they had then a notable prisoner, called Barabbas.	6 Now at ¹the feast he used to release unto them one prisoner, whom they asked of 7 him. And there was one called Barabbas, *lying* bound with them that had made insurrection, men who in the insurrection had committed mur- 8 der. And the multitude went up and began to ask him *to do* as he was wont to do unto them.	13 And Pilate called together the chief priests and the rulers and the 14 people, and	

*Comp. §56.

LAST WEEK OF OUR LORD'S MINISTRY,

Matt. 27:15-30.	Mark 15:6-19.	Luke 23:13-25.	John 18:39-19:16.
		said unto them, Ye brought unto me this man, as one that perverteth the people: and behold, I, having examined him before you, found no fault in this man touching those things whereof ye accuse him: 15 no, nor yet Herod: for he sent him back unto us; and behold, nothing worthy of death hath been done by him.	
			39 But ye have a custom, that I should release unto you one at the passover: will ye therefore that I release unto you the King of the Jews?
17 When therefore they were gathered together, Pilate said unto them, Whom will ye that I release unto you? Barabbas, or Jesus which is called 18 Christ? For he knew that for envy they had delivered him 19 up. And while he was sitting on the judgement seat, his wife sent unto him, saying, Have thou nothing to do with that righteous man:	9 And Pilate answered them, saying, Will ye that I release unto you the King of the Jews? 10 For he perceived that for envy the chief priests had delivered him up.	16 I will therefore chastise him, and release him⁷.	

AND HIS CRUCIFIXION.

Matt. 27:15-30.	Mark 15:6-19.	Luke 23:13-25.	John 18:39-19:16.
for I have suffered many things this day in a dream because of him. 20 Now the chief priests and the elders persuaded the multitudes that they should ask for Barabbas, and destroy Jesus. 21 But the governor answered and said unto them, Whether of the twain will ye that I release unto you? And they said, Barabbas.	11 But the chief priests stirred up the multitude, that he should rather release Barabbas unto them.	18 But they cried out all together, saying, Away with this man, and release unto us 19 Barabbas: one who for a certain insurrection made in the city, and for murder, was cast into prison.	40 They cried out therefore again, saying, Not this man, but Barabbas. Now Barabbas was a robber. 19. Then Pilate therefore took Jesus, and scourged him. 2 And the soldiers plaited a crown of thorns, and put it on his head, and arrayed him in a purple 3 garment; and they came unto him, and said, Hail, King of the Jews! and they struck

LAST WEEK OF OUR LORD'S MINISTRY,

Matt. 27:15–30.	Mark 15:6–19.	Luke 23:13–25.	John 18:39–19:16.
			him ⁸with their 4 hands. And Pilate went out again, and saith unto them, Behold, I bring him out to you, that ye may know that I find no crime in 5 him. Jesus therefore came out, wearing the crown of thorns and the purple garment. And *Pilate* saith unto them, Behold, 6 the man! When therefore the chief priests and the officers saw him, they cried out, saying, Crucify *him*, crucify *him*. Pilate saith unto them, Take him yourselves, and crucify him, for I find no crime 7 in him. The Jews answered him, We have a law, and by that law he ought to die, because he made himself the Son of 8 God. When Pilate therefore heard this
22 Pilate saith unto them, What then shall I do unto Jesus which is called Christ? They all say, Let him be crucified. 23 And he said, Why, what evil hath he done?	12 And Pilate again answered and said unto them, What then shall I do unto him whom ye call the King of 13 the Jews? And they cried out again, Crucify 14 him. And Pilate said unto them, Why, what evil hath he done?	20 And Pilate spake unto them again, desiring to release Jesus; 21 but they shouted, saying, Crucify, crucify 22 him. And he said unto them the third time, Why, what evil hath this man done? I have found no cause of death in him: I will therefore chastise him and release him.	
But they cried out exceedingly, saying, Let him be crucified.	But they cried out exceedingly, Crucify him.		

9 saying, he was the more afraid; and he entered into the ³palace again,
10 and saith unto Jesus, Whence art thou? But Jesus gave him no answer. Pilate therefore saith unto him, Speakest thou not unto me? knowest thou not that I have ⁶power to release thee, and have ⁶power to
11 crucify thee? Jesus answered him, Thou wouldest have no ⁶power against me, except it were given thee from above: therefore he that delivered me unto thee hath greater sin.

AND HIS CRUCIFIXION.

Matt. 27:15–30.   Mark 15:6–19.   Luke 23:13–25.   John 18:39–19:16.

12 Upon this Pilate sought to release him: but the Jews cried out, saying, If thou release this man, thou art not Cæsar's friend: every
13 one that maketh himself a king ¹⁰speaketh against Cæsar. When Pilate therefore heard these words, he brought Jesus out, and sat down on the judgement seat at a place called The Pavement, but in
14 Hebrew, Gabbatha. Now it was the Preparation of the passover: it was about the sixth hour.* And he saith unto the Jews, Behold, your King!

		23 But they were instant with loud voices, asking that he might be crucified.	15 They therefore cried out, Away with *him*, away with *him*, crucify him. Pilate saith unto them, Shall I crucify your King? The chief priests answered, We have no king but Cæsar.
24 So when Pilate saw that he prevailed nothing, but rather that a tumult was arising, he took water, and washed his hands before the multitude, saying, I am innocent ²of the blood of this righteous man: see ye *to* 25 *it*. And all the people answered and said, His blood *be* on us, and on our children.		And their voices prevailed.	
	15 And Pilate, wishing to content the multitude,	24 And Pilate gave sentence that what they ask-	

*It appears that John, who wrote in Asia Minor, long after the destruction of Jerusalem, makes the day begin at midnight, as the Greeks and Romans did. We seem compelled so to understand him in 20:19 (comp. Luke 24:29-39); and in no passage of his Gospel is that view unsuitable. Here then we understand that Pilate passed the sentence about sunrise, which at the Passover, near the vernal equinox, would be 6 o'clock. The intervening three hours might be occupied in preparations, and the Crucifixion occurred at 9 o'clock, viz. the third hour as counted by the Jews (¶133, Mark 15:25).

Matt. 27:15-30.	Mark 15:6-19.	Luke 23:13-25.	John 18:39-19:16.
26 Then released he unto them Barabbas:	released unto them Barabbas,	ed for should 25 be done. And he released him that for insurrection and murder had been cast into prison, whom they asked for;	
but Jesus he scourged and delivered to be crucified.	and delivered Jesus, when he had scourged him, to be crucified.	but Jesus he delivered up to their will.	16 Then therefore he delivered him unto them to be crucified.
27 Then the soldiers of the governor took Jesus into the ³palace, and gathered unto him the whole 28 ⁴band. And they ⁵stripped him, and put on him a scarlet 29 robe. And they plaited a crown of thorns and put it upon his head, and a reed in his right hand; and they kneeled down before him, and mocked him, saying, Hail, King of 30 the Jews! And they spat upon him, and took the reed and smote him on the head.	16 And the soldiers led him away within the court, which is the ⁶Prætorium; and they call together the whole 17 ⁴band. And they clothe him with purple, and plaiting a crown of thorns, they put it on him; 18 and they began to salute him, Hail, King of 19 the Jews! And they smote his head with a reed, and did spit upon him, and bowing their knees worshipped him.		

1. Or, *a feast.* 2. Some ancient authorities read *of this blood: see ye,* etc. 3. Gr. *Prætorium.* See Mark 15:16. 4. Or, *cohort.* 5. Some ancient authorities read *clothed him.* 6. Or, *palace.* 7. Many ancient authorities insert ver. 17 *Now he must needs release unto them at the feast one* prisoner. Others add the same words after ver. 19. 8. Or, *with rods.* 9. Or, *authority.* 10. Or, *opposeth Cæsar.*

§ 133. The Crucifixion.

Outside of Jerusalem. Friday.

(a) He is led out to Golgotha.*

Matt. 27:31–34.	Mark 15:20–23.	Luke 23:26–33.	John 19:16, 17.
31 And when they had mocked him, they took off from him the robe, and put on him his garments, and led him away to crucify him.	20 And when they had mocked him, they took off from him the purple, and put on him his garments. And they lead him out to crucify him.		16 They took Jesus therefore; 17 and he went out bearing the cross for himself,
32 And as they came out, they found a man of Cyrene, Simon by name: him they ¹compelled to go *with them*, that he might bear his cross.	21 And they ²compel one passing by, Simon of Cyrene, coming from the country, the father of Alexander and Rufus, to go *with them*, that he might bear his cross.	26 And when they led him away, they laid hold upon one Simon of Cyrene, coming from the country, and laid on him the cross, to bear it after Jesus. 27 And there followed him a great multitude of the people, and of women who bewailed and lamented him. 28 But Jesus turning unto them said, Daughters of Jerusalem, weep not for me, but weep for yourselves, and for your children. 29 For behold, the days are com-	

*Golgotha is the Aramaic word for 'skull,' and Calvary is the Latin word. The place cannot have been where the so-called "Church of the Holy Sepulchre" stands, far within the walls. There is of late a rapidly growing agreement that it was the northern end of the Temple hill, whose rounded summit (without the city wall), and southern face with holes in the rock, looks at a little distance much like a skull. This place fulfils all the conditions.

Matt. 27:31-34.	Mark 15:20-23.	Luke 23:26-33.	John 19:16,17.
		ing, in which they shall say, Blessed are the barren, and the wombs that never bare, and the breasts that never gave suck. 30 Then shall they begin to say to the mountains, Fall on us; and to the hills, Cover 31 us. For if they do these things in the green tree, what shall be done in the dry? 32 And there were also two others, malefactors, led with him to be put to death.	
33 And when they were come unto a place called Golgotha, that is to say, The place of a 34 skull, they gave him wine to drink mingled with gall: and when he had tasted it, he would not drink.	22 And they bring him unto the place Golgotha, which is, being interpreted, The place 23 of a skull. And they offered him wine mingled with myrrh: but he received it not.	33 And when they came unto the place which is called ³The skull,	unto the place called The place of a skull, which is called in Hebrew Golgotha:

1. Gr. *impressed.* 2. Gr. *impress.* 3. According to the Latin, *Calvary,* which has the same meaning.

AND HIS CRUCIFIXION.

(b) He is crucified. Many revile.

His three sayings* during the first three hours.

Matt. 27:35-44.	Mark 15:24-32.	Luke 23:33-43.	John 19:18-27.
	25 And it was the third hour, and they crucified him.	33 there they crucified him,	18 where they crucified him,
38 Then are there crucified with him two robbers, one on the right hand, and one on the left.	27 And with him they crucify two robbers; one on his right hand, and one on his left³.	and the malefactors, one on the right hand and the other on 34 the left. ⁴And Jesus said, Father, forgive them; for they know not what they do.	and with him two others, on either side one, and Jesus in the midst.
35 And when they had crucified him, they parted his garments among them, casting lots: 36 and they sat and watched him there.	24 And they crucify him, and part his garments among them, casting lots upon them, what each should take.	And parting his garments among them, they cast lots.	23 The soldiers therefore, when they had crucified Jesus, took his garments, and made four parts, to every soldier a part; and also the ⁵coat: now the ⁵coat was without seam, woven from the top throughout. 24 They said therefore one to another, Let us not rend it, but cast lots for it, whose it shall be: that the scripture might be fulfilled, which saith, They parted my garments among them, And upon my vesture did they cast lots. These things therefore the

*The apparent order of the three sayings is (1) Luke 23:34; (2) John 19:26,27; (3) Luke 23:43.

Matt. 27:35–44.	Mark 15:24–32.	Luke 23:33–43.	John 19:18–27.
			soldiers did.
			19 And Pilate wrote a title also, and put it on the cross.
37 And they set up over his head his accusation written, THIS IS JESUS THE KING OF THE JEWS.	26 And the superscription of his accusation was written over, THE KING OF THE JEWS.	38 And there was also a superscription over him, THIS IS THE KING OF THE JEWS.	And there was written, JESUS OF NAZARETH, THE KING OF 20 THE JEWS. This title therefore read many of the Jews: ⁷for the place where Jesus was crucified was nigh to the city: and it was written in Hebrew, *and* in Latin, *and* in 21 Greek. The chief priests of the Jews therefore said to Pilate, Write not, The King of the Jews; but, that he said, I am King of 22 the Jews. Pilate answered, What I have written I have 25 written. But

there were standing by the cross of Jesus his mother, and his mother's
26 sister, Mary the *wife* of Clopas, and Mary Magdalene. When Jesus
therefore saw his mother, and the disciple standing by, whom he loved,
27 he saith unto his mother, Woman, behold, thy son! Then saith he
to the disciple, Behold, thy mother! And from that hour the disciple
took her unto his own *home.*

39 And they that passed by railed on him, wagging their 40 heads, and saying, Thou that destroyest the ¹temple, and buildest it in three days, save thyself: if	29 And they that passed by railed on him, wagging their heads, and saying, Ha! thou that destroyest the ¹temple, and buildest it in three days, 30 save thyself,	35 And the people stood beholding.

AND HIS CRUCIFIXION.

Matt. 27:35-44.	Mark 15:24-32.	Luke 23:33-43.
thou art the Son of God, come down from the cross. 41 In like manner also the chief priests mocking *him*, with the scribes and 42 elders, said, He saved others; ²himself he cannot save. He is the King of Israel; let him now come down from the cross, and we will believe on 43 him. He trusteth on God; let him deliver him now, if he desireth him: for he said, I am the Son of 44 God. And the robbers also that were crucified with him cast upon him the same reproach.	and come down from the cross. 31 In like manner also the chief priests mocking *him* among themselves with the scribes said, He saved others; ²himself he cannot save. 32 Let the Christ, the King of Israel, now come down from the cross, that we may see and believe. And they that were crucified with him reproached him.	And the rulers also scoffed at him, saying, He saved others: let him save himself, if this is the Christ of God, his 36 chosen. And the soldiers also mocked him, coming to him, offering 37 him vinegar, and saying, If thou art the King of the Jews, save thyself. 39 And one of the malefactors which were hanged railed on him, saying, Art not thou the Christ? save thyself and us. 40 But the other answered, and rebuking him said, Dost thou not even fear God, seeing thou art in the same condem-41 nation? And we indeed justly;

211

Luke 23:33–43.

for we receive
the due reward
of our deeds:
but this man
hath done no-
thing amiss.
42 And he said,
Jesus, remem-
ber me when
thou comest⁶in
thy kingdom.
43 And he said
unto him, Ver-
ily I say unto
thee, To-day
shalt thou be
with me in
Paradise.

1. Or, *sanctuary.* 2. Or, *can he not save himself?* 3. Many ancient authorities insert ver. 28 *And the scripture was fulfilled, which saith, And he was reckoned with transgressors.* See Luke 22:37. 4. Some ancient authorities omit *And Jesus said, Father, forgive them; for they know not what they do.* 5. Or, *tunic.* 6. Some ancient authorities read *into thy kingdom.* 7. Or, *for the place of the city where Jesus was crucified was nigh at hand.*

(c) Darkness for three hours. After four more sayings,* he expires.

Strange events attending his death.

Matt. 27:45–56.	Mark 15:33–41.	Luke 23:44–49.	John 19:28–30.
45 Now from the sixth hour there was darkness over all the ¹land until the ninth 46 hour. And a-bout the ninth hour Jesus cried with a loud voice, say-ing Eli, Eli, lama sabach-thani? that is, My God, my God, ²why hast thou forsaken me?	33 And when the sixth hour was come, there was darkness over the whole ¹land until the ninth hour. 34 And at the ninth hour Je-sus cried with a loud voice, Eloi, Eloi, la-ma sabachtha-ni? which is, being inter-preted, My God, my God, ²why hast thou forsaken me?	44 And it was now about the sixth hour, and a darkness came over the whole ¹land un-til the ninth 45 hour, ⁸the sun's light failing.	

*These came all close together, near the end. The probable order is (1) Matt. 27:46 (Mark 15:34); (2) John 19:28; (3) John 19:30; (4) Luke 23:46.

AND HIS CRUCIFIXION.

Matt. 27:45-56.	Mark 15:33-41.	Luke 23:44-49.	John 19:28-30.
47 And some of them that stood there, when they heard it, said, This man calleth Elijah.	35 And some of them that stood by, when they heard it, said, Behold, he calleth Elijah.		
			28 After this Jesus, knowing that all things are now finished, that the scripture might be accomplished, saith, I
48 And straightway one of them ran, and took a sponge, and filled it with vinegar, and put it on a reed, and gave him to drink. 49 And the rest said, Let be; let us see whether Elijah cometh to save him.³	36 And one ran, and filling a sponge full of vinegar, put it on a reed, and gave him to drink, saying, Let be; let us see whether Elijah cometh to take him down.		27 thirst. There was set there a vessel full of vinegar: so they put a sponge full of the vinegar upon hyssop, and brought it to his mouth.
			30 When Jesus therefore had received the vinegar,
50 And Jesus cried again with a loud voice,	37 And Jesus uttered a loud voice,	46 ⁹And when Jesus had cried with a loud voice, he said, Father, into thy hands I commend my spirit; and having said this,	he said, It is finished:
			and he bowed his head,
and yielded up his spirit.	and gave up the ghost.	he gave up the ghost.	and gave up his spirit.
51 And behold, the veil of the ¹temple was rent in twain	38 And the veil of the ¹temple was rent in twain from the	45 And the veil of the ¹temple was rent in the midst.	

Matt. 27:45-56.	Mark 15:33-41.	Luke 23:44-49.
from the top to the bottom; and the earth did quake; and the rocks were 52 rent; and the tombs were opened; and many bodies of the saints that had fallen asleep were 53 raised; and coming forth out of the tombs after his resurrection they entered into the holy city and appeared unto 54 many. Now the centurion, and they that were with him watching Jesus, when they saw the earthquake, and the things that were done, feared exceedingly, saying, Truly this was ⁵the Son of 55 God. And many women were there beholding from afar, which had followed Jesus from Galilee, ministering unto 56 him: among whom was Mary Magdalene, and Mary the mother of James and Joses, and the mother of the	top to the bottom. 39 And when the centurion, which stood by over against him, saw that he ⁶so gave up the ghost, he said, Truly this man was ⁵the Son of God. 40 And there were also women beholding from afar: among whom were both Mary Magdalene, and Mary the mother of James the ⁷less and of Joses, and Salome;	47 And when the centurion saw what was done, he glorified God, saying, Certainly this was a righteous 48 man. And all the multitudes that came together to this sight, when they beheld the things that were done, returned smiting their 49 breasts. And all his acquaintance, and the women that followed with him from Galilee, stood afar

AND HIS CRUCIFIXION.

Matt. 27:45-56.	Mark 15:33-41.	Luke 23:44-49.
sons of Zebedee.	41 who, when he was in Galilee, followed him, and ministered unto him: and many other women which came up with him unto Jerusalem.	off, seeing these things.

1. Or, *earth*. 2. Or, *why didst thou forsake me?* 3. Many ancient authorities add *And another took a spear and pierced his side, and there came out water and blood*. See John 19:34. 4. Or, *sanctuary*. 5. Or, *a son of God*. 6. Many ancient authorities read, *so cried out and gave up the ghost*. 7. Gr. *little*. 8. Gr. *the sun failing*. 9. Or, *And Jesus, crying with a loud voice, said*.

(d) Found to be dead, he is buried. A guard is set over the tomb.

Matt. 27:57-66. Mark 15:42-47. Luke 23:50-56. John 19:31-42.

31 The Jews, therefore, because it was the Preparation, that the bodies should not remain on the cross upon the sabbath (for the day of that sabbath was a high *day*), asked of Pilate that their legs might be broken, and *that* they might be taken
32 away. The soldiers therefore came, and brake the legs of the first,
33 and of the other which was crucified with him: but when they came to Jesus, and saw that he was dead already, they brake not his legs:
34 howbeit one of the soldiers with a spear pierced his side, and straight-
35 way there came out blood and water. And he that hath seen hath borne witness, and his witness is true: and he knoweth that he saith
36 true, that ye also may believe. For these things came to pass, that the scripture might be fulfilled, A bone of him shall not be ⁶broken.
37 And again another scripture saith, They shall look on him whom they pierced.

57 And when even was come,	42 And when even was now come, because it was the Preparation, that is, the day before the sabbath,		
	43 there came Joseph of Arimathæa, a councillor of honourable estate,	50 And behold, a man named Joseph, who was a councillor, a good man and a	38 And after these things Joseph of Arimathæa,
there came a rich man from Arimathæa, named Joseph,		51 righteous (he had not consented to their	

Matt. 27:57-66.	Mark 15:42-47.	Luke 23:50-56.	John 19:31-42.
		counsel and deed), *a man* of Arimathæa, a city of the Jews, who was	
who also himself was Jesus' disciple:	who also himself was looking for the kingdom of God;	looking for the kingdom of God:	being a disciple of Jesus, but secretly for fear of the Jews, asked
58 this man went to Pilate, and asked for the body of Jesus.	and 52 he boldly went in unto Pilate, and asked for the body of Jesus. And Pilate marvelled if he were already dead: and calling unto him the centurion, he asked him whether he ³had been any while dead. 45 And when he learned it of the centurion,	this man went to Pilate, and asked for the body of Jesus.	of Pilate that he might take away the body of Jesus:
Then Pilate commanded it to be given up.	he granted the corpse to Joseph.		
			and Pilate gave *him* leave. He came therefore, and took away 39 his body. And there came also Nicodemus, he who at the first came to him by night, bringing a ⁶mixture of myrrh and aloes, about a hundred pound
59 And Joseph took the body, and wrapped it in a clean linen cloth,	46 And he bought a linen cloth, and taking him down, wound him in the linen cloth,	53 And he took it down, and wrapped it in a linen cloth,	40 *weight.* So they took the body of Jesus, and bound it in linen cloths with the spices, as

AND HIS CRUCIFIXION.

Matt. 27:57-66.	Mark 15:42-47.	Luke 23:50-56.	John 19:31-42.
			the custom of the Jews is to bury. Now in the place where he was crucified there was a
60 and laid it in his own new tomb, which he had hewn out in the rock: and he rolled a great stone to the door of the tomb and departed.	and laid him in a tomb which had been hewn out of a rock; and he rolled a stone against the door of the tomb.	and laid him in a tomb that was hewn in stone, where never man had 54 yet lain. And it was the day of the Preparation, and the sabbath ⁴drew on.	garden; and in the garden a new tomb wherein was never man yet 42 laid. There then because of the Jews' Preparation (for the tomb was nigh at hand) they laid Jesus.
61 And Mary Magdalene was there, and the other Mary, sitting over against the sepulchre.	47 And Mary Magdalene and Mary the *mother* of Joses beheld where he was laid.	55 And the women, which had come with him out of Galilee, followed after, and beheld the tomb, and how his body was laid. 56 And they returned, and prepared spices and ointments. And on the sabbath they rested according to the commandment.	

62 Now on the morrow, which is the day after the Preparation, the chief priests and the Phari-
63 sees were gathered together unto Pilate, saying, Sir, we remember that that deceiver said, while he
64 was yet alive, After three days I rise again. Command therefore that the sepulchre be made sure until the third day, lest haply his disciples come and steal him away, and say unto the people, He is risen
65 from the dead: and the last error will be worse than the first. Pilate said unto them, ¹Ye have a guard: go your way, ²make it *as* sure as ye
66 can. So they went, and made the sepulchre sure, sealing the stone, the guard being with them.

1. Or, *take a guard.*   2. Gr. *make it sure, as ye know.*   3. Many ancient authorities read, *were already dead.*   4. Gr. *began to dawn.*   5. Or, *crushed.*   6. Some ancient authorities read *roll.*

PART VIII.

OUR LORD'S RESURRECTION, APPEARANCES AND ASCENSION.

Judea and Galilee.   Forty days.*   Probably Spring of A.D. 30 (or 29).

§134. ANGELS ANNOUNCE TO CERTAIN WOMEN THAT JESUS IS RISEN, AND PETER AND JOHN ENTER THE EMPTY TOMB.

Golgotha.   First day of the week, very early.

Matt. 28:1–8.	Mark 16:1–8.	Luke 24:1–8.	John 20:1–10.
1 Now late on the sabbath day, as it began to dawn toward the first *day* of the week, came Mary Magdalene and the other Mary to see the sepulchre. 2 And behold, there was a great earthquake; for an angel of the Lord descended from heaven, and came and rolled away the stone, and sat upon it. 3 His appearance was as lightning, and his raiment white as snow: 4 and for fear of	1 And when the sabbath was past, Mary Magdalene, and Mary the *mother* of James, and Salome, brought spices, that they might come and anoint him. 2 And very early on the first day of the week they come to the tomb when the sun was risen. 3 And they were saying	1 But on the first day of the week, at early dawn,† they came unto the tomb, bringing the spices which they had prepared.	1 Now on the first *day* of the week cometh Mary Magdalene early, while it was yet dark, unto the tomb,

*Of this period we see that he remained at or near Jerusalem for a week (§139). Then he probably left at once for Galilee (Matt. 28:7; Mark 16:7). In the month that followed we cannot fix the exact time of the events that occurred in Galilee (§140, 141), but just at the end of the forty days we find him again in Jerusalem (§142-3).

†So he had already risen at early dawn on the first day of the week. He was buried (§133d) shortly before sunset on Friday, and at sunset the sabbath began. So he lay in the tomb a small part of Friday, all of Saturday, and 10 or 11 hours of Sunday. This corresponds exactly with the seven times repeated statement that he would or did rise "on the third day," which *could not possibly* mean after 72 hours. The phrase 2 or 3 times given, "after three days," naturally denoted for Jews, as for Greeks and Romans, a whole central day and any part of a first and third, thus agreeing with "on the third day." Even the "three days and three nights" of Matt. 12:40 need not, according to known Jewish usage, mean more than we have described. So these expressions *can* be reconciled with "on the third day," and with the facts as recorded, while "on the third day" *cannot* mean after 72 hours.

APPEARANCES AND ASCENSION.

Matt. 28:1-8.	Mark 16:1-8.	Luke 24:1-8.	John 20:1-10.
him the watchers did quake, and became as dead men.	among themselves, Who shall roll us away the stone from the door of the tomb?	2 And they found the stone rolled away from 3 the tomb. And they entered in, and found not the body ²of the Lord Jesus.	and seeth the stone taken away from the tomb.
	4 and looking up they see that the stone is rolled back: for it was exceeding great.		
	5 And entering into the tomb, they saw a young man sitting on the right side, arrayed in a white robe; and they were 6 amazed. And he saith unto them, Be not amazed: ye seek Jesus, the Nazarene, which hath been crucified: he is risen; he is not here: behold, the place where they 7 laid him! But go, tell his disciples and Peter, He goeth before you into Galilee: there shall ye see him, as he said unto you.	4 And it came to pass, while they were perplexed thereabout, behold, two men stood by them in dazzling apparel: 5 and as they were affrighted, and bowed down their faces to the earth, they said unto them, Why seek ye ⁸the living among 6 the dead? ⁴He is not here, but is risen: remember how he spake unto you when he was yet in Gal- 7 ilee, saying that the Son of man must be delivered up into the hands of sinful men, and be crucified, and the third day rise 8 again. And they remembered his words.	
5 And the angel answered and said unto the women, Fear not ye: for I know that ye seek Jesus, which hath been crucified. 6 He is not here; for he is risen, even as he said. Come, see the place ¹where the 7 Lord lay. And go quickly, and tell his disciples, He is risen from the dead: and lo, he goeth before you into Galilee; there shall ye see him: lo, I have 8 told you. And they departed quickly from the tomb with fear and great joy, and ran to bring his disciples word.			
	8 And they went out, and fled from the tomb; for trembling and astonishment had come upon them; and they said nothing to any one; for they were afraid.		

OUR LORD'S RESURRECTION,

John 20:1–10.

2 She runneth therefore, and cometh to Simon Peter, and to the other disciple, whom Jesus loved, and saith unto them, They have taken away the Lord out of the tomb, and we 3 know not where they have laid him. Peter therefore went forth, and 4 the other disciple, and they went toward the tomb. And they ran both together; and the other disciple outran Peter, and came first to 5 the tomb; and stooping and looking in, he seeth the linen cloths lying; 6 yet entered he not in. Simon Peter therefore also cometh, following him, and entered into the tomb; and he beholdeth the linen cloths 7 lying, and the napkin, that was upon his head, not lying with the 8 linen cloths, but rolled up in a place by itself. Then entered in therefore the other disciple also, which came first to the tomb, and he saw, 9 and believed. For as yet they knew not the scripture, that he must 10 rise again from the dead. So the disciples went away again unto their own home.

1. Many ancient authorities read *where he lay*. 2. Some ancient authorities omit *of the Lord Jesus*. 3. Gr. *him that liveth*. 4. Some ancient authorities omit *He is not here, but is risen*.

Five appearances are given as occurring on the day of his resurrection, and five subsequently during the forty days.

§ 135. THE RISEN LORD APPEARS TO THE WOMEN*, AND SEPARATELY TO MARY MAGDALENE. THESE REPORT TO THE APOSTLES.

Jerusalem. First day of the week (Sunday).

Matt. 28:9,10.	Mark 16:9–11.	Luke 24:9–11.	John 20:11–18.
		[8 And they remembered his 9 words] and returned ³from the tomb, and told all these things to the eleven, and to all the rest. 10 Now they were Mary Magdalene, and Joanna, and Mary the *mother* of James: and	11 But Mary was standing without at the tomb weeping: so, as she wept, she stooped and looked into the 12 tomb; and she beholdeth two angels in white sitting, one at the head, and one at the feet, where the body of Jesus had

*The five appearances on this day were (1) to Mary Magdalene (John and Mark); (2) to other women (Matthew); (3) to Simon Peter, (§ 137. Luke 24:34); (4) to the two going to Emmaus (§ 137); (5) to ten apostles, and others (§ 138).

APPEARANCES AND ASCENSION.

Matt. 28:9,10.	Mark 16:9–11.	Luke 24:9–11.	John 20:11–18.
	9 ¹Now when he was risen early on the first day of the week, he appeared first to Mary Magdalene, from whom he had cast out seven ²devils.	the other women with them told these things unto the apostles. 11 And these words appeared in their sight as idle talk; and they disbelieved them.	13 lain. And they say unto her, Woman, why weepest thou? She saith unto them, Because they have taken away my Lord, and I know not where they have laid him. 14 When she had thus said, she turned herself back, and beholdeth Jesus standing, and knew not that it was Jesus. 15 Jesus saith unto her, Woman, why weepest thou? whom seekest thou? She, supposing him to be the gardener, saith unto him, Sir, if thou hast borne him hence, tell me where thou hast laid him, and I will take him away. 16 Jesus saith unto her, Mary. She turneth herself, and saith unto him in Hebrew, Rabboni; which is to say, ⁴Master. 17 Jesus saith to her, ⁵Touch me not; for I am not yet ascended unto the Father: but go unto my brethren, and say to them, I ascend unto my Father

Matt. 28:9,10.	Mark 16:9-11.	John 20:11-18.
		and your Father, and my God and your God.
	10 She went and told them that had been with him, as they mourned and wept.	18 Mary Magdalene cometh and telleth the disciples, I have seen the Lord; and *how that* he had said these things unto her.
	11 And they, when they heard that he was alive, and had been seen of her, disbelieved.	
9 And behold, Jesus met them, saying, All hail. And they came and took hold of his feet, and worshipped him. 10 Then saith Jesus unto them, Fear not: go tell my brethren that they depart into Galilee, and there shall they see me.		

1. The two oldest Greek manuscripts, and some other authorities, omit from ver. 9 to the end. Some other authorities have a different ending to the Gospel. 2. Gr. *demons*. 3. Some ancient authorities omit *from the tomb*. 4. Or, *Teacher*. 5. Or, *Take hold not on me*.

§ 136. SOME OF THE GUARD REPORT TO THE JEWISH RULERS.

Matt 28:11-15.

11 Now while they were going, behold, some of the guard came into the city, and told unto the chief priests all the things that were come
12 to pass. And when they were assembled with the elders, and had
13 taken counsel, they gave large money unto the soldiers, saying, Say ye, His disciples came by night, and stole him away while we slept.
14 And if this ¹come to the governor's ears, we will persuade him, and

APPEARANCES AND ASCENSION.

Matt. 28:11-15.

15 rid you of care. So they took the money, and did as they were taught: and this saying was spread abroad among the Jews, *and continueth* until this day.

1. Or, *come to a hearing before the governor.*

§137. JESUS APPEARS TO SIMON PETER, AND TO TWO DISCIPLES ON THE WAY TO EMMAUS.

First day of the week, afternoon.

Mark 16:12,13.	Luke 24:13-35.	I Cor. 15:5.

12 And after these things he was manifested in another form unto two of them, as they walked on their way into 13 the country. And they went away and told it unto the rest: neither believed they them.

13 And behold, two of them were going that very day to a village named Emmaus, which was three-score furlongs 14 from Jerusalem. And they communed with each other of all these things which 15 had happened. And it came to pass, while they communed and questioned together, that Jesus himself drew near, and went 16 with them. But their eyes were holden 17 that they should not know him. And he said unto them, ¹What communications are these that ye have one with another, as ye walk? And they stood still, looking sad. 18 And one of them, named Cleopas, answering said unto him, ²Dost thou alone sojourn in Jerusalem and not know the things which 19 are come to pass there in these days? And he said unto them, What things? And they said unto him, The things concerning Jesus of Nazareth, which was a prophet mighty in deed and word before God and all the people: 20 and how the chief priests and our rulers delivered him up to be condemned to death, 21 and crucified him. But we hoped that it was he which should redeem Israel. Yea and beside all this, it is now the third day since 22 these things came to pass. Moreover certain women of our company amazed us, hav-23 ing been early at the tomb; and when they found not his body, they came, saying, that they had also seen a vision of angels, which 24 said that he was alive. And certain of them

Luke 24:13-35.

that were with us went to the tomb, and found it even so as the women had said: but
25 him they saw not. And he said unto them, O foolish men, and slow of heart to believe
26 [3]in all that the prophets have spoken! Behoved it not the Christ to suffer these
27 things, and to enter into his glory? And beginning from Moses and from all the prophets, he interpreted to them in all the scrip-
28 tures the things concerning himself. And they drew nigh unto the village, whither they were going: and he made as though he
29 would go further. And they constrained him, saying, Abide with us: for it is toward evening, and the day is now far spent. And
30 he went in to abide with them. And it came to pass, when he had sat down with them to meat, he took the [4]bread, and blessed
31 it, and brake, and gave to them. And their eyes were opened, and they knew him; and
32 he vanished out of their sight. And they said one to another, Was not our heart burning within us, while he spake to us in the way, while he opened to us the scriptures?
33 And they rose up that very hour, and returned to Jerusalem, and found the eleven gathered together, and them that were with them,
34 saying, The Lord is risen indeed, and hath
35 appeared to Simon. And they rehearsed the things *that happened* in the way, and how he was known of them in the breaking of the bread.

I Cor. 15:5.

5 and that he appeared to Cephas.

1. Gr. *What words are these that ye exchange one with another?* 2. Or, *Dost thou sojourn alone in Jerusalem, and knowest thou not the things.* 3. Or, *after.* 4. Or, *loaf.*

§138. HE APPEARS TO THE APOSTLES (EXCEPT THOMAS), TO THE TWO RETURNED FROM EMMAUS, AND OTHERS, AND GIVES A COMMISSION.

Jerusalem. First day of the week, evening.

Mark 16:14.	Luke 24:36–43.	John 20:19–25.
14 And afterward he was manifested unto the eleven them-	36 And as they spake these things, he himself stood in the	19 When therefore it was evening, on that day, the first *day* of the week, and when the doors were shut where the disciples were, for fear of the Jews, Jesus came and

Mark 16:14.	Luke 24:36–43.	John 20:19–25.
selves as they sat at meat;	midst of them, ¹and saith unto them, Peace *be* unto you. 37 But they were terrified and affrighted, and supposed that they beheld a spirit.	stood in the midst, and saith unto them, Peace *be* unto you.
and he upbraided them with their unbelief and hardness of heart, because they believed not them which had seen him after he was risen.		
	38 And he said unto them, Why are ye troubled? and wherefore ⸰do reasonings arise in your heart? 39 See my hands and my feet, that it is I myself; handle me, and see; for a spirit hath not flesh and bones, as ye behold 40 me having. ²And when he had said this, he shewed them his hands and 41 his feet. And while they still disbelieved for joy, and wondered, he said unto them, Have ye here anything to eat? 42 And they gave him a piece of a broiled 43 fish³. And he took it, and did eat before them.	20 And when he had said this, he shewed unto them his hands and his side.

The disciples therefore were glad, when they saw
21 the Lord. Jesus therefore said to them again, Peace *be* unto you: as
22 the Father hath sent me, even so send I you. And when he had said this, he breathed on them, and saith unto them, Receive ye the ⁴Holy
23 Ghost: whosesoever sins ye forgive, they are forgiven unto them; whosesoever *sins* ye retain, they are retained.*
24 But Thomas, one of the twelve, called ⁵Didymus, was not with them

---
*Of our Lord's final commissions to the apostles and others (Luke 24:33), this is the first. See a second in § 141, and a third in § 142.

John 20:19–25.

25 when Jesus came. The other disciples therefore said unto him, We have seen the Lord. But he said unto them, Except I shall see in his hands the print of the nails, and put my finger into the print of the nails, and put my hand into his side, I will not believe.

1. Some ancient authorities omit *and saith unto them, Peace be unto you.* 2. Some ancient authorities omit ver. 40. 3. Many ancient authorities add *and a honeycomb.* 4. Or, *Holy Spirit.* 5. That is, *Twin.*

§139. HE APPEARS AGAIN TO THE DISCIPLES, INCLUDING THOMAS.

Jerusalem. A week later than the resurrection.

John 20:26–31.

26 And after eight days again his disciples were within, and Thomas with them. Jesus cometh, the doors being shut, and stood in the midst, and said, Peace *be*
27 unto you. Then saith he to Thomas, Reach hither thy finger, and see my hands; and reach *hither* thy hand, and put it into my side: and be not faithless, but
28 believing. Thomas answered and said unto him, My Lord and
29 my God. Jesus saith unto him, Because thou hast seen me, ¹thou hast believed: blessed *are* they that have not seen, and *yet* have believed.
30 Many other signs therefore did Jesus in the presence of the disciples, which are not written in
31 this book: but these are written, that ye may believe that Jesus is the Christ, the Son of God; and that believing ye may have life in his name.

I Cor. 15:5.

[and that he appeared to Cephas;] then to the twelve;

1. Or, *hast thou believed?*

§140. HE APPEARS TO SEVEN DISCIPLES BESIDE THE SEA OF GALILEE.

John 21.

1 After these things Jesus manifested himself again to the disciples
2 at the sea of Tiberias; and he manifested *himself* on this wise. There were together Simon Peter, and Thomas called ¹Didymus, and Nathanael of Cana in Galilee, and the *sons of* Zebedee, and two other
3 of his disciples. Simon Peter saith unto them, I go a fishing. They say unto him, We also come with thee. They went forth, and entered
4 into the boat; and that night they took nothing. But when day was

John 21.

now breaking, Jesus stood on the beach; howbeit the disciples knew
5 not that it was Jesus. Jesus therefore said unto them, Children, have
6 ye aught to eat? They answered him, No. And he said unto them, Cast the net on the right side of the boat, and ye shall find. They cast therefore, and now they were not able to draw it for the multitude
7 of fishes. That disciple therefore whom Jesus loved saith unto Peter, It is the Lord. So when Simon Peter heard that it was the Lord, he girt his coat about him (for he was naked), and cast himself into the
8 sea. But the other disciples came in the little boat (for they were not far from the land, but about two hundred cubits off), dragging the
9 net *full* of fishes. So when they got out upon the land, they see [2]a fire
10 of coals there, and [3]fish laid thereon, and [4]bread. Jesus saith unto
11 them, Bring of the fish which ye have now taken. Simon Peter therefore went [5]up, and drew the net to land, full of great fishes, a hundred and fifty and three: and for all there were so many, the net
12 was not rent. Jesus saith unto them, Come *and* break your fast. And none of the disciples durst inquire of him, Who art thou? knowing
13 that it was the Lord. Jesus cometh, and taketh the [6]bread, and giveth
14 them, and the fish likewise. This is now the third time that Jesus was manifested to the disciples, after he was risen from the dead.
15 So when they had broken their fast, Jesus saith to Simon Peter, Simon, *son* of [7]John, [8]lovest thou me more than these? He saith unto him, Yea, Lord; thou knowest that I [9]love thee. He saith unto him,
16 Feed my lambs. He saith to him again a second time, Simon, *son* of [7]John, [8]lovest thou me? He saith unto him, Yea, Lord; thou knowest
17 that I [9]love thee. He saith unto him, Tend my sheep. He saith unto him the third time, Simon, *son* of [7]John, [9]lovest thou me? Peter was grieved because he said unto him the third time, [9]Lovest thou me? And he said unto him, Lord, thou knowest all things; thou [10]knowest that I [9]love thee. Jesus saith unto him, Feed my sheep.
18 Verily, verily, I say unto thee, When thou wast young, thou girdedst thyself, and walkedst whither thou wouldest: but when thou shalt be old, thou shalt stretch forth thy hands, and another shall gird thee,
19 and carry thee whither thou wouldest not. Now this he spake, signifying by what manner of death he should glorify God. And when he
20 had spoken this, he saith unto him, Follow me. Peter, turning about, seeth the disciple whom Jesus loved following; which also leaned back on his breast at the supper, and said, Lord, who is he
21 that betrayeth thee? Peter therefore seeing him saith to Jesus,
22 Lord, [11]and what shall this man do? Jesus saith unto him, If I will
23 that he tarry till I come, what *is that* to thee? follow thou me. This saying therefore went forth among the brethren, that that disciple should not die: yet Jesus said not unto him, that he should not die; but, If I will that he tarry till I come, what *is that* to thee?
24 This is the disciple which beareth witness of these things, and wrote these things: and we know that his witness is true.
25 And there are also many other things which Jesus did, the which if they should be written every one, I suppose that even the world itself would not contain the books that should be written.

1. That is, *Twin.* 2. Gr. *a fire of charcoal.* 3. Or, *a fish.* 4. Or, *a loaf.* 5. Or, *aboard.* 6. Or, *loaf.* 7. Gr. *Joanes.* See ch. 1:42. 8. 9. *Love* in these places represents two different Greek words. 10. Or, *perceivest.* 11. Gr. *and this man, what?*

§ 141. HE MEETS ABOVE FIVE HUNDRED* ON AN APPOINTED MOUNTAIN IN GALILEE, AND GIVES A COMMISSION.

Matt. 28:16-20.	Mark 16:15-18.	I Cor. 15:6.
16 But the eleven disciples went into Galilee, unto the mountain where Jesus had 17 appointed them. And when they saw him, they worshipped *him:* but some doubted. 18 And Jesus came to them and spake unto them, saying, All authority hath been given unto me in heaven and on earth. 19 Go ye therefore, and make disciples of all the nations, baptizing them into the name of the Father and of the Son and of the Holy Ghost: 20 teaching them to observe all things whatsoever I commanded you:	15 And he said unto them, Go ye into all the world, and preach the gospel to the whole creation. 16 He that believeth and is baptized shall be saved: but he that disbelieveth shall be con- 17 demned. And these signs shall follow them that believe: in my name shall they cast out ³devils; they shall speak with ⁴new tongues; 18 they shall take up serpents, and if they drink any deadly thing, it shall in no wise hurt them; they shall lay hands on	6 then he appeared to above five hundred brethren at once, of whom the greater part remain until now, but some are fallen asleep:

*The meeting attended by so large a number as stated by Paul, was most probably that which Jesus had appointed (Matt. 28:16, and § 131), and it could be held on an appointed mountain without attracting the attention of unbelievers.——The Commission in Mark may perhaps be reckoned the same as Matthew's here. A third Commission is given by Luke in § 142.

APPEARANCES AND ASCENSION.

Matt. 28:16-20.	Mark 16:15-18.
and lo, I am with you ¹alway, even unto ²the end of the world.	the sick, and they shall recover.

1. Gr. *all the days.* 2. Or, *the consummation of the age.* 3. Gr. *demons.* 4. Some ancient authorities omit *new.*

§ 142. HE APPEARS TO JAMES; THEN TO ALL THE APOSTLES, AND GIVES THEM A COMMISSION.

Jerusalem.

Luke 24:44-49.	Acts 1:3-8.	I Cor. 15:7.
44 And he said unto them, These are my words which I spake unto you, while I was yet with you, how that all things must needs be fulfilled, which are written in the law of Moses, and the prophets, and the psalms, concerning me. 45 Then opened he their mind, that they might understand 46 the scriptures; and he said unto them, Thus it is written, that the Christ should suffer, and rise again from the dead the third day; 47 and that repentance ¹and remission of sins should be preached in his name unto all ²nations, beginning 48 from Jerusalem. Ye are witnesses of these 49 things. And behold, I send forth the promise of my Father upon you: but tarry ye in the city, until ye be clothed with power from on high.	3 to whom he also ³shewed himself alive after his passion by many proofs, appearing unto them by the space of forty days, and speaking the things concerning the kingdom of 4 God: and ⁴being assembled together with them he charged them not to depart from Jerusalem, but to wait for the promise of the Father, which, *said he*, ye heard from me: 5 for John indeed baptized with water; but ye shall be baptized ⁵with the Holy Ghost not many days hence. 6 They therefore, when they were come together, asked him, saying, Lord, dost thou at this time restore the kingdom to Israel? 7 And he said unto them, It is not for you to know times or seasons, which the Father hath ⁶set	Then he appeared to James; then to all the apostles.

Acts 1:3-8.

within his own au-
8 thority. But ye
shall receive power,
when the Holy
Ghost is come upon
you: and ye shall be
my witnesses both in
Jerusalem, and in all
Judea and Samaria,
and unto the utter-
most part of the
earth.

1. Some ancient authorities read *unto.* 2. Or, *nations. Beginning from Jerusalem, ye are witnesses.* 3. Gr. *presented.* 4. Or, *eating with them.* 5. Or, *in.* 6. Or, *appointed by.*

§143. THE ASCENSION.

Between Jerusalem and Bethany.

Mark 16:19,20.	Luke 24:50-53.	Acts 1:9-12.
	50 And he led them out until *they were* over against Bethany, and he lifted up his hands, and blessed them. 51 And it came to pass,	
19 So then the Lord Jesus, after he had spoken unto them, was received up in- to heaven,	while he blessed them, he parted from them, ¹and was carried up into heaven.	9 And when he had said these things, as they were looking, he was taken up; and a cloud received him out of their sight.
and sat down at the right hand of God.		10 And while they were looking stedfastly into heaven as he went, behold two men stood by them in 11 white apparel; which also said, Ye men of Galilee, why stand ye looking into heaven? this Jesus, which was received up from you into heaven, shall so

APPEARANCES AND ASCENSION.

Mark 16:19,20.	Luke 24:50-53.	Acts 1:9-12.
		come in like manner as ye beheld him going into heaven.
	52 And they ²worshipped him, and returned to Jerusalem with great 53 joy: and were continually in the temple, blessing God.	12 Then returned they unto Jerusalem.
20 And they went forth, and preached everywhere, the Lord working with them, and confirming the word by the signs that followed. Amen.		

1. Some ancient authorities omit *and was carried up into heaven*. 2. Some ancient authorities omit *worshipped him, and*.

EXPLANATORY NOTES ON POINTS OF SPECIAL DIFFICULTY IN THE HARMONY OF THE GOSPELS.

In explaining a difficulty, it is always to be remembered that even a possible explanation is sufficient to meet the objector. If several possible explanations are suggested, it becomes all the more unreasonable for one to contend that the discrepancy is irreconcilable. It is a work of supererogation to proceed to show that this or that explanation is the real solution of the problem. Sometimes, owing to new light, this might be possible, but it is never necessary. And by reason of the meagre information we have on many points in the gospel narrative, it may always be impossible in various cases to present a solution satisfactory in every point. The harmonist has done his duty, if he can show a reasonable explanation of the problem before him. Let no one be upset by the numerous theories about such matters, nor be seized with a nervous anxiety to apply the square and rule to every expression of different witnesses about the life of Christ. They are all true, and simply present different views of the perfect and so many-sided Man.

§1, c. THE GENEALOGIES OF CHRIST.

Sceptics of all ages, from Porphyry and Celsus to Strauss, have urged the impossibility of reconciling the difficulties in the two accounts of the descent of Jesus. Even Alford says it is impossible to reconcile them. But certainly several possible explanations have been suggested. The chief difficulties will be discussed.

1. In Matthew's list several discrepancies are pointed out.

(*a*) It is objected that Matthew is mistaken in making three sets of fourteen each. There are only forty-one names, and this would leave one set with only thirteen. But does Matthew say he has mentioned forty-two names? He does say (1:17) that there are three sets of fourteen and divides them for us himself: "So all the generations from

Abraham unto David are fourteen generations; and from David unto the carrying away to Babylon fourteen generations; and from the carrying away to Babylon unto the Christ fourteen generations." The points of division are David and the captivity; in the one case a man, in the other an event. He mentions David in each of the first two sets, and hence David is to be counted in each. David was the connecting link between the patriarchal line and the royal line. But he does not say "from David to Jechoniah," but "from David to the carrying away unto Babylon," and Josiah is the last name he mentions before that event. And so the first name after this same event is Jechoniah. Thus Matthew deliberately puts David in two places to give symmetry to the division, which made an easy help to the memory.

(*b*) The omissions in Matthew's list have occasioned some trouble. These omissions are after Joram, the names of Ahaziah, Joash, Amaziah, and after Josiah, that of Jehoiakim. (II. Kings 8:24; I. Chron. 3:11; II. Chron. 22: 1, 11; 24:27; II. Kings 23:34; 24:6). But such omissions were very common in the Old Testament genealogies. See II. Chron. 22:9. Here "son of Jehoshaphat" means "grandson of Jehoshaphat." So in Matt. 1:1 Jesus is called the son of David, the son of Abraham. A direct line of descent is all that it is designed to express. This is all that the term "begat" necessarily means here. It is a real descent. Whatever omissions were made for various reasons, would not invalidate the line. The fact that Ahaziah, Joash, and Amaziah were the sons of Ahab and Jezebel would be sufficient ground for omitting them.

(c) Matthew mentions four women in his list, which is contrary to Jewish custom, viz. Tamar, Rahab, Ruth, and the wife of Uriah. But neither one is counted in the lists of fourteen, and each one has something remarkable in her case (Broadus, Comm. on Matt. *in loco*). Three were guilty of gross sin, and one, Ruth, was of Gentile origin and deserved mention for that reason. This circumstance would seem to indicate that Matthew did not simply copy the genealogical history of Joseph. He did this, omitting what suited his purpose and adding likewise remarks of his own. His record is thus reliable and yet made a part of his own story.

2. A comparison of the lists of Matthew and Luke.

If no list had been given by Luke, no further explanations would be necessary. But Luke not only gives a list, but one radically different from Matthew's, and in inverse order. Matthew begins with Abraham and comes to Jesus; Luke begins with Jesus and concludes with Adam [the son of God]. Several explanations are offered to remove the apparent contradiction.

(*a*) As early as Julius Africanus it was suggested that the two lines had united in accordance with the law of Levirate marriage. By this theory, Heli and Jacob being stepbrothers, Jacob married Heli's widow and was the real father of Joseph. Thus both genealogies would be the descent of Joseph, one the real, the other the legal. This theory is ably advocated by McClellan, p. 416ff., and Waddy, p. xvii. It is argued that Jechoniah's children were born in captivity and so, being slaves, lost both his royal dignity and his legal status. Stress is laid upon the word "begat" to show that Matthew's descent must be the natural pedigree of Joseph, and upon the use of the expression "son (as was supposed) of Joseph." Hence both Joseph's real and legal standing are shown, for by Luke's account he had an undisputed legal title to descend from David. This is certainly possible, although it rests on the hypothesis of the Levirate marriage.

(b) Lord Arthur Hervey, in his volume on the Genealogies of Our Lord, and in Smith's Dictionary, argues that Matthew gives Joseph's legal descent as successor to the throne of David. According to this theory Solomon's line failed in Jechoniah (Jer. 22:30) and Shealtiel of Matthew's line took his place. Luke's account, on the other hand, gives Joseph's real parentage. Matthew's Matthan and Luke's Mattathias are identified as one, and the law of Levirate marriage comes into service with Jacob and Heli. This explanation has received favor with such writers as Mill, Alford, Wordsworth, Ellicott, Westcott, Fairbairn. The chief objection seems to be the most natural meaning of "begat," implying direct descent, and the necessity for two suppositions, one about Shealtiel and another about Jacob and Heli. It is even fairly probable that the Shealtiel and Zerubbabel of Matthew and Luke are different persons.

(c) The third and most plausible solution yet suggested makes Matthew give the real descent of Joseph, and Luke the real descent of Mary. Several arguments of more or less weight can be adduced for this hypothesis.

(1) The most natural meaning of "begat" in Matthew is preserved. Jesus goes through David's royal line and so fulfils prophecy. It is not elsewhere stated that Mary was of Davidic descent, although presumptive evidence exists in the language of the angel (Luke 1:32) and the enrollment of Mary (Luke 2:5). So Robinson (Revised edition).

(2) The use of Joseph without the article, while it is used with every other name in the list. "The absence of the article puts the name outside of the genealogical series properly so-called."—Godet. This would seem to indicate that Joseph belonged to the parenthesis, "as was supposed." It would read thus, "being son (as was supposed of Joseph) of Heli." Luke had already clearly stated the manner of Christ's birth, so

that no one would think he was the son of Joseph. Jesus would thus be Heli's grandson, an allowable meaning of "son." See Andrews' (new edition) Life of Our Lord, p. 63.

(3) It would seem proper that Matthew should give the *legal* descent of Jesus, since he wrote chiefly for Jews. This, of course, could only be through Joseph.

(4) And it would seem equally fitting that Luke should give the *real* genealogy of Jesus, since he was writing for all. And this could come only through Mary. If it is objected that a woman's genealogy is never given, it may be replied that women are mentioned for special reasons in Matthew's list, though not counted, and that Mary's name is not mentioned in this list. The genealogy goes back to her father either by skipping her as suggested above and making son mean the grandson of Heli, or by allowing Joseph to stand in her place in the list, as he would have to do anyhow. On the whole, then, this theory seems the most plausible and pleasing. So practically Luther, Bengel, Olshausen, Lightfoot, Wieseler, Robinson, Alexander, Godet, Weiss, Andrews (new edition, p. 65), Broadus, Clark.

§ 7. THE PROBABLE TIME OF THE SAVIOUR'S BIRTH.

Every one now understands that the accepted date of our Lord's birth is wrong by several years. The estimates of the true date vary all the way from one to seven years B.C. There are various data that fix the year with more or less certainty, but none of them with absolute precision. They do, however, agree in marking pretty clearly a narrow limit for this notable occurrence.

1. The death of Herod the Great is relied on with most certainty to fix the year of Christ's birth. Josephus, who gives a full account of Herod's death, mentions an eclipse of the moon which occurred shortly before he died. Ant. xvii. 6, 4. This eclipse is the only one alluded to by Josephus, and fixes with absolute certainty the time after which the birth of Jesus could not have occurred, since, according to Matt. 2:1-6, Jesus was born while Herod was still living. The question to be determined would be the year of this eclipse. Astronomical calculations name an eclipse of the moon March 12 and 13, in the year of Rome 750, and no eclipse occurred the following year that was visible in Palestine. Josephus (Ant. xvii. 8, 1,) says that Herod died thirty-seven years after he was declared king by the Romans. In 714 he was proclaimed king, and this would bring his death, counting from Nisan to Nisan, as Josephus usually does, "in the year from 1st Nisan 750 to 1st Nisan 751, according to Jewish computation, at the age of seventy" (Andrews). Herod

died shortly before the Passover of 750, then, according to the eclipse and the length of his reign. Caspari contends for Jan. 24, 753, as the date of Herod's death, because there was a total eclipse of the moon Jan. 10. So he puts his death fourteen days later. Mr. Page (*New Light from Old Eclipses*) argues for the eclipse that occurred July 17, 752, as the one preceding Herod's death. He thinks that this makes unnecessary the subtraction of two years from the reign of Tiberius on the theory that Tiberius was contemporary ruler with Augustus for two years. But he finds difficulty in lengthening Herod's reign so long, and his theory has gained no great acceptance as yet. Our present era makes the birth of Christ in the year of Rome 754, and is due to the Abbot Dionysius Exiguus in the Sixth Century. Hence it is clear that if Herod died in the early spring of 750, Jesus must have been born *at least* four years before 754, the common era, and likely in the year 749.

2. It has been inferred by some that Jesus was at least two or three years old when Herod slaughtered the infants in Bethlehem, Matt. 2:16. Thus the year would be put two years further back to the end of 747 or beginning of 748. But this is not demanded by the "two years" of Matthew, for Herod would naturally extend the limit so as to be sure to include the child in the number slain, and a child just entering the second year would be called "two years" old by Jewish custom. No more definite note of time comes from this circumstance, save that the massacre probably took place some months before Herod's death, which fact would bring the Saviour's birth back some time into the year 749.

3. The appearance of the "star in the east" (Matt. 2:2). This, of course, was before Herod's death, and would agree in time with the slaughter of the children, if the star be looked upon as a supernatural phenomenon, and not the wise men's interpretation of a natural conjunction of planets. Kepler first suggested that, as there was a conjunction of Jupiter and Saturn in 747, to which Mars was added in 748, this conjunction might have been the bright star that led on the wise men. See Wieseler, Synopsis, p. 57. Kepler had also suggested that a periodical star or a comet might have joined the constellation. The Chinese records preserve the account of the appearance of a comet in the spring of 749. Either of these theories is fascinating in itself, especially to those minds that prefer a natural explanation of anything that looks miraculous. Both phenomena are possible in themselves, but they hardly meet the requirements of the record in Matthew. (1) The word used is *aster*, star, and not *astron*, a group of stars. (2) Rev. C. Pritchard, whose calculations have been verified at Greenwich (Smith's Dict.), has shown that those "planets could never have appeared as one star, for they never approached each other within double the apparent diameter of

the moon." So Ideler's hypothesis that the wise men all had weak eyes seems rather feeble. (3) The year 747 would conflict slightly with other evidence for Christ's birth that favors 749, although Wieseler, p. 53, note 4, contends that the star first appeared to the wise men two years before their visit, and a second time on their visit to Bethlehem. (4) Besides, the star is said to have stood over "where the young child was," v. 9. If it were a natural star it would have kept going as they went, and would not have stopped till they stopped. Even then it would appear as far away as ever from Bethlehem. It seems best, therefore, to admit the existence of a miracle here, and hence gain nothing from the visit of the Magi to establish the date of the Saviour's birth, save that it was not long before the slaughter of the infants, and would at least agree with the date 749. See Broadus, Comm. *in loco*.

4. The language of the heavenly host in Luke 2:14 is urged by some as fixing the birth at a time when there was universal peace throughout the world. The closing of the temple of Janus in the time of Augustus is also adduced, but it is not certainly known when it was closed apart from 725 and 729. It was intended to be closed at the end of 744, but was delayed on account of trouble among the Daci and Dalmatae. See Greswell i. 469. Nothing specific can be obtained from this fact, save that there was a time of comparative quiet in the Roman world from 746 to 752. There was a hush in the clangor of war when Jesus was born.

5. The entrance of John the Baptist upon his ministry gives us another note of time. See Luke 3:1 f. John emerged from the wilderness seclusion in the fifteenth year of the reign of Tiberius. Augustus died August 29, 767. Adding fifteen years to this, the fifteenth year of Tiberius would begin August 29, 781. John was of a priestly family and so could naturally enter upon his work when thirty years of age. Thirty years subtracted from this gives 751, as the date of John's birth. But that is too late by two years to agree with the other date. Here, however, the Roman histories come to our help. Tacitus, Ann. 1,3: "Tiberius is adopted by Augustus as his son, and *colleague in empire*." Vell. Pat. 2, 121; "At the request of Augustus, Tiberius was invested with equal authority in all the provinces." So Suetonius Aug. 97 and Tib. 21. It is clear then, that Tiberius reigned jointly with Augustus about two years before he assumed full control of the empire at the death of Augustus. Luke could have used either date, but Tiberius' power was already equal to that of Augustus in the provinces two years before his death. Hence Luke is strictly accurate in giving this date. Taking off the two years from the joint reign of Augustus, we again come to the year 749, as John was born six months before Jesus. So if

238   HARMONY OF THE GOSPELS.

John was born in the early part of the spring, Jesus would have been born in the summer or fall of 749.

6. The age of Jesus at his entrance upon his ministry, Luke 3:23. "And Jesus himself, when he began to teach, was about thirty years of age." So most modern scholars, Meyer, Wieseler, Alford, Ellicott, Wordsworth, etc. Origen refers it to the beginning of a new life, by the second birth of baptism, after his spiritualizing fashion. The Authorized Version has it: "And Jesus himself began to be about thirty years of age," applying the "beginning" to the period of thirty years. McClellan argues that it means "about thirty years, beginning;" that is, a little the rise of thirty years. The Revised Version seems to be preferable and the only doubt would be as to what is included in the phrase "about thirty years." It has been variously argued that Jesus was from one to three years younger or older than thirty. It seems more reasonable to give the words the meaning that he was just about thirty, a few months under or over. So Edersheim, Meyer, Alford, Tischendorf, DeWette, Norton. The argument that Jesus had to be exactly thirty years old because the priest had to be so, when he entered upon his work, has no great force. For Jesus was not a priest save in a spiritual sense. John had been preaching no great while when Jesus was baptized by him and so entered upon his public ministry. If John began his ministry when he was thirty years old in the fifteenth year of Tiberius, then Jesus's ministry would begin about six months later. His birth would then come in the latter part of 749, unless John was born in the latter part of 748, when it would be earlier in the year.

7. The building of the temple of Herod gives a further clue to the date of Christ's birth. In John 2:20, the Jews say, "Forty and six years was this temple in building." Josephus tells us in one place that Herod began rebuilding the temple in the fifteenth year of his reign, War. I. 21,1, and in another that he did so in the eighteenth year of his reign, Ant. XV. 11,1. In the account of Herod's death, Ant. XVII. 8,1, he used two dates for his reign, according as he counted from his declaration as king by the Romans 714, or the death of Antigonus 717. Eighteen and fifteen would both be correct, according as he reckoned from the one date or the other. Eighteen added to forty-six and both to 714 would make 778. It was at the first Passover in his ministry that this expression is used. It has been probably six months since his baptism. If thirty and a half years be taken from 778, his birth would be thrown back to the year 747, unless the forty-six years be taken as completed, when it would be 748. So Robinson. But this does not quite agree with the other notes of time we have. Many modern harmonists count the eighteen years from 717, and so bring the whole number, adding forty-

six, down to 780, or, if the years are complete, 781. Thirty and a half from this would give the autumn of 749 or 750. So substantially McClellan, Andrews, Clark, Thomson (Smith's Dict.), Meyer, Wieseler, Weiss, Godet, Edersheim, Lardner, Tischendorf. This is done because Josephus usually reckons Herod's reign from the death of Antigonus, 717. But it cannot be done without making Josephus mistaken and self-contradictory in War I. 21, 1, for if the eighteen years be added, not to the year 714, but to the year 717, the fifteen years there mentioned will fall three years short of the eighteen. It is possible that Josephus may be mistaken. So all that we can say from this note of time is that it speaks for a rather earlier date than 749, unless Josephus contradicts himself, when it favors that date. Caspari urges the year 713 as the time when Herod was proclaimed king by the Romans. This would make the year 748 or 749.

8. The census of Augustus Cæsar mentioned in Luke 2:1 f., furnishes the last note of time for this event. This subject is involved in a great many difficulties, and for a full discussion, the reader is referred to McClellan, who presents quite an array of testimony.

(1) It used to be said that no census was ever taken by Augustus, but heathen writers mention three, in 726, 746, 767. One of these, 746, may be the one here mentioned, which was delayed for various reasons, or which was executed slowly in the distant provinces. But it is not necessary that the phrase "all the world" should be pressed to its literal meaning, though this is more natural. Nor does the argument from silence prove that no other general census was taken by Augustus.

(2) It is not a "taxing," but an "enrollment" (Rev. Ver.) that was taken. There was a taxing later (Acts 5:37). And if it were done while Herod was king, Augustus could not have taxed Judea without Herod's consent.

(3) This helps to explain another objection that the enrollment would not have included Judea anyhow, because it was not yet a province, but a kingdom. But it is not likely that Herod would have displeased Augustus by refusing such information if it was desired. Tacitus asserts that the *regna*, the dependent kingdoms, were included in the census taken by Augustus.

(4) Hence, also, it is natural that the enrollment should have taken place according to the Jewish and not according to the Roman method, because Herod would wish it to be in accordance with the customs of his kingdom. So every one went to his own city.

(5) We now have to meet the objection that Quirinius was not governor till ten years later, A.D. 6, when a taxing did occur. (See Acts 5:37.) Various answers are given. (*a*) Two statements are made here; one is

that the decree went forth, which was begun by Herod, but was interrupted by his death. This enrollment was completed by Quirinius ten years later. This seems hardly likely since Luke specially says "first" and seems to point to the second in Acts 5:37. (b) But the first enrollment may have been undertaken by Herod, which was completed about 750 by Quirinius, who might thus have succeeded Varus as Procurator of Judea. We may suppose that Quirinius was twice governor of Syria. A gap exists in the history of Quirinius in the years 748–752, so that it is possible. (c) The term "governor" may have a special meaning. Quirinius, as the superior officer, may have had special powers granted for this census, which they both may have carried on after Herod's death. McClellan suggests the possibility of a plurality of Procurators, Varus, Legatine governorship, and Quirinius, the Fiscal governorship. At any rate, it is not made out that Luke was mistaken. The date must be before Herod's death, and would seem to be later than 747 and agrees well with 749.

Few subjects have excited as much interest, even needless curiosity, as the date of the birth of the Saviour. But it is noticeable that by the masses of Christians more interest is taken in the day of Christ's birth than in the year. The Christmas festivities and the natural desire to make that the birthday of Jesus cause this widespread interest in December 25. Not only is it impossible to determine with any degree of certainty the day of the month, but the time of the year also is equally uncertain. The chief thing that appears proved is that December 25 is not the time, since the shepherds would hardly be in the fields at night with the flocks, which were usually taken into the folds in November and kept in till March. The nights of December would scarcely allow watching in the mountain fields even as far South as Bethlehem. And besides, the long journey from Nazareth to Bethlehem would hardly be made by Joseph and Mary in winter, the rainy season. McClellan argues for December 25, but his arguments are not convincing. The ancients had various days for Christ's birth: May 20 (Clement of Alexandria), April 20, December 25, January 5. Tertullian and others even say that the day of his birth (December 25) was kept in the register at Rome. But chronologists attach little weight to this testimony, since the same tradition puts the birth of John, June 24; the annunciation of Mary, March 25, and Elizabeth's conception, September 25—the four cardinal points of the year. If one might hazard an opinion, it would be that the birth of Jesus occurred in the summer or early in the fall of 749.

§ 37. THE FEAST OF JOHN 5:1, AND THE DURATION OF OUR LORD'S MINISTRY.

It seems almost impossible to decide with certainty what feast is alluded to in John 5:1. One can only speak with moderation where everything is so doubtful. Various feasts have been suggested as solving the problem.

1. The Feast of Dedication has been proposed by Kepler and Petavius. But this view has met with no great amount of favor, for there is too short an interval between the first Passover and December, when it occurred. It might be a later Feast of Dedication, but this feast was not one of the great feasts and would hardly have drawn Jesus all the way from Galilee to attend it. He did attend this feast once, (John 10:22), but he was already in Judea at this time, having come up to attend the Feast of Tabernacles (John 7:2, 14). So Robinson, Clark, etc. So this feast seems to be ruled out of the question.

2. The Feast of Tabernacles is advocated by Ebrard, Ewald, Patritius. It is very unlikely that the Feast of Tabernacles after the first Passover could be meant, as the Saviour did not return to Galilee for sometime afterwards. He could hardly have come back so soon to Jerusalem. But the Feast of Tabernacles after the Passover of John 6:4 is mentioned later, John 7:2 f., which Jesus attended, it seems, because he was hindered from going up to the previous Passover by the murderous designs of the Jews. It is possible that the feast of John 5:1 may have been the Feast of Tabernacles after a Passover not mentioned, and so would come after the second Passover of his public ministry. But we do not know that Jesus attended any other Feast of Tabernacles save the one in John 7:2, which he may have done because he missed the preceding Passover.

3. The Feast of Purim, first suggested by Kepler, has had great favor with modern harmonists. So Lange, Tholuck, Ellicott, Wieseler, Tischendorf, Winer, Neander, Olshausen, Meyer, who says, "Without doubt it was Purim." But it is by no means so certain as Meyer would have us believe. (*a*) Meyer relies on John 4:35 and 6:4 to show that this was the Feast of Purim just before John 6:4. But the expression, "Say not ye, There are yet four months and then cometh the harvest?" may be, and probably is, a proverbial saying indicating the usual length of time between sowing and reaping, which, as a matter of fact, was about four months. Hence nothing can be determined by this note of time. And, besides, the four months could precede the Passover just as well as Purim, because the sowing lasted a month or so. (*b*) The Feast of Purim occurred a month before the Passover. Is it at all likely that two circuits of all Galilee were made in the meantime, besides much work of other kinds? See Luke 8:1 and Matt. 9:25-38. The three gen-

eral circuits throughout Galilee, besides the mission of the twelve and a large part of their training, the general statements about the Master's work of preaching and healing, require an expansion rather than a contraction of the time for this period of his ministry. It seems then quite unreasonable, when once the mind takes in this enlarged conception of the missionary work of Jesus, as recorded by the Synoptic Gospels, to limit it to the amount of work mentioned by John, since he omits much of the early ministry, because, it would seem, the others are so full just here. (c) The Feast of Purim, moreover, was observed at home in the synagogues, and not by going to Jerusalem. See Esther 9:22 and Jos. Ant. xi. 6, 13. But "the multitude" (John 5:13) seems to imply (Robinson) a concourse of strangers at one of the great festivals. (d) It seems hardly probable, besides, that Jesus would go to any feast just a month before the Passover and come back to Galilee and not go to the Passover itself (John 6:4). Least of all would he do this in the case of Purim. (e) The man who was healed at this feast was healed on the Sabbath (John 5:9), and this occasioned the outburst among the people. But the Feast of Purim was never celebrated on the Sabbath, and when it came on a Sabbath it was postponed. See Reland, Antiq. Sacr. 4, 9. So Robinson and Clark.

4. Pentecost is held to be the feast here alluded to by many early and some later writers, such as Chrysostom, Cyril of Alex., Erasmus, Calvin, Bengel, Norris, McClellan. Norris makes it the Pentecost after the first Passover, but to do this, has to crowd into this short interval Christ's first Judean ministry, the journey through Samaria together with the first part of his Galilean ministry. So this idea has little weight. McClellan argues that the allusions of Jesus in John 5:17-47, "infallibly point to Pentecost," meaning the Pentecost after a second Passover that is not mentioned. He further contends that this best suits the chronological arrangement and the term "a feast of the Jews." This view is certainly possible and cannot be positively disproved, although it is not so "infallibly" clear as McClellan imagines.

5. The Passover has always met with many adherents, being the second Passover in the Saviour's ministry and making four in all (John 2:13; 5:1; 6:4; 12:1). So Luther, Grotius, Lightfoot, LeClerc, Hengstenberg, Greswell, Robinson, Clark, Smith's B. D., Broadus, etc. The arguments in favor of this interpretation are the most satisfactory We cannot consider them as absolutely conclusive, yet the Passover meets all sides of the case better than any of the other feasts. (a) The plucking of ears from standing grain by the disciples (Luke 6:1.) would indicate a time after the Passover and before Pentecost. This incident appears to have happened after the feast mentioned in John 5:1. (b) It

is fairly implied (John 5:1) that the feast took Jesus to Jerusalem. The Passover would more likely be the one to lead him there. It is expressly stated that he attended two Passovers and a special reason is given for his not attending a third. If there was another passover in his ministry, this would naturally be the one. (c) This suits best the hostility manifested at this feast, which would have time to become acute (Broadus' Comm. on Matt.) and break out with increased vigor in Galilee and prevent his attending the next Passover (John 6:4; 7:1). (d) If this Passover be a second Passover of the ministry, sufficient time is afforded for the great Galilean ministry without artificial crowding. His ministry would be long enough to allow the great work recorded as done by him. Only two serious objections can be urged to this idea. (1) It is objected that the article would be used with "feast," if the Passover were thus mentioned as *the* feast. But to this we can reply: (a) The article is sometimes omitted when the Passover is meant (Matt. 27:15; Mark 15:6). (b) The use of the article with "Jews" makes the "Feast" definite without it, after a common idiom of the N. T. See Winer, p. 125. The article is not really necessary when the noun is made definite otherwise. (c) The article does occur in many manuscripts, including the Sinaitic, and is put in the margin of the Revised Version. So nothing can be gained against this theory here. (2) The chief objection is that Jesus would not have remained so long away from Jerusalem, a year and six months, from the Second Passover till the Feast of Tabernacles after the Third Passover. But (a) we do not know that he did not attend any other feast in that time, for silence proves nothing; and (b) a good reason is given for his failure to attend the third Passover, which may have applied to the others, if he did not go, viz., the desire of the Jews to kill him (John 7:1).

Hence it is natural that there should be a variety of opinions as to the length of the Saviour's ministry, varying all the way from one to four years, leaving out mere guesses based on five and more Passovers. McKnight argues that the ministry may have lasted five or more full years, since all the Passovers of Christ's ministry may not be mentioned.

(1) The *Bi-paschal* theory makes the time of the public life of Jesus one year, allowing only two Passovers to the Gospel of John. Browne in his *Ordo Saeclorum* advocates this view. But the words, "the Passover," in John 6:4 must be omitted, and for this there is not enough documentary evidence. If this could be done, Westcott thinks Browne would make out a good case. But with the present text, his view cannot be entertained.

(2) The *Tri-paschal* theory finds only three Passovers in the life of Christ. Hence the public work of Jesus would be from two to two and a

half years in length. So Wieseler, Godet, Caspari, Tischendorf, Stier, Ellicott, Farrar, etc. These writers usually make the feast of John 5:1 Purim before the Passover of John 6:4, or Pentecost after it.

(3) The *Quadri-paschal* theory contends for four Passovers and a ministry of from three to three and a half years. This theory follows from making John 5:1 a Passover or Purim before or Pentecost after an unnamed Passover. This seems to be the more probable length of the Saviour's public work on earth. How short a space was even this to compass such a marvellous work. So Robinson, Andrews, McClellan, Clark, Broadus, Waddy, Smith's B. D. It would be certain that the Saviour's public life lasted about three years and a half, if it was admitted that John 5:1 referred to a Passover. Various writers seek to find an allusion to the three years of the Saviour's ministry in the Parable of the Barren Fig Tree (Luke 13:6), but this application of the parable is by no means certain, since three might naturally be used as a round number.

§ 41. THE FOUR LISTS OF THE TWELVE APOSTLES.

It is interesting to compare the four lists of Jesus' chosen apostles as given by Matthew, Mark, Luke, and Acts.

	Matthew 10:2f.	Mark 3:16f.	Luke 6:14f.	Acts 1:13f.
1.	Simon Peter.	Simon Peter.	Simon Peter.	Simon Peter.
2.	Andrew.	James.	Andrew.	James.
3.	James.	John.	James.	John.
4.	John.	Andrew.	John.	Andrew.
5.	Philip.	Philip.	Philip.	Philip.
6.	Bartholomew.	Bartholomew.	Bartholomew.	Thomas.
7.	Thomas.	Matthew.	Matthew.	Bartholomew.
8.	Matthew.	Thomas.	Thomas.	Matthew.
9.	James the son of Alpheus.	James the son of Alpheus.	James the son of Alpheus.	James the son of Alpheus.
10.	Thaddeus.	Thaddeus.	Simon the Zealot.	Simon the Zealot.
11.	Simon the Cananæan.	Simon the Cananæan.	Judas the brother of James.	Judas the brother of James.
12.	Judas Iscariot.	Judas Iscariot.	Judas Iscariot.	

Let us examine the names here given.

(1) The lists are given some time after the selection was made, and hence may represent a later grouping according to later developments in this inner circle.

(2) One mark of an apostle was that he should have been with the Lord from the baptism of John until the day that he was received up (Acts 1:21f). Perhaps no great stress is to be laid on any exact time here, provided it began in the time of John. An apostle must know the Lord. Hence Paul received the vision of Christ. We have some knowledge of seven of these apostles before this time. If we infer from John 1:41 that John followed the example of Andrew in finding his own brother, it was not long till James was a disciple as well as John, Andrew, and Peter. Philip and Nathanael are soon added to the list (John 1:43f). Later Matthew hears the call of the Saviour, too (Matt. 9:9; Mark 2:13f). Of the other five we have no knowledge previous to this occasion. Jesus had "found" them by the same insight that led to his other selections. He chose Judas, though knowing that he was a devil.

(3) Observe the three groups of four, headed by Simon Peter, Philip, and James the son of Alpheus, respectively. The great variety in the arrangement of the other names makes this uniformity significant. It seems clear that there are three recognized groups among the apostles (Bengel, Broadus, Clark). Each group has the same persons in every list, although there is such a variety in the order. In the first group Matthew and Luke have the same order, while Mark and Acts agree. In the second group Mark and Luke have a like order, while Matthew and Acts agree in putting Matthew at the end of this group. In the third group Matthew and Mark agree exactly, while Luke and Acts are identical save the dropping out of Judas Iscariot from the list in Acts because of his apostasy and death. No great importance can be attached to the precise order within the groups since Luke, in the Gospel and Acts, gives a different arrangement in the first and second groups.

(4) Observe also that Simon Peter not only stands at the head of his group, but at the head of all the groups, while Judas Iscariot is always at the bottom till he drops out entirely. Simon occupied a position of precedence of some sort. He was one of the inner circle of three that was so close to the Saviour's heart. Perhaps it was this, rather than any notion of primacy in authority or power. He was the spokesman because of his natural impetuosity. The question as to who should be greatest among the apostles illustrates the spirit of rivalry about precedence that existed among them.

(5) There are among the Twelve three pairs of brothers—Simon and Andrew, James and John, James the son of Alpheus and Judas the brother of James. The first two pairs form the first group of the Twelve. It is, however, uncertain whether Judas is the brother or the son of James. The Greek is ambiguous, James's Judas. The Revised Version translated it "Judas son of James," but the Epistle of Jude begins

"Judas a servant of Jesus Christ and brother of James." So it is perhaps best to regard it as brother. Cf. Broadus, Comm. on Matt., p. 216.

(6) There are some apparent discrepancies in the names in the various lists. Bartholomew occurs in every list, but is generally understood to be another name for Nathanael. Thaddeus is also called Judas the brother of James. Matthew and Mark give Thaddeus, and Luke in Gospel and Acts gives Judas the brother of James. It was a very common circumstance for one to have two names. Lebbeus, given in some MSS. in Matthew and Mark, is only a marginal explanation of Thaddeus. Both are terms of endearment. Matthew and Mark again call Simon the Cananæan, while Luke in the Gospel and Acts speaks of him as Simon the Zealot. But "Zealot" is simply a translation into Greek of the Aramaic "Cananæan." Jesus gave the other Simon the name "Cephas," which was translated into the Greek "Peter," meaning rock. He is called by all three names in the New Testament. Matthew likewise had another name, Levi, and Thomas was also called Didymus, which was a Greek translation of Thomas, meaning "twin."

§42. THE SERMON ON THE MOUNT.

Do Matthew and Luke record the same discourse? Let us consider the several theories on this subject. My own view will be stated last.

1. Some hold that the two discourses are entirely distinct in time, place, circumstances and audience. So Greswell, Anger, Patritius, Clark. The arguments for this theory usually presented are these.

(*a*) The time of delivery of the two sermons appears to be different. Matthew gives the sermon before his call (Matt. 9:9), while Luke precedes his sermon by the call of the twelve. Hence Matthew's discourse comes quite a while before Luke's in the early Galilean ministry. But it may be well replied that, inasmuch as Matthew's arrangement in ch. 8–13 is not chronological, but topical, it is entirely possible, even likely, that the same arrangement should prevail in ch. 5–7. It is perfectly natural that Matthew, writing for Jewish readers and about the Messianic reign, should give at the beginning of his account of that reign the formal principles that rule in this new state of affairs, as proclaimed by Jesus on a later occasion. In the early part of the ministry of Jesus, besides, the hearers would hardly be prepared for so advanced and radical ideas. Besides, Matthew makes no note of time whatever for this discourse.

(*b*) The place appears to be different. One is on a mountain (Matt. 5:1), while the other is on a plain (Luke 6:17). Hence the one is called by Clark the Sermon on the Mount, and the other the Sermon on the Plain. If it is necessary that "plain" here shall mean a place away from a mountain, down in a valley, this would seem to refer to a different place. McClellan seeks to show that Luke uses "and" in 6:17-20 by way of anticipation. He presents for effective grouping events that happened after Jesus came down out of the mountain before he gives the sermon delivered to the whole body of disciples up in the mountain. This is possible, but another interpretation is much more likely. The plain here is really simply "a level place" (Rev. Ver.). So then the two accounts of Matthew and Luke will harmonize quite well. Jesus first went up into the mountain to pray (Luke 6:12) and selected and instructed the Twelve. Afterwards he came down to a level place on the mountain side whither the crowds had gathered, and stood there and wrought miracles (Luke 6:17). He then went up a little higher into the mountain where he could sit down and see and teach the multitudes (Matt. 5:1). Matthew gives the multitudes as the reason for his going up into the mountain. By this arrangement any discrepancy between "sat" in Matthew and "stood" in Luke disappears. Waddy has given an admirable arrangement of the material at this point in Note C, p. xix. Many writers affirm that the tradition mentioned by Jerome, making the Horns of Hattin the place where the Sermon on the Mount was delivered, suits this explanation exactly. There is a level place on it where the crowds could have assembled. It is not necessary to insist that this mountain is the Mount of Beatitudes, nor need we contend, as Robinson does, that the mountain must be very close to Capernaum.

(c) The audience is different. Matthew (4:25) states that his audience was composed of "great multitudes from Galilee and Decapolis and Jerusalem and Judea and from beyond Jordan," while Luke (6:17) says that there was "a great multitude of his disciples, and a great number of the people from all Judea and Jerusalem, and the sea coast of Tyre and Sidon." Matthew says (5:1) also that "his disciples came unto him." Hence both assemblages were composed of great multitudes from many regions besides many of his disciples, but in neither case is Jesus said to address himself to any save his disciples, his followers (Matt. 5:1 and Luke 6:20). So in both accounts the Saviour seems to withdraw a little from the great outside crowd of curiosity seekers. But the multitudes also must have heard something of what he said, for they were astonished at his teaching (Matt. 7:28). Andrews well shows that the audience in Matthew were not mostly Jews (according to Kraft), and the audience in Luke mostly heathen. Matthew omits Tyre and Sidon, but he had already mentioned Syria (4:24), which includes Tyre and Sidon. Neither list may be complete. Hence nothing can be made out of Luke's omission of Galilee, Decapolis, and beyond Jordan. Great multitudes from the same general regions are alluded to as being present.

(d) The contents are radically different. It is objected by Alford, Greswell, etc., that Luke omits large portions of what Matthew has, so that Luke has only thirty verses, while Matthew has one hundred and seven. But this leaves out of consideration the several large portions of the same matter which Luke has placed elsewhere, or which Jesus repeated on other occasions (cf. Matt. 6:9–13 and Luke 11:2–4; Matt. 6:25–34 and Luke 12:22–31). Jesus often repeated his sayings on other occasions as all teachers do and ought to do. Neither evangelist gives a complete report of this wonderful discourse. So Matthew omits some things which Luke records (cf. Matt. 5:12 with Luke 6:23–6; Matt. 7:12 with Luke 6:31–40). Nor need we be surprised that Luke, writing generally for all Christians, omits large portions towards the beginning of the sermon that were designed especially for Jews (see Matt. 5:17–27; 6:1–18). These Matthew would be sure to record. Luke adds four woes to the beatitudes. It is unnecessary to remark upon minor variations of language, since the gospels manifestly aim to give the sense of what the Saviour said and not the *verbatim* words. They make no mistakes, for they quote freely, yet correctly. In each case they are incorporated into the narrative in hand. Moreover, to offset these variations, which admit of explanation, it ought to be remembered that the two discourses begin alike and end alike, that they have a general similarity in the order of the different parts, and that they show a general likeness and often absolute identity of expression.

So these differences all melt away on careful comparison, and it is not proved that there are two distinct sermons.

2. Another theory holds that the two sermons are distinct, but spoken on the same day, and near together. So Augustine, who is followed by Lange. The further points of this theory are two. (a) The one (Matt.) was spoken before the choice of the Apostles, to the disciples alone, and while Jesus was sitting on the mountain. (b) The other (Luke) was spoken after the choice of the Apostles, to the multitudes, and standing upon the plain. It is not hard to see that these points do not solve the question. In Matt. 7:28 we are told that the multitudes were astonished at his teaching and in Luke 6:20 that "he lifted up his eyes on his disciples, and said." So this distinction vanishes. The question of the mountain and the plain has been already discussed, and another more probable explanation suggested. It is only a conjecture that the discourse in Matthew was before the appointment of the Twelve. This theory has had no great following.

3. Wieseler holds that Matthew has simply brought together detached sayings of Jesus on different occasions and does not mean to present the whole as one discourse; Luke's account being only one of the discourses

used by Matthew. But this violates the evident notes of place and audience and surroundings by which Matthew gives local color and cast to the entire discourse. See Matt. 5:1 and 8:1. The case of the grouping of the miracles in chapters 8 and 9 is not parallel, since there Matthew does not state that they occurred on one occasion. The fact that various portions of this discourse are repeated elsewhere by Matthew is immaterial, because this was a common habit of Jesus in his discourses.

4. Both Matthew and Luke give substantially similar accounts of the same discourse. So Robinson, Tischendorf, Tholuck, Lewin, Wordsworth, Andrews, Broadus, McClellan, and most modern writers. Most of the arguments for this interpretation have been mentioned in rebuttal of the previously mentioned theories. (*a*) This is the most natural explanation in view of the large volume of similar matter in both, in the beginning, progress, and close of the discourse. It is always best to give the Scripture the most natural and manifest setting, when possible. (*b*) This theory is the most probable one, since it is hardly likely that Jesus would again make the same sermon to the same audience, and under the same circumstances. (*c*) There are no objections to this theory that do not admit of a probable explanation. See the discussion above. The omissions and additions in each case suit the specific purpose of the writer. The apparent contradictions, when studied carefully, blend into a harmonious whole. Hence we seem to be justified in maintaining the identity of the discourses recorded by Matthew and Luke. For a careful outline of this matchless discourse see Broadus on Matthew.

§ 75. THE COMBINATION OF LUKE AND JOHN.

We now have to deal with the most perplexing question in harmonistic study, the proper disposal of the mass of material furnished by Luke in 9:51-18:14. McClellan discusses ten schemes, pushes them all aside, and then suggests another which is no more convincing and equally complicated. Nothing can be attempted here but a presentation of the chief points in this endless discussion. All the principal plans for arranging this part of Luke proceed on one or the other of the following ideas:

1. Some hold that this portion of Luke is neither orderly nor chronological. Hence many of the incidents, here recorded as apparently belonging to the last six months of the Saviour's ministry, in reality are to be placed earlier. They are put here as a sort of summing up of things not mentioned elsewhere. So Robinson and others. In favor of this

theory it is urged that Luke here speaks of some things that Matthew and Mark put before the third passover, such as the healing of a demoniac (Luke 11:14-36) and the blasphemy following. But it may be well replied.

(a) It is not at all clear that we have here the same events that are recorded in Matthew and Mark. Similar miracles were often wrought in the Master's work and similar sayings were frequently repeated on similar or different occasions. This was a common habit with him, as we have heretofore seen.

(b) This portion of Luke is his distinctive contribution to the ministry of Christ in addition to his account of the nativity. He has condensed his account of the withdrawals from Galilee, apparently to make room for the description of another part of Christ's work. Matthew and Mark almost confine themselves to the ministry in Galilee, while Luke thus devotes the bulk of his narrative to what seems to be a later ministry, after Jesus has left Galilee. It is hardly likely that this account should be a mere jumble of scattered details.

(c) Especially is this unlikely in view of Luke's express statement (1:3) that he was going to write an orderly narrative. In no real sense could this be true, if this large section is dislocated in time and order of events.

2. Others refer the entire narrative (Luke 9:51-18:14) to the last journey of the Saviour to Jerusalem. So Andrews, Greswell, Lewin, McClellan, who all refer it to the last journey to the Passover. Others prefer to understand it as meaning the journey to the Feast of the Tabernacles or Dedication. Some would combine this idea with the unchronological plan noticed above. In favor of this journey being continuous and the last one to Jerusalem, the following arguments are adduced:

(a) The language of Luke 9:51, "when the days were being completed that he should be received up," implies that the end was drawing near, and that he was setting his face towards Jerusalem to meet it. This is true without doubt, for Wieseler's interpretation of "received up" as meaning Christ's reception by man is entirely too forced. The expression points to the end of Christ's earthly career. But what does the vague expression, "the days were being completed," mean? Does it have to mean only a few weeks? May it not include as much as six months? For we know that Jesus had been instructing his disciples on this very subject expressly and pointedly, and at the Transfiguration he had spoken of his "decease." Henceforward this was the uppermost subject in his mind. So the interpretation is correct, but the inference is not necessary. This journey in Luke 9:51 need not be either just before the Passover or the Dedication. It could be as early as Tabernacles and be thus described.

(b) It is insisted that this is Jesus' final departure from Galilee, the one described by Matthew and Mark. No place is allowed for a return to Galilee after the departure in Luke 9:51. Robinson urges that Luke 9:51 naturally means a final departure from Galilee. But it may simply mean that he left it as a sphere of activity, not that he never entered Galilee again. And then Luke 17:11 expressly says that Jesus went "through the midst of Samaria and Galilee." This means more than going on the border between the two countries, as McClellan argues. He went through some portions of Samaria and Galilee. In order for McClellan to carry out his scheme he has to resort to the artificial device of referring part of John 10:40 to the departure from Galilee, and the other half to the Perean ministry after a diversion of considerable length into Samaria and back into Galilee. So the effort is not convincing to place all the material in this large section of Luke in one last journey to Jerusalem.

3. The combination of Luke's narrative with that of John. Wieseler was the first to point out a possible parallel between Luke and John. John gives us three journeys,—the Feast of Tabernacles (John 7:2ff), the journey to Bethany at the raising of Lazarus (John 11:17f), the final Passover (John 12:1). Luke likewise three times in this section speaks of Jesus going to Jerusalem, 9:51; 13:22; 17:11. Hence it would seem possible, even probable, that their journeys corresponded. If so, John 7:2-11:54 is to be taken as parallel to Luke 9:51-18:14. This plan is followed by Ellicott, Tischendorf, Clark, Broadus.

According to John's chronology, Jesus was in Jerusalem at the Feast of Tabernacles (7:2), at the Feast of Dedication (10:22), and at the Passover (12:1). Just after the Feast of the Dedication we find him abiding beyond Jordan, where John had baptized (John 10:40). From this point he comes to Bethany near Jerusalem at the raising of Lazarus (John 11:17), whence he withdraws to a little town called Ephraim in the hills north of Jerusalem (John 11:54). Here he abides awhile with his disciples away from his enemies till he goes to the Passover. Such is John's outline of these last six months of the Saviour's life.

(a) But how is all this to be reconciled with the statement of Luke (17:11) that Jesus went through Samaria and Galilee? If Jesus went back to Galilee, John would have mentioned it, we are told. Not necessarily, not unless it fell in with his plan to do so. Hence no conflict need exist between Luke and John. Luke says he went through Galilee and John permits it by the break in his narrative at 11:54. Various points in the six months have been suggested as the point when the return to Galilee was made. The most natural point is from Ephraim, whither he had withdrawn (John 11:54). It was not far to go up through Samaria and join in Galilee (Luke 17:11) the pilgrims from his own country who were in the habit of going to the Passover through Perea, to avoid passing through Samaria. This supposition is not improbable, as Robinson and McClellan urge, but very natural; it makes Luke and John both agree, and allows Luke 9:51 to mean that Jesus then left Galilee as a field of operations. Various other theories are suggested for this return to Galilee, but none of them appear as fitting as this one. It was just before the Passover, when such a journey from Galilee to Jerusalem would be made.

(b) One other point needs to be considered. The theory we hold makes the journey in Luke 9:51 identical with the one in John 7:2-10, viz., to Tabernacles. Many hold such identity to be impossible. So Andrews, Meyer, Godet, Groswell, Farrar, McClellan, etc. Andrews makes three objections against this identity: (1) That the Lord refused to go with his brethren (John 7:6). But it was his brothers who were not favorable to him that he refused to go with. He simply wished to avoid publicity. His face was set (Luke 9:51) all the time, but he was not going with them. (2) That the manner of the going is unlike; the one in John is secret, while the one in Luke is public. But the secrecy in John may merely mean the avoidance of the caravan routes and so through Samaria (Luke). The messengers sent before were not to herald his coming to gather crowds simply, but to make ready for him. It was needed, since the Samaritans saw that his face was as if he were going to Jerusalem. (3) That he went rapidly according to John and slowly according to Luke. He does, according to John, appear in Jerusalem before the feast is over, but Luke does not make him move slowly. Nor is it necessary to connect the sending of the seventy (Luke 10:1ff) with this journey. It belongs rather to the interval between Tabernacles and Dedication. So the secret going of John and the going through Samaria of Luke agree. So substantially Ellicott, Robinson, Wieseler, Gardiner, Caspari, Edersheim, etc. This theory is held irrespective of this being the final departure from Galilee. It is not necessary to fill out every detail in this programme and show where Jesus was between Tabernacles and Dedication. The main outlines remain clear and harmonious and are fairly satisfactory. This combination of Luke and John preserves the integrity of both narratives and fills up a large blank that would otherwise exist in these closing months of the Saviour's life. Upon the whole, therefore, this view seems decidedly preferable, though nothing like absolute certainty can be claimed in regard to the question.

NOTES ON SPECIAL POINTS.

§ 118. DID CHRIST EAT THE PASSOVER?

To put this question in another form, it would be, On what day of the month was Jesus crucified? For the crucifixion occurred on the same Jewish day as the eating of the meal recorded by all four Evangelists. Nearly all agree that the crucifixion occurred on Friday and the meal was eaten the evening before, our Thursday, but the beginning of the Jewish day, counting from sunset to sunset. But what day of the month was it? The Passover feast began on the 15th Nisan, the lamb being slain in the afternoon of the 14th. But the day of the week would vary with the new moon. If Jesus ate the regular Passover supper, he was crucified on the 15th Nisan. If he ate an anticipatory meal a day in advance and was himself slain at the hour of killing the paschal lamb, he was crucified on the 14th Nisan. In that case he did not really eat the Passover supper at all. So then we must seek to determine the truth about this matter, because express statements are made about it in the Gospels.

1. Some sentimental views of the question need to be disposed of first. A great controversy once raged in the early churches about the Passover.

(*a*) In the latter part of the second century some of the churches of Asia Minor, largely composed of Jewish Christians, kept up the Passover on the ground that Jesus had eaten it the night before his crucifixion. Polycarp, the disciple of John, expresses the persuasion that Jesus ate the Passover.

(*b*) But some of the churches were afraid of this example and its application to the discussion about the relation of the Mosaic laws to Christianity. So they took the position that Jesus did not eat the Passover himself, but as the Paschal Lamb, was crucified at the time the lamb was slain. He was our Passover. The Greek churches now hold this position, while the Latin churches hold that Jesus ate the Passover. But those arguments are purely subjective and do not affect the question of fact. Hence we waive this old time controversy and come to the testimony of the Gospels themselves.

2. The testimony of the Synoptists, Matthew, Mark, and Luke. The evidence they give is abundant and explicit to the effect that Jesus ate the regular Paschal Supper on the evening after the 14th Nisan.

(*a*) Jesus predicted that his death would occur during the Feast of the Passover. See Matthew 26:2, "Ye know that after two days the Passover cometh, and the Son of Man is delivered up to be crucified." See also Mark 14:1 and Luke 22:1, where the fact is alluded to. Passover is used in the general sense of the feast of unleavened bread, as Luke explains. The feast of unleavened bread followed the Passover meal, beginning the next morning and lasting a week. But the one term was used to include the other. The Passover was expanded to mean the entire feast that followed, and *vice versa*.

(*b*) It is true that the Jewish authorities decided not to put Jesus to death during the feast (Matthew 26:5; Mark 14:2). But this decision was reached not because of any compunctions of conscience in the matter, but because they were afraid of a tumult among the people, owing to the great crowds, many of whom were friendly to Christ. But so soon as Judas offered his services, their fears vanished and they proceeded with their murderous designs (Matthew 26:14; Mark 14:11). The rulers did expedite matters at the crucifixion that the bodies might not be exposed on the Sabbath. But they had often tried to slay Jesus on the Sabbath heretofore. Public executions did take place during the feasts (Deut. 17:12f).

(*c*) The Synoptists flatly say (Matthew 26:17,20; Mark 14:12,17; Luke 22:7,14) that on the first day of unleavened bread Jesus sent Peter and John from Bethany into the city to make preparations for eating the Passover, and that on the evening of the same day he ate it with his disciples. Luke calls it "the hour." Now, the first day of unleavened bread was the 14th Nisan. There is no question about this. Josephus speaks of the feast lasting eight days. The lamb of the supper being slain on the afternoon of this day, it was regarded as the beginning of the feast. Besides, Mark and Luke end the whole matter by saying that on this day they sacrificed the Passover. Jesus himself calls it the Passover (Luke 22:15). It is useless to say that Jesus ate the Passover a day in advance. This could not be done, especially by one to whom the temple authorities were hostile. Equally useless is it to say that the Jews ate the Passover a day too late. If a mistake was made about the new moon, they would hardly keep the Passover on two different days, nor would Jesus be apt to make a point about the matter.

3. The testimony of John. If we had only the evidence of the Synoptists, no serious trouble would ever arise on this question. Strauss has strenuously urged that John is on this point in hopeless conflict with the other Evangelists, since he makes Jesus eat the Passover on the evening after the 13th Nisan (Wednesday), and not the evening after the 14th (Thursday). This idea has gained a foothold among many orthodox or semi-orthodox writers, such as Ellicott, Westcott, Alford, Godet, Farrar, Greswell, Meyer, Bleek, Weiss. Some of these evidently do so because they hold that the Paschal controversy in Asia Minor arose from this supposed conflict of John with the Synoptists, and that this shows John's Gospel to have been in existence when that controversy began. But as many able men hold that John and the Synoptists are in perfect harmony

on the question. So Wieseler, Robinson, Andrews, McClellan, Tholuck, Clark, Broadus, Edersheim, etc. Andrews, Robinson, and McClellan have elaborate and convincing discussions of the whole subject. It is not worth while to maintain that John in chapter 13 alludes to a different meal on a different occasion. The points of contact with the Synoptists are too sharp and clear, such as the sop given to Judas. But five passages in John are produced as being in direct opposition to the statements of the Synoptic Gospels. Let us examine them.

(*a*) John 13:1f., "Now before the feast of the Passover, Jesus knowing, etc." Here, it is alleged, a distinct statement is made that this supper was before the Passover, and consequently twenty-four hours before. But several things are taken for granted in this inference. One is that the phrase "feast of the Passover" is to be confined to this particular meal, and is not to include the entire festival of unleavened bread (cf. Luke 22:1). Often by a metonymy of speech the name of a part is given to the whole. Besides, it is not certain that verse 1 is to be connected with verse 2. The best exegetes agree that a complete idea may be presented therein, either a general statement that Jesus loved his own before the Passover and until the end, or that he came into special consciousness of this love just before the Passover. And if the more natural interpretation be taken and the application of this love be made in verse 2, it is not necessary that the "before" be as much as twenty-four hours. Observe also the text adopted in the Revised Version in verse 2, not "supper being ended," but "during supper." With this reading agree the other references in 13:3, "riseth from supper," 13:12, "sat down again," 13:23, "There was at the table reclining in Jesus' bosom." So the natural meaning is that just before the meal began, Jesus purposed to show his love for his own by a practical illustration. So, after they had all reclined at the table according to custom, Jesus arose and passed around the tables, washing their feet; then he reclined again and proceeded with the meal. So nothing at all can be made out of this passage against the view that this was the regular Passover; but, on the other hand, the most natural meaning is that John is here describing what took place at this Passover meal. Else, why should he mention the Passover at all?

(*b*) John 13:27, "That thou doest, do quickly." The objection is made that the disciples would not have thought that Jesus referred to the feast (13:29), if the Passover meal was already going on or was over. So, it is urged, this remark must have been made a day before the Passover was celebrated. But if that were the case, where would be the necessity for hurry, as there would be plenty of time on the morrow? The word "feast" here need not be confined to the paschal supper, but more naturally refers to the whole of the feast, of which the supper was a part. So this haste was needed to provide for the feast of unleavened bread which began on the next morning. No real force lies in the fact that this day was a holy day, being the first day of the Passover festival. The Mishna expressly allows the procuring even on a Sabbath what was needed for the Passover. If this could be done on a Sabbath, much more could it be done on a feast day which was not a Sabbath. Hence not only was it possible for the disciples to have misunderstood the remark of Jesus on the Passover evening, but it was far more natural that such misapprehensions should arise then than a day before. So this passage, like the preceding, when rightly understood, really confirms the Synoptists.

(c) John 18:28, "They themselves entered not into the palace, that they might not be defiled, but might eat the Passover." At first sight this does look like a contradiction. For this was certainly after the feast of John 13:2, and if they had not eaten the Passover meal, why here is a clear case of conflict of authorities. But it is by no means certain that the phrase "eat the Passover" means simply the paschal supper. This phrase occurs five times in the New Testament besides this, but all in Matthew, Mark, and Luke (Matt. 26:17; Mark 14:12,14; Luke 22:11,15). In all of these the reference is to the paschal supper. But the word "passover" is used in three senses in the New Testament, the paschal supper, the paschal lamb, or the paschal festival. The word is used eight times in John besides this instance, and in every case the Passover festival is meant. So we may fairly infer that the usage of John must determine his own meaning rather than that of the Synoptists. This becomes more probable when we remember that John wrote much later than they, after the destruction of Jerusalem, when these terms were not used so strictly. He always speaks of "the Jews" as separate from Christians. And this very expression is used in II. Chronicles 30:22, "And they did eat the festival seven days." The Septuagint translates it, "And they fulfilled (kept) the festival of unleavened bread seven days." See Robinson. So it is entirely possible for the phrase, "eat the Passover," to mean in this instance also the celebration of the Passover festival. Some have urged that the Sanhedrin had not eaten the Passover at the regular hour because of the excitement of the trial. But this is hardly tenable. And, moreover, since this remark was made early in the morning, how could that affect the eating of the supper in the evening? For whatever impurities one had during the day passed away at evening. Hence this uncleanness must belong to the same day on which it was incurred. If the Passover festival had begun, this would be true, for they would wish to participate in the offerings of that day. So this passage likewise becomes an argument in favor of agreement with the Synoptists.

(d) John 19:14, "Now it was the Preparation of the Passover." This is claimed to mean the day preceding the Passover festival. Hence Christ was crucified on the 14th Nisan, in opposition to the Synoptists. The afternoon before the Passover was used as a preparation, but it was not technically so-called. This phrase "Preparation" was really the name of a day in the week, the day before the Sabbath, our Friday. We are not left to conjecture about this question. The Evangelists all use it in this sense alone. Matthew uses it for Friday (27:62), Mark expressly says that the Preparation was the day before the Sabbath (15:42), Luke says that it was the day of the Preparation and the Sabbath drew on (23:54), and John himself so uses the word in two other passages (19:31,42), in both of which haste is exercised on the Preparation, because the Sabbath was at hand. The New Testament usage is conclusive, therefore, on this point. This, then, was the Friday of Passover week. And this agrees with the Synoptists. Besides, the term "Preparation" has long been the regular name for Friday in the Greek language, caused by the New Testament usage. It is so in the Modern Greek to-day. It was the Sabbath eve, just as the Germans have Sonnabend for Sunday eve, *i. e.*, Saturday afternoon. So this passage also becomes a positive argument for the agreement between John and the Synoptists.

(e) John 19:31, "For the day of that Sabbath was a high day." From this passage it has been argued that at this Passover the first day of the Passover festival coincided with the weekly Sabbath. But that is an entirely gratuitous inference. This coincidence would, of course, be a "high day," but so would the first day of the feast, the last day, or the Sabbath of the feast. In John 7:37 the last day is called "the great day of the feast." The Sabbath occurring during the festival would be a high day likewise. Robinson's arguments on this point are quite conclusive. Nothing can be made out of the expression against the position of the Synoptists.

McClellan discusses various other passages in John which show that the crucifixion occurred on Friday, and that this was the first day of the feast (John 18:39,40; 19:31,42; 20:1,19, etc.). We conclude then that a fair interpretation of the passages alleged not only removes all contradiction between John and the Synoptists, but rather decidedly favors the view that they have the same date for the Passover meal, and that Jesus ate the Passover at the regular hour and was crucified on Friday, 15th Nisan.

§ 132. THE HOUR OF THE CRUCIFIXION.

In John 19:14 it is stated that the time when Pilate sentenced Jesus to be crucified, or rather when he began the last trial in which he sentenced him, was about the sixth hour. We read, however, in Mark 15:25 that it was the third hour when Christ was crucified. The Synoptists all unite in saying that the darkness began at the sixth hour. The Jewish way of counting the hours was to divide the night and day into twelve divisions each, beginning at sunrise and sunset. The hours would thus vary in length with the time of year. Just after the vernal equinox the third hour of Mark would be about 9 A.M., and the sixth hour of the Synoptists would be about noon. The ninth hour, when Jesus gave his piteous cry to God (Mark 15:34) would be about 3 P.M. But how can the sixth hour of John, the time when Jesus was sentenced by Pilate, be reconciled to this schedule? A real difficulty is here presented, but by no means an insuperable one, as Alford and Meyer hold. Let us discuss some of the more usual explanations. Andrews and McClellan give quite a variety of suggested solutions.

1. Some hold that "sixth" in John is a textual error for "third." This could easily happen, since the gamma and the digamma of the Greek are very similar. Eusebius said that the accurate copies had it "third" in John. Various writers have held this position, such as Beza, Bengel, Alford, Robinson (given up by Riddle), Olshausen, (Farrar). But the textual evidence is overwhelmingly against it, and, besides, the difficulty would not be removed. John is evidently speaking of the time at the last trial and Mark of the time after Jesus has been led out to the crucifixion. So nothing is gained by this hypothesis.

2. Others would change the punctuation in John 19:14 so as to make "of the Passover" belong to "sixth hour," beginning from midnight. But there is no evidence that the Passover began with midnight. So Hofmann. This is very forced and unnatural.

3. Views that hinge on the word "preparation." Some would hold that John simply says that about noon the preparation time of the Passover begins. But Preparation here means Friday, and noon is not the hour needed to harmonize with Mark. Equally arbitrary is it to count six hours backward from noon so as to reach six o'clock.

Augustine suggested that the six hours are to be counted from 3 A.M. This would make 9 A.M., and would concur with the hour of Mark. But this is wholly arbitrary and unsatisfactory, and would not relieve the trouble.

4. Equally arbitrary is the solution that makes Mark refer to the hour of the sentence and John to the crucifixion, just the reverse of the Scripture account. Augustine also proposed that Jesus was crucified at

the third hour by the tongues of the Jews, and at the sixth by the hands of the soldiers.

5. Others hold that Mark and John both speak in general terms. Hence the crucifixion may have taken place between 9 and 12 in the morning. Mark looks in one direction and John in the other. So Hengstenberg, Krafft, Ellicott, Campbell. The Jews, it is true, were not as exact in the use of expressions of time as we are to-day, but this solution hardly meets the requirements of the case. Mark puts his *third* hour at the beginning of the crucifixion, and John his *sixth* hour at the beginning of the last trial. This reconciliation does not reconcile.

6. The most satisfactory solution of the difficulty is to be found in the idea that John here uses the Roman computation of time, from midnight to noon and noon to midnight, just as we do now. Hence the sixth hour would be our six o'clock in the morning. If this hour was the beginning of the last trial of Jesus, we then have enough, but not too much, time for the completion of the trial, the carrying away of Jesus outside the city walls, together with the procuring of the crosses, etc. All the events, moreover, narrated by the Evangelists, could have occurred between dawn (John 18:27) and six or seven.

For a long time it was doubted whether the Romans ever used this method of computing time for civil days. Farrar vehemently opposes this idea. But Plutarch, Pliny, Aulus Gellius, and Macrobius expressly say that the Roman civil day was reckoned from midnight to midnight. So the question of fact may be considered as settled. The only remaining question is whether John used this mode of reckoning. Of course, the Romans had also the natural day and the natural night just as we do now. In favor of the idea that John uses the Roman way of counting the hours in the civil day, several things may be said.

(*a*) He wrote the Gospel late in the century, probably in Asia Minor, long after the destruction of Jerusalem, when the Jewish method would not likely be preserved. Roman ideas were prevalent in Asia Minor. John evidently is not writing for the Jews primarily, since he constantly speaks of "the Jews" as outsiders. John is writing to be understood by the people, and this is the way it would be understood in Asia Minor.

(*b*) All the passages in John, where the hour is mentioned, allow this computation. John 1:39 would be 10 A.M.; 4:6f. would be 6 P.M., counting from noon also (as we do). This hour suits best the circumstances. In the evening the women would come to get water, Jesus would have time for his journey thither, and would be tired and hungry. In John 4:52 the hour would be 7 P.M. This hour likewise suits the circumstances better. John 11:9, Are there not twelve hours in the day? is not against this idea, since here obviously the natural day, as opposed to night, is meant. The Romans used both methods and so do we.

(c) Moreover, one passage in John (20:19), when compared with Luke 24:29,36, makes it necessary to understand that John used the Roman method in this instance. It was toward evening, and the day had declined, according to Luke, when Jesus and the disciples drew near to Emmaus. Here he ate supper and, "rising up that very hour," the disciples returned seven miles to Jerusalem and told these things to the eleven who were together. But while they were narrating these things Jesus appeared to them. Now John, in mentioning this very appearance of Jesus (20:19) says that it "was evening on *that day*, the first day of the week," *i. e.*, evening of the day when Mary Magdalene had seen the Lord. But with the Jews the evening began the day. Hence John, here at least, is *bound* to mean the Roman day. It was the evening of the same day in the morning of which Mary had seen Jesus. This appears conclusive. John did use the Roman method here, may have done so always, almost certainly did so in 19:14. Besides, as McClellan shows, the natural meaning of John's phrase is that it was the sixth hour of the Friday (Preparation) of the Passover. But we have just seen that John in 20:19 counts according to the Roman day. Hence the sixth hour of Friday would be six o'clock in the morning.

This is the only solution that really harmonizes John and Mark. The rest make the hours agree, but the hours bring together different events. This method harmonizes the whole narrative, and seems entirely probable. So substantially Greswell, McClellan, Ebrard, Tischendorf, Tholuck, Wieseler, Broadus, Gardiner, Clark, Andrews (new edition), and others.

Prof. W. M. Ramsay, in *The Expositor* for March, 1893, contends that Mark and John are at variance, but that it is of small moment, since the ancients had little notion about hours. He seeks to show that the martyrdom of Polycarp and Pronius, usually relied on to prove that in Asia Minor the hours were counted from midnight, took place in the afternoon, instead of the morning, the usual time. Hence the eighth and tenth hours respectively would be 2 P.M. and 4 P.M. But his arguments are not sufficient to set aside the established custom in such cases. He claims, moreover, that the Roman civil day was just a day and was not divided into hours. But this is mere assertion, and would besides be an anomaly. How else could divisions of time be marked in the civil day?

§ 134. THE TIME OF THE RESURRECTION OF CHRIST.

1. Mark, Luke, and John unite in stating that the resurrection of Jesus took place early on the first day of the week, *i. e.* early Sunday morning. Mark (16:9) says that Jesus, "having risen early, on the first

day of the week, appeared, etc." This passage is early testimony, even if not a part of Mark's gospel. Mark (16:2) states that it was very early on the first day of the week, the sun having risen, when the women came to the sepulchre. Luke (24:1) says that the women came to the tomb at early dawn on the first day of the week. John (20:1) says that Mary Magdalene came to the tomb in the morning on the first day of the week. So then, there is no doubt that these three Evangelists mean to say that Jesus rose very early on Sunday morning, and that shortly after that event came the two Marys and some other women to anoint his body with spices.

Sceptics make objection to some of the details in the accounts of Mark and John especially as being inconsistent. John (20:1) says that Mary comes while it is yet dark, while Mark says (16:2) that the sun was risen. But Mark also says in the same verse that it was very early, which would agree with John's statement that it was yet dark. Hence Mark's other statement, that the sun was risen, must be interpreted in the light of his own words. Two solutions can be offered.

(a) We may suppose, as McClellan and others, that John's note of time refers to the starting from Bethany, while it was yet dark or very early (Mark). In a few minutes it would be early dawn (Luke), and by the time the women come to the tomb, the sun would be up. All this is entirely possible and looks even probable, for in the twilight of early dawn, the border line is very narrow between darkness and sunrise. A stiff morning walk would pass through all the stages. It all depends on where you take your stand in this fleeting interim. Mark covers both sides and so includes it all from the first glimmering light till the full light of day.

(b) Or the expression, "the sun was risen" (aorist participle), may simply be a general expression applicable to the phenomena of sunrise. The first gleam of daylight comes from the rising sun, though not yet completely risen. So Robinson, Ellicott, Clark. Robinson gives several examples from the Septuagint, where the same phrase is used in the aorist tense in a general way for the dawning light of day (Judges 9:33; 2 Kings 3:22; Ps. 104:22). Either of these explanations is entirely possible and removes the difficulty.

2. But Matthew seems to put the resurrection on the evening after the Sabbath, our Saturday evening. He says (28:1), "But late on the Sabbath day, as it was dawning into the first day of the week, came Mary Magdalene and the other Mary to view the sepulchre." If this passage means that the visit was made at the end of the Sabbath day (evening) and after the resurrection of Jesus, then Matthew is in plain contradiction to the other Evangelists. Some have taken the position that Jesus

rose at sunset on the Sabbath day, forgetting that Mark (16:9) says that he rose early in the morning. There are several ways of reconciling Matthew with the other gospels.

(a) Greswell, Alford and others would translate "late on the Sabbath day" by "late in the week." The Greek word is the same in this verse for Sabbath and week. In both cases, therefore, the translation could be the same. But little sense would result from this translation. "Late in the week" and "dawning into the first day of the week" hardly fit well. By this explanation the latter expression is used for the first part of Sunday, and the visit occurred in this dawning part of the day.

(b) Others would translate "late on the Sabbath day" by "after the Sabbath day." Godet, Grimm and others contend that the Greek idiom could mean this, and it is so translated by several English translators such as Newcome, Sharpe, Wakefield, Norton, etc. But it is extremely doubtful whether the Greek will permit such a rendering. So it seems that we must choose between the two following explanations.

(c) Matthew does not clearly say that this visit was made after the resurrection of the Saviour although his words may mean that. Hence the words may have their natural meaning. Late in the Sabbath day, about sundown say, the two Marys go to view the sepulchre (Matt. 28:1), having rested through the day (Luke 23:56). The women who had come with Jesus from Galilee had gone thither on Friday, after his burial, to see where he was laid and had prepared spices. If the two Marys were with them they may well have gone again at nightfall at the close of the Sabbath to see if their Lord was still there. In the early morning, they rose and took the spices and went to anoint his body. It was then that they saw the angel (Matt. 28:5). Matthew does not say that in the visit of 28:1 the angel appeared to them. He speaks of the earthquake having come, and the resurrection, and then resumes. This view gains some support from the use of the same Greek word in Luke 23:54, "And it was the day of the Preparation (Friday) and the Sabbath drew on (was dawning)." Here the meaning seems to be that the Sabbath *dawned* at the close of the day. So Westcott, McClellan and others. McClellan has an elaborate and vigorous presentation of this position. However it may be about the visit of the women in Matt. 28:1, Matthew certainly does not mean to say that Jesus rose at sunset on the Sabbath. The whole course of his narrative in the rest of the chapter shows that it was the morning of Sunday when the angel appeared. The women ran quickly to the disciples. The soldiers ran to the chief priests (Matt. 28:13) and said that the disciples came by *night* and stole him while they slept, clearly implying that it was now day. Hence Matthew does not teach that Jesus rose at sunset, but the reverse. Besides, Matthew expressly says that Jesus rose on the third day, which would not be true, if he rose on the Sabbath.

(*d*) Sabbath day may be used of the day followed by the night, according to popular reckoning prevailing in the Saviour's time. The Jews originally counted from evening to evening, but this custom did not prevail universally. Jonah (1:17) and Matthew (12:40) speak of three days and three nights, following the day by the night. Meyer, Morison, Clark and others hold this view, and it is possible at least, but hardly so satisfactory as the view of McClellan above. At any rate, it remains clear that Matthew agrees with the other Evangelists in putting the resurrection of Jesus Sunday morning. The chief point of difficulty is Matthew's visit of the women in 28:1, whether this was in the evening before simply "to view the sepulchre," or in the morning to anoint the body of the Saviour. The condensed account of Matthew leaves this question unsettled, and there we too shall have to leave it. And this last matter does not affect the question as to the time of the Lord's resurrection, but only the number of the visits made by the women.

§ 134. THE LENGTH OF OUR LORD'S STAY IN THE TOMB.

Quite an effort is made in some quarters to show that Jesus remained in the tomb seventy-two hours, three full days and nights. There are three sets of expressions used about the matter, besides the express statements of the Gospels about the days of the crucifixion and resurrection. Let us examine these lines of evidence.

1. Luke settles the matter pointedly by mentioning all the time between the crucifixion and the resurrection (Luke 23:50–24:3). The burial took place Friday afternoon just before the Sabbath drew on (Luke 23:54). The women rested on the Sabbath (Saturday) (Luke 23:56), and went to the sepulchre early Sunday morning, the first day of the week (Luke 24:1). There is no escaping this piece of chronology. This is all the time there was between the two events. Jesus then lay in the tomb from late in the afternoon of Friday till early Sunday morning. The other Gospels agree with this reckoning of the time, as we have already seen.

2. But how about the prediction of Jesus, repeatedly made, and once illustrated by the case of Jonah, that he would rise after three days? Are two nights and a day and two pieces of days three days? Let us see.

(*a*) The well-known custom of the Jews was to count a part of a day as a whole day of twenty-four hours. Hence a part of a day or night would be counted as a whole day, the term day obviously having two senses, as night and day, or day contrasted with night. So then the part of Friday would count as one day, Saturday another, and the part of Sunday the third day. This method of reckoning gives no trouble to a Jew.

(b) Besides, the phrase "on the third day" is obliged to mean that the resurrection took place on that day, for, if it occurred after the third day, it would be on the fourth day and not on the third. Now it so happens that this term "third day" is applied *seven* times to the resurrection of Christ (Matt. 16:21; Matt. 17:23; Matt. 20:19; Luke 27: 7,21,46; I. Cor. 15:4). These numerous passages of Scripture, both prophecy and statement of history, agree with the record of the fact that Jesus did rise on the third day.

(c) Moreover, the phrase "after three days" is used by the same writers (Matthew and Luke) in connection with the former one, "the third day," as meaning the same thing. Hence the definite and clear expression must explain the one that is less so. The chief priests and Pharisees remember (Matt. 27:63) that Jesus said, after three days I rise again. Hence they urge Pilate to keep a guard over the tomb until the *third day* (Matt. 27:64). This is their own interpretation of the Saviour's words. Besides, in parallel passages in the different Gospels, one will have one expression and another the other, naturally suggesting that they regarded them as equivalent. (Cf. Mark 9:31 with Matt. 16:21, Luke 9:22 with Mark 10:34.) On the third day cannot mean three whole days, while after three days can be used as meaning parts of the first and third days.

(d) Matthew 12:40 is urged as conclusive the other way. But the "three days and three nights" may be nothing more than a longer way of saying three days, using day in its long sense. And we have already seen that the Jews counted any part of this full day (day and night) as a whole day (day and night). Hence this passage may mean nothing more than the common "after three days" above mentioned, and, like that expression, must be interpreted in accordance with the definite term "on the third day" and with the clear chronological data given by Luke and the rest. They seemed to be conscious of no discrepancy in these various expressions. Most likely they understood them as well as we do at any rate.

www.ingramcontent.com/pod-product-compliance
Lightning Source LLC
Chambersburg PA
CBHW032108230426
43672CB00009B/1674